Electoral
Participation
A Comparative
Analysis

Sage Studies in
Contemporary Political Sociology

Trends Toward Corporatist Intermediation
edited by Philippe C. Schmitter and Gerhard Lehmbruch

Political Clientelism, Patronage and Development
edited by S. N. Eisenstadt and R. Lemarchand

Electoral Participation: A Comparative Analysis
edited by Richard Rose

Sponsored by the Committee on Political Sociology,
International Political Science/
International Sociological Association

Electoral Participation
A Comparative Analysis

Edited by

Richard Rose

Secretary, Committee on Political Sociology
IPSA/ISA

SAGE Publications • Beverly Hills • London

Copyright © 1980 by
SAGE Publications Ltd

For information address

SAGE Publications Ltd
28 Banner Street
London EC1Y 8QE

SAGE Publications Inc
275 South Beverly Drive
Beverly Hills California 90212

British Library Cataloguing in Publication Data

Electoral participation.
  1. Voting
  2. Democracy
  I.Rose, Richard *b. 1933*
  324'.242   JF1001   80-41015

ISBN 0-8039-9811-2

First Printing

Contents

In Memoriam

Stein Rokkan

1921-1979

Preface

Elections are the central institution for popular participation in government. Without elections, the mass of the population has no means to influence the choice of a nation's governors. The meaning of popular participation is, however, ambiguous. While scholars agree that participation is important, they disagree about its meaning. Conventionally, participation has been thought a good indicator of democratic government. But some social scientists have argued that "too much" participation may be a sign of political crisis. A society in which many people do not feel it necessary to invest time, effort and emotions in politics may show a higher level of popular satisfaction than a political system where nearly everyone is mobilized electorally.

The purpose of this book is to provide fresh insights into classic questions of electoral participation. This can be done by looking afresh at conventional questions of voter turnout, and by looking at familiar questions in unfamiliar contexts, such as Mediterranean societies now acquiring or regaining representative systems of government. The chapters in this volume demonstrate the value of exploring these questions in a comparative context. For example, it is impossible to know whether voting turnout in a country such as America is "high" or "low", except by comparison with other countries. It is not necessary to ascend to the stratosphere to survey the whole of the world's political institutions. Much can be learned by examining generic questions of the social sciences intensively and in depth in the context of one nation. The resulting findings can test general theories of social science — and amend them as necessary.

The book opens by focussing upon voter turnout, the classic measure of electoral participation. G. Bingham Powell's study of voting in thirty democracies is a pioneering, systematic effort to find out what causes the very real differences in electoral participation around the world. By comparison, Walter Dean Burnham's study focusses primarily upon the American experience, in which non-participation is as important as participation. Burnham uses his wide knowledge of American and European experience to highlight the distinctiveness of low levels of voting in America. William Schneider further expands the discussion by considering varieties and styles of electoral competition, a reminder that parties contribute at least as much to the meaning of elections as do voters.

The long central chapter by Juan Linz about the new Spanish party system presents a uniquely informed review of the most important emerging democratic government in Europe in a generation. Linz shows how truly new the parties of the Spanish state are; presents a wealth of detail about electoral behaviour and party competition in the 1977 and 1979 Spanish elections; and relates events in Spain to developments in other Mediterranean countries. The Danish election expert Ole Borre shows to what extent developments in Denmark question the idea of a "stable" party system there, because of a proliferation of parties across the political spectrum.

The more complex the society, the more important is the viewpoint of political sociology, giving equal attention to the role of parties and of social groups in structuring electoral participation. The chapter about Israel by Ofira Seliktar gives a rounded picture of the importance of religious cleavages within a nominally Jewish state, and the complexities of party alignments in a society gathering in citizens from throughout Europe and beyond. Arend Lijphart's study of the electoral importance of language by comparison with class and religion introduces data about Switzerland and South Africa, two countries rarely studied by political survey research, as well as the Netherlands and Belgium. The concluding chapter by Ilja Scholten critically examines the concept of "consociationalism", developed by Lijphart as a description of democratic political participation in the Netherlands.

While the contents of any scholarly book must be written by individuals, this volume is the product of a collective effort, namely, research meetings, organized for two decades by the Committee on Political Sociology. As the list of Committee publications on p. 355 illustrates, the Committee has pioneered comparative electoral analysis under the inspiration of its founding Chairman and Secretary, S. M. Lipset and Stein Rokkan. We particularly regret that Stein Rokkan, who edited the first volume of the Committee on political participation, following a conference in Bergen in 1961, did not live to see this substantial monument to continuities and developments in his field of work.

As the title page and acknowledgements of various chapters illustrate, the activities of the Committee are themselves part of the institutional framework of international social science. The Committee is established as part of the International Sociological Association and of the International Political Science Association. It holds meetings at the World Congresses of each of these Associations. Drafts of several papers herein were first presented at a panel on party politics organized by Professor Giovanni Sartori for the 1978 World Congress of the International Sociological Association in Uppsala, Sweden. Others have been presented as first drafts at national or international conferences in Europe and America, and a few have been written without any spur from the calendar. Scholarly conferences and meetings can serve as a means of bringing scholars from many lands together for discussion and for reflecting and sifting ideas.

This volume is intended to represent the cumulation of knowledge across time and space, and not simply be a record of a "one-off" conference. In preparing it, the editor is not only indebted to individual authors for their ideas and patience in revising manuscripts, but also to the staff of the Centre for the Study of Public Policy at the University of Strathclyde, Glasgow, which provides an unusually good home for the furtherance of comparative scholarship.

Richard Rose
Secretary, Committee on Political Sociology
IPSA/ISA

—————————— *1* ——————————

Voting Turnout in Thirty Democracies: Partisan, Legal, and Socio-Economic Influences

G. Bingham Powell, Jr.

University of Rochester

Voting occupies a central place in democratic politics and in contemporary political science. Increasingly sophisticated studies have analyzed the sources of partisan support and political participation, especially voting, among different individuals and groups within nations (e.g., Campbell, et al., 1960, 1966; Verba, Nie, and Kim, 1971; Rose, 1974; Pomper, 1975; Nie, Verba and Petrocik, 1976; Milbrath and Goel, 1977; Verba, Nie, and Kim, 1978). Who chooses to stay home and who goes to the polls can often determine who wins an election, and voting is a major instrument by which leaders are compelled to be attentive to citizens (Eulau and Prewitt, 1973; Verba and Nie, 1972). Moreover, voting turnout is a critical indication of the involvement of citizens in the national political life of a society (Deutsch, 1961).

Yet, there have been few, if any, attempts to compare and explain the large and rather stable differences in voting turnout across the full range of democratic nations. Average turnout levels in recent decades ranged from 60 percent or less in nations such as India, Lebanon, Switzerland, and the United States, to around 90 percent in Italy, the Netherlands, and Austria.

VOTING TURNOUT IN DEMOCRACIES

A brief survey of the political systems of the world in the early 1960s suggests that some 30 nations of over one million in population have

                                      Electoral Participation

TABLE 1

Voting Participation in Thirty Democracies, 1960-1978

Nation	Democratic elections included in study[1]	Average turnout as percentage registered[2] %	Average turnout as percentage eligible age groups[3] %
Australia	1961,63,66,69,72,75	95	86
Austria	1962,66,70,71,75	93	89
Belgium	1961,65,68,71,74,77	92	88
Canada	1962,63,65,68,72,74	77	71
Ceylon (S.L.)	1960,60,65,70	80	72
Chile	1964,70	84	71
Costa Rica	1962,66,70,78	81	73
Denmark	1960,64,66,68,71,73,75,77	88	87
Finland	1962,66,70,72,75	83	84
France	1962,67,68,73,78	77	70
Germany (W.)	1961,65,69,72,76	89	84
Greece	1963,64,74,78	81	85
India	1962,67,71,77	58	60
Ireland	1961,65,69,73,77	75	75
Israel	1961,65,69,73,77	81	81
Italy	1963,68,72,76	93	94
Jamaica	1962,67,72	72	61
Japan	1960,63,67,69,72,76	72	71
Lebanon	1960,64,68,72	53	56
Netherlands	1959,63,67 // 71,72,77	95[2]	90[2]
New Zealand	1960,63,66,69,72,75	88	81
Norway	1961,65,69,73,77	82	82
Philippines	1957,61,65	77	77
Sweden	1960,64,68,70,73,76	88	86
Switzerland	1963,67,71,75	60	53
Turkey	1965,69,73	67	62
United Kingdom	1964,66,70,74,74	75	74
United States	1960,64,68,72,76	n.a.	59
Uruguay	1958,63,68,71	77	71
Venezuela	1958,63,68,73	95	80

1. Figures are for national legislative elections, unless there is a strong President, nonparliamentary system. Figures for Chile, Philippines, and United States are for presidential elections only; Uruguay, 1971, is presidential. Data were not available for Ceylon (Sri Lanka) 1977, Costa Rica 1974, Jamaica 1976, Philippines 1969, Turkey 1977, Venezuela 1978, and New Zealand 1978.

2. Averages for the Netherlands are for years in which voting was compulsory.

3. In the Philippines and pre-1970 Chile the eligibles exclude illiterates. In Ceylon (Sri Lanka) the eligibles exclude the Indian Tamils.

met for a substantial period of time the criteria of competitive, mass
party politics and relative freedom of communication and organization that roughly constitute contemporary standards of democracy.
Although democratic regimes were overthrown or temporarily
suspended in some of these nations, their experience while working
democracies remains a useful source of material for comparative
analysis. Table 1 lists these countries in alphabetical order, and
indicates the years during which national elections took place from
1960 to the present. While country experts and theorists alike will
probably disagree on the inclusion or exclusion of some particular
countries as "democracies", there is substantial agreement on most
of this universe. (For comparisons, see Dahl, 1971.)

Table 1 also presents data on average voting participation. The
data include, insofar as possible, all voters who went to the polls,
whether they cast valid or invalid ballots. There are two reasons for
looking at all votes. First, in some cases casting a blank or spoiled
ballot may be a deliberate act that meets our definition of participation in every respect, e.g. a protest at some party being excluded from
the ballot. Second, countries vary greatly in how they judge ballots as
valid; hence the same actions can result in valid or invalid ballots in
different countries. In some countries with compulsory voting the
percentage of invalid ballots is relatively high; e.g. it runs around
seven percent in Belgium.

The calculation of turnout depends on one's definition of the
universe of potential voters. In conducting this research it became
gradually clear that different studies were reporting different
"electorates" in calculating voting participation. Although the
differences in reported absolute numbers of votes were seldom very
great, the differences in turnout percentages were often notable,
especially in Latin American democracies. In European nations,
scholars and journalists invariably offer percent of the registered
electorate as their measure of turnout. In discussing the United
States, it is always percent of the population of voting age, national
registration figures are not available; elsewhere practices vary.

In Table 1 the third column shows the average turnout as a percentage of registered voters; the fourth column shows turnout as a
percentage of citizens of eligible age, calculated from United Nations
census data. [1] We can see that there are some sharp discrepancies
between the two figures. Such differences are most pronounced in
nations where registration is a citizen's responsibility, rather than an
automatic process carried out by the government: Australia, Chile,

Costa Rica, France, post-1962 Jamaica, New Zealand, the United
States, Uruguay, and Venezuela. [2] These differences, whose effect on
turnout itself is discussed at more length below, shape both size and
make-up of the registered electorate. In countries such as the USA,
where registration is for many citizens more difficult than voting, the
registered electorate clearly represents a more interested and
involved subset of potential eligibles than in countries with automatic
registration. Thus, despite some error in census-based estimates of
eligibles, the last column, voting participation as percent of all
citizens of enfranchized age, is the most appropriate figure for
comparative analysis across the full range of countries. We shall use
it throughout.

It is important to note that in general turnout from election to
election is consistent within nations. For the most part, the averages
in Table 1 do not conceal precipitous swings. A turnout increase or
decrease of five percent is a large shift in most of these nations. Some
important exceptions, such as the step level changes in turnout in
Costa Rica and the Netherlands caused by changes in penalties for
non-voting, and the shift in Jamaica caused by altering registration
laws, are discussed below. But normally campaigning seems to result
in rather small turnout differences. Of course, the effects of dramatic
party contests can occasionally be found. A good example is the
"surge" in Indian turnout in 1967, when the opposition parties first
united to challenge seriously Congress's dominance: turnout
increased from 55 to 61 percent of the registered electorate, a level
reached again in the dramatic election which ousted Mrs. Ghandi in
1977.

Scholars noting the relative stability of turnout rates within individual nations frequently characterize a country's turnout as "high"
or "low." Comparisons are often made to well-known, but
statistically deviant, cases such as the United States or Italy. Table 1
suggest more useful comparative benchmarks. Turnout averages 76
percent of the eligible age groups (about 80 percent of the registered
electorate), across elections in thirty countries.

We expect the average levels of voting participation in a society to
be shaped by a wide variety of factors. These would include the values
and skills of its citizens, the issues and problems of the society, the
legal and constitutional rules, and the political structures which link
the individual voters to collective outcomes. We do not have
available comparative data on the citizen's normative beliefs about
the importance of participation, although some studies of voting

participation within individual countries have demonstrated the importance of such attitudes (see Milbrath and Goel, 1977). However, the broad environmental setting for citizen choice does explain a great deal of the cross-national variation. The two aspects of that environment most immediately proximate to the citzen seem to be the national party system, which presents the voting options, and the incentives or costs created by the legal system.

FACTORS SHAPING COMPARATIVE VOTING TURNOUT: THE LEGAL SETTING

Penalties for Failure to Vote

In comparing voting participation across nations, we need to put "first things first" and consider the legal incentives or hindrances acting directly on the individual citizen. In over a quarter of the democracies substantial penalties exist, or did exist during several elections, for individual citizens failing to vote in national elections. [3] As Tingsten (1937) demonstrated quite clearly forty years ago, the imposition of relatively small fines or other penalties can have a major impact on voting turnout. Although this effect is hardly surprising, it is a factor we must take account of before we can assess the impact of other political and social conditions.

In Australia, Belgium, and Venezuela non-voters are in violation of the law and subject to fines and other penalties for failure to vote unless excused by illness. The potential sanctions in Venezuela are particularly harsh. Such penalties have also existed in Costa Rica since 1960 and were in effect in the Netherlands until the 1971 election. Similar penalties and requirements also existed in Chile before its democracy was overthrown, and apparently in Greece before the 1967 military coup, as well as presently. Italy does not have legally designated compulsory voting, but non-voters are stamped as such on their official work and identification papers. It is widely believed, at least, that such non-voters are subject to discrimination in receiving employment and other benefits. (See Galli and Prandi, 1970: 28-32; Zariski, 1972: 75) The potential penalties for not voting are apparently quite substantial.

The impact of these sanctions can be seen in Table 2. None of the countries with penalties for non-voting had average turnout levels under 70 percent of the eligible electorate, or under 80 percent of the registered electorate. The average turnout was about 10 percent higher in the countries with penalties for non-voting. The relationship is strong and statistically significant at the 0.01 level. Further, two nations changed their laws on penalties for non-voting: Costa Rica and the Netherlands. The introduction of penalties for non-voting increased turnout in Costa Rica by about 15 percent. Elimination of penalties in the Netherlands led to an initial decrease of 16 percent, although turnout has leveled off at 10 percent below earlier levels. (See also Tingsten, 1937)

We have, therefore, both cross-sectional and longitudinal evidence that penalties for non-voting have a major and significant impact on turnout across the contemporary democracies. We need to recognize, however, that establishing such penalties does not guarantee turnout. The extent of enforcement and magnitude of penalties vary greatly. Moreover, different penalties affect different parts of the population. The aged and unemployed, those in remote villages or those outside the cash economy will often be untouched by various penalties for non-voting and/or even unnoticed by registration officials.

TABLE 2

Voting Laws and Turnout of Eligible Age Group [1]

Types of Voting Laws		Level of Voting Turnout of Eligibles					
Compulsion penalties	Automatic registration	50-65%	66-75%	76-85%	86-95%	Total %	(N)
NO	NO	40%	40%	20%	0	100	(5)
NO	YES	24	29	29	18	100	(17)
YES	NO	0	50	25	25	100	(4)
YES	YES	0	0	25	75	100	(4)

1. Turnout data from Table 1. Countries with penalties for failure to vote are Australia, Belgium, Chile, Costa Rica, Greece, Italy, Netherlands, and Venezuela. Countries in which registration is by application of citizens, rather than automatic, are Australia, Chile, Costa Rica, France, Jamaica, New Zealand, United States, Uruguay, and Venezuela. New Zealand and Uruguay, as well as the compulsory voting countries, provide some penalties for failure to make registration application.

Registration Laws: Application or Automatic Registration

A second way in which the legal setting may affect voting turnout is through variations in registration laws and bureaucratic machinery. In about two-thirds of the democracies, the government assumes the responsibility for voter registration, either through maintaining continually updated lists of registered citizens compiled from census and other official materials, or through periodic and systematic canvasses of all citizens to create or update registration rolls. In other countries it is up to the potential voter to apply to the proper authorities to be entered on the registration lists. In most of the latter countries, there is some legal requirement for citizens to become registered, either in conjunction with compulsory voting, or as a citizenship duty where voting itself is voluntary (New Zealand and Uruguay). Only the United States, France, and post-1962 Jamaica rely totally on the initiative of citizens, sometimes encouraged by their political parties, to get on the electoral rolls. (See Herman, 1976, for comparison of registration laws in 22 of the democracies considered here.) Clearly, when citizens must make the double effort to register and to vote, voting becomes a significantly more difficult act, and we would expect turnout to be lower.

Table 2 shows that the presence of automatic registration procedures, in contrast to citizen application, facilitates citizen turnout, even within countries having penalties for non-voting. These effects are also confirmed in multivariate analysis,[4] and Spackman (1969) describes vividly the drop in citizen registration in Jamaica in areas where "enumerated" citizens were additionally required to take their enumeration certificate and a photograph to a registration center to be enrolled.

Studies within the United States have demonstrated that in some states the registration laws are much more facilitating than in others, although these differences have probably declined. Kelley, Ayers, and Bowen (1967) found that differences in registration laws were a major factor in explaining turnout differences across cities, as did Kim, Petrocik and Enokson (1975) across states. (Also see Campbell et al., 1960: ch. 11; and Rose, 1978.) Rosenstone and Wolfinger (1978:41) estimate that voting turnout in the 1972 Presidential election might have been about nine percent higher if all states had registration laws as facilitative as those in a few states.

Other effects of the legal arrangements for voting seem much less significant than the various experiments with compulsory voting and the provision of automatic registration of eligible citizens. Different arrangements for absentee voting do not seem associated with major turnout differences, although data are incomplete and these may be important in a few specific cases. Baaklini (1976) suggests that the absence of any provisions for absentee balloting in Lebanon depressed turnout, especially as many citizens lived and worked away from their home villages.

**The Legal Environment: Single Member
Districts or Multimember Proportional
Representation**

It has frequently been suggested that voting participation is or would
be enhanced by the introduction of multimember legislative districts
and proportional representation of parties, as opposed to single
member district plurality or majority representation. (For example,
see Lakeman, 1974:151-163.) A variety of arguments to this effect
has been offered. Among the more plausible are the following: (1)
with single member districts, it is likely that some districts will be non-
competitive, giving citizens less incentive to vote; parties, less
incentive to campaign there; (2) the single member district system of
representation can lead to great distortion between votes given to a
party and the legislative representation it receives (see Rae, 1967:74);
these distortions may alienate and discourage sympathizers of
disadvantaged parties; (3) single member districts may encourage the
formation of more diffusely based political parties, whose ability to
mobilize easily identifiable demographic groups of supporters,
especially social class groups, will be inhibited.

In counter-argument, it can be said that with single member
districts the individual representatives may seem closer to
constituents, more identifiable as personal linkages to the national
centres of power. Observers of such complex PR systems as those in
Finland and Switzerland have also suggested that the very complexity
of the voters' choice situation may serve to discourage participation
by some citizens.

We shall use Blondel (1969) to classify electoral systems as either
providing single representatives for most districts (whether through
majority, plurality, or preferential mechanisms) or some form of
multimember PR arrangement. We find that there is a substantial
association between PR and turnout of enfranchised citizens.
Turnout averages about 78 percent in the PR systems, but only about
71 percent in the single member district systems. The Pearson
correlation between electoral laws and turnout is 0.30, significant at
the 0.05 level across the 30 countries. However, controlling for
compulsory voting and the registration laws reduces this relationship
sharply; a multiple regression with the two voting law variables
produces an insignificant Beta of 0.07 for the electoral laws. Thus,
while PR is on average associated with higher turnout, much of the
association seems to be due to facilitating registration and
compulsory voting, which are more frequently present in the PR
systems.

FACTORS SHAPING COMPARATIVE
VOTING TURNOUT: PARTY SYSTEMS

Political parties are the institutions meant to link individual citizen voting choices and aggregate electoral outcomes in the competitive democracies. The political parties set the alternatives offered citizens and their organized activities encourage voting. Studies of voting participation have emphasized the key role of citizens' ties to political parties in explaining different participation levels of individuals and social groups (e.g., Campbell et al., 1960; Verba, Nie and Kim, 1968; and the various party identification studies reviewed by Milbrath and Goel, 1977:53-55). Indeed, in their comparative analyses of participation in seven nations, Verba, Nie and Kim note that "with the exception of the United States, then, we find that (party) institutions are dominant over voting activity; they both mobilize the affiliated and restrict the unaffiliated" (1978:121). Voting is in this respect contrasted with other forms of campaign activity, where both party affiliation and socioeconomic resources shape citizens' activities.

Party Systems and Cleavage Alignments

In explaining the role of parties in shaping voting participation, we expect the relationships between party systems and national cleavage structures to play a major role. In some countries the national parties have developed close and enduring ties to particular demographic groups. In other countries, the different parties have relied upon more diffuse, less differentiated support, as in the United States, or upon varying alliances with local organizations and factions, as in many developing nations.

Theoretically, where strong linkages exist between national parties, or blocs of parties, and demographic groups, voting participation should be encouraged. Alford suggested in his analysis of class voting that "where workers have a party clearly appealing to their interests, their participation and sense of political efficacy is as great as middle-class persons" (1963:302). Thus, where the national parties represent different, meaningful, cleavage groups, the electoral outcomes take on an easily identifiable significance. Where these linkages are relatively stable, they provide cues to even poorly informed and less interested voters as to the interpretation of issue and candidate choices in given elections. That such linkages can be

highly durable has been demonstrated by Lipset and Rokkan (1967),
who point out that the efforts of particular Western European parties
to organize and mobilize particular demographic groups — workers,
farmers, believing Catholics, businessmen — in the period between
1880 and 1920, had continuing effects on voting alignments through
the 1960s. Moreover, the presence of strong, continuing expectations
about parties and cleavage alignments not only creates easily
identifiable choices for citizens, but also makes it easier for parties to
seek out supporters and mobilize them at election time. The creation
of enduring relationships between parties and organized social and
economic groups, such as trade unions and economic and religious
organizations, also contributes to linkages.

Therefore we expect that voting participation will increase to the
extent that political parties are linked with nationally identifiable
cleavage groups. The critical empirical question here is not one of
party labels and aspirations, but of the de facto success of the parties
in creating these linkages. We are not concerned, then, with the
presence of "Socialist" or "Catholic" parties as such, but with
differential success achieved by such parties in building linkages to
workers, believing Catholics, and so on. Perhaps surprisingly, given
the plausibility of the argument and the influence of the work of
Alford (1963) and Lipset and Rokkan (1967), the comparative effects
of cleavage alignments on voting turnout have not been previously
explored.

A simple and straightforward measure of the strength of the
alignment between parties and cleavage groups is the degree to which
we can predict individuals' partisan preferences from knowledge of
their demographic characteristics. Where our predictive capacity is
high, then cleavage group alignments are strong and we expect rather
high levels of voting participation. Where knowledge of individuals'
cleavage group membership is of little help in predicting their
partisanship, then cleavage group alignments are weak, and, ceteris
paribus, we expect lower levels of electoral participation.

Reliable construction of measures of *national party-group
linkages* requires survey data within each country to link an
individual's party preferences to his demographic characteristics.
The closest approximation to such data is provided by Rose
(1974:17), who offers a table showing the percent of variance in
partisanship explained by various demographic characteristics in 15
countries. In fact, the correlation between Rose's measure of
variance explained for these 15 countries and their average voting

turnout as reported in the last column of Table 1 is 0.66. (If we add the percent variance explained for Japan provided by Flanigan and Richardson — 19 percent — it fits perfectly and the correlation is unaltered.) If we exclude the five cases with compulsory voting, the correlation increases somewhat. Even with so few cases, these relationships are significant at the 0.01 level.

Using a cruder set of measures based on published tables of the relationship between occupation and partisanship, and religiosity and partisanship, as shown in Table 3, it is possible to extend a measure of party-group linkages to 24 nations. The measures here are based on the work of Alford (1963) and his "index of class voting." Alford's well-known index is the percentage of manual workers voting for "left" parties, minus the percentage of non-manual workers voting for "left" parties. For example, in Sweden in 1964, some 84 percent of workers supported the Communists or the Social Democrats, whereas only 32 percent of these in all other occupations did so — yielding a "class support index" of 52 for that year. In the United States, in contrast, in that same year 78 percent of the manual workers favoured the Democrats over the Republicans, while 61 percent of those in other occupations did so — yielding a "class support" index of only 17 for that year.

TABLE 3

Social Cleavage and Party Support Alignments in Twenty-Four Democracies

Nation	Years of survey	Major cleavage alignment of party system	National party-cleavage group linkage index[1]
Netherlands	1968	Religion: Relig. Parties v. Other	64
Finland	1966,72	Occupation: Comm./Socialist v. Other	55
Belgium	1968,71	Religion: Catholic v. Other	50
Austria	1967,69	Religion: OeVP v. Socialist	49
Denmark	1964,71,73	Occupation: SPP/Socialist v. Other	47
Sweden	1964,68,73	Occupation: Comm./Socialist v. Other	46
Switzerland	1972	Religion: Catholic v. Other	45
New Zealand	1966*	Occupation: Labour v. National	42
Italy	1968,71,75	Religion: Christ. Dem. v. Other	40
Norway	1965,73	Occupation: SPP/Labour v. Other	40

TABLE 3 (continued)

Nation	Years of survey	Major cleavage alignment of party system	National party-cleavage group linkage index[1]
United Kingdom	1964-74	Occupation: Labour v. Conservative	38
W. Germany	1967,71	Religion: CDU/CSU v. SPD	36
Israel	1969	Religion: Alignment v. Other	34
France	1967,71,73	Religion: Gaullist/Rep./Cent. v. Other	34
Australia	1967	Occupation: Labour/DLP v. Other	33
Canada	1965,68	Religion: Liberal v. Other	28
Chile	1972*	Income: Allende v. Other	25
Japan	1967	Occupation: Liberal/Dem. Soc. v. Other	24
Ireland	1969	Occupation: Labour v. Other	21
Philippines	1969	Language: Marcos v. Other	20
United States	1960-72	Religion: Republican v. Democratic	20
Jamaica	1967*	Occupation: PNP v. JLP	18
India	1971*	Landholding: JS/Swatranta v. Other	13
Venezuela	1973	Religion: COPEI v. Other	13

* Sub-national sample. Indian sample is national, but of males only.

1. Index for occupation is percent of manual workers supporting the left parties, minus percent of those in other occupations supporting the left parties. For religion, the index is usually the percent regular church attenders supporting religious parties, minus non-regular attenders supporting such parties; in the US, Canada, and Switzerland the religious cleavage contrasts Catholics and Protestants. Support is measured by party preference or intended vote; don't know and independent responses, not reported in many countries, are excluded from percentages. Unlike Alford (1963) and Lijphart (1971), the rural populations are included.

Sources: Indices are calculated from published tabled in Rose (1974) for the Netherlands, Finland, Belgium, Sweden, Italy, Norway, Germany, Australia, Canada, and Ireland; from tables for Finland, Denmark, Sweden, and Norway in Berglund and Lindstrom (1978); from tables for Belgium, France, and Germany in Inglehart (1977:199,224). Where equivalent data were available for several years or sources, these were averaged to provide the best estimate. Data for these and other countries for the 1960 to 1978 period were calculated from tables in the following: Austria (Inglehart, 1971; Powell, 1976); Canada (Meisel, 1974); Chile (Prothro and Chappario, 1974); Denmark (Damgaard, 1974; Thomas, 1973); France (Sondages, 1967, 1973); Israel (Arian, 1973); India (Sheth, 1975), Italy (Sani, 1977); Jamaica (Stone, 1973); New Zealand (Mitchell, 1969); Philippines (Averch, Koehler and Denton, 1971); Switzerland (Kerr, 1974); United Kingdom (Crewe, Sarlvik, and Alt,

1977); United States (Pomper, 1975). The Philippine tables were re-estimated for the size of language groups as given by census data. Data for Japan were generously provided by Norman H. Nie and Sidney Verba (also see Watanuki, 1967). Tables for Venezuela were contributed with great kindness by Enrique Baloyra and John Martz; the study is described in Martz and Baloyra (1976).

In most countries with strong linkages, one cleavage was clearly more important than the second. In Austria, Israel, and the United States, however, occupation and religion were of about equal strength. In India size of landholding was somewhat stronger than either caste or occupation. In all countries, cutting points were chosen to divide the population into roughly equal size groups where possible.

As described in the footnote to Table 3, we have replicated that index in as many nations as possible. Where equivalent original data were available from several sources, or over several elections in the appropriate time period, all the scores were averaged to improve the estimate. In a few countries it was necessary to use alternative measures of the occupation of the head of the household, and religion was not available in all cases. As most data sources did not report class and religion jointly, and hence the interactions could not be estimated, the measure of national party-group linkage, shown in the last column in Table 3, is either the class or religious support index, whichever is higher. The Pearson correlation between this group support index and voting turnout (as a percent of citizens of voting age) is 0.58 for the twenty-four countries, significant at the 0.01 level.

As the measure of group support involves dichotomizing both the independent and dependent variables, and the exclusion of the uncertain respondents, there is some element of judgment in coding and creating the indices. There is, however, a very high correlation (0.85 for 14 cases) between the scores reported here and those reported by Lijphart (1971) in his sophisticated effort to extend and replicate the work of Alford. (Also see Inglehart, 1977:chs. 7,8.) The major differences among the subset of fourteen cases for which Lijphart reports data are in Belgium, where the rise of ethnic parties has decreased the power of religion, and in France, where religion has become somewhat less important in the Fifth Republic than it was in the Fourth. Comparison of Lijphart's scores, based usually on surveys about five years earlier, with the data in Rose and with later data in Inglehart (1977) and Berglund and Lindstrom (1978) suggests that the relative magnitude of these linkages tends to be rather stable over time, at least in modernized systems. At a general level this conclusion is also supported by the time series analyses in Britain by

Crewe, Sarlvik and Alt (1977), in Scandinavia by Berglund and Lindstrom (1978), and in the United States by Pomper (1975). Although Crewe et al., demonstrate that class voting was declining in Britain from the 1950s to the 1970s, as was turnout, the size of the shifts is such that Britain's comparative rank in both respects does not change greatly. The tendency of demographic party-group alignments to be "frozen" for substantial time periods, so powerfully argued by Lipset and Rokkan (1967) is quite evident here, even as regards the magnitude of the linkages.[5]

The strong association between the measure of party-group linkage and voting turnout is shown in Table 4. Controlling for required voting increases the relationships: the zero-order gamma between group linkage and turnout is 0.84 for the twenty-four countries; controlling for required voting, the first-order partial gamma is 0.87.

TABLE 4

Linkages Between Cleavage Groups and Parties and Average Voting Turnout of Eligibles in Twenty-Four Democracies[1]

National cleavage group-party linkage index		Average Turnout of Eligible Age Group					
		50-65%	66-75%	76-85%	86-95%	Total %	(N)
Compulsory Voting	NO 0-30	43%	43%	14%	0	100	(7)
	NO 31-45	14	29	57	0	100	(7)
	46-70	0	0	25	75	100	(4)
	0-30	0	50	50	0	100	(2)
	YES 31-45	0	0	0	100	100	(2)
	46-70	0	0	0	100	100	(2)

1. Average turnout data from Table 1. National Cleavage Group-Party Linkage index scores from Table 3. Tau-C for 18 nations without compulsory voting penalties is 0.69, significant at the 0.01 level. Tau-C for all 24 nations combined is 0.68, also significant at 0.01. Relationships are also significant using turnout as percent of registered electorate.

In short, the examination of the relationship between strength of party-group linkages and voting turnout yields a consistent and robust conclusion: strong linkages between citizens' cleavage group memberships and their party preferences are a powerful predictor of voting turnout across nations. This relationship holds up well using several different statistical measures of linkage, using several alternative subsets of countries and various tests of association, and in multiple regression analysis controlling for registration laws and compulsory voting (Beta = 0.47).

Party Competition

Among students of voting participation, it seems largely agreed that increased levels of party competition should be associated with higher voting turnout. A number of studies across cities and states in the USA support that conclusion (e.g., Kelley, Ayres and Bowen, 1967; Kim, Petrosik, and Enokson, 1975; and the review by Milbrath and Goel, 1977). Unfortunately, it seems to be difficult to find agreement on the meaning of competitiveness once one moves beyond the simplicity of two-party dominated elections. In the American case, researchers have assumed that where one of the two major parties predominates, interest will be less among both voters and party activists, and turnout lessened. Where a given election outcome seems a foregone conclusion, turnout will decline in that election (see Aldrich, 1976). In a Third World perspective, Huntington has argued that citizen mobilization should be greatest in two-party systems, followed by predominant party situations, with least mobilization in multiparty situations (Huntington, 1968:428 ff.), an argument somewhat supported by McDonough's findings in India (1971), although the differences are not great. Huntington notes, however, that multiparty systems in modernized nations may develop strong ties between parties and special constituencies of the sort we have explored above, and these would facilitate mobilization.

In general the problem of theoretical expectations about voting turnout in multiparty systems is compounded by the variety of coalition arrangements, formal and informal, in such systems. In Denmark in the 1960s, for example, the complex system of five substantial parties took on virtually a two-party clarity for voters and activists with the consolidation of pro- and anti-Socialist blocs. The emergence of these apparently sharply contrasted opposing blocs, evenly balanced in voting strength, was associated with a moderate increase in voting turnout, as was the situation of evenly balanced bloc-confrontation in Sweden in the 1970s, and Norway from 1965.

At the other extreme of the complex relationship between multiparty competition and legislative/electoral outcomes, we find

Switzerland. The Swiss case is extremely "deviant" in terms of
voting turnout. Switzerland is a highly economically developed,
small country, with automatic registration and rather strong linkages
between parties and cleavage groups along religious lines. Four
cantons even have required voting. Most of our theoretical
arguments lead us to predict high voting turnout in Switzerland. But
in fact it is very low, even before the enfranchisement of inex-
perienced female voters in the early 1970s. Turnout has been steadily
declining, moreover, several percent in each election, since the 1930s.
The most likely explanation is offered by Przeworski (1974): the
deliberate demobilization of party competition by the major national
parties themselves. Since the late 1930s, the four major parties, each
linked to a cleavage group, have guaranteed themselves roughly
equal place in the shared collective national executive, which has a
rotating chairmanship. Unless a new party should suddenly break
into the big four, the electoral outcomes at the national level are
virtually meaningless. There is not the intense juggling of ministries
and party balances which marked the responsiveness of the German
and Austrian Grand Coalitions to electoral outcomes. Moreover,
most important policy decisions are made at the Cantonal level.
There is little incentive for voters to go to the polls, or for the major
parties to try to mobilize them. (See Steiner, 1974.)

The Swiss case, and consideration of changes in coalition competitiveness in the Scandinavian nations, support the idea that intensity
of competition is associated with increased voting turnout. However,
they also suggest the difficulty of finding unambiguous measures of
such competition. One attempt to classify party systems by types of
competition is that of Sartori (1976:314). Of our democracies he
identifies six party systems as "two-party", another six as "predominant," and another eleven as having some form of multi-
partyism. We find turnout averages 77 percent in the two-party
systems, 79 percent in the multiparty systems, and 72 percent in the
predominant systems. The purported advantages of two-party
competition in mobilizing support seems to hold up vis-à-vis one-
party predominance. But the multiparty systems do not seem
disadvantaged, except in the case of Switzerland. Moreover, each
type shows substantial variation, relating in part to the cleavage
alignment and voting law differences. Moreover, most of the Third
World nations in Sartori's analysis are predominant system
countries, which weighs down the turnout level of that type of party
system. In multivariate analysis, the impact of single-party
predominance is insignificant.

Another approach is to look at the apparent connection between elections and legislative/executive outcomes. If a single party dominates the electoral process, or if deliberate inter-party agreements predetermine the electoral outcomes, we might expect the lesser importance of elections to reduce voting participation. In four countries such dominance or pre-election agreements seemed virtually to determine the cabinet and chief executive before the elections: India, where the Congress Party dominated national politics until 1977; Japan, where the Liberal Democrats have dominated national politics throughout the post-war period; Switzerland, where the four large parties have had a predetermined share in the collective executive; and Lebanon, where the constitution guarantees sets to religious subfactions and personalistic "parties" have represented these. Average turnout in these four countries was, respectively, 60, 71, 53 and 56 percent, all well below the general average for the democracies. In these rather extreme cases of limited electoral/executive connections, we seem to see some sharp effects in lowering election participation. However, if we construct a typology for the remaining countries, in which we classify countries in terms of the frequency with which elections lead directly and unambiguously to executive change, we find no simple anticipated differences in turnout levels. [6]

FACTORS SHAPING COMPARATIVE VOTING TURNOUT: SOCIAL STRUCTURE

Economic Development and Social Modernization

Probably the largest body of writing on theories of cross-national participation is the literature on social modernization and political mobilization (See Lerner, 1958; Deutsch, 1961; Almond and Powell, 1978; Huntington, 1968; Nie, Powell and Prewitt, 1969; and Inkles and Smith, 1974.) The various approaches suggest that "economic development" has important consequences for mass political activity, as the achievement of higher levels of economic development is associated with major transformations of the social and economic structure of the society. Some analyses emphasize the exposure of individuals to a modern, secular political culture, which stresses the ability of human beings to transform their physical and social environment. Others stress the creation and dispersion of personal social resources, such as information, status, and social awareness. While yet other studies discuss the transformation of group relationships within the society, the networks and dependencies which link individuals together in various ways.

Despite the vast body of theory, the only published studies which examine the relationship between economic development and voting turnout across a large set of countries draw on the data in Russett et al. (1964). In the original analysis Russett et al., report a strong (Pearson) correlation of 0.47 between economic development and voting participation of citizens in enfranchised age groups for a single election (p. 83). However, the majority of their 90 countries are not democracies; franchises vary sharply; the meaning of the voting act, as well as inducements and penalties for participation, no doubt varies widely. Other studies using these data, with similar conclusions, include Alker (1966) and Tanter (1967).

In Figure 1 we show a scattergram of GNP/Capita level and average voting turnout as a percent of the eligible age groups for the thirty democracies. As sanctions for non-voting are quite important, the countries which tend to compel voting through legal penalties are indicated with stars, rather than dots. The best-fit regression lines for turnout with log GNP per Capita — the most commonly used measure of economic development — are shown separately for countries with required and voluntary voting. Both sets show relationships significant at the 0.05 level. The simple Pearson correlation between log GNP/Capita and turnout is 0.35, significant at the 0.05 level. Other measures of modernization, such as literacy level (r = 0.40) and percent employed in non-agricultural occupations (r = 0.36), are similarly related to voting turnout.

A rough but useful indication of the magnitude of the modernization effect is provided by breaking down the countries into two major groups of developing and developed nations as of 1965. The former group includes the twelve nations with 1965 GNP/Capita under $900, the wealthiest of which was Venezuela. The latter includes the eighteen nations with GNP/Capita at $1,000 or more, the poorest of which were Ireland and Italy. The average turnout levels are about 12 percent higher in the developed nations, controlling for legal penalties:

Nations without penalties for non-voting
GNP/Capita $100 — $900 Average Turnout 66% (8 nations)
GNP/Capita $901 — $3,600 Average Turnout 77% (14 nations)

Nations with penalties for non-voting
GNP/Capita $100 — $900 Average Turnout 77% (4 nations)
GNP/Capita $901 — $3,600 Average Turnout 90% (4 nations)

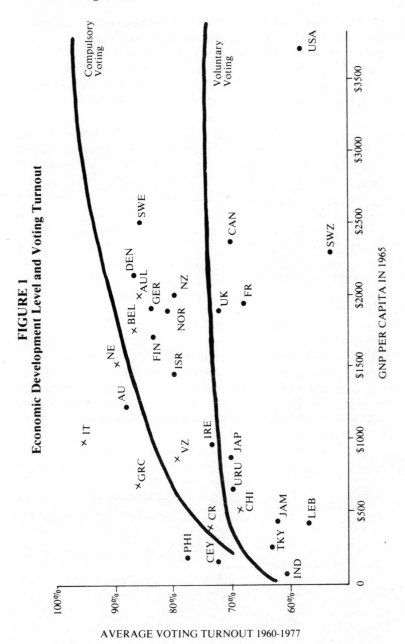

FIGURE 1
Economic Development Level and Voting Turnout

All of these results support the expectation that economic development and turnout are associated in the democratic political systems, although they do not resolve theoretical issues regarding the individual level linkages or dynamic relationships involved. We might add, too, that as the poorer countries are more likely to employ compulsory voting to get their citizens to the polls, the effect of the compulsory voting laws has been to diminish the depressing effect of low economic development on voting turnout. The most striking example is Venezuela, which has very harsh penalties for unexcused non-voting and high turnout. Baloyra (1977) reports that over 40 percent of the citizens say they would not vote if the penalties were removed. The simple gamma between dichotomized GNP/Capita and turnout was 0.68, and the first-order partial controlling for compulsory voting was 0.77. Similarly, when GNP per capita (log) is entered into a regression analysis with registration laws and compulsory voting, its impact on turnout increases, with the Beta up to a highly significant 0.41.

MULTIVARIATE ANALYSIS

Multivariate analysis can show how much of the total variance in voting turnout is explained by environmental characteristics. We can use simultaneous multiple regression to guard against accepting or rejecting associations spuriously. Causal modeling can also be of help in dealing with direct and indirect relationships.

Multiple Regression

We have survey evidence on the linkages between cleavage groups and parties in only twenty-four of our thirty democracies. The missing cases are without exception nations at lower levels of wealth and socio-economic modernization. Our conclusions must, therefore, be drawn with some care.

1. If we enter GNP/Capita (log), Electoral Laws (PR Dummy), Compulsory Voting, and Registration Laws into a multiple regression equation with voting turnout, the Beta for electoral laws is insignificant. The other three variables are each significant at the 0.05 level. Running the equations with and without log Population Size yields the same result. Re-running the equation only with

GNP/Capita (log), Compulsory Voting, and Registration Laws finds each of them clearly significant, with the Bs well over twice the standard error (Betas of 0.41, 0.47, and 0.39). The three variables yield a multiple R of 0.67, explaining some 45 percent of the variance in voting turnout for the thirty democracies. These results support our previous conclusions that PR electoral laws have no direct significant effects, while the level of economic development and compulsory voting and registration do.

2. The simple competitiveness dichotomy does establish itself as a powerful and significant variable, along with compulsory voting and registration laws. Although only four nations were classified as non-competitive, they clearly had turnout below the levels otherwise anticipated. Addition of the competitiveness dummy variable to GNP/Capita, Compulsory Voting, and Registration Laws increases the percent variance explained from 45 percent to 69 percent for the thirty countries. Interestingly enough, the impact of GNP per capita is weakened, although still significant ($\beta = 0.29$).

3. In the smaller set of 24 countries for which we have survey data on the relationships between cleavage groups and parties, first-stage analysis, before considering party factors, basically confirms the above findings. When we introduce the measure of linkage between parties and cleavage groups, the variance explained increases sharply. Party Linkage replaces GNP/Capita in importance; the latter loses all significance. This result strongly suggests that much of the effect of modernization operates through the creation or maintenance of more clear-cut linkages between parties and cleavage groups in the more modernized societies. The secondary literature on party systems in those nations for which we do not have data certainly suggests that linkages between parties and national cleavage groups tends to be weak in the less developed countries. Personalism and patronage dominate party politics in the democracies such as Costa Rica, Uruguay, the Philippines, Lebanon, Greece, and Turkey. (See McDonald, 1972, for some limited survey evidence for Uruguay.)

Introducing the dichotomous competitiveness variable yields four significant variables explaining turnout in the twenty-four countries: Competitiveness (dummy), Party Linkage, Compulsory Voting, and Registration Laws. The multiple R is 0.85, explaining 73 percent of the variance in voting turnout, and the respective Bs are all twice the size of the standard error, Betas being respectively, 0.52, 0.28, 0.31, and 0.41. (Additional consideration of GNP/Capita, Population Size, and Electoral Laws does not increase the explanatory power or yield additional significant coefficients.)

However, given our theoretical understanding of the working of the party linkages to cleavage groups — that they will make it easier to identify mobilizable supporters, and that elections will be more clearly significant in their effects to citizen group members — it is not clear that we should expect such influences to operate *within* highly non-competitive situations. It is appropriate, then, to recognize the impact of non-competitiveness in its own right — in this rather extreme version where election outcomes are largely predetermined — and to run the multivariate model only on the twenty-one competitive cases, the twenty-four for which survey data is available less Switzerland, India and Japan. If we do so, we find that Party Linkages, Compulsory Voting, and Registration Laws alone explain 74 percent of the variance in turnout, with highly significant Betas of respectively, 0.47, 0.36, and 0.43. It is interesting to see that compulsory voting, although strong and significant, is the least powerful of these three. No other influence is significant when added to this model.

CONCLUDING COMMENTS

We can explain a substantial amount of the variance in average voting turnout across democracies by a few characteristics of the party system and electoral laws. The specific tactics of candidates and the specific issues and alliances of individual elections play a lesser role in shaping voting participation. Linkages between parties and cleavage groups, the presence of successful party competition, automatic registration, and compulsory voting account for nearly 75 percent of the variance in turnout across the twenty-four democracies for which data were available.

The literature on voting participation suggested a number of factors which should affect cross-national turnout differences. Some of these expectations, such as those regarding registration laws and compulsory voting, were confirmed. On the other hand, such frequently cited factors as small population size, proportional representation, and the number of competitive parties did not have any direct effect on turnout after controlling for legal factors. In analyzing the effects of party competition, only the general dichotomy between systems with and without a recent history of elections altering the composition of the executive had a notable impact on turnout. As only four countries qualified as "non-competitive," this variable retains a somewhat doubtful status. Linkages between parties and cleavage groups, however, had strong and consistent effects in mobilizing voters.

Given the large literature describing the mobilizing role of economic development and social modernization, we expected to find average voting turnout related to measures of modernization in the democracies. So it was, and modernization variables remained significant after controlling for the legal factors. At best we can judge from these data, however, that much of the modernization effect seemed to occur through the shaping of ties between parties and national cleavage groups, rather than through individual level increases in status or information. This conclusion seems consistent with the most recent individual level studies of voting participation in modernizing countries. (See Huntington and Nelson, 1976; and especially, Verba, Nie and Kim, 1978.) Individual resources and status changes may have major impact on non-partisan participation and on the more difficult participatory acts, but the relation of the party system to individuals and social groups is critical for voting.

A full scale causal model has not been presented. The assumptions of causal modeling require an analysis of the sources of registration laws and compulsory voting which is beyond the scope of this study. But the data are consistent with causal effects in which both modernization and, to a lessor extent, proportional representation, act to increase the likelihood of close ties developing between parties and national cleavage groups. The religious and ethnic compositions of the population, as well as historical events, help determine whether these linkages will be primarily based on social class alone, or based on other demographic groups as well. The strength of these linkages, then, together with registration laws and penalties for non-voting, strongly determine the average voting turnout levels in countries with even moderate degrees of party competition. This argument can be summarized in the following sketch:[7]

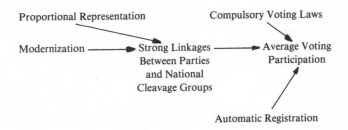

The absence of proportional representation is usually associated (r = 0.9) with British or American culture (or colonial tutelage) at the time of constitution making. The countries with single-member district electoral systems in 1959-1977 are Australia, Canada, Ceylon (Sri Lanka), France, India, Jamaica, New Zealand, Philippines, the United Kingdom and the United States. Cultural assumptions about representation are a major influence upon electoral laws; calculation of political advantage is also present and occasionally overriding.

It is also revealing to replicate all of the analysis in this paper using the turnout of registered voters (Column 3, in Table 1), rather than voters as a percent of the enfranchised age groups. We have to delete the United States from such analysis, as reliable national registration figures are not available. For some countries, however, the difference between turnout of registered voters and turnout of enfranchised eligibles is quite substantial. Not surprisingly, we find that the effects of the registration laws themselves are negligible in predicting turnout of those registered. The predictive power of compulsory voting, on the other hand, increases sharply. Penalties for non-voting seem particularly effective in getting those already on the registration rolls to the voting booth. Party variables remain about equally significant in explaining the turnout of registered as of enfranchised voters. The party effects seem quite robust. However, as so few of the democracies were notably non-competitive, we cannot be as confident of competitiveness as of party-group linkages. Modernization plays a similar role in explaining the turnout of registered as of eligible voters: it is significant until the party linkage is introduced, and apparently mediated through it to a large extent.

Whichever version of the dependent variable we use, the effects of modernization, seem to have impact on the turnout-enhancing development of party ties to demographic groups. The positive indirect effects on turnout appear even in the more modernized sub-set of nations where zero-order relationships are negligible. However, there is evidence that the strength of occupational group linkages to parties has declined somewhat in recent years in at least some Western nations, especially in Britain and Denmark. And in many of the European nations religion continues to be the primary orienting cleavage at a time when church attendence is falling. These facts suggest that a post-industrial society may see a decline in the strength of party-group linkages, or a period of uncertainty as re-alignment occurs and new linkages are developed. One might expect such events to produce lower voting turnout.

The data here indeed emphasize the direct and immediate effects on voting turnout of party ties to identifiable demographic groups. Among several sub-sets of countries and with several measures of the group basis of party preference, this influence is a major predictor of turnout. Group-based partisanship also has important connections to other aspects of democratic politics, such as the patterns of conflict and the stability of party and voting coalitions. We need to explore further the basis of the party-group linkage relationship, its sensitivity to change, and the extent to which it is founded on citizen's incentives or the mobilizing effectiveness of political parties, or both.

NOTES

I should like to thank Peter H. Lemieux, Lynda W. Powell, Seymour Martin Lipset, and Richard Rose for helpful comments and suggestions at various stages of this analysis.

1. The population of appropriate age was calculated from the United Nations *Demographic Yearbook 1970* and later editions. The *World Book Atlas* (1977) was used for estimating population size for several elections after 1976. Some interpolation was necessary in many countries and data are clearly more accurate for years close to those of general national censuses. However, average turnout changes from election to election correspond quite systematically to differences in turnout of registered voters in most countries. (In Venezuela the registration roles were expanded from 1958 to 1968.) Raw turnout figures are largely from Mackie and Rose (1974); the *European Journal of Political Research; Keesing's Archives;* and individual country studies listed in the bibliography, especially the excellent AEI "At the Polls" series. The ages of eligibility were derived primarily from Mackie and Rose (1974); United Nations Secretary General's Report, 1968; and Herman (1976).

2. A major exception is Ceylon, with automatic registration and a substantial discrepancy between "eligibles" and the electorate registered. This difference may be due in part to the need to estimate size of the voting age Indian Tamil population (10.6 percent of total population in the 1963 Census) who are disenfranchised in these elections, and for whom age distribution figures were not available. (See Kearney, 1973.) Analysis deleting Ceylon does not materially change any results reported below.

3. Two other countries, Austria and Switzerland, had compulsory voting for citizens residing in several Provinces or Cantons. These made up less than 10 percent of the total national population, and their inclusion or exclusion does not greatly alter the national averages in the two countries. Hence, they are classified as non-penalty countries. But within each nation, it is true that average turnout is higher in the subunits where penalties exist.

4. The registration law variable in multivariate results reported below is trichotomized: Automatic registration = 3; Required citizen-initiated application = 2;

voluntary citizen-initiated application = 1. See the footnote to Table 2 for countries in each category. Jamaica, a "3" in 1962 and a "1" in part of 1967 and 1972, is coded "2". The same conclusions follow, with a slightly weaker Beta for registration laws, using a dichotomized "Dummy" variable distinguishing only automatic and voluntary registration.

5. More recently, a sharp drop in the absolute level of linkage between parties and cleavage groups took place in Denmark. The sudden emergence of the Progress Party, general weakening in the strength of the Social Democrats, and decline in the size of the agricultural population, reduced the strength of occupation-party ties from an index figure of over 50 (Berglund and Lindstrom, 1958; Thomas, 1973) to around 40 (Berglund and Lindstrom, 1978; Damgaard, 1974), between the late 1960s and mid-1970s. However, even the latter figure is relatively high in comparative perspective, double that of the USA.

6. The initial competitiveness analysis distinguished four levels of effects on executive control: (1) systems in which during all elections there had been at least one example of direct responsiveness to an election in the decade before; (2) systems in which such a responsiveness history was present during only part of the elections averaged; (3) systems in which such effects were discernible in at least a few elections, but of a complex type, as in the Italian cabinet changes: (4) systems in which no responsiveness had been present in the decade before any election averaged into the study. Respectively, the countries so classified were: (1) Australia, Austria, Belgium, Ceylon, Chile, Costa Rica, W. Germany, Jamaica, New Zealand, Philippines, Turkey, UK, USA; (2) Canada, Denmark, France, Greece, Ireland, Norway, Uruguay, Venezuela; (3) Finland, Italy, Netherlands, Sweden, Israel; (4) India, Japan, Lebanon, Switzerland. As pointed out in the text, although some over-time differences in the expected direction can be found *within* countries in category (2), only category (4) clearly is distinguished by lower average turnout.

7. We can, of course, offer a partial causal model of the "sketch" in the text, in which it is described by two simultaneous regression equations. In one equation, Voting Participation is the dependent variable, and all other five variables are independent. In this equation, the R for Voting Participation is 0.87, and the only significant Beta's are those for Linkages (0.44), Compulsory Voting (0.32) and Registration Laws (0.36), each with a B over twice the standard error. In the second equation, Linkages is the dependent variable, predicted only by Modernization (GNP/Capita) and Proportional Representation. In this equation the R for Linkages is 0.58, and the Beta's for both GNP/Capita (0.42) and Proportional Representation (0.38) are significant. That is, given the assumptions of causal priority implied, each of the arrows shown in the causal sketch yields a significant coefficient, and no other possible causal connections do so.

REFERENCES

ALDRICH, J. H. (1976) "Some Problems in Testing Two Rational Models of Partici-
    pation." *American Journal of Political Science,* XX: 713-734.
ALFORD, R. R. (1963) *Party and Society: The Anglo-American Democracies.*
    Chicago: Rand McNally.

ALKER, H. R., Jr., (1966) "Causal Inferences and Political Analysis." In J. Bernd, ed., *Mathematical Applications in Political Science*. Dallas: SMU Press.

ALISKY, M. (1969) *Uruguay: A Contemporary Survey*. New York: Praeger.

ALMOND, G. A. and G. BINGHAM POWELL, Jr. (1966) *Comparative Politics: A Developmental Approach*. Boston, Little, Brown.

— — (1978) *Comparative Politics: System, Process, and Policy*. Boston: Little, Brown.

ARIAN, A. (1973) *The Choosing People: Voting Behavior in Israel*. Cleveland: Case Western Press.

AVERCH, H., J. E. KOEHLER, and F.H. DENTON (1971) *The Matrix of Policy in the Philippines*. Princeton: Princeton University Press.

BAAKLINI, A. (1976) *Legislative and Political Development: Lebanon, 1842-1972*. Durham: Duke University Press.

BALOYRA, E. A. (1977) "Public Attitudes Toward the Democratic Regime," in John D. Martz and David J. Myers, *Venezuela: The Democratic Experience*. New York: Praeger.

BERGLUND, S. and U. LINDSTROM (1978) *The Scandinavian Party System(s)*. Lund (Sweden): Studentlitteratur.

BLONDEL, J. (1969) *Introduction to Comparative Government*. New York: Praeger.

CAMPBELL, A., P. E. CONVERSE, W. E. MILLER, and D. E. STOKES (1960) *The American Voter*. New York: John Wiley.

— — (1966) *Elections and the Political Order*. New York: John Wiley.

CREWE, I., B. SARLVIK, and J. ALT (1977) "Partisan Dealignment in Britain," *British Journal of Political Science*, 7 (April): 129-190.

DAHL, R. E. (1971) *Polyarchy: Participation and Opposition*. New Haven: Yale University Press.

DAMGAARD, E. (1974) "Stability and Change in the Danish Party System Over Half a Century," *Scandinavian Political Studies*, 9: 103-125.

DENTON, C. F. (1971) *Patterns of Costa Rican Politics*. Boston: Allyn and Bacon.

DEUTSCH, K. (1961) "Social Mobilization and Political Development," *American Political Science Review*, LV (September): 493-514.

EULAU, H. and K. PREWITT (1973) *Labyrinths of Democracy*. Indianapolis: Bobbs-Merrill.

FLANIGAN, S. C. and B. M. RICHARDSON (1977) *Japanese Electoral Behavior: Social Cleavages, Social Networks, and Partisanship*. Beverley Hills, Ca.: Sage Publications.

GALLI, G. and A. PRANDI (1970) *Patterns of Political Participation in Italy*. New Haven: Yale University Press.

GOEL, M. L (1974) "Social Bases of Party Support and Political Participation in India," *Political Science Review*, 13 (Jan.-Dec.): 58-87.

GOLDEY, D. B. and R. W. JOHNSON (1978) "The French General Election of March 1978", *Parliamentary Affairs*, XXXI (Summer): 294-313.

HERMAN, V. (1976) *Parliaments of the World*. New York: De Gruyter.

HIROFUMI, A. (1969) "Voting Turnout in the Philippines," *Philippines Journal of Public Administration*, XII (October): 424-441.

HUNTINGTON, S. P. (1968) *Political Order in Changing Societies*. New Haven: Yale University Press.

— — and J. P. NELSON (1976) *No Easy Choice: Political Participation in Developing Countries*. Cambridge: Harvard University Press.

INGLEHART, R. (1977) *The Silent Revolution: Changing Values and Political Styles among Western Publics.* Princeton: Princeton University Press.

KEARNEY, R. (1973) *The Politics of Ceylon (Sri Lanka).* Ithaca: Cornell University Press.

KELLEY, S., Jr., R. AYRES, and W.G. BOWEN (1967) "Registration and Voting: Putting First Things First," *American Political Science Review,* LXI (March): 359-379.

KERR, H. H., Jr. (1974) *Switzerland: Social Cleavages and Partisan Conflict.* Beverly Hills: Sage Publications.

KIM, J. O., J. R. PETROCIK, S. N. ENOKSON (1975) "Voter Turnout Among the American States," *American Political Science Review,* LXIX (March): 107-123.

LAKEMAN, E. (1974) *How Democracies Vote.* London: Faber and Faber. (Rev. ed.)

LANDES, C. (1965) *Leaders, Factions and Parties.* New Haven: Yale University S. E. Asian Series.

LEGG, K. R. (1969) *Politics in Modern Greece.* Stanford: Stanford University Press.

LERNER, D. (1958) *The Passing of Traditional Society.* New York: Free Press of Glencoe.

LEVINE, S. and J. LODGE (1976) "The New Zealand Election of 1975," *Parliamentary Affairs,* XXIX (Summer): 310-326.

LIJPHART, A. (1971) *Class and Religious Voting in the European Democracies.* Occasional Paper No. 8, Survey Research Centre, University of Strathclyde.

LIPSET, S. M. and S. ROKKAN (eds.) (1967) *Party Systems and Voter Alignments.* New York: Free Press.

MacDONALD, R. H. (1972) "Electoral Politics and Uruguayan Political Decay," *Inter-American Economic Affairs,* XXVI (Summer): 25-46.

MACKIE, T. and R. ROSE (1974) *The International Almanac of Electoral History.* New York: Free Press.

MARTZ, J. D. (1967) "Costa Rican Electoral Trends, 1953-1966," *Western Political Quarterly* (Dec.): 886-888.

— — and E. BALOYRA (1976) *The Venezuelan Election of 1973.* Chapel Hill: University of North Carolina Press.

McDONOUGH, P. (1971) "Electoral Competition and Participation in India," *Comparative Politics,* 4 (October): 77-88.

McGLEN. N. E. (1974) "Strategy Choices for Political Participation." Unpublished Ph.D. Dissertation. University of Rochester.

McHALE, V. (1977) "Community Characteristics and Voting Patterns in Urban Greece." Paper presented at the Annual Meeting of the Midwest Political Science Association, Chicago.

MEISEL, J. (1974) *Cleavages, Parties and Values in Canada.* Beverly Hills: Sage Publications.

MILBRATH, L. W. and M. L. GOEL (1977) *Political Participation.* Chicago: Rand McNally. (Rev. ed.)

MITCHELL, A. (1969) *Politics and People in New Zealand.* Christchurch: Whitecombe and Tombs.

NIE, N. H., G. BINGHAM POWELL, Jr., and K. PREWITT (1969) "Social Structure and Political Participation," *American Political Science Review,* LXIII (June and Sept.): 361-378, 808-832.

— — S. VERBA, and J. PETROSIK (1967) *Changing American Voter.* Cambridge: Harvard University Press.

OZBUDUN, E. (1976) *Social Change and Political Participation in Turkey.* Princeton: Princeton University Press.

POMPER, G. (1975) *Voters Choice.* New York: Dodd, Mead.

POWELL, G.B., Jr. (1976) "Political Cleavage Structure, Cross-Pressure Processes and Partisanship," *American Journal of Political Science,* XX (Feb.): 1-23.

PROTHRO, J. W., and P. E. CHAPPERIO (1974) "Public Opinion and the Movement of Chilean Government to the Left," *Journal of Politics,* 36 (Feb.): 2-43.

PRZEWORSKI, A. (1975) "Institutionalization of Voting Patterns," *American Political Science Review,* LXIX (March): 49-67.

RAE, D. (1967, 1974) *The Political Consequences of Electoral Laws.* New Haven: Yale University Press.

ROSE, R. (ed.) (1974) *Electoral Behavior: A Comparative Handbook.* New York: Free Press.

— — (1978) *Citizen Participation in the Electoral Process.* Strathclyde: Center for the Study of Public Policy.

ROSENSTONE, S. J. and R. E. WOLFINGER (1978) "The Effect of Registration Laws on Voter Turnout," *American Political Science Review,* 72 (March): 22-45.

RUSSETT, B. M. and H. R. ALKER, K. W. DEUTSCH, H. D. LASSWELL (1964) *World Handbook of Political and Social Indicators.* New Haven: Yale University Press.

SALEM, E. A. (1973) *Modernization Without Revolution: Lebanon's Experience.* Bloomington: Indiana University Press.

SANI, G. (1977) "The Italian Electorate in the Mid-1970's," pp. 31-122 in H. Penninman, (ed.) *Italy at the Polls: 1976.* Washington: AEI.

SARTORI, G. (1976) *Parties and Party Systems.* Cambridge: Cambridge University Press.

SHETH, D. L. (1975) "Social Bases of Party Support," pp. 135-164 in D. L. Sheth, (ed.) *Citizens and Parties: Aspects of Campaign Politics in India,* New Delhi: Allied Publications.

Sondages. 1966, 1967, 1973.

SPACKMAN, A. (1969) "Electoral Law and Administration in Jamaica," *Social and Economics Studies,* 18 (March): 1-53.

STEINER, J. (1974) *Amicable Agreement Versus Majority Rule: Conflict Resolution in Switzerland.* Chapel Hill: University of North Carolina Press.

STONE, C. (1973) *Class, Race and Political Behavior in Urban Jamaica.* Jamaica: University of West Indies.

TANTER, R. (1967)) "Toward a Theory of Political Development," *Midwest Journal of Political Science,* XI (May): 145-172.

TAYLOR, C. and M. HUDSON (1972) *World Handbook of Political and Social Indicators.* New Haven: Yale University Press.

TINGSTEN, H. (1937) *Political Behavior: Studies in Election Statistics.* Totow, NJ: Bedminster Press (US issued, 1963).

UNITED NATIONS, Secretary General's Report. (1968) *Constitutions, Electoral Laws and Other Legal Instruments Relating to the Political Rights of Women.* New York: United Nations.

VERBA, S. and N. H. NIE (1972) *Participation in America.* New York: Harper and Row.

— — N. H. NIE and J.O. KIM (1971) *The Modes of Democratic Participation.* Beverley Hills: Sage Publications.

VERBA, S., 'N. H. NIE and J.O. KIM (1978) *Participation and Political Equality: A Seven Nation Comparison*. New York: Cambridge University Press.

WATANUKI, J. (1967) "Patterns of Politics in Present Day Japan," in Lipset and Rokkan, (eds.) *Party Systems and Voter Alignments*. New York: Free Press.

WOODWARD, C. A. (1969) *The Growth of a Party System in Ceylon*. Providence: Brown University Press.

ZARISKI, R. (1972) *Italy: The Politics of Uneven Development*. Hinsdale: Dryden Press.

2

The Appearance and Disappearance of the American Voter

Walter Dean Burnham
Massachusetts Institute of Technology

It has long been appreciated among analysts of comparative politics that generalizations drawn from a larger political cosmos often fit the American case very badly. In particular, the American case deviates in many crucial respects from developmental models based on Western European historical experience. These models suggest a cumulative penetration and organization of the society by increasingly elaborate partisan structures, and thus a long-term trend toward the maximization of electoral participation. In the United States, on the other hand, saturation was reached a century ago. Since then, electoral demobilization has occurred in several waves, and is still going on. Thus, we may speak of the appearance and disappearance of the American voter. Such an extraordinary peculiarity requires both documentation and explanation.

We begin with several propositions. Firstly, electoral mobilization of the mass electorate in pluralistic political systems is contingent on the competition between and organizational vitality of political parties. The one cannot be understood in isolation from the other. Secondly, one widely and rightly used index of democratization in a political system is the proportion of the potential electorate that actually votes. Thirdly, by this criterion, the United States is significantly less democratized today than any other polity of consequence holding more or less free elections. This is the more striking in view of the enormous aggregate American advantage in wealth, education and the like, which normally increase the comparative level of mass mobilization. Bingham Powell's essay in this volume shows how very much the United States stands out from this generalization.

There are two features of American electoral participation particularly worthy of note. For one thing, turnout in contemporary American elections is very much concentrated in the middle and upper classes. For another, long-term trends in American participation run exactly counter to historical developments in other Western countries.[1] The American shift toward functional disfranchisement — especially of the lower classes — is an anomaly historically as well as comparatively. It implies that the less wealthy and well-educated the population was (at least back to the middle of the last century), the higher were the participation rates. Moreover, the disappearance continues: by 1978, the non-Southern regions of the country showed the smallest participation rate (about 38 percent for House races) since data was first compiled in 1824.

An extensive polemical and analytical literature has grown up on the subject of American electoral participation during the past decade.[2] Some has attempted to discount the anomalously high nineteenth-century participation rate by arguing that it was grossly inflated by the kind of electoral corruption known as ballot-box stuffing.[3] No one doubts the occasional appearance of these abuses, but neither the work of the present author nor the judgement of leading historians of the period lends credence to the view that this was overwelmingly common.[4]

A good deal of effort has gone into the analysis of the influence of specifically American rules governing access to the ballot box — particularly the personal-registration statute — upon depressing and skewing turnout, both in the 1900-1920 period of initial decline and in the contemporary era.[5] In a recent article, Rosenstone and Wolfinger estimate that removal of these peculiarly American legal barriers would lead, ceteris paribus, to an increase of slightly more than nine percent in the participation rate.[6] On the whole, this literature does not seek to evaluate why such procedures should have come into existence, nor does it deal with the problem that more than one-fifth of the 1960 participation base outside the South had disappeared by 1976, despite significant marginal relaxations in the impact of registration rules between those two dates. But it identifies nevertheless a significant and measurable component of the problem.

Certain other writings, especially diring the 1950s and early 1960s, not only accepted both the low participation rate and the heavy class skew, but in fact celebrated it as part of a "politics of happiness" — pragmatic, low-keyed politics in a contented middle-class political culture.[7] In the wake of the events which convulsed American politics from 1965 to 1974, such views have understandably tended to go out of fashion. Moreover, the current decline in turnout approaching all-time lows is closely associated chronologically — and perhaps causally — with an even steeper and well-documented decline in the public's affective support for national political leaders and institutions.[8] The reasons for electoral abstention almost certainly vary with the specific historical situation. But even without the present atmosphere of distrust, hostility, and bafflement which appears to dominate public opinion, it requires an exceptionally distorted view of democratic procedure to accept with equanimity both the extreme class skewing of participation and its policy implications.

In sum, it is the argument of this essay that the decay in participation during this century has been real, that the high levels of democratization during the nineteenth century were also real, and that the decay — an essentially unique property of modern American politics — is largely the artifact of political decisions in a context of uncontested hegemony. In what follows, we shall first establish several comparative benchmarks, then examine the history of American electoral participation in some detail, and finally evaluate the contemporary situation.

I. COMPARISONS WITH OTHER COUNTRIES TODAY

A major theme of the literature of comparative electoral politics is the existence of a close link between party organization and other politically relevant social organizations, and the mobilization of voters.[9] It is virtually axiomatic that organizations penetrating and mobilizing the American working classes are much feebler than they typically are in Europe. Gunnar Myrdal, has gone so far as to comment that the United States has the most disorganized social infrastructure (or, if one prefers, the largest *Lumpenproletariat*) to be found in any advanced industrial society.[10] Table 1 contrasts contemporary Swedish and American turnout patterns by occupational class.

The data in Table I are unambiguous. Turnout in Sweden is essentially invariant along class lines, and is extremely high in each category. In the United States, there is a massive class skew in turnout. The Swedish turnout ratio between manual workers and

TABLE 1
Voting Participation in Sweden, 1960,
and in the United States, 1968 and 1976, by Broad
Occupational Category

Socio-occupational classification	Voting, Sweden, 1960	Voting, USA 1968	1976	Difference between Sweden and USA: 1968	1976
	%	%	%	%	%
Propertied middle class (professional, managerial, farm owners)	89.6	81.7	76.9	- 7.9	12.7
Non-properted ("white-collar") middle class[1]	90.4	77.4	70.4	-13.0	-20.0
Subtotal: middle class	90.0	79.9	73.6	-10.1	-16.4
Craftsmen, foremen[2]	93.3	66.9	58.0	-26.4	-35.3
Workers (incl. farm labourers)[3]	87.0	57.5	46.7	-29.5	-40.3
Working class	87.4	62.0	52.3	-25.4	-35.1
Total turnout from survey	86.6	67.8	59.2	-18.8	-27.4

1. The occupational categories are not quite the same as between the countries. Non-propertied "white collar" (salaried employees) includes two categories in the US and three in Sweden.
2. Craftsmen, foremen. In the US this has been expanded in this table to include also service employees. For the craftsman-foreman category alone in the US, the turnouts were 68.6 percent in 1968 and 56.1 percent in 1976, with differences with Sweden of -24.7 in 1968 and -37.2 in 1976.
3. Workers (including farm labourers). In the Swedish sample, this includes two categories: all non-craftsman blue-collar workers and farm labourers. In the American case, it includes three categories: operatives, labourers (except farm) and farm labourers. It should also be noted that the Swedish survey contains a substantial category of people not in the labour force (independents, members of families), with a turnout rate of 75.5 percent, reducing the overall to 86.6 percent.

Sources: Sweden, 1960: *Statistisk Arsbok for Sverige,* 1964, p. 380. Based on a 1/30th sample of total voting-age population. United States, 1968: US Bureau of the Census, Current Population Reports, Series P-20, No. 192 (2 December 1969), *Voting and Registration in the Election of November 1968,* p. 22; 1976 ibid., Series P-20, No. 322 (March 1978), *Voting and Registration in the Election of November 1976,* pp. 63-64.

propertied middle-class voters is 1.03 to 1 in favour of the latter; in the United States, this ratio was 1.42 to 1 in 1968 and 1.65 to 1 in 1976. Even more extreme American skews can be found when cross-tabulating educational and occupational levels. Where such cross-tabulation can be performed in 1972 the turnout rate among white male labourers with a grade-school education was 40.9 percent compared with 86.6 percent among people in managerial occupations and with a degree — a ratio of 2.12 to 1. This class skew also shows up in the 1976 survey among adults who have never voted in elections. Among white males, 6 percent of the propertied middle classes reported that they never voted, compared with 13.5 percent of the subaltern middle classes ("white collar" salaried workers), 20.2 percent of craftsmen and service workers, and 30.4 percent of people in lower working-class occupations. While race differences are most often commented about in discussions of turnout in America, in fact class differences are greater.[11]

Two other points should be made about Table 1. Turnout patterns in Sweden and elsewhere in Europe have not only been very high but also invariant from election to election in recent decades. This reflects the capacity of the Social Democrats and other parties to penetrate and mobilize the lower classes, and two rules of the electoral game which facilitate mass participation in elections. The first of these is automatic state registration of voters, a practice universal in one form or another in every Western democratic system except for the United States. The second is proportional representation, which essentially eliminates "wasted votes" and the potential turnout-depressing effects of "safe" seats in the first-past-the-post representation systems like the American or the British.

In the United States the combination of personal-registration and first-past-the-post balloting is no doubt an important contributing factor in depressing the participation rate. But it should be noted that their contribution is marginal at best. Moreover, there has been a notable relaxation of barriers to the franchise since the early 1960s in the whole country. Yet this has not been associated with increased participation (except in the South) but with declining participation. In contemporary America, turnout is not only low, but also highly variable. The primary explanation for this must be found not so much in structural factors (which in any case are not without political causes) but in politics itself. What is it about? How relevant is electoral politics in the United States to the latent or manifest needs of the lower classes?

As with class, so with age. It is well-known that younger voters in the United States participate much less than those of middle age. But this is not an inexorable law. A review of American participation rates in the nineteenth century makes it clear that class differentials in participation then must have been much closer to the contemporary Swedish example than to the current American situation. The same considerations apply to age stratification in voting participation. If the authentic aggregate turnout rate is 90 percent or better, it is trivial to show that the participation of the youngest age cohorts varies by a few percent from middle-aged people. An obvious comparative case involves two elections held at the same time (1972) in the United States and West Germany, both of which had enfranchised 18-year-olds since their last general election. In Germany, the ratio between the participation rate of the 18 to 20-year-old age group and the highest-turnout group (50 to 59) is 1.11 to 1. In the United States, the ratio between the participation of the newly-enfranchised and the highest-participation group (45 to 54) is 1.47 to 1. (See Table 2.)

TABLE 2
Turnout Rates by Age: United States, 1972,
West Germany, 1972

Age group	United States			Age group	W. Germany		
	M %	**W** %	**Total** %		**M** %	**W** %	**Total** %
18-20	47.7	48.8	48.2	18-20	85.0	84.3	84.6
21-24	49.7	51.7	50.7	21-24	83.9	85.0	84.4
25-29	57.6	58.0	57.8	25-29	87.6	88.8	88.2
30-34	62.1	61.7	61.9	30-34	90.4	91.3	90.8
35-44	65.9	66.7	66.3	35-39	92.4	92.3	92.3
				40-44	93.4	92.8	93.1
45-54	72.0	69.9	70.9	45-49	94.5	93.5	93.9
				50-59	95.2	93.3	94.1
55-64	72.4	69.2	70.7	60-69	94.5	92.2	93.2
65-74	73.1	64.3	68.1				
75 & over	65.9	49.1	55.6	70 & over	90.2	83.3	85.9
Total	64.1	62.0	63.0	Total	91.4	90.2	90.8
Actual turnout, % of pot. elect.			55.7				91.1

Sources: US Bureau of the Census, Current Population Reports, *Population Chactertistics*, 'Voting and Registration in the Election of November 1972, Series P-20, No. 253 (October 1973). W. Germany: Statistisches Bundesamt, *Statistisches Jahrbuch 1975 fur die Bundesrepublik Deutschland,* p. 143.

With an aggregate turnout rate of 91 percent, the maximum age-cohort gap in German turnout is less than 10 percent. With an aggregate survey turnout rate of 63 per cent (7 percent over-reporting), the maximum age-cohort gap in American turnout is nearly 23 percent. This point is supported by the age-stratified data in *The Changing American Voter* which stresses the magnitude of rejection of political parties among the youngest age cohorts.[12] We conclude that in addition to a massive failure in political *incorporation* of the lower classes, there is today an almost equally massive failure in political *socialization* of the young into participation in the American electoral process.

II. THE EVOLUTION OF VOTING PARTICIPATION IN THE UNITED STATES

The Nineteenth Century

In general, there is a great and irreducible difference between American participation rates in the nineteenth and twentieth centuries. The United States was the first major Western country to adopt substantially universal male suffrage.[13] A major comparative distinction exists between the situation in the United States in this period and in most other Western political systems. In the latter, it was not until the period 1885-1918 that full enfranchisement of the adult male population was accomplished. In all cases, the struggle to expand or to contain the franchise was intensely, and explicitly political. It was closely linked with the emergence of socialist mass movements whose first demand, naturally, was for class equality in political participation.

As the European franchise was broadened under this kind of pressure, the simple, often dualistic, competition between middle-class "parties of notables" was immensely complicated by the entry of socialist — and in some cases, notably Ireland and Austria — nationalist mass movements. The transition to the European party systems which we take for granted today was by no means a smooth or gradual process. In some countries (notably Germany, Italy and Spain) it was derailed by Fascist counter-revolutions. In Britain it led to a highly volatile multiparty system which came to pivot on the Irish question, and toward a civil war which was averted only by the international explosion of August 1914. Britain's problem was settled (at least for the next 50 years) only by the separation of southern Ireland from the British polity in 1921.

In the United States, on the other hand, matters were far different. Firstly, as J.R. Pole has demonstrated, the proportion of adults legally able to participate in electoral politics was generally very large even in the colonial era, and especially so by contemporary British standards.[14] Secondly, the period from 1818 to 1830 was marked by a very rapid elimination of old property barriers to universal white male suffrage in virtually all states where these had existed except for Louisiana, Rhode Island and South Carolina. This "constitutional revolution" was not associated with the emergence of mass movements hostile to the foundations of the economy or the state. It occurred at a time when four-fifths of the population lived in rural areas. Moreover, with the sole if important exception of the issue of black participation in the electoral system, the reform was not only speedily carried through but almost instantly won universal acceptance. Even in the antebellum South this was very largely the case. So long as the institution of slavery was not threatened by organized electoral movements elsewhere in the country, participation and the closeness of interparty competition reached heights fully comparable with those found elsewhere at the same time. If, after 1860 and 1877, Southern cultural norms turned away from democracy, it seems fair to say that this happened because there was no way to preserve it without accepting the presence of large numbers of blacks in the active electorate.

These differences are largely explicable by the difference between what Louis Hartz calls the American "fragment culture" and the much more complex European "matrix."[15] This "fragment culture" has involved a consensus about the nature of the political economy, the organization of the political system, and the place of religion in public life which was and is quite absent in any European context, even the British. Put another way, the United States is a very conspicuous example of *uncontested hegemony*. If one were to find a single term which might describe this hegemony most concisely, it would be *liberal capitalism:* a consensual value-system based on support for private property, and political democracy. The primordial value is that of *self-regulation* extended to the individual level; hence, for example, the enduring vitality of Western movies in the popular culture. In Europe, on the other hand, the hegemony of the middle classes (the bourgeoisie) has been anything but uncontested. They have had to fight a two-front war against organized traditionalist social forces (the curch, the nobility, and to a large extent the peasantry), and subsequently against a socialism which seeks the speedy or eventual replacement of capitalism.

These differences are fundamental, and have enormous ramifications. With regard to democratization and the suffrage, it is enough to make a few points. First, in the United States there was a paucity of traditionalist social forces threatened by, and resisting mass enfranchisement. Second, unlike Europe, the propertied classes in the United States accomodated themselves both speedily and effectively to the democratic dispensation, since it rapidly became clear that the democracy which came into being offered no serious threat to themselves or their property. Third, substantially full democratization occurred — radically differently from Europe — well before the onset of urbanization and concentrated industrial capitalist development, which was to create a sensation of acute vulnerability among the propertied classes of the industrial Northeast by the end of the century.

Fourth, as Hartz suggests, the absence of effective organized opposition to the liberal-capitalist consensus involved a significant blurring of ideas and of alternatives. So far as popular participation was concerned, property-holding barriers to the ballot-box were removed quickly and easily. By the end of the nineteenth century, the growth of huge ethnically polyglot urban "masses" led to the creation of personal-registration legislation — ostensibly, at least, to combat corruption, i.e., stuffing the ballot box. This legislation was not only created, but varied extremely widely in its incidence and effects (like all other electoral legislation) from state and locality to locality. Moreover, it too was accepted consensually: it is very hard to find any critical literature of political science on this subject until as late as the 1960s.[16]

In Europe and other democratic political systems, on the other hand, the burden of registering electors is universally borne, in one way or another, by the state. There are two obvious reasons for this. First, the epic struggles over the state, lasting several centuries, had produced a "hard" or "internally sovereign" state with elaborate and prestigious bureaucracies. The sheer physical competence required for the state to enroll voters was in place. Second, struggles among social groups produced great clarity about the political uses to which electoral legislation could be put by those in power, and an insistence that individuals (especially of lower and dependent classes) not be burdened by cumbersome procedures which might easily lead to their abstention. In the United States, on the other hand, personal registration appears to have come into being as beyond organized political criticism because it fits so well with the underlying, hegemonic ideology. The other side of the coin of individual self-regulation is individual responsibility: if an individual wants to vote, it is up to him to prove to the electoral officials that he is legally qualified to do so.

Finally, one may speculate that political parties could develop their organizational capacities to penetrate and mobilize an individualistic electorate only up to a point. Maurice Duverger points out that American parties have a "very archaic general structure" compared with newer types of mass parties in the European context.[17] If so, an essential reason for this is that these newer parties reflect a *collectivist* organizational capacity which cannot strike root in the United States so long as the consensual ideology of liberal capitalism retains its uncontested hegemonic position. So long as the demographic structure and the political economy were of American nineteenth-century type, the traditional major parties could and did mobilize very effectively indeed. In the radically different social and economic conditions of today, their mobilization capacity would almost inevitably be seriously impaired: neither their organizational form nor their leadership are geared to do so, and the cultural conditions for a serious effort along those lines do not exist.

The most notable point about nineteenth-century participation is its rapid growth with the spread of organized, mass-based democratic politics in the 1830s. One case among many which could be chosen is Connecticut's presidential vote between 1820 and 1844. (See Table 3.)

TABLE 3
Classic Mobilization in the Jacksonian Period:
the Case of Connecticut

| Year | Of Potential Electorate | | | | |
	Voting %	Non-voting %	Jacksonian (Dem.) %	Opposition %	Other %
1820	7.6	92.4	6.4 (Monroe)		1.2
1824	14.9	85.1	—	11.8 (Adams)	3.1 (Crawford)
1828	27.2	72.8	6.6	20.6 (Adams)	—
1832	46.0	54.0	16.0	25.2 (Clay)	4.7 (Wirt)
1836	52.3	47.7	26.5 D	25.8 W	—
1840	75.7	24.3	33.6	42.0	0.1
1844	80.0	20.0	36.9	39.1	2.4 (Liberty)

The process of growth in this period took extremely diverse forms from state to state. By the early 1840s, a moderate to very full mobilization had occurred in most states. It is possible to give a modal description. Essential to the new parties of this period was their use of a variety of devices to get voters to the polls. Throughout most of the nineteenth century, party identification was obviously much more complete throughout the voting population, and much more intense, than it is today. This meant, typically, that parties could not expect very many conversions from already-active opposition voters, and that they could not count upon a large pool of free-floating independent voters. Propaganda, torchlight parades, and other activities were designed to secure a maximum turnout of their own voters, since that was normally the way to win elections. This accounts, amoung other things, for the creation of Tammany's Naturalization Bureau in 1840, since it was already clear to this organization that most immigrants, if naturalized in time for the election as required by New York law, would vote the Democratic ticket. The resultant turnout rates in closely contested states like New York throughout this period, or Indiana from 1860 on, were truly awesome. (See Table 4.)

In this period there were effectively no personal-registration statutes or other significant barriers to the franchise in most states. What amounted to freehold or property qualifications survived in Louisiana and South Carolina until the Civil War, and in Rhode Island until after 1888. In a few states (Massachusetts, Connecticut and Rhode Island), anti-Irish sentiment led by the American ("Know-Nothing") party resulted in the adoption of literacy qualifications of varying effectiveness in the mid-1850s.

Similarly, the conduct of elections was very largely a party matter. Printed tickets were typically produced by the parties and distributed to their voters — initially, before the election, but toward the end of the century on election day near the polls. Such tickets, of course, immensely simplified the act of voting for the plethora of candidates and officers which are elective in the complex American system. They could be and often were "scratched" by voters dissatisfied with one or more of the candidates on the printed ticket. It was possible in effect to cast a "split ticket" under this system; but in general, it facilitated straight-ticket voting, reflecting the intense partisanship of the age.

In a great many jurisdictions, the act of voting itself was at best only semi-secret: often, separate ballot urns were maintained for the supporters of each candidate. This kind of system could and did lend itself to abuse on occasion. But typically this occurred when a party organization was willing to terrorize or bribe officials belonging to the opposition (as well as the police). This sort of thing was episodic. Well-known cases include the Placquemines Parish frauds of 1844, which helped Polk win the Presidency, and the New York frauds of 1868, when the Tweed Machine produced turnouts of well over 100 percent in many election jurisdictions, helping Seymour carry New York state by exactly 10,000 votes, it was said, in order for a leading city politician to win an election bet! But Jensen is obviously right: these cases were episodic rather than the norm.[18] Normally, it would seem that the system worked without excessive ballot-box stuffing because in the rural areas of North and West people knew each other and because in the cities the two parties had every incentive to watch each other. Moreover, each organization's cadres had an extremely precise idea of just how many troops the other army had.

In general, turnout rates reached their historic high in the United States during the last quarter of the nineteenth century. The broad reason for this is obvious. The most traumatic collective experience through which Americans have ever passed was the Civil War (and, for Southerners, the Reconstruction which followed the war). In many respects, it was, as Barrington Moore has argued, the "last capitalist revolution" in modern world history,[19] and it partook of many of the characteristics of revolution — not only in the South. The Civil War produced a much higher tax of men than did World War II. Using as a benchmark the total male population 21 and over, about two-fifths served in the Union army, and probably somewhat more than half in the Confederate army, compared with about one-third of the age and sex group during World War II. Even more dramatic were the differentials in casualty rates: 18.0 percent of those who served in the Union army died during the war, while another 13.8 percent were wounded. The Confederate toll was still more ghastly: about 34 percent in its army died, and another 26 percent were wounded. By comparison, only 1.1 percent of all those who served in World War II died, and another 1.6 percent were wounded.

In retrospect, the most important collective tasks of our party system were the creation of the political preconditions for this conflict and, then, its political management.[20] In view of the magnitude of this trauma and the fundamental issues at stake in it, it is hardly surprising that in the North the quality and quantity of party organizational effectiveness reached levels never seen before or since.

In the wartime era, the trauma in the South was vastly greater, because of the victors' requirement of incorporating the just-freed black population into the electorate. In this esoteric — almost "third world" — context, its effects were to destroy any long-term stable basis for electoral competition, and to encourage the white population to get rid of the region's black voters.

Another concomitant of the Civil War period was the shift toward urbanization and concentrated industrial capitalism which achieved a temporary maximum velocity during the 1880s. (1) Devotion by most Americans to the premises of our uncontested hegemony — self-regulation and business in the broader sense of the term — continued after the Civil War as it did before. In politics, this was manifested in the increasingly machine-dominated character of party organizations, fuelled both by the rapid increase in the concentrated power of money and by the growth of dependent immigrant urban populations which were used effectively as electoral cannon-fodder. (2) The growth of the "new" capitalist and the "new" political boss, along with the "new", i.e., post-1882 immigration, led to a massive sense of loss — in cultural values, prestige and status — among older-stock middle-class elements. The forces promoting this alienation eventually produced a reaction with major consequences for the electoral mechanism and for representation itself. (3) The shift toward new industrial-urban concentrations of power produced many of the same social-issue strains among farmers, and massive economic dislocation as well. These were byproducts not only of general processes by which rural areas were subordinated to the industrial-capitalist city, but of public policy too. The Civil War had left an enormous public debt behind, and this was largely funded by inflation. The twin objectives of Treasury policy under both parties from 1865 to the 1890s were to shrink the money supply, returning to and then defending an implicit gold standard; and to retire the national debt. The result was a generation-long deflation which was particularly damaging to Southern and Western cash-crop farmers because they were so often undercapitalized and in debt. The stage was thus set for a massive agrarian insurrection against the new capitalist order. The extraordinary anxieties which defenders of that order displayed during the crisis of the 1890s becomes somewhat more explicable when it is recalled that an absolute majority of the work-force was employed in agriculture until about 1879, and nearly a majority until after 1900.

The political explosion which struck the United States was ignited in this highly-politicized and mobilized setting. Just how comparatively full this mobilization was can be gauged from Table 4, which provides mean turnout values by state for the 1874-1892 period and, for contrast, "stable" turnout patterns of the 1952-1970 era and the shrunken rates of the 1970s.

TABLE 4
Changes in Electoral Participation by State, United States, 1874-1978

Rank State (1874-1892)		1874-1892 (Mean)		1952-1970 (Mean)		1972-1978 (Mean)	
		Presi-dential	Off-year congres-sional	Presi-dential	Off-year congres-sional	Presi-dential	Off-year congres-sional
		%	%	%	%	%	%
1	Ind.	92.7	83.5	73.5	59.9	60.6	43.2
2	N.J.	92.2	76.6	69.6	49.7	59.0	37.5
3	Ohio	92.1	76.8	67.1	48.7	56.0	38.4
4	Iowa	91.8	73.4	72.9	49.0	63.9	43.0
5	N.H.	89.7	83.0	74.7	53.8	61.6	41.3
6	N.Y.	89.0	68.4	66.0	49.5	53.3	34.9
7	W.Va.	87.5	72.6	74.2	50.5	61.5	34.3
8	Ill.	86.1	67.4	73.4	54.2	61.8	37.2
9	N.C.	84.5	67.3	51.8	28.8	43.5	26.6
10	Conn.	82.8	69.7	74.8	61.2	64.1	47.1
11	Pa.	82.7	70.5	66.7	54.8	55.4	41.2
12	Md.	81.4	65.3	56.1	37.7	50.3	30.5
13	Wis.	81.3	64.4	69.6	50.1	64.1	41.4
14	Kans.	80.1	66.6	67.6	50.3	59.5	43.5
15	Mo.	78.2	64.9	68.7	42.3	57.6	39.7
16	Fla.	76.6	67.9	49.4	25.1	50.1	29.0
17	Va.	76.4	54.2	37.6	22.5	46.8	28.3
18	Ky.	76.3	45.6	56.8	30.7	51.2	25.4
19	Del.	76.1	65.8	72.7	56.1	61.0	39.6
20	Mont.	74.2	70.0	70.8	61.9	66.2	53.3
21	Nev.	73.9	73.4	62.5	50.9	49.9	40.6
22	Calif.	73.4	65.1	65.9	53.1	55.7	40.0
23	Vt.	73.3	56.2	67.2	53.5	58.3	39.3
24	Me.	73.2	70.1	66.1	49.2	63.9	49.9
25	Tenn.	72.7	54.9	49.1	28.0	47.1	33.5
26	Texas	72.3	54.9	43.2	20.5	46.5	20.9
27	Mass.	71.8	58.2	71.7	54.7	61.6	41.3
28	Mich.	71.5	63.3	68.7	51.3	58.8	40.3
29	S.D.	70.7	80.4	75.3	61.5	67.4	56.7
30	Minn.	70.3	60.3	72.8	58.5	69.7	47.7
31	Wash.	67.3	48.2	69.4	50.2	61.7	36.7

TABLE 4 (continued)

Rank State (1874-1892)	1874-1892 (Mean)		1952-1970 (Mean)		1972-1978 (Mean)	
	Presidential %	Off-year congressional %	Presidential %	Off-year congressional %	Presidential %	Off-year congressional %
32 Neb.	66.1	55.2	67.6	50.3	56.3	42.9
33 Ore.	64.9	70.2	69.0	55.0	62.0	48.9
34 Idaho	63.1	67.0	76.4	63.0	62.7	49.4
35 Ala.	62.2	47.0	34.4	25.4	45.7	23.2
36 Ark.	61.4	34.9	44.3	36.9	50.4	32.4
37 S.C.	58.2	54.8	34.0	19.9	40.4	23.2
38 N.D.	56.6	66.4	73.8	55.4	69.3	51.1
39 Colo.	55.4	51.4	69.7	52.9	61.1	44.5
40 La.	54.6	49.7	44.7	17.6	47.7	22.5
41 R.I.[1]	52.5	26.4	73.0	59.0	62.6	44.2
42 Ga.	48.9	30.6	37.2	19.5	40.6	21.6
43 Miss.	48.3	35.3	31.6	16.7	47.9	26.6
44 Wyo.	47.7	49.1	70.6	60.5	61.7	50.2
Admitted since 1892:						
Ariz.			52.6	41.1	49.0	36.1
N.M.			60.9	50.9	57.4	43.2
Okla.			63.3	40.9	56.6	32.4
Utah			78.4	63.1	69.2	51.6
Alaska			53.4	43.6	50.5	40.3
Hawaii			55.0	47.4	49.7	42.3
North and West[2]	85.4	70.8	68.5	52.6	58.4	40.3
Non-South	84.5	69.2	68.0	51.2	58.0	39.5
Border	79.1	60.3	63.2	39.7	54.9	32.3
South	65.6	49.9	42.6	23.3	46.1	25.7
USA	78.5	64.7	62.0	44.5	55.1	36.0

1. Rhode Island: freehold qualifiction for voting until 1892.
2. Regions: Border: Ky., Md., Okla., Mo., W. Va.; South: Ala., Ark., Fla., Ga., La., Miss., N.C., S.C., Tenn., Texas, Va.; Non-South: North and West plus Border. North and West: all states not in South and Border.

The first and obvious thing to note about the 1874-1892 period is that aggregate presidential turnouts in the non-Southern states were then about as high as they are today in such high participation European countries as Norway and Sweden, and higher than in Britain, France or Canada. Indeed, turnouts in these areas of the country were higher for off-year congressional elections during this period than they were for the Presidency in the 1952-1970 period — to say nothing of later figures.

Secondly, on the whole, the most densely-populated states were also those those with the highest turnouts.[21] Among the 14 states whose mean presidential turnout rates ranged from 80.1 percent to 92.7 percent (roughly equivalent to a range from France to Italy in contemporary Europe), only two — Iowa and Kansas — could be described as overwhelmingly rural. Of the ten largest cities in the United States in the 1890 census, eight were in states whose mean presidential turnout was 80 percent or greater during this period. The South was already moving toward the extremely low turnouts of the succeeding era (six of its eleven states fall in the lowest quartile), a move only consolidated shortly after 1900. Outside the South, the peripheries, and especially the frontier areas, tended to have the lowest turnout rates. (Table 5 provides a sense of this concentration of participation in the most densely-populated and socio-economically developed parts of the country — and what has happened on this dimension more recently.)

Both the relative and absolute drop off from presidential to off-year congressional participation was significantly smaller in all parts of the country in the last quarter of the nineteenth century than it has ever been since. For example, the relative presidential/off-year decline in the Northern and Western states was 17.1 percent then, compared with 23.8 percent in 1952-1970 and 31.0 percent in 1972-78. Turnouts of 80 to 90 percent are prima facie evidence that the contemporary American class skew did not then exist in such areas. A similar assumption seems warranted about the absence of an age skew as well. (Cf. Tables 1-2.)

Quite a different pattern emerges when we compare that mobilized universe with the patterns of 1952-1970 and 1972-1978; the latter reinforcing the characteristics of the former. Drop-off rates between presidential and off-year elections are uniformly higher in every comparable state during the second period than during the first, except for the very special case of Rhode Island. In some cases, especially in the Southern and Border states, they are very much larger, even absolutely, despite the notable overall shrinkage in the active electorate as measured by presidential turnouts. The political effects of this shrinkage at the state level may be magnified significantly by another development: the wholesale movement of state gubernatorial elections for four-year terms to off-years. Granted current participation patterns, this typically means that the chief state executive officer (and most other elective state officials) will be chosen by one-third to two-fifths of the potential electorate.

Another and most suggestive change can be seen in the distribution of states in the top and bottom quartiles. The movement in the bottom quartile is perfectly straightforward. In the 1874-1892 period, this quartile was a mixture of some Southern states,[22] Rhode Island (which uniquely maintained a freehold qualification for voting until after 1888), and frontier states of the West. Movements in the top quartile are in some respects more interesting and are certainly less well-known. With the sole exceptions of North Carolina and West Virginia, the 1874-1892 top quartile was concentratyed in the emerging "metropole" of the country, and included the four most populous states: Illinois, New York, Ohio, and Pennsylvania. By 1952-70 the only American "megastate" to qualify in the top quartile turnout is Illinois. To it must be added Connecticut, Rhode Island and Indiana within the ex-metropole; the other nine are Plains, Mountain, and Pacific states. Table 5 graphically demonstrates the shift in the top turnout quartile's distribution toward smaller and, on the whole, sparsely-populated peripheral regions of the country.

TABLE 5
The Long-term Shift away from the Metropole:
Number of Representatives in States
in Top Turnout Quartile, 1874-1976 (Presidential)

Period	Range of turnout, top quartile	No. of representatives	% of total	Mean no. of reps. per state
1874-1892	82.7-92.7	158	44.4	14.4
1894-1910	81.5-91.7	154	39.4	14.7
1912-1930	67.7-77.8	120	27.6	10.0
1932-1950	71.0-78.4	90	20.7	7.5
1952-1970	72.8-78.4	77	17.7	6.4
1972-1976	62.0-69.7	46	10.6	3.8

The Disappearing American Electorate, 1896-1930: Social Crisis and Political Response

The late nineteenth-century electorate we have been describing was fully mobilized. Its participation was the fruit of several generations of effective work by America's traditional, party organizations. But it presented dangers for elites, chronic and growing irritation among old-stock middle-class elements who saw themselves between the hammer of corporate giantism and the anvil of machine corruption, and serious impediments to the realization of technocratic and bureaucratic ambitions. The great socio-economic crisis of the 1890s appeared to demonstrate that this electorate was not only large but might also be a mortal danger to emergent hegemonic interests.

The United States was unique in that it had a fully operating set of mass-democratic institutions and values before the onset of industrial-capitalist development.[23] In every other industrializing nation of the 1850-1950 period, modernizing elites were effectively insulated from mass pressures. In most of the West this insulation was accomplished by the *régime censitaire* or other formal devices for keeping lower classes out of electoral politics, supplemented in some cases by ingenious *trasformismo*-type manipulation and corruption of both electorates and of legislatures. In the Communist world, insulation involved dictatorship and the use of elections as devices of acclamation for the regime rather than choice. In today's third world, a mixture of the two — coupled with the entry of the Army where "necessary" as an ultimate control — generally prevails.

Since the processes of capitalist development can be exploitative, harsh, and even brutal, it is not surprising that so wide a range of devices has been employed to prevent modernizing elites being overthrown by an outraged population, and that the quest for such insulation has been universal. This was a problem with particular urgency in the American context, because of the relative breadth of popular participation, and because so many participants were agrarian. Alexander Hamilton's policy, from beginning to end, betrays preoccupation with an overriding question: How can one find a legitimate way to win mass acquiescence for measures designed to promote the creation of what Madison, Monroe, and others quite correctly called "empire" and to accumulate movable capital? It is hardly surprising that Jefferson suspected Hamilton of harboring dictatorial designs. It is still less surprising that the turn-of-the-century Progressives — particularly those of a technocratic-corporatist bent — revered Hamilton as their hero and rejected Jefferson as a tribune of all the backward agrarian forces in American society.[24]

How, then, does one tame a fickle, numerous, and dangerous electorate without outright overthrow of the engrained democratic tradition in American politics? It is not suggested that any of our corporte elites or the organic intellecuals and politicans who supported them at the turn of the century ever put the question in such nakedly self-conscious terms. Still more doubtful is it that what happened to participation and the nature of the party system in this period was the result of a conspiracy among elites who knew just what they wanted and how to get it — though localized conspiracies abounded, chiefly in the South, where the stakes were higher and the social structure primitive.

The questions to ask ourselves, then, are these. What was done? Against whom was it done? What was the convergence of interests making it possible to do things at all? What were the effects of what was done? And finally, why was what was done so rapidly and fully legitimated that it remained beyond criticism for more than a half-century or even today?

We may begin by identifying schematically the major targets of legislative changes affecting elections and their opponents.

Whether or not elites conspired, the pattern of political change which emerged during the first third of this century functioned as though its proponents and beneficiaries agreed on a number of points which are scarcely in accord with participatory-democratic policical theory. (1) The greater preliminary hurdles which a potential voter had to cross in order to vote, the fewer voters there would be. (2) These hurdles would be easily cleared by people in the native-stock middle classes, would not exist at all in small towns and rural areas, would be serious impediments to urban lower-class voting, and would be virtually impassable for Southern blacks. (3) Political parties were dangerous anachronisms when it came to giving cities efficient, expert government. They were to be abolished where possible (especially at the urban level), and were elsewhere to be heavily regulated by the state. In particular, their monopoly over nominations would be stripped from them, so that "the people" (between 5 and 35 percent of the potential electorate as a rule) could choose candidates in direct primaries. (4) Close partisan competition was generally undesirable, though for different reasons as between the South (where a quasi-absolute prohibition of party competition developed) and the North and West. Desirable or not, it was substantially abolished down through 1932 in the South and in vast reaches of the North from Pennsylvania to California.

The basic legal devices which were adopted — particularly the device of personal registration — without question contributed to the massive decline in voter participation after 1900. In the extreme case of the South, the result was that by the mid-1920s, presidential

TABLE 6

The Socio-political Thrust of Electoral Reform

Target groups	Opponents	Rationale	Sanctions
I. Urban machines	Middle-class WASPS (Status-anxiety) Technocratic progressives Upstate agrarians	Anti-corruption Inefficiency "Sodom & Gomorrah"	ballot reforms; special prosecutors; nonpartisanship malapportionment, discriminatory registration laws
II. Political Parties	Progressives; many of the above	Unrepresentativeness; "old politics", corruption	detailed legislative regulation; direct primaries
III. Immigrants	Agrarians (upstate in NY); small-town & metropolitan middle-class WASPS	Not adequately culturally developed; Romanism; "Anarcho-Communism", lazy, drunk, etc.	Elimination of alien voting (Midwest and West); Personal periodic registration for cities only; literacy tests
IV. Populist agrarians (North & West)	Corporate elites, urban/town middle-classes	Danger of "revolution" by the "backward"	Electoral activity plus some corruption and "pressure" on dependent voting pop.
V. Populist agrarians (South)	Elites (regional & local), Democratic organization	Same as above	Same, but massive use of fraud and force, & sanctions below
VI. Blacks (South)	Southern white progressives; gradually, ex-Populist white agrarians	Racism; "traditionalist Southernism"; anti-corruption	Violence & terror; later largely replaced by poll tax, literacy tests, "white primaries", grandfather clause, etc.

turnout had declined to about 18 percent of the potential electorate, while in the off-year congressional election of 1926 only 8.5 percent of the South's potential voters actually went to the polls. Participation fell in the North and West as well, but very unevenly. How much of this was attributable to these rules-of-game changes? In an earlier study, I concluded that in the period prior to the enfranchisement of women (nationally adopted in 1920) no more than one-third of the decline could be attributed to these causes alone.[25] It is possible from recent Ohio data to give a more precise estimate of the effect of introducing personal-registration requirements on the participation rate.

Ohio is a state, like many others, where until 1977 the basic electoral law prescribed personal registration in counties of a certain size, and allowed local option in all other counties. In some counties, registration applied only to one or two small towns, with the rural areas having no such requirement for voting. In the period from 1960 to 1976, a significant number of counties shifted from non-registration to registration status. It is therefore possible to derive a relatively good estimate of the effects of registration by comparative analysis (see Table 7).

TABLE 7
Turnouts in Ohio Counties,
1960-1976 by Registration Category*

Category type: registration began	No. of counties	Turnout 1960 %	1964 %	1968 %	1972 %	1976 %
Before 1960	28	69.0	64.0	62.3	57.7	57.1
Before 1964	5	75.5	60.4	57.9	54.6	53.8
Before 1968	4	77.7	72.1	63.3	57.9	58.3
Before 1972	10	79.2	72.3	69.3	59.9	59.0
Before 1976	5	79.5	72.7	70.6	63.7	57.1
Never	23	79.8	73.0	70.0	65.8	71.4

*Does not include counties with partial registration coverage during this period.

Taking the transitions in each group but subtracting the year-on-year turnout change for full-registration counties yields a differential of 6.1 percent. Another approach is a straightforward year-on-year comparison between those counties fully covered and those never covered across the period. Not surprisingly, this yields the highest general differential of 10.0 percent, though it provides no basis for estimating possible turnout differentials arising from the rurality of the 23 counties which do not have registration as a requisite for voting. Still another way of analyzing the data in Table 7 is to estimate the positive deviation in pre-registration turnout in each category with "before" and "after" experience. This produces a positive deviation of 7.8 percent, which — when one attempts such crude controls for the downward movement in turnout — seems perhaps to be the most accurate estimate of the three. It is worth noting that all of these measures, except the simple comparison between full and non-registration counties, are at their maximum in 1960, the election with the highest overall turnout rate. Equally noteworthy, a substantial decline in turnout occurred across the board between 1960 and 1968. In those counties with personal registration throughout the period under review, this decline was 6.7 percent. In those where this requirement did not exist at any time, the decline was 9.8 percent between 1960 and 1968, i.e., prior to the enfranchisement of the 18-20 age group.

Rosenstone and Wolfinger conclude that if the laws of all states were brought into conformity with the registration statutes of the most permissive states, the estimated increased in turnout would be 9.1 percent.[26] It could be assumed that a fully automatic state-enrollment system of the type normally found in other Western nations would eliminate any residual burdens associated with these laws, and add several more points to the estimated increase. The anlysis of our Ohio data would suggest that the latter condition (approximated, of course, by a situation in which no registration is required at all for voting) would increase turnout by a rather small figure, that is, by between 7 and 9 percent. Applied to the states of North and West for the 1952-1970 period (see Table 4), this latter estimate would yield a mean presidential turnout in the 75 to 77 percent range. This is a considerable improvement, but would still leave unaccounted for half of the difference between the actual 1952-1970 average turnout and the 85.4 percent of the 1874-1892 average. Moreover, such estimates are implicitly static in character. They give no information about the causes of the marked decline in turnout after 1960 shown in the bottom two rows of Table 7. Nor do they, for example, explain why turnout declined in New York City by a full 21.3 percent (34 percent of the 1960 electoral base) from 1960 to 1976, despite continuity or marginal liberalization of electoral law.

Viewed over the long run, the same considerations apply to expansions of the size of the electorate — notably to the enfranchisement of women, which was legally completed in 1920. There is no doubt at all that the enfranchisement of women initally reduced sharply the participation rate. This too, however, appears to have varied widely in accordance with the extent of political mobilization (or "socialization") prevailing in a given society at the time of enfranchisement. It is well known that women participated much less than men, especially in ethnically polyglot cities, from the time of enfranchisement until the 1928 election, which involved the issue of Al Smith's Catholicism, and substantially less than men thereafter down to the early 1950s, when contemporary survey data becomes available. Thus, in his pioneering study, *Political Behavior,*[27] H.L.A. Tingsten reports a female participation rate immediately after enfranchisement of 61.8 percent in Sweden (1919), 68.1 percent in New Zealand (1896) and 82.1 percent in Austria (1919). This meant that female participation trailed male turnout by 7.1 percent in the first case, 7.8 percent in the second, and 4.9 percent in the third. The data in the United States is largely limited to Chicago, where separate returns by sex were published for the 1916-1920 period. Without going into exhaustive analysis of this case, it is enough to report that the 1916 turnout in Chicago was 77.1 percent of estimated potential electorate among men and 47.3 percent among women, a sex differential of 29.8 percent.[28]

Such data makes it very easy — indeed, too easy — to assume that the post-1928 mobilization of women and other previously non-participating groups were in some sense the overwhelmingly dominant electoral "cause" of the New Deal realignment. The issues involved are much more complex than that, though the importance of these mobilizations cannot be denied.[29] Secondly, there is an interesting implication in the 1976 finding that the participation differential between men and women had virtually disappeared. In the historical context, the turnout rates in 1976 and 1978 mean that while women are turning out somewhat more than fifty years ago, men are participating vastly less, perhaps by a factor of 20 percent or more.

Thus, by the end of World War I, an essentially oligarchic electoral universe had come into being, with a hegemonic sectionalism and the disappearance of socialism as an even marginal electoral force. Table 8 reveals the magnitude of the transformation. Essentially, a political system which was congruent with the hegemony of laissez-faire corporate capitalism over the whole society had come into being. This system rested on two non-competitive party hegemonies and upon a huge mass of non-voters.

This implies, of course, that an American electorate had come into

TABLE 8
The Achievement of Normalcy: Turnouts in
the North and West, 1880-90 and 1920-30

Year	President %	Congress %	Drop off %
1880	87.6	86.8	
1882		71.4	18.5
1884	84.9	84.2	
1886		71.6	15.7
1888	86.4	87.7	
1890		71.3	17.5
1920	56.3	53.5	
1922		42.8	24.0
1924	57.4	52.4	
1926		39.7	30.8
1928	66.7	61.6	
1930		43.7	34.5

being: that is, one heavily skewed toward the middle classes *in the absence of an organizable socialist mass movement capable of mobilizing lower-class voters.* This is implicit in a comparison of contemporary turnout rates with those prevailing in the normalcy era. Individual-level data for the 1920s is, naturally, extremely fragmentary, but, such as it is, it supports the inference. Tingsten reports one study of 1925 which focussed on the small and overwhelmingly native-stock city of Delaware, Ohio.[30] This study found a turnout rate of 86 percent among the local upper class (corporate and banking elites), compared with 63 percent among the "mass of industrial workers". Since, as it happens, personal registration requirements were not imposed there until 1965, this class gap in the 1920s supports the view that the interaction of social change and organizable political alternatives, rather than rules change, was *primarily* responsible for what happened to American electoral participation after 1900. Where one finds a disappearance or even reversal of this class-structured turnout pattern during the 1920s — and one does find such cases — the inversion can be linked directly to the existence and motivations of political machines able to deliver votes as need arose.[31]

Incomplete Remobilization and the
(So-called) New Deal Revolution

The "system of 1896" was composed of a series of mutually

reinforcing parts, bound together by a common belief in the corporate-capitalist path to economic development and individual affluence. It was destroyed by the Depression which undermined its ideological and operational base, laissez faire. The emergence of the Democrats as the new majority party was associated with a relatively huge mobilization of population groups which had not voted in the 1920s.[32] The examination of registration by party in San Francisco in the 1928-1940 period illuminates this transition (see Table 9).

TABLE 9
Mobilization and Conversion in the
New Deal Period: the Case of San Francisco,
1928-1940

Year	Estimated potential electorate	Percentage of potential electorate			
		Non-registered	Dem.	Registered Rep.	Misc., decl. to state
1928	393,600	35.7	19.1	41.9	3.3
1930	401,933	43.1	8.4	46.2	2.3
1932	410,200	33.3	30.5	34.5	1.7
1934	418,500	25.1	38.9	34.0	2.0
1936	426,800	25.9	47.0	25.5	1.6
1938	435,100	21.7	50.7	25.7	1.9
1940	443,386	12.9	56.2	29.1	1.8

If we were to make two most unrealistic assumptions — that all conversions and mobilizations favoured the Democrats only and that the electorate was wholly stationary during this twelve-year period — we could conclude that the 56 percent Democratic registration of 1940 had the following origins in the 1928-30 period; 14 percent Democratic,15 percent Republican, 26 percent non-registered, and 1 percent miscellaneous. Obviously these are in no way the true figures. But in a city where growth was comparatively tightly constrained, they suggest something of what happened. It is not off the mark to suggest that about three-fifths of the accretions to the Democratic registration pool came from the mobilization of people not registered before, and about two-fifths from Republican conversions.

But if remobilization formed a central part of constructing a nationwide Democratic majority in the 1930s, there are important parts of the story which are less frequently emphasized. In the first place, one extremely important component of the "system of 1896" not only survived the New Deal era but was actually reinforced: the "solid South", composed of eleven ex-Confederate states retained their antipartisan, antiparticipatory structure until after 1950. The pro-Democratic thrust of the New Deal realignment drastically weakened what was left of the Republican opposition in the few states — like Tennessee and North Carolina — where it had been relatively strong in the preceding period. Turnouts in these states, as in the Border states where similar realignments occurred, fell subsequently below the levels reached in the 1920s. Moreover, the ascendancy of the Democratic party nationally entailed normal Democratic majorities in both houses of Congress. Granted the salience of seniority and the effects of occasional Republican sweeps in the North (as in 1946 and 1952), the result was that Democratic ascendancy nationally meant Southern ascendancy in Congress. As events after 1938 were to demonstrate, this involved a critical limitation on the reformist potential of the New Deal until well into the 1960s.

Earlier we saw that the turnout patterns of the late nineteenth century involved both very high levels of mass mobilization and extremely stable levels as well. (See Table 8.) By contrast, the period between 1940 and 1950 showed major fluctuations in turnout and the post-1970 period a precipitous decline from already mediocre levels. Thus, while turnout in the North and West reached 58.6 percent in the congressional elections of 1938 and 73.7 percent in the presidential election of 1940, participation skidded to 43.2 percent in 1942 and 48.4 percent in 1946, while by 1948 only 62.2 percent of the Northern-Western electorate bothered to vote for President. Certainly neither war nor women's suffrage can be held accountable for the low turnout in the latter two elections.[33] One is led to suspect instead that the replacement of "Dr. New Deal" by "Dr. Win-the-War" may have had something to do with this. The off-year election of 1938 was marked by a turnout which has never since been equalled outside the South, a turnout fully 18 percent higher than the 38.0 percent voting in 1978.

The Contemporary Period:
1952 to the Present

From many aspects of contemporary electoral participation, we will select three major themes: (1) regional change involving civil rights and the South; (2) longitudinal change in the Northern and Western states, especially the recent decline in participation to historically low levels; (3) certain attributes of voters and non-voters in the mid-1970s.

(1) As we have indicated, the New Deal "revolution" in voting participation almost wholly bypassed the South, whose elites had long since set up the oligarchic conditions epitomized by the 1.5 percent turnout rate in the South Carolina gubernatorial election of 1925. This extraordinary regional deviation from democratic norms was enforced by a dense network of exclusionary legislation and — especially in the early years of this system — by the widespread use of extralegal violence. This unfinished business was finally taken in hand in the Civil Rights Acts of 1965 and 1970. In the black-belt areas of worst electoral repression, local authorities were simply bypassed and federal registration machinery set up to enroll voters. More generally, abolition of such barriers to the franchise as literacy and poll-tax requirements opened the sluice-gates throughout the region. It should be stressed that these laws came at the end of a process of development rather than at the beginning. The crumbling of the Solid South and the urbanization of the electorate had already brought considerable mobilization by the early 1950s; these laws completed the job. As a result, there was a major improvement in Southern turnout — from abysmally low levels — between 1948 and 1970, followed thereafter by stagnation or decline. (See Table 10.)

(2) Civil rights acts significantly lowered access thresholds outside the South too, for example, reducing residency requirements in presidential elections to 30 days and suspending literacy tests in those non-Southern states (like New York), which had them. Table 11 should be read bearing in mind that since the early 1960s a number of states have simplified the registration process to make the act of voting easier than it was in 1960.

Overall, the participation rate in these states was stable between 1950 and 1966, with a mean in presidential elections of 69.6 percent, in congressional elections held in presidential years of 66.7 percent and in off-year congressional elections of 53 percent. Thereafter a substantial decline occurred, bringing the latest rates down to 57.2 percent, 53.4 percent, and 38.6 percent respectively. By 1976, 21.4 percent of the 1960 active-electorate base was not voting; by 1978, 29.4 percent of the 1962 active-electorate base was no longer participating. The general enfranchisement of the 18-20 age group in 1971 does not begin to account for the magnitude of these declines. Analysis of the Census Bureau participation surveys by age cohorts makes it clear that the addition of this cohort has depressed post-1971 presidential turnout by not more than 1.5 percent, leaving nine-tenths of the drop from 1960 to 1976 unaccounted for.

TABLE 10
Mandated Remobilization:
Southern Turnouts, 1948-1978

Year	President	Percentage of potential electorate voting for:		
		US House, Presidential years	US House, Off-years	Drop off
1948	24.6	21.2		
1950			12.4	49.6
1952	38.5	32.2		
1954			16.1	58.2
1956	36.6	29.2		
1958			15.1	58.7
1960	41.2	33.6		
1962			24.0	41.7
1964	45.6	39.3		
1966			29.0	36.4
1968	51.0	41.5		
1970			32.2	34.9
1972	44.9	39.3		
1974			25.1	44.1
1976	47.6	41.8		
1978			26.3	44.7

Decline in voting participation outside the special mandated case of the South has been nearly universal since 1960, but it has proceeded at very different rates, both in terms of social stratification and geography. As Table 12 shows, the lower the social class the more rapid the decline, both in presidential and off-year elections.

A complementary pattern of decline emerges along geographical lines when comparing participation rates in the early 1960s with the late 1970s. To take an extreme local case, New York City in 1976 reached its lowest turnout rate in 150 years, at 42.1 percent of the potential electorate, compared with a 72.6 percent turnout in 1940 and 63.4 percent as late as 1960.[34] Much of this effects the influx of non-white dependent populations whose turnout rates are extremely low, and also in decline. But there are broader issues at work. Thus, for example, turnout in white assembly districts for the 1977 mayoral election appears to have reached a low without precedent since the first mayor was elected in 1834.

TABLE 11
Surges, Declines and Decays: Turnouts in
the Northern and Western States, 1948-1978

Year	President	Percentage of potential electorate voting for:		
		US House, Presidential years	US House, Off-years	Drop off
1948	62.2	59.8		
1950			52.8	15.1
1952	71.1	68.2		
1954			51.4	27.7
1956	68.4	65.6		
1958			53.8	21.3
1960	71.7	68.2		
1962			54.7	23.7
1964	67.3	64.9		
1966			52.3	22.3
1968	64.1	60.7		
1970			50.7	20.9
1972	59.7	56.8		
1974			41.9	29.8
1976	57.2	53.4		
1978			38.6	32.5

On a national basis, the relative rate of decline in states, from 1962 to 1978 shows marked geographic concentrations. As might be expected, the quartile of states with smallest losses or actual gains in this 16-year interval include nine of the Southern states plus Missouri, Maine, and Oregon. The bottom quartile is heavily concentrated in the urbanized states of the East and near Midwest from Massachusetts to Illinois; two other very large states (Ohio and California) show attrition rates not much smaller than these. If one rearranges the analysis to deal with non-Southern states only, the top quartile of states (relative declines of 2.9 to 18.8) shows a mean of 4.9 House members per state, and 13.5 percent of all non-Southern House members. The bottom quartile, on the other hand (relative declines from 1962 to 1978 of between 32.2 and 41.4) has a mean of 14.9 House members per state, and 45.6 percent) of all non-Southern congressional representation. This bottom quartile contains both states which have traditionally had very strong party organization (e.g., Illinois, Indiana, and West Virginia), and those with weak or very weak organizations (e.g., Massachusetts and Washington).

TABLE 12
Class Differentials in Abstentions:
Turnout Rates by Occupation, United States, 1966-1974

Categories	Presidential years				Off years			
	1968	1972	Shift	Norm- alized shift**	1966	1974	Shift	Norm- alized shift**
	%	%	%	%	%	%	%	%
Propertied middle class	81.7	79.7	-2.0	-2.4	69.8	59.8	-10.0	-14.3
Dependent middle class	77.4	72.8	-4.6	-5.9	64.9	50.3	-14.6	-22.5
Upper working class	66.9	60.4	-6.5	-9.7	55.8	41.1	-14.7	-26.3
Lower working class	57.5	49.5	-8.0	-13.9	46.2	33.7	-12.5	-27.1
Middle class	79.9	76.5	-3.4	-4.3	67.9	55.3	-12.6	-18.6
Working class	62.0	55.0	-7.0	-11.3	51.0	37.4	-13.6	-26.7
USA, Census/ CPS Survey	67.8	63.0	-4.8	-7.1	55.4	44.7	-9.7	-19.3
USA, Aggregate data*	60.7	55.7	-5.0	-8.2	45.3	37.1	-8.2	-18.1

*Off-year aggregate data: House elections only. Total turnouts (including those for Governor, Senator, etc.) typically 1.5 to 2 percent higher.

**Calculated as the shift as a proportion of the actual participation rate at time 1.

Classifications of occupations:

Propertied middle class: professional, managerial, farm owners
Dependent middle class: clerical, sales
Upper working class: craftsmen & kindred workers, service workers
Lower working class: operatives, labourers, farm labourers

(3) Chronologically, this is a period during which very large and well-documented changes occurred in individual political cognitions and responses to political stimuli. So large and substantively important were these changes that they led to a complete rewriting of *The American Voter* since 1964, and to a growing crisis of explanatory paradigms

within the voting-behaviour research community as a whole.[35] The 1964-1976 period, as issue-polarization dramatically rose, the salience of political parties and their acceptability to wide strata of the mass public steeply declined. This decay of party was associated with a marked fragmentation of electoral response along office-specific lines, yielding a multi-tiered structure of electoral alignments. So far as congressional elections are concerned, the chief aggregate change of the past fifteen years has been the emergence of a dominant incumbency effect as a significant "cue" to electoral decision as the collective, cross-district bonds of party deteriorated.[36]

Borrowing from the work of Anthony Downs and other rational-choice theorists, it could be argued that (a) party is a particularly vital aggregate short-cut device for calculating utilities among those who have little other information to rely on; (b) access to politically-relevant information is strongly class-skewed in a capitalist society; (c) therefore, the disappearance of party as a meaningful vehicle for calculating utilities is likely to result not only in increasing abstention generally, but also to an increase in abstention among those who already vote least. On the other hand, a different analytical tradition would suggest that the rise in abstention is not only chronologically but causally associated with stimuli which have produced growing waves of alienation with politics, politicians, and political institutions among the public.

Arthur T. Hadley suggests another view even though he fails to take class variables into account.[37] Hadley observes that alienated voters — so similar to the alienated segment of non-voters in attitudes and other characteristics — might well provide the basis for even further large-scale increases in abstentions under the right circumstances. What, then, discriminates? It appears that the most powerful single attitudinal variable is a question about the respondent's attitude toward his or her personal life: does a respondent believe that luck determines most of what happens to him or her, or is one's life susceptible of personal control through planning? Those who believe that their lives are largely determined by chance will tend to be non-voters, those who believe otherwise will tend to vote.

This singular finding has an a priori fit with an argument in survey-research analysis: it is not differentials in individual political trust that divides voters from non-voters, but differentials in their sense of political efficacy. Those who believe that nothing they can do will make much difference, will tend to vote less often than those with similar demographic characteristics but a sense of political efficacy.

Since the late 1960s that internal composition of the non-voter population has changed as the pool of non-voters has grown. The classic formulation of the early survey-research studies — non-voters are people who are essentially "out of it" politically — is no longer remotely adequate to describe this pool. Finally, if we assume even that the proportion of politically inefficacious or luck-orientated people has remained constant within the non-voter pool since, say, 1968 (and much more so if we assume that this component has increased) we are left with the following naked proposition: *The structure of political choices offered the electorate in the United States, and the major decisions made by political elites, have together produced more and more baffled ineffective citizens who believe that chance rules their world.* This not only implies the long-term paralysis of democracy, but also a rapid speed-up of this paralysis in the most recent period of our history.

CONCLUSION

It has long been argued that American politics is not organized in class-struggle terms. At the most, social class is one among a wide variety of competing variables explaining voters' decisions. This conventional wisdom is very largely right. Lack of explicit class-consciousness among the large majority of the population is an essential linchpin of uncontested hegemony in the United States. But in that case, it would be logical to suppose that the "real" class struggle, the point at which class polarization is most salient, is not found in the contests between Democrats and Republicans in the active electorate, but *between* the active electorate as a whole *and* the non-voting half of the adult population as a whole. As in nineteenth-century Europe, there is a major difference in American today between *le pays légal* and *le pays réel*. That difference was razor-sharp in Europe a century ago, but is blurred and indeed nearly invisible in the United States. In America, it is possible to devote a whole book to the problem of non-voting without seriously addressing the class issue at all.

Given a large and enduring comparative deficiency in political consciousness among Americans, what difference does it make?

One set of objections arises from the evident collision between the realities of the case and the postulates of democratic theory. The current and until now fruitless debates in Congress about electoral-law reform are part of the characteristically obscure but never-ending struggle about the first principles of electoral democracy. This struggle has continued in the United States for decades after its counterparts elsewhere were concluded.[38] Comparative analysis make it clear that there are significant and conservative implications for the shape of American public policy.[39]

But one may also take a position much closer to that of *Real-politik* in international relations. Giovanni Sartori, himself no left-wing ideologue, has restated a well-known axiom of politics.[40] Political parties and large-scale mass participation in politics appear to be functional requisites of a modern state. First, they provide a means of channeling demands and socializing adult citizens into the possibilities and limits of political action in a given system. Second, they provide a means of communication or linkage between rulers and ruled, reducing the great distance which otherwise can produce popular alienation from government. Third, parties and participation are not only important to rulers as means to penetrate the society for purposes of government; they are also essential feedback mechanisms through which the rulers can gain legitimacy for themselves, their policies, and their rule. But it should be emphasized that there is a price for all this. That price is the creation of mass party organizations and the shaping of public policies and policy conflicts in the terms meaningful to the electorate, and particularly to those living in the lower half of a class society.

Quite different conditions now prevail in the United States today. The channels to which Sartori refers are in an advanced state of decay. With this decay has come an explosion of highly intense, narrowly-focussed sectoral demands on political elites. This rancourous *hyper*pluralism coexists with a steep decline in mass participation from relatively low levels, and a decline in popular support for governing elites. In the process, the state is seriously impaired at a time when the longer-term interests of the political economy — both at home and abroad — require its strengthening. It is therefore hardly surprising that the media has discovered a "governability crisis" in the 1970s. But this "crisis", whatever it is, has not come into being because of the immoderate demands of fickle and inconstant masses. It has come into being because of a contra-

diction, now becoming increasingly evident, between the maintenance of uncontested hegemony on one hand and the requirements
of the modern state for coherence, stability, and legitimacy on the
other.

The problem of participation in the United States today probably
cannot be resolved within the existing framework of organizable
political alternatives. It is structural in origin, and a major change in
political consciousness would be needed to overcome it. But the
shape of electoral law clearly makes a difference. Personal
registration requirements did not descend from the skies. They were
made by men, and are now defended by men who see no particular
advantage to themselves in making it easier for ordinary Americans
to get to the polls. Their abolition and replacement by automatic
state-enrollment procedures is only a first step, but a necessary one.

We simply do not know with any great clarity what it would take to
bring the missing adults, 40 million or more of them, back into the
active American electorate. Presumably, political structures would
have to be developed for the representation of interests which are
now feebly or not at all represented in electoral politics. This could
not be accomplished without fundamental changes in political consciousness and equally fundamental challenges to things which
upper- and upper-middle-class Americans believe to be sacrosanct.
The United States appears to be moving into an historical era during
which, at some point, uncontested hegemony will cease to exist. If so,
that stability of the regime will be more secure if organized channels
for representing the interests of the lower half of the population have
come into being.[41] This point, to which Sartori is justly sensitive, is
precisely identified by E. E. Shattschneider:

> A greatly expanded popular base of political participation is the essential
> condition for public support of the government. This is the modern problem of
> democratic government. The price of support is participation. The choice is
> between participation and propaganda, between democratic and dictatorial ways
> of *changing consent into support, because consent is no longer enough.*[42]

NOTES

1. For good discussions of the European cases, see Seymour M. Lipset and Stein Rokkan (eds.), *Party Systems and Voter Alignments* (New York: Free Press, 1967), and Stein Rokkan, *Citizens, Elections, Parties* (New York: David McKay, 1970). An early long-range review of American turnout, in which the developmental "movie" runs backwards, is contained in Walter Dean Burnham, "The Changing Shape of the American Political Universe," *American Political Science Review*, (1965): 7-28.

2. The most complete contemporary analysis thus far is Sidney Verba and Norman Nie, *Participation in America: Political Democracy and Social Equality* (New York: Harper & Row, 1972). See also the controversy between the present author and Professors Philip E. Converse and Jerrold G. Rusk: "Theory and Voting Research: Some Reflections on Converse's 'Change in the American Electorate'," *American Political Science Review*, 68 (1974): 1002-1023; comments by Converse and Rusk, ibid., 1024-1049; and author's rejoinder, ibid.: 1050-1057.

3. Cf. Philip E. Converse's contribution, "Change in the American Electorate," (ch. 8), in Angus Campbell and Philip E. Converse (eds.), *The Human Meaning of Social Change* (New York: Russell Sage, 1972), and the present author's discussion in "Theory and Voting Research," op. cit.

4. For example, Richard Jensen has observed that "The myth of massive corruption so cleverly conceived that it cannot be detected is a ghost story . . . By nineteenth-century standards, American or European, the midwestern elections were quiet, decorous affairs — hard-fought, but basically honest." Richard Jensen, *The Winning of the Midwest* (Chicago, 1971): 35-36.

5. Converse, op. cit. Similar reliance on rules changes as a sufficient explanation of post-1900 change in turnout rates is to be found in Rusk, "Comment," op. cit.; and, though not directly related to the turnout question, Rusk raises interesting collateral issues in "The Effect of the Australian Ballot on Split-Ticket Voting: 1876-1908," *American Political Science Review*, 64 (1970): 1220-1238.

6. Steven J. Rosenstone and Raymond E. Wolfinger, "The Effect of Registration Laws on Voter Turnout," *American Political Science Review*, 72, (1978): 22-45.

7. The phrase is Heinz Eulau's; but the locus classicus is probably Seymour M. Lipset, *Political Man* (New York: Doubleday, 1960): 179-263.

8. The most recent installment of this story is found in *Public Opinion*, 1 (2) (May/June 1978), p. 23.

9. The work of Stein Rokkan and his associates, op. cit., is particularly helpful. See also Dieter Nohlen, Bernhard Vogel et al., *Die Wahl der Parlamente*, Vol. I (Europa), (Berlin: Walter de Gruyter, 1969).

10. Gunnar Myrdal, *Challenge to Affluence* (New York: Pantheon, 1963), esp. pp. 92-193. Myrdal comments that ". . . it is fatal for democracy, and not only demoralizing for the individual members of this under-class, that they are so mute and without initiative, and that they are not becoming organized to fight for their interests." (p. 39).

11. There is a well-known general tendency for blacks to participate less than whites at all income levels. Thus, in 1976 the racial stratification by income was:

1976 Income Level	Whites		Blacks	
	Registered %	Voted %	Registered %	Voted %
Under $5,000	57.7	46.2	54.2	41.7
$5,000-9,999	62.6	54.2	58.5	48.8
$10,000-14,999	68.8	61.4	63.3	54.7
$15,000-24,999	76.9	71.2	69.9	64.6
$25,000 and over	83.4	77.8	77.6	73.1
Total (including not reported)	68.7	61.4	59.1	49.5

But the importance of social-class related factors for the turnout of both racial groups is obvious. In this connection, it should be noted that 32.5 percent of black respondents reported incomes of less than $5,000, compared with 13.2 percent of whites. US Bureau of the Census, "Voting and Registration in the Election of November 1976," p. 66.

12. Norman H. Nie, Sidney Verba, and John R. Petrocik, *The Changing American Voter,* (Cambridge: Harvard University Press, 1976): 59-73.

13. Samuel P. Huntington, *Political Order in Changing Societies* (New Haven: Yale University Press, 1968), pp. 122-133; J. R. Pole, *Political Representation in England and the Origins of the American Republic* (Berkeley: University of California Press, 1966), especially pp. 172-213.

14. Pole, ibid., Appendix II, "Voting Statistics in America": 543-564.

15. Louis Hartz, *The Liberal Tradition in America* (New York: Harcourt, Brace, 1955); cf. also his articulated theory of the "fragment culture" in Louis Hartz (ed.), *The Founding of New Societies* (New York: Harcourt, Brace & World, 1964): 3-122.

16. But note Dudley O. McGovney, *The American Suffrage Medley* (Chicago: University of Chicago Press, 1949).

17. Maurice Duverger, *Political Parties* (New York: Wiley, 1961): 21-22, 217-220.

18. Jensen, op. cit., ch. 2.

19. Barrington Moore, Jr., *Social Origins of Dictatorship and Democracy* (Boston: Beacon Press, 1966): 111-155.

20. See the important article by Eric McKitrick, "Party Politics and the Union and Confederate War Efforts," in William N. Chambers and Walter Dean Burnham (eds.), *The American Party Systems* (New York: Oxford University Press, 1967, 1975): 117-151.

21. Rhode Island was in a class by itself. It retained an essentially freeholder suffrage qualification until after 1888, and the last vestiges of its peculiar *régime censitaire* electoral law were not removed until 1928. It is, therefore, the only state in the union to show a longitudinal upward trend in voter participation from the mid-nineteenth century to the 1952-1970 period.

22. V. O. Key, Jr., *Southern Politics in State and Nation* (New York: Knopf, 1949). See especially Part Five, "Restrictions on Voting," pp. 531-663, for a comprehensive discussion of the full range of suffrage-restricting devices then in place in the ex-Confederate states. Mean Southern presidential turnouts from 1912 to 1928 were 24.8 percent; from 1932 to 1948, 25 percent; from 1952 to 1968, 42.6 percent.

23. The basic argument is made, if rather crudely, in Burnham, "The Changing Shape of the American Political Universe," op. cit.

24. This is a chief theme of the so-called "Bible of Progressivism," Herbert Croly's *The Promise of American Life* (New York: Macmillan, 1909).

25. Burnham, "Theory and Voting Research," op. cit.

26. Rosenstone and Wolfinger, op. cit., pp. 33, 41. These authors also argue that movement toward a "most permissive" standard would enlarge the electorate without changing its internal composition very much. This of course is true, granted both the social structure and the very large but still marginal numbers involved. It would be somewhat less true on the assumption that the class differential in participation, at whatever aggregate level of turnout, were to disappear altogether. Comparison of the male labour-force categories in Table 12 in terms of their share of the total adult male population on one hand, and 1972 reported Census Bureau turnouts on the other, would give the following:

Category	Percentage of population 1972	Percentage of active electorate 1972	Discrepancy
Propertied middle class	31.6	38.1	+ 6.5
Dependent middle class	13.2	14.9	+ 1.7
Middle class total	44.8	53.0	+ 8.2
Upper working class	28.3	26.5	− 1.8
Lower working class	27.0	20.6	− 6.4
Working class total	55.2	47.0	− 8.2

A shift toward full equality of participation along class lines — certainly not a matter of registration law alone, as we argue here — would thus produce marginal but not inconsequential changes in the aggregate class composition of the active electorate.

27. H. L. A. Tingsten, *Political Behavior* (London: King, 1937): 10-78.

28. The Chicago data make clear the truth of the axiom that if people go to the trouble of registering, the probability is high that they will vote. Male registration in 1916 was 82.7 percent of estimated potential electorate, female registration was 51.1 percent, a discrepancy of 31.6 percent. Subsequent data for 1920 and 1924 are essentially identical. In 1928, however, male registration was 80.5 percent, while female registration rose to 64.2 percent, closing the gap to 16.3 percent. It would appear that very similar results were obtained in Philadelphia.

29. See e.g., Samuel Lubell, *The Future of American Politics* (New York: Harper, 1952), which concentrates its attention on the influx from 1928 on of formerly non-participant foreign-born and foreign-stock voters; and Kristi Anderson, "Generation, Partisan Shift, and Realignment: A Glance back to the New Deal," in Nie et al., *The Changing American Voter,* op cit.: 74-95.

30. Tingsten, op cit.: 157-158.

31. Detailed data analysis can normally pick up such cases without difficulty. Thus, in the 1902 gubernatorial election, eight notoriously machine-controlled wards of Philadelphia produced a turnout rate of 105.3 percent, with 85.4 percent of their vote going to the machine's candidate (this turnout was 37.5 percent higher than in

Pennsylvania as a whole). Again, in the 1926 Republican gubernatorial primary, the turnout in these largely proletarian, "river" wards was 60.1 percent (30.2 percent higher than in the state as a whole); and the organization's candidate got 96.7 percent of the votes case in these wards.

32. Anderson, op. cit.; David F. Prindle, "Turnout: An Historical Investigation," doctoral dissertation, Massachusetts Institute of Technology, 1977.

33. The contrast between the turnouts in the "war elections" of 1918 and 1942 on one hand, and that of 1862 on the other, is striking. Despite the intensity of the demographic effort involved in the Civil War, and despite the fact that laws in many states did not permit soldiers in the field to vote, 68.8 percent of the estimated potential (exclusively male) electorate voted in the North and West in the 1862 election. The all-time high turnout in any off-year election was reached in 1866 (75.8 percent in North and West), reflecting the intense struggle then going on between Andrew Johnson and the radical Republicans over Reconstruction policy.

34. The basic methodology employed in the construction of the population-base denominators for turnout estimates is explained in detail in the author's note, "Voter Participation in Presidential Elections, by State, 1924-1968," in Bureau of the Census, *Historical Statistics of the United States, Colonial Times to 1970,* vol. II (Washington: Government Printing Office, 1975): 1067-1069. For the most recent period, problems exist not only with census undercounts of the "underclass population," but with the identification of aliens in 1960 and in some jurisdictions in 1970. For 1970, an exclusion of those aliens counted can be made for New York City, and a proportionate approximation made for 1960 in constructing the denominator. The undercount problem involving "underclass" (especially nonwhite) adults is a more serious one. See David M. Heer, (ed.), *Social Statistics and the City* (Cambridge: Joint Center, 1968). It almost certainly means that the turnouts reported for New York City and other central-city areas are substantially *higher* than the true rates of participation; though one wonders how much lower one can go than the 24.7 percent of estimated adult population voting for president in 1976 in Shirley Chisholm's Brooklyn district (CD 12).

35. The study referred to is, of course, Nie et al., *The Changing American Voter,* op. cit. In addition to the controversies referred to in notes 2 and 3 above, the pardigm crisis is reflected in a recent exchange of views: one one side, the Michigan CPS group, Arthur H. Miller et al., "A Majority Party in Disarray: Policy Polarization in the 1972 Election," *American Political Science Review,* 70 (1976): 753-778; and on the other, Samuel Popkin et al., "Comment: What Have You Done for Me Lately? Toward an Investment Theory of Voting," ibid.: 779-805.

36. Cf. the extensive discussion of this phenomenon and its background in Morris P. Fiorina, *Congress: Keystone of the Washington Establishment* (New Haven: Yale Fastback, 1976); and also, Walter Dean Burnham, "The 1976 Election: Has the Crisis Been Adjourned?" in W. D. Burnham and Martha Weinberg (eds.), *American Politics and Public Policy* (Cambridge: MIT Press, 1978), esp.: 14-21.

37. Arthur T. Hadley, *The Empty Polling Booth* (Englewood Cliffs: Prentice-Hall, 1978).

38. The fullest recent discussion of the philosophical issues involved in this obscure struggle is found in my "A Political Scientist and Voting-Rights Litigation: The Case of the 1966 Texas Registration Statute," *Washington University Law Quarterly,* 1971 (1971): 335-358.

39. Douglas A. Hibbs, Jr., "Political Parties and Macroeconomic Policy,"

American Political Science Review, 71 (1977): 1467-1487. This study demonstrates that American macroeconomic policy is much more sensitive to inflation (a particular concern among middle- and upper-status voters), and much less sensitive to unemployment (of particular concern among working-class voters) than is the case in European political contexts.

40. Giovanni Sartori, *Parties and Party Systems,* Vol. I (Cambridge: Cambridge University Press, 1976): 39-51.

41. This point is thoroughly discussed in a pioneering work which needs more professional attention than it has thus far received: the chapter by William McPhee and Jack Ferguson, "Political Immunization," in William McPhee et al., *Public Opinion and Congressional Elections* (Glencoe: The Free Press, 1962): 155-179.

42. E. E. Schattschneider, *The Semisovereign People* (New York: Holt, Rinehart and Winston, 1960): 109.

3

Styles of Electoral Competition

William Schneider
Hoover Institution, Stanford

As an institution of democratic politics, elections perform two different functions. In the first place, elections give voice to the principal political cleavages and issue conflicts in society; they reflect major political divisions — liberal versus conservative; middle class versus working class; clerical versus secular; tribal, regional, racial, or religious antagonisms. In its purest form this ideological function requires that elections produce a microcosm of the larger society in which all major interests receive due representation, at least to the extent that such interests are expressed as divisions over political issues. Historically, this view of elections derives from the constitutional practice of electing a "constituent assembly" of the nation, in which all major social forces are represented. Legislators then strike whatever bargains are necessary to form a coalition government which will receive majority support or majority toleration. The voter's relation to the government is essentially indirect. He votes for the individual or party that will best represent his interests in the process of forming a government. The government is responsible to the legislature, which in turn is "constituted" from the electorate. The purpose of elections here is accurate and complete representation.

Secondly, elections have a plebiscitary function. An election is a referendum, a passing of popular judgement on the performance of the incumbent government. In its simplest version, people vote for the government if times are good and against the government if times are bad. The constitutional principle reflected here is that of a direct relationship between the government and the electorate. In a presidential system, this direct relationship is a matter of formal requirement. It is also consistent with parliamentary systems as long as the voter has a reasonably clear sense of which party or parties should be identified as the government and which as the opposition.

At first glance, there appears to be a certain incompatibility between ideological voting and plebiscitary voting at the individual level. When the voter enters the polling booth, two kinds of factors influence his choice. He selects the candidate or party that most closely represents his views and interests, and he passes judgement on "how things are going" when assessing the performance of the incumbent government. Logically, there is no reason why these factors should be consistent. Empirically, however, there is an important source of constraint: assessment of performance, the plebiscitary function, is strongly correlated with partisanship. For a substantial proportion of the electorate, the evaluation of "how the government is doing" is a reflection of long-term partisan or ideological identification. If it is a government of "my" party, then it is doing relatively well. This important relationship was first demonstrated in *The American Voter,* where it was shown that "responses to each element of national politics are deeply affected by the individual's enduring party attachments" (Campbell et al., 1964: 73). By distinguishing short-term evaluational elements from long-term partisanship, the researchers were able to infer causal priority in the relationship:

> In the period of our studies (1952-1956) the influence of party identification on attitudes toward the perceived elements of politics has been far more important than the influence of these attitudes on party identification itself. We are convinced that the relationships in our data reflect primarily the role of enduring partisan commitments in shaping attitudes toward political objects (Campbell et al., 1964: 78).

This solves the problem of inconsistency between ideological voting and plebiscitary voting for many electors. (One of them was Harry S. Truman, who was once asked: "Mr. President, do you believe in voting for the man or for the party?" "I always vote for the best man," Truman replied. "He is the Democrat.") If the correlation were perfect, with short-term evaluation determined entirely by long-term partisanship, then the political system would be reduced to immobility, with the only sources of change being long-term shifts in partisan allegiance (realignment) and in the demographic balance between the partisan camps.

But even allowing for measurement error, the correlation between long-term commitment and short-term evaluation is not perfect, a point recognized in *The American Voter:* "However great its impact, partisan loyalty does not by any means express the total influence of factors antecedent in a causal sense to the attitudes we have studied" (Campbell et al., 1964: 74-75). There are two forces which weaken the correlation. For one thing, every child that is born alive is *not* "either a little Liberal or else a little Conservative." Many are independents and uncommitted partisans who, by definition, have few long-term commitments colouring their evaluations of political objects. They exist partly because of the weak intergenerational transmission of party loyalties. Even in the strong party culture of Great Britain, among voting-age respondents whose parents both supported the same party, 12 percent claimed to have no party loyalty themselves in a 1964 survey. Moreover, 24 percent of respondents could not recall the party loyalty of either parent (Rose, 1974a: 149).

Second, there is the phenomenon of defection. Even the strongest partisans will inevitably be affected by the short-term forces at work in the larger electorate. In the 1968 Presidential election, the year of Vietnam, 15 percent of strong Democratic voters defected from their party. Precisely the same percentage of strong Republican voters defected to Democratic Congressional candidates in 1974, the year of Watergate.[1] (Inter-University Consortium for Political and Social Research, 1968 and 1974 American National Election Studies).

The phenomenon of defection was the central focus of V. O. Key, Jr.'s analysis in *The Responsible Electorate* (1966). Key looked at marginal shifts from election to election in order to demonstrate that voter movements are highly responsive to short-term political forces, including performance evaluation. Table 1 (from Key) shows that voter movement between the 1948 and 1952 Presidential elections was correlated with the evaluation of the Administration's foreign policy. Those who felt that the US had made a mistake in going into the war in Korea were more likely to switch to the Republican candidate if they had voted for the Democrat in 1948, or stay with the Republicans if they had voted Republican in 1948, or cast their first Presidential vote for a Republican, than were those who felt that getting involved in Korea was not a mistake, or those who had no opinion.

The critical feature of Key's methodology was to control for

TABLE 1

Switches in Presidential Voting Preference, 1948-1952, in Relation to Response to Question: "Do you think the US made a mistake in going into the war in Korea or not?"

Response	% of 1948 D's, D-R	% of 1948 R's, R-D	% of new voters, R
Yes, mistake	37 (821)	5 (912)	64 (622)
No	20 (1,032)	11 (462)	46 (550)
No opinion	18 (420)	9 (250)	38 (247)

D = Democrat
R = Republican
D-R = Switch Democrat 1948 to Republican 1952
R-D = Switch Republican 1948 to Democrat 1952
Source: V. O. Key, Jr., *The Responsible Electorate* (New York: Vintage Books, 1966), p. 75.

previous vote, which functioned like a control for party identification. The point is to hold past commitments constant and look for responsiveness to short-term issue forces. The finding of *The American Voter* — that short-term issue evaluations are strongly correlated with long-term partisanship — is confirmed by Table 1. The table shows a total of 2,273 respondents who had voted for the Democrat in 1948. Of these "previous Democrats," 36 percent (821) felt in 1952 that the US made a mistake going into the Korean war. They were outnumbered by the 45 percent (1,032) of 1948 Democratic voters who felt that getting involved in Korea was not a mistake, supporting the policy of the Democratic Administration which they had helped put into office. Among 1948 Republican voters, the balance was two-to-one in the opposite direction. Fifty-six percent of the 1948 Republican voters (912 out of 1,624) felt that the Korean war was a mistake, whereas 28 percent (462) felt that it was not a mistake. New voters in 1952 were closely divided, with 44 percent calling Korea a mistake and 39 percent approving the policy. In sum, previous Democratic voters tended to support the Democratic Administration's foreign policy and previous Republican voters tended to oppose it. (See also Campbell et al., 1964: 78.) Key, of course, simply drew attention to a different feature of the table — that *if* a voter felt that going into Korea was a mistake, no matter what his previous political commitment, he tended to move in a pro-Republican direction in 1952.

Other percentages not included in Key's table are also revealing. For instance, while 37 percent of former Democratic voters who felt that Korea was a mistake switched to the Republican candidate in 1952, 63 percent stayed with the Democrats despite their reservations over Korea. And 89 percent of former Republican voters who approved the Democrats' Korea policy continued to vote Republican in 1952. Whatever their issue position on Korea, most 1948 Democrats continued to vote Democratic in 1952, and most 1948 Republicans continued to vote Republican. Key wished to stress the fact that issues do produce change on the margins of long-term partisan stability. These short-term issue fluctuations represent the plebiscitary function of elections.

Thus, it is the strength of the correlation between short-term evaluations and long-term partisanship that makes the two influences consistent at the individual level. It is the weakness or, more precisely, the *indeterminacy,* of this same correlation that allows both functions to operate at the aggregate level.

TWO TYPES OF ISSUES

The short-term issues analyzed by Key in relation to governmental performance were for the most part valence issues, according to a distinction first made by Stokes:

> Let us call "*position* issues" those that involve advocacy of government actions from a set of alternatives over which a distribution of voter preferences is defined. And . . . let us call "*valence* issues" those that merely involve the linking of the parties with some condition that is positively or negatively valued by the electorate. (Stokes, 1966: 170-171)

Divisiveness is central to this distinction (Schneider, 1974: 112). Position issues are inherently divisive in that they involve explicit alternative values — for or against state support of church schools, continued membership in the European Economic Community, a gay rights ordinance, or higher military spending. Valence issues do not entail legitimate alternative values. Only one value is involved; that value may be positive (prosperity, peace) or negative (unemployment, corruption, ineffective leadership).

This distinction is a true dichotomy, a difference of kind and not degree. But is it not possible to speak of issues as being more or less divisive? In fact, the intensity of division — or the degree of polarization — is a characteristic of position issues as a group. Class polarization clearly varies in intensity over time. Indeed, one of the important contributions of *The American Voter* was to treat "status polarization" in American politics as a variable rather than a constant (Campbell et al., 1964: chapter 12). A position issue that fails to polarize the electorate to any great degree is not the same as a valence issue. It is simply a position issue with low salience, whereas the defining characteristic of a valence issue is that it is *essentially non-divisive*.

For example, the Keynesian trade-off between inflation and unemployment represents a positional economic issue: one must choose between alternatives. There is a good economic argument to suggest that, if voters knew their best interests, the Keynesian trade-off would polarize along class lines, with working class voters more fearful of unemployment and middle class voters more fearful of inflation. But there is not much evidence that the trade-off between inflation and unemployment polarizes voters very intensely along class lines. To most rank-and-file voters, the trade-off is not a clear one; both inflation and unemployment are considered undesirable, with no compelling sense that one must "choose" one evil or the other.

On the day of the 1976 US Presidential election, NBC News asked over 15,000 voters to select "the single issue that led you to vote for your Presidential candidate." Inflation was the issue most frequently chosen from a list of eighteen. The 21 percent of the voters who said "inflation" voted 58 percent for Carter, the Democrat, and 41 percent for Ford, the Republican. In another question on the same survey, voters were asked whether inflation or unemployment "is the more important problem facing the country today." The group who said inflation, 24 percent, voted 35 percent for Carter and 63 percent for Ford (NBC News, 1976). Carter, the candidate of the out-party, benefited from the generalized concern over inflation, which seems to have been a valence issue working against the incumbent. Ford did well among a different group of voters, those who endorsed the ideological position that inflation is more important than unemployment.

Thus, an issue such as inflation can be represented as either a valence or a position issue. The same might be said of Vietnam at the time of the 1968 US Presidential election. The positional aspect of the Vietnam issue was the widely discussed hawk-dove distinction, immediate withdrawal versus a more vigorous application of military force. The intensely divisive quality of this issue led both major party candidates in 1968 to avoid clear definition as either a hawk or a dove. On the other hand, the protest candidates of the left and of the right in 1968 — Eugene McCarthy and George Wallace — could be easily identified in hawk-dove terms by the electorate (Page and Brody, 1972: 986-993; Schneider, 1974: 140-144). But there was also a valence aspect to the Vietnam issue that year, namely, the widespread sentiment that the United States had made a mistake getting involved in Vietnam and that the war should be ended as quickly as possible. While both major party candidates avoided ideological definition as a hawk or a dove, both competed for identification as the candidate most likely to end the war.

Social scientists have a tendency to impose a positional conception on all political issues, as if all issues relate to underlying divisions of values. But as Stokes pointed out:

> It will not do simply to exclude valence-issues from the discussion of party competition. The people's choice too often depends on them. At least in American Presidential elections of the past generation it is remarkable how many valence-issues have held the center of the stage. (Stokes, 1966: 171)

Since valence issues are not usually associated with long-term realignment effects, there is a temptation to treat them as trivial — the "ephemera" of politics. But valence issues are frequently of overwhelming salience to the electorate, entailing substantial shifts in voting behaviour, the revision of normal ideological alignments, and even profound changes in the structure of political conflict.

The fact that valence issues are non-divisive does not mean that they are not controversial. On what grounds can there be debate about issues which do not involve alternative values?

(1) *Salience.* How serious is the problem? Is there cause for concern over the value in question — peace, national prestige, corruption, competence, etc.? The issues of "Communism, Korea, and corruption" in the 1952 Presidential election and the missile gap in 1960 were both salient and controversial, even though both parties agreed in endorsing the same values.

(2) *Responsibility.* Who is to blame for the problem? Who should receive credit for the solution? Harry Truman tried to shift the blame for the nation's problems in 1948 by running against a "do-nothing" Congress, while Hubert Humphrey made an effort in the 1968 campaign to dissociate himself from the most unpopular policies of his party's Administration. Prime Minister Edward Heath called the British General Election of February 1974 on the issue of "Who governs Britain?" — i.e., the government or the unions. But whereas

most voters disapproved of the crippling strike called by the miners' union, many also blamed the Conservative Government for polarizing the situation and precipitating a national crisis (Butler and Kavanagh, 1974: 139-143; Crewe et al., 1974).

(3) *Choice.* Do the voters perceive a difference between the parties, not in ideological terms, but in terms of their priorities and performance? If times are bad under the current government, is there an alternative government whose promise to make things better is widely believed? If the country is engaged in an unpopular war, will the election of a different government bring peace? The essential logic of democracy in V. O. Key's terms is that the way to change the policy is the change the government.

The notion that the parties must present a choice is usually interpreted in ideological terms — that the voters must have a clear basis for anticipating what each party will do in office. A "choice" in valence terms is simply the anticipation that one party can solve the problems created by the other, and that it therefore makes sense to change governments. The choice of specific remedies is left to the experts. But the voters reserve the right to judge for themselves whether the policies and solutions work. When the voters want relief from rampant inflation, *most* of them do not care whether the government solves the problem by balancing the budget or by wage-and price controls: they care only whether the problem is solved. When the voters want an end to a disastrous foreign war, *most* do not care whether this is done by withdrawing troops or by applying greater military pressure, so long as the war is ended. In the case of valence issues, choice really comes down to the question of whether one party can do better than the other what the the great majority agrees needs to be done. The failure of choice would be evidenced by the widespread perception that no alternative government will work: the decision to vote one way or the other could mean little in terms of anticipated performance.

A shift in the aggregate vote can signify either a temporary defection or a long-term realignment. Valence issues produce across-the-board shifts in a party's vote that do not disturb the correlations with past votes or with social and demographic variables. Position issues usually affect correlations because they set in motion group antagonisms that change a party's strength in different areas of the electorate. One normally associates political realignments with changes in the group basis of voting behaviour. But valence issues, too, may have long-term effects. Americans have ranked the

Democratic Party as better for "keeping the country prosperous" more or less consistently for the past twenty-five years. The Republican Party has enjoyed a somewhat less consistent advantage in the area of foreign affairs (*Gallup Opinion Index,* 1976: 3-6). These evaluations are based not so much on group conflict as on the perception that each party has performed well on different issues while in office. In several European countries, it is the parties of the right that have been associated with prosperity since these parties were in office during the periods of greatest economic growth following World War II.

The valence category also includes the whole range of "style" and "candidate image" issues that profoundly affect electoral outcomes. In fact, one of the enduring problems of a system of candidate voting like that of the United States is the tendency for non-substantive image and style factors to dominate elections. Candidates spend most of their time dwelling upon their own strengths and decrying the incompetence of their opponents precisely because such issues involve valence sentiments (competence, character, reliability, etc.) and therefore low risk. Once a candidate has been established in the public mind as incompetent or unappealing, few issues of substance are likely to make a difference to the outcome. In his discussion of extreme factionalism in Southern politics, V. O. Key criticized this attribute of the system: "Competence is undoubtedly important, but the placing of great, almost sole, emphasis on 'qualifications' carries with it the tacit assumption that all issues are either settled or quiescent" (Key, 1949: 186-187).

Candidate-image politics usually means valence-issue politics ("the selling of the President"), but not always. President Eisenhower's positive image drew generalized support across the American electorate in the 1950s without polarizing the electorate or disturbing the underlying bases of partisanship.

By contrast since 1958 in France the reaction to President De Gaulle was a "relatively clear polarization of French politics along a single dimension: Gaullism versus anti-Gaullism" (Inglehart and Hochstein, 1972: 361). Attitudes toward De Gaulle gave a new coherence to French partisanship; evidence of a divisive issue conflict was captured in a candidate image, rather than a transient reaction to personality and competence (Charlot, 1971: 38-40; Wright, 1975; Campbell, 1976; McHale and Shaber, 1976).

Similarly, it would be misleading to analyze the candidate images of US Presidents Franklin D. Roosevelt or Andrew Jackson as simply positive or negative. Sentiments about both men involved deep divisions in the electorate, to the point where feelings about them — as about De Gaulle in France — were the basis of a new partisanship (the Whig Party emerged as the anti-Jackson party, the party of Roosevelt became the New Deal Democratic Party). In matters of candidate image, as with other issues, "the question whether a given problem poses a position or valence issues is a matter to be settled empirically and not on a priori logical grounds" (Stokes, 1966: 172).

TWO STYLES OF ELECTORAL COMPETITION

Position and valence issues may be associated with alternative styles of political competition. One style may be called *ideological,* the use of position issues to define a segment of the electorate and mobilize its support. There is empirical justification for linking ideology with position-issue conflict. While ideology is usually associated with abstract conceptual thinking at the elite level, at the mass level it is almost always characterized by a sense of group conflict, of "us" versus "them," of a fundamental opposition of beliefs and interests.

Whereas abstract conceptual thinking does not penetrate very deeply below the elite level, involvement in group conflict does (Converse, 1964). Moreover, Nie (1974) notes a marked increase in the level of attitude consistency in the American electorate in the period from 1956 to 1972. In a discussion of Nie's findings, Converse distinguishes between attitude consistency on the one hand and ideological thinking, "the active use of ordering abstractions," on the other (1975: 103-107). This distinction corresponds to the difference between "ideological thinking" at the mass and elite levels. Converse points out that "attitude consistency may become dramatically heightened without any correspondingly large increase in the active use of ordering abstractions" (1975: 103). This is precisely what happened in the United States between 1956 and 1968: a slight increase in ideological thinking within the more sophisticated half of the electorate, accompanied by an enormous increase in attitude consistency across all levels of the electorate (Converse, 1975: 102-194). The reason why the two vary independently, Converse suggests, is that they have different causes. Level of conceptualization ("the recognition and use of capping abstractions") is fundamentally a product of education. Attitude consistency, on the other hand, is related to the salience of politics. As the salience of politics increases, political involvement increases, and political involvement, according to Nie's and Converse's evidence, leads to an increase in attitude consistency.

One must then ask: what produced an increase in the salience of politics during the 1960s? The answer, Converse suggests, is group antagonisms. At first, the sharp issue differentiation between the major parties in 1964 "cued" the electorate to the emerging issue conflicts between liberals and conservatives. "However, by 1968 group antagonisms within the electorate itself had reached a sufficiently politicized peak that high levels of consistency across issue domains could be maintained." The electorate, Converse continued, "fell into positions of heightened ideological clarity without any clear recognition of the fact that they were doing so. This is simply social polarization, with the motive force being less ideological reasoning than group antagonism" (Converse, 1975: 106-107).

Thus, ideological division at the mass level is the end product of a chain of causation beginning with conflict over position issues, such as race and Vietnam in the 1960s. Conflict over position issues creates group antagonisms, which raise the salience of politics; salience increases political involvement, which, in turn, creates greater attitude consistency. The inception of the process, Pomper argues, is the decision by party elites to offer choices that are increasingly differentiated in positional terms (Pomper, 1975: 166-185): in other words, to follow the strategy of ideological politics. Such a strategy makes use of divisive issue positions to define supporters, maximize their enthusiasm, and draw the line between "us" and "them."

In a two-party system, the incentives for ideological politics are weak; pressure for ideological coherence usually comes from activist factions within the parties or from extra-partisan protest groups which demand that the parties take sides on position issues. The ideological strategy tends to prevail in highly fractionated multiparty systems with proportional representation, where each party attempts to develop a secure base in one segment of the electorate and where there are few incentives for a party to adopt a majoritarian appeal. Rose has compared the degree to which party choice is structured by basic social characteristics in fifteen Western democracies. Multiparty systems such as the Netherlands, Sweden, Norway, Belgium, and Fourth-Republic France show a relatively high degree of social structuring of the vote, at least in terms of the percentage of the variance in individual party choice explained by occupation, religion, and region. Systems that approximate a two-party model (Great Britain, the United States, Australia, Canada, and West Germany) fall near the bottom of the list (Rose, 1974: 16-17). Parties that claim to be capable of governing more or less alone usually cannot afford to limit their appeal to polarized and antagonistic social groups.

Partisan conflict is an institutionalized form of ideological conflict. Partisanship usually originates in a situation of deeply divisive group conflict over position issues — class conflict, religious antagonism, sectional animosity, etc. Parties sustain such divisions long after the original issue conflicts have faded by turning them into the normal basis of political opposition. Thus, some form of ideological politics is present in all. Republicans and Democrats continued to revive the bitter antagonisms of the Civil War ("waving the bloody shirt") as the most efficient means of mobilizing party supporters until well into the 1890s. The two major parties in Britain have similarly used class conflict. When new ideological conflicts emerge, that is, conflicts over new position issues, it is their uninstitutionalized quality that makes them dangerous; such issues may generate protest activity in the short run (third party movements in the United States, "flash parties" in Europe). If the conflicts persist, they may alter the basis of partisanship in the long run.

The second style of electoral competition may be labeled *coalition politics*. The strategy of coalition politics is to appeal to *all* voters as potential supporters. This approach uses non-divisive valence issues that appeal to the broadest range of voters without necessarily excluding any supporters at all. Ideological strategists may claim to build coalitions, but they are coalitions in which only those who agree with particular positions are welcome; supporters must join the movement on its own terms. As the term is used here, a coalition defines its goals in all-inclusive terms: to achieve peace or prosperity, or to root out corruption or incompetence. Generally, one thinks of political parties as facing a choice. A party can close ranks and stress its ideological appeal through position issues, and thereby stabilize a core bloc of party supporters, or it can open ranks and construct shifting coalitions from election to election, in which case the party appeals to floating voters by stressing valence themes. The latter approach was aptly termed "catch-all politics" by the later Otto Kirchheimer (1966: 184-195). The activation of a party's ideological base commonly involves rallies, parades, meetings, and a stirring up of group antagonisms in the face of a common threat. Coalition strategists eschew such dramatic appeals since they will frighten away potential supporters. Coalition parties prefer the techniques of advertising and education to persuade voters to approve the best man or the best party.

Which strategy a party uses depends on the nature of the party, the incentives and disincentives created by the electoral rules, and the availability of opportunities to win wider support. In 1959 the German Social Democratic Party rewrote its programme to give it a coalitional rather than an ideological appeal. In the 1970s the Italian Communists decided to support a Christian Democratic government in order to reduce their ideological position and broaden their potential coalition appeal. In each case, one reason was the widespread perception that there were many voters disenchanted with the performance of the incumbent bourgeois parties who might consider switching to a moderate opposition party. In a multiparty system with proportional representation, however, a small party may "go for safety" by mobilizing its hard-core supporters and guaranteeing for itself a determinate minority share of the vote.

One generalization seems to stand out: every major theoretical analysis of two-party systems — Dahl (1967), Downs (1957), Key (1966), Stokes (1966), Schattschneider (1960) — has pointed to the inherent tendency of both parties to "go for the centre." However, "going for the centre" does not mean finding a middle position on position issues. It means avoiding position issues altogether and, instead, competing in valence-issue terms by finding salient coalition themes that will attract a broad majority of the electorate. In a two-party system, both parties have an incentive to avoid taking a position on any issue where there is a risk of losing some votes. The more divisive the issue, the greater the risk. Even if polls show a two-thirds majority on one side of an issue, an incentive against taking a position would still exist. So long as an issue is in any degree divisive, i.e., so long as there are voters on both sides, then votes may be lost by taking one side. The coalition strategy minimizes the risk of losing votes; there is no support to be "written off" on the other side of valence issues for there is only one side. A party does not write off any votes by coming out in favour of better government, greater national security, or lower inflation, even if no one believes that it can accomplish these objectives.

The principal reform movements of late nineteenth- and early twentieth-century America, Populism and Progressivism, exemplify the distinction between ideological and coalition politics. Populism is probably the most dramatic example in American history of a truly radical ideological movement. The core of the movement was agrarian anti-capitalism, and its ideology was permeated with the sense of conspiracy and confrontation. Hofstadter, for instance, describes the "dualistic version of social struggles" which pervaded Populist ideology, the tendency to conceptualize conflict in the starkest "us versus them" terms (Hofstadter, 1955: 64). The Populist movement was infused with the spirit of agrarianism and evangelical Protestantism. While its principal target was monopoly capital and "the money power," many Populist spokesmen expressed a broader antagonism to all the symbols of urban, industrial civilization. The movement was widely perceived as anti-urban, anti-Eastern, anti-immigrant, and, most damaging of all, anti-business. Its sectional and agrarian exclusivity, as well as its radical quality as a moral crusade, clearly frightened away many potential supporters.

There is considerable substantive continuity between the Populism of the 1890s and the Progressivism of the 1910s, for many Populist programs — including such radical proposals as government ownership of public utilities — were incorporated into Progressivism. But in political style and strategy, there was a sharp break between the two movements. One clue to the difference between them is the fact that, while scholars have had little difficulty defining the social basis of Populist support, it has proved much more difficult to define Progressive support in class or cultural terms. Detailed quantitative studies of voting behaviour during the Progressive era show no clear correlation between class or ethnic background and Progressivism (Rogin and Shover, 1970; Thelen, 1972; Wyman, 1974).

Whereas Populist leaders exploited social divisions in defining the battle as class against class, Progressives wrote and spoke in terms of "the public interest" and "the public good." Progressives tried to define the common denominator of public sentiment and avoided social polarization at all costs. They did so by choosing specific targets of protest — party bosses, arrogant corporate leaders, corrupt industrialists — who were not identified with any class or group. The Progressives were indeed a protest movement like the Populists, but they appealed to *universal* sentiments. Thelen concluded:

Perhaps there are, after all, times and places where issues cut across class lines . . .

The attitude of moral indignation, such an obvious feature of the early stages of progressivism, was not rooted in social tensions but in *the universal emotion of anger.* (1972: 179, 180; emphasis added)

According to Rogin and Shover:

Antirailroad sentiment was diffused throughout the population, from poor farmers to San Francisco merchants and industrialists. The community could be mobilized against a common foe: *no need to stir up more divisive feelings* ... The language of progressivism remained 'classless,' oriented toward moral virtue and fearful of conflict. (1970: 53, 56; emphasis added)

Certainly many conservatives and business leaders regarded the Progressives as ideological crusaders and creators of "division." But that is not the way the Progressives viewed or publicized themselves, and the nature of their support reveals little in the way of group antagonism. There was no important group in society — including businessmen — who opposed the values that the Progressives stood for.

In the end, the Populists accomplished little in substantive or programmatic terms. Indeed, much of what the Populists stood for, like "free silver," seems curiously antiquated today. But the Populists did succeed in realigning the bases of support for the two major parties for a generation to follow. In fusing their movement with the Democratic Party, the Populists institutionalized a new axis of political conflict: sectional, urban versus rural, and industrial versus agrarian. The effects of Progressivism were just the reverse. By using a coalition strategy, the Progressives brought about an immense amount of reform at the municipal, state, and federal levels: child labour laws, government regulatory agencies, non-partisan municipal government, primary elections, and a whole host of other measures that have profoundly transformed the nature of American government. When a Populist-originated measure such as government regulation of railroad rates was presented as a Progressive reform and dramatized by tangible abuses — and not presented as an attack on capitalism — implementation was much more easily achieved. But the Progressives did not realign the basis of party support in any significant way. There were Progressive wings in both major parties, but these did not represent group antagonisms capable of shifting the enduring basis of partisanship.[2]

In *The Responsible Electorate* (1966) Key elaborates the logic of coalition politics. A system of competing coalitions allows for

"rational" voter choice despite the parties' conscientious avoidance
of clear-cut ideological differences. In Key's system, the parties
create temporary coalitions out of each other's mistakes. Key
emphasized the plebiscitary function of elections. Voters choose
Presidential candidates according to their evaluation of the
performance of the incumbent Administration.

> The major streams of shifting voters graphically reflect the electorate in its great,
> and perhaps principal, role as an appraiser of past events, past performance, and
> past actions. It judges retrospectively; it commands prospectively only insofar as it
> expresses either approval or disapproval of that which has happened before.
> (1966: 61-62)

"Responsible" behaviour on the part of the electorate means
throwing the rascals out when they have done a bad job and giving
them a vote of confidence when they have done well. But if this
system is to work properly, the opposition must always be a usable
opposition, that is, acceptable to a majority of the electorate. To
Key, the parties are real alternatives if voters can switch from one
party to the other according to their assessment of performance. If
parties or candidates are too far apart ideologically then the coalition
system cannot work.

The most cogent alternative to Key's model is that presented by E.
E. Schattschneider in *The Semi-Sovereign People* (1960). In striking
contrast to Key's confidence, Schattschneider's essay is bitterly
pessimistic about the prospects for democracy in a system where the
major parties exclude a whole range of issues and fail to represent the
interests of a vast segment of the population. To Schattschneider, the
systematic avoidance of clear-cut policy alternatives was an effective
cause of mass disenfranchisement.

> The root of the problem of nonvoting is to be found in the way in which the alterna-
> tives in American politics are defined, the way in which issues get referred to the
> public, the scale of competition and organization, and above all by what issues are
> developed. (110)

Schattschneider wanted a system of ideological politics, so that
elections would serve, on the British model, as a choice between
programmes and policy mandates: "The [American] political system
has never assigned to the elective process a role as overwhelmingly
important as that played by the British elections. The US political
system is not well designed to bring great issues to a head in a national

election" (110). Thus Schattschneider anticipated the finding reported by Nie and by Converse that political involvement depends on the salience of politics, and that salience, in turn, is related to the perception of group antagonism and group interest. Without ideological coherence, "group antagonism" is minimized and salience and therefore participation are likely to be quite low. In Schattschneider's estimation, the American political system remains "insensitive to the interests of the largest minority in the world," the millions of non-voters who feel no stake in the choice being offered to them (1969: 108-109).

ISSUES AND CHOICE: A TYPOLOGY

The discussion thus far has dwelt upon the position/valence issue distinction and the style of electoral competition associated with each. Two separate causal problems may be raised:

(1) What determines whether the issues which dominate the political agenda tend to be positional or valence in character? Are there cultural, institutional, or developmental factors associated with the prevalence of one issue type rather than the other?

(2) What determines whether political parties will be attracted to an ideological or a coalition strategy, that is, whether parties will tend to exploit or avoid divisiveness in their appeals to the voters? Are there factors that promote either ideological or coalition politics independent of the nature of the political issues themselves?

While a thorough investigation of these questions is beyond the scope of this essay, some comments may be offered suggesting that the nature and quality of party choice is to a large extent independent of the nature and quality of political issues.

At least one body of opinion, the so-called "decline of ideology" school, has argued that modern political issues are primarily non-divisive valence issues. According to this view, governments in the modern welfare state are held accountable by their electorates in terms of universalistic and technocratic standards of performance: efficiency, control, and impartial mediation among competing interests. Ideological conflict involving alternative moral visions of the social order is associated with an earlier stage of modernization in which the state was more a symbolic authority than an active force responsible for the management of social and economic well-being.

In his classic work on political parties, Duverger traced the development of mass ideological parties from earlier systems of clientelistic factions (1959: 63-71). Lipset and Rokkan elaborated a sequence of four great polarizing issues in the national and industrial revolutions experienced by Western democracies (1967: 47). These studies argue that ideological polarization, primarily along lines of class, region, and religion, is inherent in the process of transition from traditional to industrial society. The accompanying transition from clientelistic to mass parties corresponds to a shift in the nature of voting behaviour, from the expression of particularistic ties to the articulation of moral values and ideological positions.

The third, or post-ideological, stage of politics is characterized by the predominance of valence issues, by a coalitional style of politics, and by a strong performance orientation by voters. Kirchheimer, for instance, regarded "catch-all" politics as highly pragmatic and action-oriented, marked by a transformation of the political party from "an organization combining the defense of social position, the quality of spiritual shelter, and the vision of things to come" to "a vehicle for short-range and interstitial political choice" (1966: 195). The shift in voting behaviour from ideological expression to the critical evaluation of performance, is often labeled the "decline of ideology." However, it should be noted that recent events in the United States and Western Europe suggest that new sources of ideological polarization may be emerging in post-industrial political systems. (See Inglehart, 1977.)

The developmental sequence noted above postulates a shift from clientelistic parties for which issues are largely irrelevant, through mass parties which are highly ideological in style, to modern coalition parties that compete in valence-issue terms. Independent of this developmental sequence, however, one can identify several institutional conditions that effect the nature of party competition. Three political factors appear to increase the likelihood that parties will adopt a coalition rather than an ideological strategy:

(1) A system of single-member districts penalizes minority parties and encourages coalition-formation. In Sartori's apt formulation, proportional representation is a "weak" system which "does nothing to prevent the fragmentation of a party system," whereas a plurality electoral system introduces forces which impede party fragmentation (Sartori, 1966: 173).

(2) A unitary executive directly responsible to the electorate forces parties to present themselves as potential national governments seeking majority support. Such an executive is the defining feature of

a presidential system, but the same function may be served in parliamentary systems that have a strong tradition of party government, such as Great Britain.

(3) A coalitional style of politics is impracticable where the legitimacy of the constitutional order divides the major parties. The existence of extremist and anti-democratic parties makes it difficult for voters to switch from government to opposition in response to performance, since a change of government may also mean a change in the entire system. A similar immobilization occurs when one party identifies itself as the party of the system and forces opposition parties to oppose it in those terms, i.e., as anti-system parties. These tendencies were present for decades in post-war France and Italy.

Thus party strategies are not simply a function of prevailing issues. Parties follow a logic of their own, partly determined by the rules of the game, which may lead them to activate latent cleavages, create new issues, or, not uncommonly, ignore entirely certain issues highly salient to the electorate. A typology may be proposed distinguishing issues first, in terms of divisiveness (position and valence) and second in terms of the congruence between issue alternatives and party choice. The latter dimension, labeled quality of choice in Figure 1, raises the question whether the party choice on an issue is clear or unclear, that is, whether the electorate perceives a difference between the parties on a particular valence or position issue. Perceived party differences are capable of empirical measurement directly (the voters' ability to discriminate party positions) and indirectly (voter shifts correlated with issue positions, as in Table 1 above). (See Schneider, 1974, for a discussion of approaches to measurement.)

The four issue types are shown in Figure 1-A. *Partisan issues* are divisive issues on which the parties hold clearly identifiable positions, defining and sustaining partisan allegiances. Partisan issues include those issues that gave rise to the party alignment and therefore constitute the historical basis of partisanship, as well as new issues on which the parties have taken clear positions. An example of the latter would be the civil rights issue in the United States. Pomper's evidence shows increasing clarification of party positions on the race issue after 1960 (1975: 166-184): by the 1970s, differences on the issue of civil rights were rather clearly incorporated in the major-party choice. *Election issues* — valence issues with a clear partisan direction — account for most normal electoral change. These are the issues that V. O. Key is concerned with in *The Responsible Electorate*: changing evaluations of performance which produce

FIGURE 1
The Quality of Party Competition

A. Issue Typology

| | | Issue is . . . | |
		Divisive	Non-divisive
Party Choice is . . .	Clear	Partisan Issue	Election Issue
	Unclear	Critical Issue	Abstention Issue

B. Process Typology

| | | Issue is . . . | |
		Divisive	Non-divisive
Party Choice is . . .	Clear	Alignment	Swing
	Unclear	Realignment	Dealignment

C. Examples of Dominant Trends in Recent Years

| | | Issues have been . . . | |
		Divisive	Non-divisive
Party Choices have been . . .	Clear	France	West Germany
	Unclear	United States	Great Britain

shifts between government and opposition parties. Partisan issues and election issues provide respectively for the representation of political interests (the ideological function) and for the evaluation of government performance (the plebiscitary function).

Dysfunctions occur when issues do not find adequate expression in the available party choice. *Critical issues* are divisive issues that show no clear partisan direction, that is, polarizations in the electorate not adequately incorporated in the conventional system of party alternatives. The Vietnam issue and the race issue at the time of the 1968 US Presidential election are examples of such critical issues. Two groups of voters with specific, deeply felt issue positions — Vietnam doves (the antiwar movement) and the law-and-order backlash (the Wallace movement) — perceived that neither major party offered an acceptable choice on the issue of overriding salience to them. The emergence of critical issues is associated with periods of party realignment around new symbols of conflict. For example, Irish home rule was a critical issue in late nineteenth-century Britain. The incorporation of a critical issue into the normal terms of party conflict moves that issue into the partisan category.

Abstention issues describe valence sentiments that have no clear partisan direction. Such issues typically give rise to a generalized discontent that produces no clear transfer of votes from government to opposition, either because the opposition is unacceptable as an alternative (too extreme, too great an ideological distance) or because voters have little confidence that the opposition can handle the problem any better. Such a sense of alienation, which is not accompanied by a specific "demand," usually results in high abstention rates, as large number of voters decide that it makes no difference which way they vote. Thus alienation is typically signified by non-voting, while critical issues usually create protest activity. The difference between "protest" and "alienation" is a difference in the specificity of concern. Protesters have a position — end abortion, stop the war, get Britain out of the Common Market — while alienated voters feel generally dissatisfied about the way things are going but see no rational political response. Both protest and alienation represent failures of the party system in the sense that the parties for one reason or another fail to structure an adequate choice. This interpretation is consistent with the argument made by Burnham elsewhere in this volume that the "disappearance" of American voters in this century is due to the failure of the political system to provide a meaningful choice. As he writes,

> The structure of political choices offered the electorate in the United States, and the major decisions made by political elites, have together produced more and more baffled ineffective citizens who believe that chance rules their world. (see p. 66)

Figure 1-B extends the typology of issues for four categories of electoral change:

(1) *Alignment* is the process by which partisanship emerges through the association of parties with position issues. Lipset and Rokkan, for example, develop a general model of party alignment in Western Europe based on the sequence and intensity of position issue conflicts (1967: 37).

(2) *Swing* is the normal shift of public support from government to opposition in response to the changing evaluation of performance. Butler and Stokes, for example, analyze the phenomenon of uniform national swing in Britain (1976: 99-108).

(3) *Realignment* is caused by the emergence of new sources of polarization that are not fully incorporated in the traditional terms of partisanship. The new dimension of conflict acts as a source of pressure on the party system. This pressure may take the form of factional cleavages within the traditional parties or protest movements outside the party structure. In either case, there will be pressure on the traditional parties to realign their support around the new bases of conflict so long as the new issue polarities persist. The realignment process in the United States is described by Sundquist (1973: 26-38).

(4) *Dealignment* is signified by defection from traditional partisanship in the direction of no-party preference, or anti-party preference, as an expression of no confidence in the conventional alternatives. A rise in political independence may be a symptom of either dealignment or realignment, or both, depending on the issue motivations associated with such a shift. Dealignment in Britain in the early 1970s took the form of an upsurge of voting for Liberals and nationalist candidates (Crewe et al., 1977).

Figure 1-C attempts to classify political trends in four Western democracies. The United States experienced the emergence of a new ideological dimension of conflict stimulated by issue polarizations over race, foreign policy, and cultural radicalism between 1964 and 1974. This ideological dimension cut across the traditional partisan alignment and put pressure on the parties to realign along a "conservative-liberal" axis. (Pomper, 1975; Burnham, 1970; Schneider, 1978; Ladd, 1978; Nie, Verba and Petrocik, 1976; Converse, 1975). Britain in 1974 experienced a sharp and rather sudden decline in the class polarization that has dominated the party system since 1945. The British electorate showed signs of becoming increasingly volatile during the late 1960s and early 1970s. The long-term trend of declining turnout reversed in 1974 and turned into a surge of anti-partisan protest (Crewe et al., 1977; Butler and Stokes, 1976). The West German case shows a decline in the intensity of partisan opposition and a convergence of the social and ideological bases of party politics. Evidence from Germany indicates a growing sense of "normal" opposition between the two major parties and an acceptance of both as legitimate competitors for power (Edinger,

1970; Kaltefleiter, 1970; Conradt, 1972; Conradt and Lambert, 1974). Finally, France, like the United States, experienced a period of protest and ideological polarization in the 1960s. However, the impact of the French crisis, unlike that in the United States, has been to re-enforce the traditional left-right cleavage and intensify the "bipolarization" of political attitudes. While the presidential system of the Fifth Republic has stimulated coalition-building, institutional constraints continue to inhibit the formation of a two-party system (Charlot, 1971; Wright, 1975; Charlot, 1973; Campbell, 1976; Inglehart and Hochstein, 1972; Cameron, 1977; McHale and Shaber, 1976).

The utility of this scheme is that it promotes the functional comparison of party systems. Any argument for the "convergence" of post-industrial politics must first identify the common causal mechanisms operating in those systems — for instance, a universal trend toward valence issues or institutional changes that promote coalition behaviour. Most of the evidence indicates that the similarities among post-industrial party systems may be more apparent than real. The effort here has been to define the dimensions of comparison in order to understand the reasons behind the specificity of national patterns.

NOTES

1. The data utilized in this article were made available in part by the Inter-University Consortium for Political and Social Research. Original investigators are noted in the bibliographical listing. Neither the original sources or collectors of the data nor the Consortium bear any responsibility for the analyses or interpretations presented here.

2. There is evidence that the Progressive movement in its later, more advanced stages did develop a working-class base, mostly in response to the social legislation passed by the Progressives *after* they had been elected to office. Labour elements in California and poorer Scandinavian farmers in Wisconsin continued to support Progressive candidates and third-party movements well into the 1920s. (See Wyman, 1974: 503; and Rogin and Shover, 1970: 62-85.) Thus, at most, Progressivism gave rise to a nascent class alignment that was not fully realized until the New Deal, when the major parties redefined the basis of partisanship in class terms and the economically radical Progressive elements moved into the Democratic Party.

REFERENCES

BECK, P. A. (1977) "Partisan dealignment in the postwar South." *American Political Science Review,* 71 (June): 477-496.

BURNHAM, W. .D. (1970) *Critical Elections and the Mainsprings of American Politics.* New York: Norton.

BUTLER, D. and D. KAVANAGH (1974) *The British General Election of February 1974.* New York: St. Martin's.

BUTLER, D. and D. STOKES (1976) *Political Change in Britain,* second college edition. New York: St. Martin's.

CAMERON, D. R. (1977) "The dynamics of presidential coalition formation in France: from Gaullism to Giscardism," *Comparative Politics,* 9 (April): 253-279.

CAMPBELL, A. and P. E. CONVERSE, W. E. MILLER, and D. E. STOKES (1964) *The American Voter: An Abridgment.* New York: John Wiley.

CAMPBELL, B. (1976) "On the prospects of polarization in the French electorate," *Comparative Politics,* 8 (January): 272-290.

CHARLOT, J. (1971) *The Gaullist Phenomenon.* London: George Allen and Unwin.

CONRADT, D. P. (1972) *The West German Party System: An Ecological Analysis of Social Structure and Voting Behavior, 1961-1969* (Sage Professional Paper No. 01-028). Beverly Hills, California: Sage Publications.

CONRADT, D. R. and D. LAMBERT (1974) "Party system, social structure, and competitive politics in West Germany: an ecological analysis of the 1972 federal election," *Comparative Politics,* 7 (October): 61-86.

CONVERSE, P. E. (1964) "The nature of belief systems in mass publics," in D. E. Apter (ed.) *Ideology and Discontent.* New York: Free Press.

— — (1975) "Public opinion and voting behavior", chapter 2 in F.I. Greenstein and N. W. Polsby (eds.) *Handbook of Political Science:* Volume 4, *Nongovernmental Politics.* Reading, Massachusetts: Addison-Wesley.

CONVERSE, P. E. and G. DUPEUX (1966) "Politicization of the electorate in France and the United States," chapter 14 in A. Campbell, P. E. Converse, W. E. Miller, and D. E. Stokes, *Elections and the Political Order.* New York: John Wiley.

CREWE, I. (1976) "Party identification theory and political changes in Britain," chapter 3 in I. Budge, I. Crewe, and D. Farlie (eds.) *Party Identification and Beyond.* New York: John Wiley.

CREWE, I., B. SARLVIK, and J. ALT (1974) "The How and Why of the February Voting." *New Society,* No. 623 (September 12).

— — (1977) "Partisan dealignment in Britain, 1964-1974," *British Journal of Political Science,* 7 (April): 129-190.

DAHL, R. (1967) *Pluralist Democracy in the United States.* New York: Rand McNally.

DOWNS, A. (1957) *An Economic Theory of Democracy.* New York: Harper and Row.

DUVERGER, M. (1959) *Political Parties,* second English edition, revised. New York: John Wiley.

EDINGER, L. (1970) "Political change in Germany: the Federal Republic after the 1969 election." *Comparative Politics,* 2 (July): 549-578.

GALLUP OPINION INDEX (1976) Report No. 135 (October).

HOFSTADTER, R. (1955) *The Age of Reform.* New York: Vintage Books.

INGLEHART, R. and A. HOCHSTEIN (1972) "Alignment and dealignment of the electorate in France and the United States." *Comparative Political Studies,* 5 (October): 343-372.

INTER-UNIVERSITY CONSORTIUM FOR POLITICAL AND SOCIAL RE-SEARCH (1968) *American National Election Study* (Survey Research Center, University of Michigan). Ann Arbor, Michigan: ICPSR.

— — (1974) *American National Election Study* (Center for Political Studies, University of Michigan). Ann Arbor, Michigan: ICPSR.

KALTEFLEITER, W. (1970) "The impact of the election of 1969 and the formation of the new government on the German party system," *Comparative Politics,* 2 (July): 593-604.

KEY, V. O., Jr. (1966) *The Responsible Electorate.* New York: Vintage Books.

— — (1949) *Southern Politics.* New York: Vintage Books.

KIRCHHEIMER, O. (1966) "The transformation of the Western European party systems," chapter 6 in J. La Palombara and M. Weiner (eds.) *Political Parties and Political Development.* Princeton, New Jersey: Princeton University Press.

LADD, E. C., Jr., with C. D. HADLEY (1978) *Transformation of the American Party System,* Second edition. New York: Norton.

LIPSET, S. M. and S. ROKKAN (1967) "Cleavage structures, party systems, and voter alignments: an introduction," pp. 1-64 in S. M. Lipset and S. Rokkan (eds.) *Party Systems and Voter Alignments.* New York: Free Press.

McHALE, V. E. and S. SHABER (1976) "From aggressive to defensive Gaullism: the electoral dynamics of a 'catch-all' party." *Comparative Politics,* 8 (January): 291-306.

NBC NEWS (1976) *Street Poll of Voters in the November 2, 1976, Presidential Election.* New York: NBC News Election Unit.

NIE, N. H. with K. ANDERSEN (1974) "Mass belief systems revisited: political change and attitude structure," *Journal of Politics,* 36 (September): 541-591.

NIE, N. H., S. VERBA, and J. R. PETROCIK (1976) *The Changing American Voter.* Cambridge, Massachusetts: Harvard University Press.

PAGE, B. I. and R. A. BRODY (1972) "Policy voting and the electoral process: the Vietnam War issue," *American Political Science Review,* 66 (September): 979-995.

POMPER, G. M. (1975) *Voters' Choice.* New York: Dodd, Mead.

ROGIN, M. P. and J. L. SHOVER (1970) *Political Change in California.* Westport, Connecticut: Greenwood.

ROSE, R. (1974) "Comparability in electoral studies," chapter 1 in R. Rose (ed.) *Electoral Behavior: A Comparative Handbook.* New York: Free Press.

— — (1974a) *Politics in England,* second edition. Boston: Little, Brown.

SARTORI, G. (1966) "European political parties: the case of polarized pluralism," chapter 5 in J. LaPalombara and M. Weiner, (ed.) *Political Parties and Political Development.* Princeton, NJ: Princeton University Press.

SCHATTSCHNEIDER, E. E. (1960) *The Semi-Sovereign People.* New York: Holt, Rinehart, and Winston.

SCHNEIDER, W. (1974) "Issues, voting, and cleavages: a methodology and some tests," *American Behavioral Scientist,* 18 (September): 111-146.

— — (1978) "Democrats and Republicans, liberals and conservatives," chapter 8 in S. M. Lipset (ed.) *Emerging Coalitions in American Politics.* San Francisco: Institute for Contemporary Studies.

STOKES, D. E. (1966) "Spatial models of party competition," chapter 9 in A.

Campbell, P. E. Converse, W. E. Miller, and D. E. Stokes, *Elections and the Political Order*. New York: John Wiley.

SUNDQUIST, J. L. (1973) *Dynamics of the Party System*. Washington, DC: The Brookings Institution.

THELEN, D. P. (1972) "Progressives and the issues: social tensions and the origins of Progressivism," pp. 161-183 in F. O. Gatell, P. Goodman, and A. Weinstein (eds.) *The Growth of American Politics:* Volume II, *Since the Civil War*. New York: Oxford University Press.

WRIGHT, V. (1975) "Presidentialism and the parties in the French Fifth Republic," *Government and Opposition,* 10 (Winter): 24-45.

WYMAN, R. E. (1974) "The growth of U.S. political culture," *American Political Science Review,* 68 (June): 488-504.

4
The New Spanish Party System

Juan J. Linz
Yale University
in collaboration with DATA

I. HISTORICAL ANTECEDENTS

Modern Spanish political history is characterized by discontinuity. The nineteenth century was a period of civil wars, *pronunciamientos* and even a short-lived Republican experiment in the then dominantly monarchical Europe. The slow transition from estate representation to parliaments of notables and constitutional monarchies, the gradual transformation of political clubs into parties of notables, could take place only imperfectly. The most successful liberal experiment, the Restoration monarchy established in 1875, lasted until the dictatorship of Primo de Rivera (1923), that forestalled the internal transformation of the great parties of the early phase of the Restoration and the emergence and consolidation of new political forces. It in turn was displaced in 1931 by a republic with new parties whose leaders often had no parliamentary experience, and by a rapid mobilization of the electorate and social forces in a period of crisis.[1] While it is possible to establish links between the parties over this period, there were obvious discontinuities in organization and leadership.

The 40 years between the last free election (1936)[2] and the death of Franco represent an even greater discontinuity, in contrast to Germany where after some 12 years of Nazi rule a number of democratic politicians who had played already an important role in the Weimar Republic could contribute to the re-establishment of democracy, and in Italy where after 19 years of fully consolidated fascist rule a number of parliamentarians of the pre-fascist era would sit in the Constituente and participate actively in the building of democracy.[3]

It is symbolic that while the establishment of the Federal Republic would be presided over by a politician like Adenauer who started his career under the Kaiser's Empire, in Spain that process would be led by a young man (born in 1932) who had grown up in the Franco period, Adolfo Suárez. Even the youngest of the political leaders of the Republic, José María Gil Robles, who for many years had been active in the opposition to Franco, did not succeed in gaining a seat in parliament. Among the outstanding leaders of the new democracy only Santiago Carrillo of the Partido Comunista de España (PCE), Ajuriaguerra of the Partido Nacionalista Vasco (PNV), and Tarradellas, President of the Generalitat of Catalonia, had played an important role before 1936, only a few of the deputies were militants of their parties before 1936. The already advanced age of the top leadership of the Partido Socialista Obrero Español (PSOE) before the Civil War and the long years of Franco rule did not allow any of them to return to play an important role. Even in the Socialist Party, which can claim the longest historical continuity, there has been a renewal of leadership and a loss of historical memory. The PCE, a small fringe party during the Republic by comparison with the Italian and the German communists, grew during the Civil War and despite purges in exile has a continuity with the past symbolized by its president, Dolores Ibárruri, and its leader, Santiago Carrillo, head of the socialist youth before its unification with that of the PCE. The continuity in name and in membership is reflected particularly for the PSOE in continuities in political behaviour as the correlations between their vote in 1936 and 1977 prove. Even so, there have been fundamental changes in their areas of strength. The PSOE, federated with the Partit Socialista de Catalunya, has made gigantic gains in that region where before the Civil War, much of the working class supported the anti-parliamentary Confederación Nacional del Trabajo (CNT), and those ready to vote for the left gave their support to the Catalanist Esquerra.

The most striking discontinuity has been the disappearance in 1977 of left bourgeois republicanism. The dominant parties in the Cortes between 1931 and 1936 on the centre left have found no direct heirs. In contrast to the changeover from the Third to the Fourth Republic in France, the whole bourgeois left side of the spectrum of Spanish

TABLE 1
Correlation Between the Vote in June 1977 and in February 1936 at the Provincial Level

Historical voting: 1936 Vote for:	1977 vote for:			
	PCE	PSOE	UCD	AP
Left	0.68	0.54	− 0.36	− 0.45
Centre	− 0.17	− 0.32	0.11	− 0.00
Right	− 0.40	− 0.18	0.20	0.38
PSOE	0.22	0.60	0.04	− 0.07
CEDA	− 0.32	− 0.08	0.46	0.35

Source: Calculations by DATA.

politics has been unable to articulate an appeal to the electorate,[4] and been largely replaced by a PSOE, whose electoral strength has grown from some 16 percent to 29 percent, particularly thanks to replacing the Catalan left. Even the conservative expression of bourgeois liberalism, always relatively weak (if we ignore the rightist turn of the Radical Party of Lerroux that had already disintegrated in the 1936 election) is also absent, quite in contrast to the continuities between the Deutsche Demokratische Partei (DDP), the Deutsche Volkspartei (DVP), and the post-war Freie Demokratische Partei (FDP) in Germany.

The weakness and late birth of a true Christian democratic or Christian social party and its absorption in the 1930s by a conservative clerical party, Confederación Española de Derechas Autónomas (CEDA), many of whose leaders died in the Civil War or joined the Franco side, and the subsequent defeat of the revived Christian democrats in the 1977 election, has produced another great discontinuity which stands in sharp contrast to the continuity between the German Zentrum and the CDU-CSU, or the Italian Populari and the Christian Democrats (DC).[5] Many changes in the Church and its role in Spanish politics, as well as in the Catholic Church generally, account for this discontinuity. However, as the electoral correlations show, there is a continuity between the support for the CEDA in 1936 and for the Unión de Centro Democrático (UCD) in 1977, reflecting continuities in the social structure and the political culture, in spite of discontinuities in leadership and organization. (See Table 1.)

The ideological heritage of the extreme right, Renovación Española, transmitted by the intellectual group of Acción Española, that contributed so much to the Franco regime, has in part been carried over into Alianza Popular (AP) by some of its leaders. But the explicit links with that past are not prominent. Electorally, correlations between the vote for candidates to the right of the CEDA in 1936 and for AP candidates in 1977 reflect this continuity. The case of the Carlists is perhaps one of the most paradoxical we can encounter, with considerable continuity reflected in correlations, for example in Navarra between the strongholds of this right wing pro-Franco movement in 1936 and the support for the left-oriented *auto-gestionnaire* (self-management) party led by the royal pretender today.[6]

At the regional level we find a clear-cut case of continuity in name, largely in leadership, and even more in areas of maximum electoral support in the case of the Basque nationalist PNV, that on the other hand has continued the leftward drift initiated under the Republic. There is, however, a great deal of discontinuity in the Basque country due to the appearance of an important left nationalist movement ready to compete with the PNV, the Euskadiko-Ezkerra (EE), which had no parallel during the Republic, as well as other still illegal Basque ultra-nationalist parties that in 1979 joined the coalition Herri Batasuna (HB). Even when the ecological analysis might show interesting continuities between the electorate of the Catalanist parties during the Republic and the coalition led by Jordi Pujol, there is no clear continuity between his party and those appealing to Catalans in the thirties. The proud conservative bourgeois Catalanist party, Lliga, led by Cambó, in 1977 had been reduced to a miniscule survival, and the same is true for those appealing to the traditions of the Esquerra led by Companys. Only the small Christian democratic group in Catalonia could link with a past in which one of its leaders was executed by Franco and another on the Republican side, but by 1979 its most distinguished leader was a deputy of UCD.

The picture therefore is one of discontinuity with the democratic past, except for the PSOE and to a lesser extent the PCE, and to an outstanding degree, for the PNV. But even in that party the old leaders have been fading away. Too many years have passed between 1936 and 1976. On the other hand, we find impressive continuities in the areas of strength of parties and between certain of the newly created and those of the past.

The relative discontinuity, however, has important advantages. The parties today are less burdened by the ghosts of the past, the debates and the failures that preceded a civil war. But there are also disadvantages — the lack of historical memory of past mistakes, and above all, the lack of experience in parliamentary and democratic politics of the new leadership.

The discontinuity between the parties does not mean, however, that the memory of the past and particularly the Civil War is not present and linked with today's political alignments. In 1979, 22 percent of the respondents in a national sample could not or did not want to say with which side their family had sympathized in that War, and another 26 percent say that it was with neither of the two contenders. The remainder, except for a small proportion that reported their family divided, split between sympathizers of the Popular Front, 21 percent, and of the nationalists, 27 percent. The supporters of the different parties did not divide that evenly. Among those of the PCE-PSUC (Partit Socialista Unificat de Catalunya) 51 percent recorded their family on the Popular Front side and only 9 percent on the Franco side, while among the socialists the division was respectively 28 percent and 19 percent. Across the dividing line between left and right, the alignment changes: 44 percent of the UCD supporters remember their family siding with the nationalists and only 10 percent with the Popular Front, and among those voting for the Coalición Democrática (CD), the party led by Fraga, the proportions were 62 and 8 percent respectively. It is not surprising that the two parties in the centre of the spectrum should be less homogeneous in the political background in their families and more dependent on less committed families, as a number of "none of the two sides" and of those who did not know where their family stood indicates. The Civil War has not been a lively issue in the campaigning and in the politics of the post-Franco era, but the tacit agreement not to fight about the past, except on the part of the extreme right, cannot hide the fact that those memories exist and that the party choice and even more party activism is associated with those family memories.

The more recent past of the Franco regime is obviously seen very differently by the supporters of different parties (see Table 3). Communist voters express almost unanimous disapproval of all his actions, while supporters of the PSOE are already much less intense in their disapproval and a minority among them is far from totally critical. The UCD supporters are divided in their opinions and more often than those of any other party hold an intermediate position. In this the voters are not different from the leadership in which we find men, like Prime Minister Suárez, who initiated their political career

TABLE 2
Vote in the 1979 Legislative Election and Political Sympathies of the Family in the 1937 Civil War, According to the Respondent

	Extreme left %	PCE/ PSUC %	PSC- PSOE %	UCD %	CD %	Extreme right %	Regional parties %	Other parties %	Did not vote %	d.k. n.a. %	Total %
Nationalist;	15	9	19	44	62	70	16	33	22	15	27
Popular Front	50	51	28	10	8	11	38	17	18	12	21
Both	4	6	4	5	4		8		5	2	4
None	17	17	26	23	12	8	23	33	33	28	26
No answer	13	18	22	18	14	8	14	17	23	44	22
	(46)	(394)	(1300)	(1486)	(162)	(37)	(369)	(12)	(1089)	(606)	(5499)

Source: The data of this and subsequent tables are based on national sample surveys designed and executed by DATA in July 1978 and July 1979.

TABLE 3
Opinion of the Voters of Different Parties in 1979 about Franco

	Extreme left %	PCE/ PSUC %	PSOE %	UCD %	CD %	Extreme right %	Regional parties %	Did not vote %	d.k. n.a. %	Total %
Approve totally his actions	—	0	3	18	22	32	2	5	10	9
Acted fairly well	4	5	11	36	48	38	7	19	24	21
Acted so-so without too many errors	4	4	14	16	11	5	8	14	15	13
Many errors that could have been avoided	11	24	30	17	14	14	24	20	16	21
Disapprove totally his actions	80	63	34	5	2	5	51	28	10	25
d.k.	—	2	6	4	1	—	6	8	12	6
n.a.	—	1	3	4	2	5	3	5	14	5
	(46)	(394)	(1300)	(1486)	(162)	(37)	(369)	(1089)	(606)	(5499)

in the Franco regime and were active in the opposition, like Christian Democrats or liberals. Among the voters of CD there is a clear majority having a favourable opinion, but not a very intensely favourable. The overall response of the Spanish electorate to the Franco period tends toward the negative but without too much intensity in their feeling, and only a small minority fully identifies with him. While there is an association between party preference and the opinions about that period of Spanish history, the party alignments do not correlate that clearly with pro- and anti-Franco regime positions.

The relation between the present party system and the 40 years of Francoism is complex. In 1977 only the extreme right represented electorally by the Alianza del 18 de Julio, that obtained 0.6 percent of the vote, claimed allegiance to the past and rejected the new democracy. In that Alliance, and its successor, Union Nacional, the aggressive radical neo-fascist Fuerza Nueva led by Blas Piñar closely linked with the extreme right violent groups, is the driving force. Electorally, the fascist heritage was claimed also by three groups in 1977; one of them turning to the radical social anti-capitalist, anti-monarchical and anti-democratic heritage of fascism, the Falange Auténtica, wants to be considered a party of the left; another sector that grew out of the youth organization in the Franco period, the Círculos José Antonio, took a more moderate position; and the Falange Espanola de las JONS (Juntas de Ofensiva Nacional Sindicalista), led by the former minister of party affairs and companion of the founder of the old falange, is a survival linked to Fuerza Nueva.

None of them was able to make a significant electoral showing anywhere. Fascism, *strictu sensu,* was weak in the Republic and neo-fascism today manifests itself in violent groupuscules that cannot be compared in strength and importance even to the Movimento Sociale Italiano (MSI).

AP (Alianza Popular) finds itself in a strange relation to the recent past.[7] It wants to see it respected as a period of considerable achievements in the economic and social field, but it does not propose a return to its political institutions and wants to be a "civilized right" within the new democratic framework that it wants to build, for example by the participation of its leader, Fraga, in the constitution-drafting committee. Its leaders are men who have played a prominent role in the Franco cabinets, but several of them conceive themselves more as technocrats than as ideologists. Many of them proceed from the Catholic groups that replaced the Falangists in the elite of the regime and the most distinguished among them, Fraga, can claim to have favoured already an early liberalization of the regime. The party was formed formally by an alliance and later fusion of political associations created in the last period of Franco's rule with the purpose of channeling the very limited pluralism of a decaying regime in an effort to institutionalize a process of liberalization and democratization doomed to failure from the start.[8] Those associations which enjoyed some official and financial support by the state provided the platform for different leaders and reflected some of the ideological and social heterogeneity within the Franco system.

Not only AP shows a continuity with the elite of the Franco regime. In the parliamentary benches of the UCD (Unión de Centro Democrático) we also find men who sat in the Cortes in various capacities, including the semi-opposition of the family representatives directly elected since 1968 before the death of Franco. None of them occupied positions equally prominent as those of AP deputies in that period, with one exception. A number of them started their political life in the youth organization, others in the Sindicatos and the para-state bureaucracies, while others were close to the Opus Dei. Most of them are of the younger generation grown up under the regime rather than participants in its more totalitarian phases. In contrast to the AP leadership, they do not defend the past, but in fact some try to discover a semi- or pseudo- opposition role in their past. That component of the UCD has been mixed with men of a clear trajectory of opposition to the Franco regime, particularly on the part of some of the Christian democrats that in 1976-77 refused to follow the leadership of Ruiz Giménez and Gil Robles and organized the Partido Demócrata Cristiano (PDC) as well as some liberals in the European sense of the term and some self-identified as social democrats. We should not forget that the UCD was initially an electoral coalition of 12 parties and a large number of independents that only through a painful process and under the prodding of President Suárez, fused into a single party. Undoubtedly, the different political biography of the UCD leadership accounts for some of the initial tensions within the party, particularly those who have a record of democratic opposition to the Franco regime and those who having served that regime decided to contribute to the transition to democracy from positions of power — foremost among them, Adolfo Suárez.

The split of the men that in one way or another have their lives linked with the Franco period into those who consider it still a valid experience for the future, those who want to see it and their role in it respected but accept democracy, those who without any love lost for the past have been in the forefront of the *reforma,* and those who early or late identified with a radical opposition to that past, is one of the complexities on the political scene. It would be difficult to understand the emotional undercurrents in the relationship between these leaders, the mutual rejections and suspicions, the difficulties for cooperation among them, the bitter accusations of treason and the insinuations about the past, without reference to that element of continuity.

The model of *reforma* rather than *ruptura,*[9] the passing of the Law for the reform by the Francoite Cortes, the referendum on that Law, the incorporation of AP into the constitutional consensus and its partial participation in the Moncloa pacts, and finally the syncretism of UCD incorporating men coming from the regime, from the old opposition and new men and women entering politics, has facilitated what Giuseppe Di Palma calls "backward legitimation."[10] But that same process makes what he calls "forward legitimation" more difficult. The Portuguese developments after the coup, particularly the imposition by the Movimento das Forças Armadas (MFA) of a break with the past, the revolutionary changes in the society, and the exclusion from the party system of those suspect of representing a continuity with the past, is in many respects the reverse pattern.

II. POLARIZED PLURALISM OR POTENTIAL BIPARTISM

To understand the new democratic system we have to turn our attention to the nature of the party system; that is, the number of parties and their interaction at the electoral, legislative and governmental level. The typology developed by Giovanni Sartori[11] can serve us as a starting point although we confront the difficulty of studying a party system just born in the 1977 election while his analysis very often refers to characteristics that can be observed only in the course of several elections and the dynamics of party government in the course of time.

Certainly we are not confronted with a predominant party system by any of the criteria Sartori suggests, since no party has been disproportionately stronger than others. The difference between the UCD, the party with the largest vote and the second largest, the PSOE, has only been 5.47 percent in 1977 and 4.56 in 1979, that is less than the 10 percent he suggests. The more important criterion, that one party obtains an absolute majority of seats over a certain period of time (he suggests three successive elections) or the less restrictive criterion that a party can govern over such a period as the largest party even without an absolute majority, cannot be applied since there are only two elections on record. It does not seem likely that the UCD with 34.8 percent of the vote in 1977 and 35.0 in 1979 could occupy in the political spectrum the position of the parties he describes as predominant in pluralist democracies like the Liberal Party in Japan, the Congress Party in India and the social democratic parties in Sweden and Norway over a long period of time whose representation in parliament gave them an absolute majority. Even with the unequal representation of parties in the first two legislatures, the UCD was short of an absolute majority. (See Table 4.)

If we consider the composition of the Cortes and even more the distribution of the vote, the conditions Sartori establishes for a two-party system are most unlikely to be fulfilled. The alternation in power of two parties governing alone without depending on the support of any third party has not occurred, nor is it likely in future. In addition, the modified proportional representation of the D'Hondt system does not favour the emergence of a two-party system that is generally linked with single member districts. Neither the UCD nor the PSOE are in the position to compete for an absolute majority of seats. Alternation or rotation in power without the support of third parties either with their vote or their abstention in the process of forming a government, is unlikely. There is little prospect that Spain would join the United Kingdom, the United States, New Zealand, Austria and Australia that function as a two-party system.

Spain is undoubtedly a multiparty system and the remaining question is whether it will be a polarized multiparty system or an example of what Sartori calls moderate multiparty systems. The Spanish case presents some difficulties in the analysis since, and we have to insist on it, there are only two elections on record and only one government depending on parliament for support in the new regime, and a number of the dimensions used in Sartori's analysis are based on a dynamic rather than a static picture of the party system.

If we consider the number of parties characterizing extreme multipartism, Sartori gives a figure between 5 and 6. Spain is thus on the borderline. If we consider only national parties, at the level of parliamentary representation the last election has reduced them to

TABLE 4
Party Alignments in the 1977 Lower House Election in Spain

	% of Vote	Seats
Extreme right		
Alianza Nacional 18 del Julio	0.36	
Fuerza Nueva	0.04	
FE de las JONS/Círculos José Antonio	0.21	
Total	0.61	
Right		
Alianza Popular	8.42	16
Other Right	0.27	
Total	8.69	
Centre right		
UCD	34.85	167
Equipo de la Democracia Cristiana	1.41	2
Reforma Social Española/ANEPA Centro Popular	0.45	
PNV	1.70	8
Democracia i Catalunya	3.73	11
Other Centre	0.67	
Total	42.81	
Centre left		
Alianza Socialista Democrática	0.75	
PSOE	29.38	118
Unidad Socialista	4.49	6
Left		
Partido Comunista de España and PSUC	9.28	20
Other Left	0.51	
Total	44.41	
Extreme left		
Frente Democrático de Izquierdas (PTE)	1.46	1
Agrupación Electoral de Trabajadores	0.44	
FUT	0.21	
Other Extreme Left	0.94	1
Total	3.05	
Others		
FE de las JONS (a)/Partido Carlista/Others	0.43	
Total	0.43	
Grand Total	100.00	350

four: PCE, PSOE, UCD and CD (formerly AP). It could be argued that the regional parties of the Basque country, Catalonia and Andalucía present segmental pluralism and therefore should not be taken into account to place Spain in the extreme multiparty category, since adding the PNV and the Pacte Democratic per Catalunya (now Convergencia i Unió) and the Partido Socialista de Andalucía (PSA) otherwise would increase the number to seven.

However, using Sartori's criteria of coalition use and power of intimidation, those parties should be considered part of the nationwide party system, particularly taking into account the present and likely future difficulty in aggregating a majority and a conception of democracy that makes the establishment of a pattern of stable minority governments unlikely.

The second criterion used by Sartori, the ideological distance between parties and more specifically the presence of anti-system parties, is not likely to produce consensus judgments among scholars. We should not forget that it is this dimension on which much of the debate between Sartori and his critics on the Italian case hinges. Some observers would be inclined to consider the PCE and AP as anti-system parties or at least one of them, but it could also be argued that the recent behaviour of a Eurocommunist PCE and the moderate stance taken at least in parliament of the so-called civilized right, AP, does not allow us to so characterize them. The ambiguity of AP led to a split vote of its parliamentary group (5 voted no, 8 yes, and 3 abstained) on the Constitution in 1978 and to a reorganization of the right in the 1979 election in which Fraga joined with other politicians disgruntled with UCD under the label Coalición Democrática (CD). This coalition was able to obtain only 6.12 percent of the vote. The new grouping adopted a more moderate stance than its predecessor, leading to a new crisis in AP in 1979. The role of the PNV and its relationship to the Spanish state could also be the object of a lengthy debate. Its ultimate hope for an independent Euskadi, its lack of approval of the 1978 Constitution and the call for active abstention in the constitutional referendum, its use in the negotiations on the statute of autonomy of the situation created by the extremists in the Basque country bordering on blackmail, could lead us to define it as semi-loyal or anti-system party. On the other hand, the final approval of the Autonomy Statute, and its support in a referendum, and its growing moderation would argue for a more positive view. Certainly the lack of interest in participating in governing Spain, the refusal of any public commitment to Spain as a nation, give it an ambiguous place in the party system. Let us underline once more, following Sartori, that the three parties to which we refer are not revolutionary parties; to be characterized as anti-system does not require a party to be revolutionary.

There would be less debate if we would use Sartori's criterion in its attenuated form, that is, referring to the ideological distance between parties. Certainly the distance on a left-right dimension between the PCE and the AP is still much larger than the one between the typical parties of the moderate pluralism systems of the Federal Republic of Germany, Belgium and the Scandinavian countries. There would be those who would argue that the internal changes in the PCE over the last years and particularly at its recent party congress, where it even dropped its Leninism, have narrowed those ideological distances. It seems however doubtful that in the image of the militants and even in most of the electorate those parties would not be far apart. When voters are asked about parties they would never vote for, there is some tendency toward polarization, but it is far from complete. (See Table 5.)

The presence of the PCE, AP and the PNV with its ambiguity toward the Spanish state, create a climate of the potential crisis of legitimacy of the democratic system, even against the best intentions of their leaders. Undoubtedly, the PCE has not engaged in a massive effort of delegitimation of the present political system. In fact, it is making a somewhat contrived effort to contribute to its legitimation by its acceptance of the monarchy, the national flag, its positive stance toward the armed forces, the disavowals of terrorism, and its positive responses to the reform process led by President Suárez, positions which often made it look more moderate than the PSOE, provoking the indignation of many socialists who disapproved of those in their view, cynical and opportunistic stances. They certainly distinguish the present Eurocommunist PCE from other communist parties and particularly the inter-war communist parties in Europe, including the PCE during the Second Republic in Spain. This is a deliberate policy to assure the legitimation of the party to avoid in the future the problems faced by other West European communist parties. The PCE wants to save itself the difficult and long process of relegitimation in which the PCI and to a lesser extent the PCF have engaged. This process of integration in the political system finds a parallel in the moderate stances of the party and its trade union affiliate in the social economic field in the present crisis, as reflected in the acceptance of the Moncloa pacts. There can, however, be little doubt that the PCE does not consider the present social economic

TABLE 5
Parties the Voters of Different Parties in the 1979 Legislative Elections "would never vote for"

Party they would never vote for	Extreme left %	PCE/PSUC %	PSOE %	UCD %	CD %	Extreme right %	Regionalist parties %	Did not vote %	d.k. n.a. %	Total %
					Party Vote in 1979					
ORT	39	26	34	43	50	49	38	42	21	37
PTE	33	23	30	40	51	54	38	42	19	35
PCE	37	—	25	60	75	86	44	46	23	40
PSOE	43	9	—	17	40	62	28	30	10	17
UCD	70	48	30	31	16	51	44	37	11	24
CD	74	52	47	44	—	30	44	46	18	39
Falangists	80	67	61	44	39	41	54	53	26	50
FN	89	74	72	51	44	19	64	60	28	58
	(46)	(394)	(1300)	(1486)	(162)	(37)	(369)	(1089)	(606)	(5499)

system as legitimate and that its position is one of opposition on principle rather than on issues.

There can be little doubt that for important sectors of the population and of the institutional set, particularly the so-called factic powers, and more concretely, the armed forces, the PCE is still an anti-system party and therefore an illegitimate claimant to participation in government. In fact, the strenuous efforts of the PCE to show its sense of responsibility are a reflection of that widespread perception of illegitimacy. The constant emphasis on democratic concentration government rather than on alternative government, that parallels the Italian emphasis on the *compromesso storico,* shows the awareness of the PCE of the difficulties on its way to access to government compared to other parties in Western Europe. Certainly the consequences of an entry of the PCE into the cabinet and particularly into some sensitive ministries, would at least at present provoke reactions difficult to envisage.

The situation of AP in the political system is in many respects comparable to the PCE. There is a wide gap between it and the old democratic opposition to the Franco system and even many of the new democrats of the UCD. Even though the AP leadership, particularly its forceful and distinguished leader, Manuel Fraga, try hard to show that AP is a responsible party, to reject any identification with the violent anti-system extreme right, and to contribute to the making of a consensual constitution, it is not easy to overcome its image as the heirs of Francoism and as a party potentially dangerous to democracy. Except if confronted with a solid and radicalized Popular Front, UCD would find it difficult to form a stable coalition with AP and some of its spokesmen have said so to the rage of AP leaders. The campaign against AP, and particularly against Fraga by all parties in 1977, undoubtedly has shaped a climate of opinion in which it becomes difficult for AP to enter a government without provoking a serious crisis and perhaps even alterations of public order by the left and regional nationalists. AP therefore faces the problem of legitimation as a system party that it might or might not overcome.

In 1979 the Coalición Democrática (CD), under the leadership of Fraga, Areilza (who had been linked to the opposition to Franco and been a founder of the Partido Popular — a later component of UCD) and Alfonso Osorio, and by subdued campaigning quite different to that of 1977, has moved to the centre and given parliamentary support to Suárez. This change in image might have contributed a loss of vote to the rightest Unión Nacional of Blas Piñar in the 1979 election and in October 1979 to an internal crisis in AP. The centripetal move has (Sartori would inevitably say) produced also a centrifugal reaction.

The occasional reciprocal support for the legitimate participation in the political system of the PCE and AP in parliamentary debates and in the famous presentation of Santiago Carrillo by Manuel Fraga in the Club Siglo XXI, reflect this problem common to both parties.

The participation of either the PCE or AP in any government could well create a crisis of legitimacy of the newly born democracy. In 1977 the two parties secured 17.7 percent of the vote, and 16.9 percent in 1979.

Leaving aside the question of ideological distances, the anti-system character of parties, and the delegitimating impact of their participation in the political system, there can be no question that their presence creates a situation of bilateral opposition to the central parties, the PSOE or the UCD. The UCD will always have to fight on two fronts, with AP on the right suspicious of leftist changes and not convinced anti-Francoists, and on the left with the PSOE, that can claim to be a moderate social democratic alternative attacking the UCD for the links of many of its leaders with a non-democratic past. The issues separating parties are not only pragmatic issues, questions of specific policies, but questions about the nature of the political system born out of *reforma* rather than *ruptura* with the past. It is the ambivalence of the UCD and its internal heterogeneity, as much as the denial of legitimacy to AP by the left, that makes for bilateral opposition.

The PSOE has to battle to retain a large social democratic electorate, including voters who might be centre-right in terms of their interests but could not vote for the UCD because of the links of many of its leaders with the past. The struggle of Felipe González against his leftist opponents at the May 1979 party congress and his victory at the extraordinary PSOE congress in September 1979 reflected the need to shift the course of the party toward less dogmatic Marxist positions to make it more attractive to voters in the centre in competition with the UCD.

But the PSOE has also to retain the loyalty of a Marxist, and to some extent radicalized, base of militants and the image of a socialist Marxist party capable of confronting a communist party that combines the image of a party to the left with capable leadership and organizational versatility. The relative advantage of CCOO

(Comisiones Obreras) over the socialist UGT (Unión General de Trabajadores) in the 1978 trade union elections and the apparent success of the CCOO among workers who must have voted for the PSOE in the political elections of June 1977, makes that bilateral opposition to the PSOE particularly threatening and places the party in a quite different position than the social democratic parties in moderate multiparty systems.

Because of bilateral oppositions, the Spanish party system satisfies one of the key criteria used by Sartori to characterize polarized multiparty systems. Independent of ideological or doctrinal self-definitions, there is a central political space confronted by bipolar oppositions occupied at present by the UCD and, in spite of its more radical manifestations, by the PSOE. Both parties are clearly perceived as the moderate alternatives in the centre, as the parties that can contribute to the stabilization of democracy and peaceful political co-existence among Spaniards, and in greater or lesser degree as able to handle the regional problems that plague the Spanish polity.

There are, however, some fundamental differences between the political centre position in Spain and in other Western European extreme multiparty systems. There is no dominant party in the centre with either an absolute majority of seats in parliament or close to such a majority and able to count with a number of smaller allied parties (with little alternative but to support it or have no share in power). In this respect, the defeat in 1977 of the Christian democrats of the Federación Demócrata Cristiana (FDC) and of the Alianza Socialista Democrática (ASD), and the ideological position of the Partido Socialista Popular (PSP) that since then has fused with the PSOE, differentiate the Spanish system from the Italian and the French under the Fourth Republic. It could be argued that the Catalan minority in the Congreso and the PNV could play a role similar to minor parties supporting a central political core but this would disregard the fundamental ambivalences of the PNV toward participation in governing the Spanish state, the difficulties created for the Catalans by the need for different coalition politics in Barcelona and Madrid, and the complexity of autonomist demands and latent nationalism of the periphery in its relations to the political system. The relative proportions of the vote, the UCD with its 34.8 percent in 1977 and 35.0 in 1979, and the PSOE with 29.4 and 30.5 respectively, deprive centre positions of the dominance that the larger vote for the Democrazia Cristiana in Italy, the Nea Democratia of Karamanlis in

Greece, and the Socialist Party in Portugal enjoyed in the period of consolidation of democratic institutions. The centre position in Spain does not find itself united for the defense of the system against the extremes in the way that the coalitions of the Fourth Republic found themselves in the period of the cold war and the initial rise of Gaullism. The distribution of votes has inevitably led to competition between the UCD and the PSOE in the elections, rather than a grand coalition of the centre.

A comparison of the June 1977 and the March 1979 legislative elections, to discern some of the dynamics of the party system presents many difficulties.[12] The extension of the right to vote to 18-year-old youths expanded the electorate from 23,616,421 to 26,838,500, an increase of 13.6 percent, which is a significant change particularly since the young voters were apparently more likely to abstain and when they voted had quite different preferences from their elders. To compound the difficulty, the number actually voting remained almost identical: 18,232,049 in 1977 and 18,284,948 in 1979, which means that participation dropped from 77.2 percent to 68.1 percent. Assuming that more than 52,899 of those newly eligible did vote, a large number of voters in 1977 opted for non-voting in 1979. In addition new parties appealed to the voters like Herri Batasuna, others changed their image, the PSP fused with the PSOE, and the Christian Democrats abandoned the struggle.

The main results of the 1979 elections were a consolidation at the national level of the party system that had emerged out of the 1977 poll and a simplification, with the disappearance of the Partido Socialista Popular/Unidad Socialista (PSP/US) coalition, of the Equipo de la Democracia Cristiana, and of a number of parties without representation in the Cortes. The two main moderate parties UCD and PSOE consolidated their position with 64.2 percent of the vote in 1977 and 65.5 in 1979, and 285 seats in 1977 and 289 in 1979, and the parties on their flanks made little gains, for PCE went from 20 seats to 23 and from 9.3 percent to 10.8 while the successor coalition to AP had fewer votes and seats. Even so the two unquestionably pro-system parties made few gains. CD, after moving centripetally, must have lost some of its votes to the extreme right Union Nacional. This political group obtained 379,560 votes (2.11 percent) compared to 94,948 (0.52 percent) of the three groups running in 1977 integrated into UN. The growth of the PCE and UN can be considered evidence of a centrifugal trend.

TABLE 6
Returns for the Lower House Elections of March 1979

	Votes	% of total	Seats
A) Nationwide parties			
UN (Unión Nacional)	379,560	2.11	1
CD (Coalición Democrática)	1,097,653	6.11	9
UCD (Unión de Centro Democrático)	6,293,878	35.05	168
PSOE (Partido Socialista Obrero Español)	5,475,389	30.49	121
PSOE (h) (Partido Socialista Obrero Español (sector histórico))	133,761	0.74	
PCE (Partido Comunista de España)	1,427,104	7.95	14
PSUC (Partit Socialista Unificat de Catalunya)	511,800	2.85	9
PCE + PSUC	(1,938,904)	(10.80)	
PTE (Partido del Trabajo de España)	192,440	1.07	
ORT (Organización Revolucionaria de Trabajadores (including UNAI))	138,634	0.77	
MC-OIC (Movimiento Comunista-Organización de Izquierda Comunista)	84,505	0.47	
Other Marxist Parties to the Left of PCE	136,723	0.76	
Republican Parties	55,594	0.31	
Different Falangist Parties	34,312	0.19	
Syndicalist Party	9,746	0.05	
Other non-regional parties	29,926	0.17	
PC (Partido Carlista)	50,665	0.28	
Total nationwide parties with representation	(15,185,384)	(84.56)	(322)
Total nationwide parties without representation	(866,306)	(4.82)	
Total nationwide parties	(16,051,690)	(89.38)	
B) Regional parties			
Euskadi and Navarra			
PNV (Partido Nacionalista Vasco)	296,597	1.65	7
HB (Herri Batasuna)	172,110	0.96	3
EE (Euskadiko Ezkerra)	85,677	0.48	1
UPN (Unión del Pueblo Navarro)	28,248	0.16	1
Total	(582,632)		
Catalonia			
CiU (Convergència i Unió and the coalition CiU (CDC-UDC))	482,479	2.69	8
ERC (Esquerra Republicana de Catalunya)	123,266	0.69	1
BEAN (Bloc D'Esquerra D'Alliberament Nacional)	44,688	0.25	
Other Catalan Parties (EC, DSCC, PSAN)	12,849	0.07	
Andalucía			
PSA (Partido Socialista de Andalucía)	325,842	1.81	5

TABLE 6 (continued)

	Votes	% of total	Seats
Aragón			
PAR (Partido Aragonés Regionalista)	38,042	0.21	1
CpA (Coalición por Aragón)	19,237	0.11	
Canary Islands			
UPC (Unión del Pueblo Canario)	59,342	0.33	1
PPC (Partido del País Canario)	10,099	0.06	
Galicia			
BNPG (Bloque Nacional Popular Galego)	63,446	0.35	
UG (Unidade Galega)	57,795	0.32	
País Valencià			
BEAN in PV (Bloc D'Esquerra			
D'Alliberament Nacional)	9,620	0.05	
Other Valencian Parties	33,641	0.19	
Castile and León			
Rural and PANCAL (Partido Nacionalista de			
Castilla-León)	22,555	0.13	
Balearic Islands			
Socialistes de Mallorca	10,022	0.06	
Other local parties	11,159	0.06	
Total regional parties with representation	(1,611,603)	(8.97)	(28)
Total regional parties without representation	(295,111)	(1.64)	
Total regional parties	(1,906,714)	(10.62)	
A + B Total valid votes*	17,958,404	98.21	350
C Blank votes	58.267	0.32	
D Void votes	268,277	1.47	
A + B + C + D Total votes cast	18,284,948	100.00	
Participation		68.13	
Total eligible voters	26,836,500		

In the absence of an official publication of the electoral returns for all parties and provinces the source used is the newspaper *El País,* 2 and 3 May 1979. *El País* only gives national totals for eligible voters, valid votes, blank and void votes (but the sum of the three is not identical with their figure of votes cast) and the vote for parties with representation. The only possibility for all other parties was to add the returns for them in each district. Adding the vote for the represented parties in the same way, they do not coincide with the national totals given by *El País*, 3 May, p. 17. The difference is due to the non-inclusion of lists running on a different label and to inconsistencies in the additions. The publication by the Inst i tuto Nacional de Estadistica, *Elecciones Generales Legislativas de 1° de Marzo de 1979. Resultados,* (Madrid, INE, 1979 [actually 1980]) contains the returns by province and for each municipality of Spain for the Lower House and at the provincial level for the Senate. Percentages of valid votes are given for the four leading parties in each district for every municipality. The Junta Electoral Central (JEC), on the basis of the official count sent by the provincial Juntas Electorales, reported on 17 April 1979 the returns for each of the 52 electoral

TABLE 6 (continued)

districts. These provincial figures were those used to allocate the seats. The figure for the total electorate in the table coincides with the JEC but is 50,458 larger than the one given by the INE. The number of votes cast is 29,393 more than the JEC figure but 10,870 less than the INE figure. The figures for blank and void votes for the table and JEC are identical, but respectively 519 and 3,163 less than the INE. The valid votes added by us are 25,514 more than those reported by the JEC and the INE (that is 0.095 of the total electorate). There is no difference between our data and those of the JEC for many parties and in other cases they are less than 200 votes; only in the case of eight parties they are over one thousand. The two most significant are 25,285 more votes for UCD than reported by the JEC, but only 1,176 more than by the INE. Our figures for the PCE-PSUC are 27,687 more than those of the JEC, but 1,322 less than those of the INE. This means that with respect to our figure of valid votes UCD would have 0.14 percent fewer votes and the PCE-PSUC 0.15 fewer using the JEC figures. The discrepancy between our figure and that of the JEC for UN (8,820) is large considering its small vote, but only 93 more than the one given by the INE. In the case of the PSOE the JEC gives 5,576 fewer votes and the INE 1,648 more. Among the regional parties our figure for the BNPG is 2,566 and for UG 2,240 more than those of the JEC, but identical to those given by the INE. Jorge de Esteban, Luis López Guerra, (eds.), *Las elecciones legislativas del 1 de Marzo de 1979,* (Madrid, Centro de Investigaciones Sociológicas, 1979) is a monumental work including information on electoral legislation, the parties, their platforms, polls published at the time of the election, etc. and returns by districts. The data used are derived from many sources. This accounts for the differences between their data and ours. The table on pp. 303-305 gives the vote for each party (with PRE missing) but the table *should be corrected* with the data on p. 447. DATA has prepared a tape with returns for municipalities and electoral maps (forthcoming). None of the data available will be "official" and totally consistent or accurate.

   *The figure given in *El País,* 3 May, for total votes cast is 18, 255, 555, but the same paragraph gives 17, 932, 890 valid votes, that added to the blank and void would be equal to 18, 259, 434 voters. Our figure resulting from adding the votes from *El País* by district (and in the case of no information on a party in a district — UN in Almeria and PSOE(h) in Santander — from Jorge Esteban, op. cit.) adds up to 17, 958, 404 valid votes, that is 25, 514 more than those reported in *El País.*

In Madrid with an increase in the electorate of 431,945 voters but a decrease in participation of 69,563, the PSOE gained 48,767 votes, this was only a small proportion of the 209,090 votes that in 1977 went to the PSP, which in the meantime had fused with the PSOE. Even assuming that there was considerable party loyalty, some of the PSOE vote must have come from other parties. A sign of the greater polarization in this highly politically sensitive electorate was the increased vote for the PCE (66,536 new votes) bringing their 10.59 percent up to 13.90, and that the candidates sponsored by the (Organización Revolucionaria de Trabajadores (ORT) and Partido del Trabajo de España (PTE) (that respectively had obtained 0.70 percent and 0.57) increased respectively to 2.16 percent and 1.16 (44,893 more votes). On the other end of the spectrum UN could obtain 110,730, 4.96 percent of the vote, compared to 13,587 (0.59

percent) for Falange Española de los JONS in 1977.

If we consider the growth in strength of different left nationalist parties like Herri Batasuna with 0.96 percent of the vote, the Unión del Pueblo Canario, that obtained seats, and the Bloque Nacional Popular Galego that increased its vote from 23,036 to 63,446 (that is from 1.99 percent to 5.86) of the Galician vote, the centrifugal-polarization thesis finds additional support. While at the level of nationwide parties the fragmentation was reduced, at the regional level, particularly in the Basque country, but also of other regions, like Andalucía, the fragmentation increased.

Congruent with the thesis of a centrifugal potential, despite deliberate centripetal policies pursued by the top leadership, in the PSOE, is the powerful challenge the PCE presents to it, due to four reasons: 1) the shared and close political space; 2) the ecological correlation of the vote of both parties; 3) the appeal of the Communist led union, the CCOO, to PSOE voters; and 4) many PSOE voters have the PCE as second choice. These are obviously strains in the opposite direction among PCE voters, but given the size of the electorates of the PSOE and the PCE, the tendencies among the socialists have greater political significance.

> The question is if the PSOE can overcome its historical tension between "revolution" and "reform" and move beyond dilemmas which provide a strategical paralysis — most likely, in the direction of what has been called "revolutionary reformism" or "constitutional radicalism" — then it will also disprove the thesis of the irrelevance of leftwing politics in industralized societies, while at the same time strengthen democracy in Spain.[13]

It is also clear that to the extent that alternation is being considered within the party system, it is only alternation between the centre parties. The PSOE presents itself as an alternative to the UCD without telling us from where it would be able to get the parliamentary support to achieve a majority, even if its vote would increase considerably in the next election. More realistic or cynical observers before the 1979 election were speculating that an increase in votes for the PSOE would lead to a coalition government of PSOE and UCD. One could argue that if the society would really trust the moderate Eurocommunist stance of the PCE and the left would admit that AP has a legitimate place in the democratic political system, the alternative of a Popular Front government led by the socialists and the rightist government led by the UCD would allow real alternation. In this respect, the Spanish political situation is perhaps different from the French. The Giscardians and the Gaullists can govern together as a right of centre alternative, and despite many fears, a government of the left on the basis of the *Programme Commun* was not excluded. Perhaps a political system based on unipolar alternative coalitions would serve Spanish democracy better than the reliance on minority centre governments or an internally contradictory grand coalition. But it is doubtful that at present such an alternative is available (even though it has become less "unthinkable"). The present patterns of politics are likely to lead to the complex combination of visible and invisible political bargains that has characterized the Italian system, since the dynamics of the party system have deprived the DC and even the *apertura a sinistra* of a majority, or to the other alternative suggested so often by the PCE of government of all parties on the basis of a "democratic concentration." All of these alternatives exclude effective alternative policies and real accountability of government.

A basic difference between Spain and Switzerland and the Netherlands is the fact that in those two countries we are dealing with cases of segmented pluralism based on a recognition of diversity that is institutionalized, primarily a structural construct of the social-cultural variety in which some of the parties are located on a different dimension than the left-right and ready to cooperate in the political process. There is no room here to note some of the difficulties for consociational politics as a solution to the problems of regional autonomy demands in Catalonia and the Basque country and particularly secessionist tendencies in the Basque country.

It has become fashionable to overextend the term consociational democracy to encompass even such a quite different political formula as the *compromesso storico* in Italy, and it is not unlikely that the idea might be picked up to apply it to a future understanding between the UCD and the PSOE and even to the analysis of the politics of semi- or pseudo-consensus in the constitution-making process and the Moncloa pacts. In our view such a model is not applicable to Spanish politics. As an evidence we might refer to the way in which the issue of school policy has been formulated by the PSOE. In our view, Spanish politics in the near future is likely to show the dynamics of polarized pluralism with centrifugal tendencies and the added characteristic that there is no permanent more or less stable centre around which politics turns, like in Italy, but that the situation shows a potential similarity with Chile. However, the presence of a monarch rather than an elected president is likely to make the Spanish system more stable than the Chilean in recent years. It is the awareness of these risks that leads the politicians to constantly search for consensus.

There are certainly other models which are being discussed in attempting to interpret the emerging party system. There are those like Martínez Cuadrado who turn their attention to the historical past, particularly the politics of the Restoration after 1875 in which the two great leaders of the Conservative and the Liberal parties, Cánovas and Sagasta, worked out an understanding and a pre-arranged peaceful alternation, the famous *turno pacífico,* (excluding the anti-system Carlists and Republicans and ultimately dividing them and thereby obtaining some cooperation on their flanks from the so-called *mestizos* and *posibilistas*) at the cost of real political participation and leading ultimately to the alienation of the periphery from the system and the discontented lower classes turning to radical political alternatives. There can be no question that the two-party system created by those leaders to pacify the country and stablize the monarchy assured Spain years of peace and considerable progress. The idea is that the UCD and the PSOE are reaching an under-standing between their leaders, Suárez and Felipe González, that could inaugurate a similar period. There are certainly some tendencies in this direction, but it seems doubtful that in a modern and politically more mobilized society, in a world of more ideological politics, in the absence of notable politics and with a system of proportional representation rather than single member districts, such a system could withstand the competition of parties excluded from the pact, most concretely of a dynamic and well organized PCE, and a CD capable of articulating the grievances of more conservative sectors of society. To start, the model is flawed by the fact that the two major parties in 1977 only added up to 68.7 percent of the electorate (including the PSP vote) even though claiming 291 of the 350 seats. It also ignores the ideological distance between the two main parties and the fact that the PSOE is in addition to being an electoral party, a membership party in which the militants want a right to influence party policy without leaving control exclusively to the parliamentary leadership.

Certainly, clientelistic and transformistic patterns that in many respects are congruent with the social and political culture of Spain, the availability of a para-state sector, the importance of state-related middle classes in the political leadership of all parties, the weakened legitimacy of the entrepreneurial class, etc., might favour a cooperation between UCD and PSOE. Giuseppe Di Palma has recently emphasized the importance of such tendencies in Mediterranean politics and their persistent presence in Italian politics in spite of changes of regime. But we would argue that even if such patterns are likely to emerge, they would take place more at the level of invisible politics rather than more visible parts of the political process. The visible politics will respond to the polarized pluralism model with the electoral consequences predicted by that model and the ultimate weakening of the imperfect or pseudo-bipartism in the centre with the exclusion of other parties. As the Restoration experience showed, such a system also is highly dependent on the skills and prestige of the founding leaders, and likely to enter in crisis should they fail. Limited pseudo-bipartisan politics in the context of a modern society with a polarized extreme multiparty system at the electoral level, is not likely to be stable and even less to be effective to handle the complex problems faced by the country in a period of institutional, social, and economic change.

Our discussion until now, like that in the main theoretical work of Sartori, has ignored the role of the parties not represented in parliament or weakly represented, both left of the communists and right of CD and their disruptive capacities contributing to polarization. In the case of the small parties of the left, particularly the ORT and the PTE that in March 1977 decided to fuse, with their trade union wings, their competition with the PCE cannot be ignored in the long run, (particularly since the PCE does not have the secure place in Spanish society that the PCI has achieved over many years of control of local and recently regional government in Italy). Nor can the more violent antisystem opposition of Union Nacional on the right and its potential capacity to compete with AP be neglected. The readiness of some groupuscules on both extremes and of the extreme nationalist Basque separatist movement represented by Herri Batasuna at the political level and ETA as a terrorist organization on the left of Basque politics, are another factor to be taken into account in this age of violent and terrorist politics. In the first version of this essay (1978) we predicted that the two parties farthest apart on the ideological spectrum, the PCE and the AP, might very well move in the near future closer to the political centre, but that in the process they were likely to alienate, if not important sectors of the electorate, some of their activists. We expressed the fear that they would move outside of the range of democratic electoral politics creating small but highly virulent extremes, threatening continuously even though perhaps ineffectively, the political system, contributing to the erosion of the centre and increasing its dependency on the moderate flanks to shore-up its authority, which in turn would create tensions within the centre. This factor, likely to be ignored in an analysis of the parliamentary party system, in and of itself might make the model of pseudo-bipartism questionable.

Spanish Voters and Parties on the Left-Right Dimension

The placement of individuals and parties on a left-right dimension has become one of the most interesting tools in the study of political attitudes and parties. It has been used in the study of Western mass publics and through the work of Giovanni Sartori entered the theoretical debate on the nature of party systems. The use of a spatial dimension, and in particular the left-right dimension, in the study of parties, has stimulated an interesting debate.[14] Here we shall only provide some data on one of the dimensions of Spanish politics, the left-right dimension, leaving for another occasion the intriguing problem of the relationship between this dimension, and another, more difficult to label, in which Spaniards place themselves, extending from the affirmation of the Spanish centralist state to the nationalist challenge of independence from that state.

The standard question asking the respondents to place themselves on a continuum from left to right, from 1 to 10, has been asked by DATA in four national surveys and three local and regional studies, as well as in a study of Spanish youth.[15] In several of these polls, the respondents were asked also to place a limited number of parties on that continuum. These allow us to compare the self location of the voters of particular parties and the placement of those parties by the electorate in general and their own voters.

Since the question was asked in July 1976 when the outcome of the transition to democracy was still uncertain, in January-February 1977 when parties were just beginning to be legalized and the Communist Party was still illegal, in July 1978 one year after the first election, and again in 1979, five months after the second election, we can follow the changes in the crucial period of the emergence and crystallization of the party system. A first interesting finding is that it has been a period of slow but continuous mobilization by the left that emerged from the underground to share in power at the municipal and regional level. This process is clearly reflected in the continued drift leftward in the self location of the Spanish population. In July 1976, the average score was 5.64, a little over half a year later it had

TABLE 7
Self-placement on the Left-Right Scale (1976-1979)
National Samples of DATA

		July 1976		January- February 1977		Madrid Fall 1977		July 1978		July 1979	
Left	1	2 ⎫		1 ⎫		3 ⎫		3 ⎫		4 ⎫	
	2	3 ⎬ 18		3 ⎬ 21		5 ⎬ 42		5 ⎬ 40		5 ⎬ 38	
	3	6 ⎪		7 ⎪		17 ⎪		15 ⎪		15 ⎪	
	4	7 ⎭		10 ⎭		17 ⎭		17 ⎭		17 ⎭	
	5	24 ⎫ 38		23 ⎫ 41		19 ⎫ 35		21 ⎫ 33		17 ⎫ 37	
	6	14 ⎭		18 ⎭		16 ⎭		12 ⎭		13 ⎭	
	7	6 ⎫		8 ⎫		3 ⎫		6 ⎫		5 ⎫	
	8	7 ⎬ 22		7 ⎬ 19		5 ⎬ 11		4 ⎬ 12		5 ⎬ 13	
	9	4 ⎪		2 ⎪		1 ⎪		1 ⎪		1 ⎪	
Right	10	5 ⎭		2 ⎭		2 ⎭		1 ⎭		2 ⎭	
d.k.		14		—		—		—		—	
n.a.		7		18		12		14		11	
Sample size		(6342)		(8857)		(493)		(5898)		(5499)	
Mean score		5.64		5.53		4.73		4.68		4.78	

Source: from surveys by DATA, unpublished report 1979.

moved slightly to the left to 5.53. But that score placed Spain among European nations on a point that was not to be congruent with the emerging party system, and by July 1978 Spain had occupied its place at the same point on the scale as Italy. These data raise the interesting interesting question to what extent political leadership contributed to create a climate of opinion and a party system of a certain type rather than being a reflection of the predispositions of the electorate before political mobilization, or can we assume that the similarities between the social structure of Spain and Italy, common elements in the political history of southern and western in contrast to central and northern Europe, made such a development toward the left inevitable. (See Table 8.)

The data show a considerable tendency to stay close to the centre of the spectrum but increasingly left of centre. The average location has moved left but not so much due to a strengthening of the more extreme left positions but of the centre-left, and above all, the continuous weakening of the right. In this the responses to the question do not differ that much from the election returns.

TABLE 8
Self-location of European and Spanish Voters on the
Left-Right Continuum

	Measure	
Ireland	6.30	*Most Right*
Netherlands	5.80	
Belgium	5.67	
SPAIN, July 1976	5.64	
Federal Republic of Germany	5.63	
SPAIN, January-February 1977	5.53	
Luxembourg	5.43	
Denmark	5.41	
United Kingdom	5.37	
France	5.05	
SPAIN, July 1979	4.78	
Italy	4.69	
SPAIN, July 1978	4.68	*Most Left*

Sources: Ronald Inglehart and Hans D. Klingemann, "Party Identification, Ideological Preference and Left-Right Dimension among Western Mass Publics," in Ian Budge et al., (eds.) *Party Identification and Beyond,* New York, Wiley, 1976, pp. 243 ff. and from surveys carried out by DATA.

Significantly, few Spaniards were unable or unwilling to place themselves on the left-right scale and their number has diminished with increased politicization, independently of non-participation in the elections in 1979.

The self-placement on the left-right scale already in 1976-1977 was highly correlated with the ideological tendencies that the voters felt would represent best their interests, at a time in which only one-fifth of the electorate was ready to identify with one of the political parties on the scene or emerging. In January-February 1977 those who identified with the continuators of the Franco regime had a score of 7.25. Those feeling themselves represented by conservatives, 6.63. Christian democrats placed themselves on 5.87, and the social democrats at 5.03. On the left, those who felt that socialism would be closest to their ideological preference located themselves on 3.93, practically on the same place where in 1979 we shall find the PSOE voters, 3.99. The few who dared at that time to identify with communism were at 2.89 slightly to the left of the present PCE-PSUC electorate (3.06) and the few revolutionaries placed themselves at 2.34. In 1976, self-placement correlated with religiosity, 0.46, very little with income, -0.09, and negatively, -0.21, with level of education.

A study of July 1978 allows us to compare the self-placement of those expressing a preference for each of the parties, the placement of each party by those intending to vote for it, and finally the image of the location of each party among the electorate as a whole. Our data (see Table 9) show a pattern that is already familiar from studies in other countries, that the electorate as a whole tends to place parties more distant from each other, and those on the extremes farther out on the spectrum, than the supporters of each of those parties. The voters themselves show an even greater reluctance to place themselves toward the extremes. To give just one or two examples from the table: while the electorate placed the PCE-PSUC at the point 2.52, those intending to vote for the communists placed their party on 2.61, and when it came to locate themselves their score was 3.06, clearly to the right of the public image of the party. In the case of AP, we find the same pattern. The electorate moves it far to the right, 8.46, the AP supporters already place it much more toward the centre 7.73, and they themselves turn out to be even more moderate in their rightism locating themselves on 7.08. In the public mind, the distance between AP and PCE was 5.96, between the images that the supporters of those parties had of their location 5.12, and finally the actual distance between the supporters of AP and PCE-PSUC was reduced to 4.00. There is a certain room for the parties to act centripetally even when the ideology tends to place them far apart in the public image.

In order to place those distances in perspective, let us note that the maximum distance among the voters in different countries was 6.90 in Italy, 4.93 in France, but only 3.89 in the United Kingdom, 3.70 in Belgium and 3.09 in Germany. Data confirm our image of the Spanish party system as one of polarized and potentially centrifugal multipartism rather than the moderate multiparty system of the Federal Republic or Belgium.

The perception of the position of different parties on the left-right scale is far from random but reflects the point of reference used by different social groups and the supporters of different parties. Those located on the extremes or close to the extremes tend to see the parties on the other end of the spectrum much farther out and their own party closer to the centre; so for example the communists in 1978 placed AP at 8.97 and the electorate on the whole placed it at 8.46, and the supporters of AP responded in kind by placing the PCE at 1.87 while the electorate placed it at 2.52. The process of latent and potentially actual polarization in a multiparty system like the Spanish

TABLE 9

Placement of Parties on the Left-Right Scale by the Electorate, the Potential Voters of Each Party and Self-placement of Potential Voters, 1978

	EE*	PCE/PSUC	PSOE	PNV*	CDC**	UCD	AP	Maximum distance	Distance AP/PCE
Placement by the electorate as a whole	2.28	2.52	3.84	4.46	5.76	5.96	8.46	6.18	5.94
Placement of each party by those expressing a preference for it	2.57	2.61	3.81	4.36	5.43	5.62	7.73	5.16	5.12
Self-placement of those expressing a preference for each party	3.06	3.06	3.99	4.12	4.98	5.74	7.08	4.02	4.02
Placement by those who express no party preference	2.41	2.93	4.14	4.41	6.21	6.06	8.35	5.94	5.42

*Only respondents in Basque-Navarrese region.

**Only respondents in Catalonia.

Source: survey of DATA, July-August 1978; national sample of 5,898.

is to a considerable extent the result of the distorted, polarized and centrifugal perception that the supporters of the parties closer to the extremes have of those on the other end of the continuum. In the case that such parties gain votes they contribute decisively to a polarized climate of opinion that is largely a reflection of perceptions rather than of the self-locations of the voters.

A sign of the tension in the Basque country is that the supporters of EE are those that see their own party farthest to the left, 2.57, and AP more to the right than those of any other party at the national level, 9.58, while they place the great national parties of the left, the PCE and the PSOE, far to the right from where the electorate as a whole places them. These perceptions of the Basque Marxist nationalist party are a good example of the stretching of the ideological space noted by Sartori in the cases of extreme polarized multiparty systems. In fact, even the moderate Basque nationalists, the PNV, put AP far to the right 9.33, and EE far to the left 2.08 from where the electorate as a whole places them and their own supporters do.

The very different climate of opinion in Catalonia is reflected in the fact that the supporters of the main Catalanist party Convergència Democràtica de Catalunya (CDC) tend to place all the parties closer to the centre than the electorate as a whole. The very different possibilities of cooperation between the governing party UCD and the Catalanist party of Jordi Pujol, is reflected in the fact that the CDC supporters placed UCD at 5.79 and their own party at 5.43. In contrast to the case of the PNV that pushes UCD far to the right 6.69 (even compared to the communists 6.39) and place their own party at 4.35.

If we take the overall location of Spanish parties and compare it with the location of Italian parties, we see that the Spanish electorate does not seem to place the communist as far out as the Italians did in 1972 (2.25 versus 1.74). The PSOE was located to the right of the PSI, 3.84 versus 3.31. On the other hand, the UCD, perhaps rightly so, was placed somewhat to the right of the DC, 5.96 versus 5.55, and again with good sense the electorate placed AP less to the right than the MSI, 8.46 compared to 8.83. Significantly the AP supporters placed themselves even more toward the centre, 7.08 compared to 8.04 of the MSI supporters. These last data confirm our image of AP as a party more compatible with a stable democracy and a potential system party. Let us note that this data is for 1978, before CD tried to change the image of the old AP. The far out extremist MSI would be much closer to Fuerza Nueva in Spain than to AP-CD.[16]

As an indication of the distance between parties we do not have to rely exclusively on the left-right continuum and the position of voters on it or their placement of different parties on that scale, but we ask people in which measure they consider different parties near or far from their personal, ideological position, including their own party.

To begin, the voters of different parties do not find them equally close to their own personal beliefs. Not surprisingly, communist voters find their party closest to their own position while those of the PSOE and the UCD, that is, of two less ideological parties, are somewhat less identified with the positions of their parties. A sign of the ideological ambivalences within the CD electorate can be found in the smaller number that is fully represented by the party's position. In fact, that goes very far in explaining the internal difficulties of that party a few months later.

The proximity of the parties of the left appears quite clearly even when the two extreme-left parties ORT-PTE appear relatively isolated compared to the two major parties of the left. The communist voters divide between those who feel a certain affinity but not an intense one with the parties to the left, and those who see them as rather far apart. There is no such doubt about the proximity the communist voters feel toward the PSOE. That, to some extent, is reciprocated among the PSOE voters toward the PCE even when there is almost half of them that see the two parties rather far apart. A good indicator of the hinge position of the PSOE is the fact that the same proportion of its voters see themselves close to the PCE and to the UCD. The socialist voters, however, have little doubt about their rejection of CD, the successor to AP. In fact, their rejection of the party of Fraga is equally as intense as that of the communist voters. The UCD electorate defines itself as very far apart or rather far from the communist and other parties to their left but not so with respect to the PSOE. In fact, the same proportion of UCD voters consider the PSOE as close to their positions as PSOE voters considered the UCD close to theirs. There can be little doubt that there is room for competition between those two parties and for considerable turnover in either direction. The supporters of the governing party, however, feel relatively far from CD even when about a quarter of them do not feel that far apart from the civilized right. This clearly confirms the impression from other data, including the positioning of the left-right scale, that the UCD electorate is quite shielded from appeals coming from its right, while the CD electorate's view of UCD indicates a potential affinity and appeal of the great centre party to voters to its right. The findings are not incongruous with the hostility expressed in 1977 and later by the UCD leadership to AP and the willingness of the CD to give its parliamentary support to Suárez. Their perception of Fuerza Nueva, the only nationwide party represented in parliament by one deputy that has opposed the constitution and the new democratic order, shows that the electorate of all parties considers itself far apart from the extreme right. UCD voters find themselves farther apart from FN than from the PCE. A large majority of the voters of the civilized right consider themselves very far or rather far from FN even when among them we find a minority that shows a certain affinity with that Francoist extremist group.

The overall picture that emerges is one of isolation of one of the extremes, of considerable distance of most voters from ORT-PTE, of a certain capacity of PCE to reach an understanding with PSOE that is only partially reciprocated, and a relative closeness of the two dominant parties that could result in both intense competition between them as well as a limited capacity for cooperation. Even so both the PSOE and the UCD would alienate a very large proportion of their respective voters if they worked too closely together. The data also confirm the intense rejection of CD by the left and the large proportion of UCD supporters that feel rather far from a party with which they would be obliged to ally in the case of a popular front against the centre right and the right. Certainly, alternation between two blocks in view of the distances between parties would impose serious strains on all parties but particularly on those in the centre.

The more ideological character of the communists and, to a lesser extent, of AP, is not just the perception of scholars; the voters themselves are conscious of the differences between parties in terms of ideology, programme and leadership. When asked for the reasons for their vote in 1977, and the relative importance they would assign to ideology, programme, leadership and chances of success or capacity to govern, an overwhelming majority of the PCE-PSUC supporters mention ideology, and fully 72 percent mentioned it either in first or second place, compared to only 55 percent of the PSOE voters and 24 percent of those of UCD, which in this respect differs from AP where 48 percent mention ideology. This is noteworthy, considering the strong personality of Manuel Fraga, and his prominent role in the party and its campaign. By contrast, the leader plays a very secondary role for the communist voters, despite the fact that they strongly approve of the leadership of Santiago Carrillo.

Even when the actions of Felipe González were far from unanimously approved by the voters of the PSOE, his personality was far more important for the socialist voters. Adolfo Suárez, as prime minister, was one of the main assets of UCD in 1977, with 23 percent mentioning him as a main consideration in their choice of party, and another 20 percent in the second place. However, contrary to what many observers might have thought, a large proportion of the UCD voters were attracted in the first place by the programme or by the chances of success, the capacity to govern, and the responsibility of the party, rather than by identification with the leader. The motivations for voting UCD therefore and to a lesser extent those for voting PSOE are heterogeneous by comparison with other parties. (See Table 10.)

TABLE 10
Significance Attached to the Ideology, Programme, and Leader by the Voters of Main Parties in the 1977 Election (in percent)

	PCE/ PSUC	PSOE	UCD	AP
Ideology				
1st place	62	38	11	32
2nd place	11	17	13	16
Programme				
1st place	20	20	23	22
2nd place	28	20	9	15
Leader				
1st place	3	18	23	14
2nd place	14	14	20	4
Party's chances of success, capacity to govern, sense of responsibility				
1st place	8	14	31	24
2nd place	25	32	35	42
	(599)	(1842)	(1573)	(381)

III. THE CLEAVAGES:
PRESENT AND ABSENT

1. Christian Democrats

The failure of Spanish Christian democracy, in view of the central role played in the democratic reconstruction of Europe after World War II and even in Chile and Venezuela, represents for Catholic Europe a major change. Many factors, some of them of general significance, others distinctively Spanish, concur in accounting for the fact that an ideological alternative that significant segments of the electorate understood, had given the opposition to the Franco regime outstanding leaders in the period of the transition should be absent from the Cortes.[17] There is no question that the changed position of the Church in politics after Vatican II, the erosion of the image of Christian democratic parties in other European countries, the desire of many Catholics not to mix religion and politics, the leftward turn of lay Catholic activists and some sectors of the clergy operate today in many countries. In the Spanish case, other factors contributed: the internal crisis of the church that led the hierarchy to opt for a more pastoral position and to avoid commitments in partisan politics, the internal divisions within the Christian democratic family that were overcome only shortly before the elections, the desire to accommodate the Basque PNV that had been a founding member of the Christian Democratic International, and with it the commitment to regional parties federated at the national level rather than a nationwide unified party, but perhaps more than anything else, the leftward leanings of the most distinguished leader of the party, Joaquín Ruiz Giménez in the transition period and in response to his moral convictions and his rejection of his past political career under Franco. It was those leanings that made Christian democratic unity difficult and brought some Christian democrats into the UCD camp. The ideological and programmatic positions of the Christian democrats did not respond to the predispositions of their potential electorate, and the social correlates in Spain between religion and social class left little room for a left Christian Democratic Party. An unsuccessful 1977 election campaign did the rest.

*Religion and Politics in the Absence of the
Christian Democratic Party*

The lack of success of a Christian democratic party does not mean that religious commitments are unrelated to political behaviour even without religious issues playing a major role in elections.[18] (See Table 11.) Even without an active intervention of the Church in politics, the position stated by the hierarchy on controversial issues cannot but influence the behaviour of the electorate. In fact, religiosity is one of the variables most closely associated with political attitudes, whatever indicators we might take, positions of the left-right scale, party preferences, and attitudes toward a wide range of issues. The differences in religiosity between the supporters of different parties are not only between the left and the right but even between parties like the PCE-PSUC and the PSOE they are greater on the religious dimension than even on the subjective class dimension. In every social class, in every region, and both among men and women, those who define themselves as very good Catholics give little support to the parties of the left; the same is even more true for those who define themself as indifferent and above all as atheist, giving almost no support to the UCD and even less to the AP-CD. (See Tables 12 and 13.)

There are obviously differences among those reporting the same levels of religious practice who identify their family with a different subjective class. The incompatibility between being a good Catholic and a communist is asserted by 47 percent of upper- and middle-class practicing Catholics and only by 40 percent among those identifying with the working class. (See Table 14.) In contrast, among upper and middle class persons identified as religiously indifferent or atheist, 68 percent affirmed the compatibility of being a communist and a good Catholic while 56 percent of those identified as working class and indifferent or atheist are of that opinion. In this case, we find that the lower-class leftists are closer to the traditional view than the small minority of non-religious upper- and upper-middle class. When it comes to voting for the Communist Party, the same proportion of upper- and upper-middle class persons rather than lower middle class (who defined themselves as "very good" or "practicing" Catholics), say they would never vote for the party, while the proportion is reduced somewhat among those of the same level of religiosity in the working class. Religiosity, irrespective of class, is an obstacle for the PCE in spite of all its efforts to tend its hand toward the Catholics, but not so in the case of the PSOE.

2. Eurocommunism

The PCE has defined itself a most outspoken Eurocommunist party.[19] In its line it follows closely the footsteps of the Italian

TABLE 11
Social Class, Religiosity and Report of Sympathy of the Family in the Civil War (1936-1939) among Men and Women

	Total	Upper and upper middle class				Lower middle class				Working class			
		v.g.	pr.	n.v.pr. not pr.	ind. atheist	v.g.	pr.	n.v.pr not pr.	ind. atheist	v.g.	pr.	n.v.pr not pr.	ind. atheist
	%	%	%	%	%	%	%	%	%	%	%	%	%
Nationalists	27	72	54	37	27	38	41	22	19	35	31	17	6
Popular Front	21	3	13	20	30	11	12	22	40	15	15	22	48
Both sides	4		10	9	6	2	4	6	9	2	2	3	4
None	26	16	11	19	24	27	26	29	21	25	29	27	23
n.a./d.k.	22	9	13	15	11	20	18	21	10	23	24	31	19

v.g.: "very good catholic"
pr.: "practicing"
n.v.pr.: "not very practicing"
not pr.: "not practicing"
ind.: indifferent

TABLE 12
Religiosity, Subjective Class and Vote in 1979

	Upper and middle class				Middle class				Working class			
	good	pr.	n.v.pr. not pr.	ind. atheist	good	pr.	n.v. pr not pr.	ind. atheist	good	pr.	n.v.pr. not pr.	ind. atheist
	%	%	%	%	%	%	%	%	%	%	%	%
EE-HB	—	1	1	2	—	—	1	2	—	2	1	4
PCE-PSUC	1	1	3	11	1	2	8	17	4	3	10	17
PSOE	9	9	22	18	7	11	27	30	21	19	33	31
PNV	3	2	3	—	4	2	1	0	4	2	0	1
CiU	1	1	2	2	1	2	3	1	1	2	1	1
UCD	37	47	32	8	51	52	24	8	38	37	15	6
CD	18	12	4	2	8	5	2	1	3	2	1	1
UN	6	1	2	—	—	1	1	—	1	1	0	—
Other	2	4	4	7	1	3	4	11	2	—	5	5
None	13	13	21	41	19	12	19	25	16	18	19	30
n.a./d.k.	10	9	6	9	8	10	10	5	10	14	15	4
	(68)	(216)	(257)	(124)	(167)	(627)	(996)	(260)	(240)	(669)	(1359)	(364)

TABLE 13
Mean Self-placement on the Left-Right
Dimension by Social Class and Religiosity

Religiosity	Upper and upper middle class	Middle and lower middle class	Working class	Maximum difference by class
Very good Catholic	6.83	6.04	5.41	1.42
Practicing	6.08	5.69	5.34	0.74
Not very practicing or not practicing	4.98	4.70	4.34	0.64
Indifferent or atheist	3.59	3.38	3.24	0.35
Maximum difference by religiosity	3.24	2.66	2.17	—
Difference between practicing and indifferent or atheist	2.49	2.33	2.10	—
Other religion than Catholic	5.25	4.40	4.09	1.16

Source: DATA, July 1978, national sample of 5,499. The mean for the sample was 4.78.

Communist Party. How can we account for this and what are the implications of it for the Spanish scene and internationally? These questions have no easy answer considering the history of the Spanish PCE, which was far from distinguished compared to other European communist parties, particularly the Italian.

The PCE attempted in the years after World War II a strategy of guerilla struggle against the Franco regime and failed. A bitter internal polemic arose as a consequence of which Claudín and Semprún became the spokesmen for a new line. However, when they were defeated and expelled from the party, Santiago Carrillo took over their line, as so often happens in the history of communist parties. Carrillo has been and continues to be the undisputed leader of the party that he joined after bringing into it in 1935-1936 the socialist youth organization of which he was the leader. He has the advantage of years of political experience in Spain and in exile. It would be interesting to know to what extent his experiences in Moscow and Eastern Europe and the relations between the Eastern bloc and Franco have contributed to his alienation from the Soviet leadership. The failure of subversion has obviously been a factor in a desire to build a broader coalition of social forces, in the shift toward a policy of the open hand towards the Catholics, and the decision to operate within the society through what the Italians call *presenza*

TABLE 14
Answers to the Question: Can one be a Good Catholic and a Good Communist ? by Subjective Class and Religiosity (1978)

	Upper and upper middle class				Lower middle class				Working class			
	v.g.	pr.	n.v.pr. not pr.	ind. atheist	v.g.	pr.	n.v. pr not pr.	ind. atheist	v.g.	pr.	n.v.pr. not pr.	ind. atheist
	%	%	%	%	%	%	%	%	%	%	%	%
Yes	21	48	51	68	39	46	58	60	42	50	62	56
No	75	47	42	26	53	49	35	35	46	40	27	36
d.k./n.a.	4	5	7	6	8	5	6	4	12	10	11	8
Would never vote:												
PCE	66	59	48	35	66	55	40	25	47	43	29	31
PSOE	37	31	17	25	23	17	15	21	15	15	12	24
Difference												
PCE over PSOE	29	28	31	10	43	38	25	4	32	28	17	7
	(68)	(216)	(257)	(124)	(167)	(627)	(996)	(260)	(240)	(659)	(1359)	(374)

Source: DATA, July-August 1978; national sample of 5,499.

rather than a tight vanguard party. The success of the Comisiones Obreras (CCOO) in the labour field in the last years of the Franco regime and the awareness reflected in his writings of the social and economic changes that had taken place in Spain, must have also contributed to disillusion the party of any revolutionary hopes. The Chilean experience and the advice of the Italian comrades must have added a greater awareness of the reactions that leftist demagogy can produce in the established sectors of society and above all, among the military.

The need to legitimize the party after years of anti-communist propaganda, negative memories of the Civil War, not only on the right, but also among the supporters of the Republic, the persistent cleavage between communists and Catholicism, all forced the party to devote its main efforts to its legitimation as a participant in the democratic political system. The perhaps unexpectedly limited electoral success also leads the party to think more in the long run of growth of its influence and electorate rather than immediate ambitions to assume power, except perhaps in an all party government. In this context, the Eurocommunist position, giving up of traditional commitments to the dictatorship of the proletariat and even Leninism, seem to make sense.

Certainly the behaviour in Parliament and in public of the party has gained it the respect of many who would never vote for it. There can be little doubt that a radical opposition stance would have made the instauration and process of consolidation of democracy more difficult. The party needs democracy, needs freedom and tolerance to expand and conquer positions of strength in local government, perhaps regional government and presence in different realms of society. Its present strength obliges it to wait and it can wait. In addition, the personal experience of many leaders of the PCE in the jails of Franco for many years, in exile and in the underground, leads it to value even more highly the freedom it has finally gained and the opportunities that democracy provides.

All this would lead to the conclusion that the Eurocommunist stance of the PCE responds not only to tactical considerations, but to its position in Spanish society in this moment of transition. I think that to put the question in terms of the sincerity of those ideological positions is to ask the wrong question. The question really is how far other participants in the political system and the society at large are ready to believe the party. Without such a trust, which is likely to be achieved only slowly as the Italian experience shows, communist participation in the government could provoke extreme reactions. On the other hand, the communist behaviour ultimately will depend on situational factors including the reactions of its opponents that are not under its control.

In the Spanish electorate of early 1977, a large proportion, 63 percent, mentioned communism as an alternative they would never consider voting for (in 1979 that figure had been reduced to 40 percent); only 44 percent said the same thing about those who would define themselves as the heirs of Francoism. Those placing themselves in the middle of the political spectrum — 5 on the left-right scale — answered in 1977 64 percent and 52 respectively to those alternatives. In spite of the open hand toward the Catholics, the party still has to overcome the religious barrier. Fifty-six percent of the population said in 1977 that it was impossible to be a good Catholic and a good communist, with 32 percent saying that it was possible and 12 percent with no opinion, while in Italy in 1968 the proportion saying Yes was 36 percent and in 1970 had reached 45 percent with the No's reduced to 44 percent. By 1979 in Spain the proportions were 54 percent and 37 percent. It will take the PCE time to gain even the legitimacy it has gained in the Italian political scene.

The future of Spanish Eurocommunism hinges much more on the relationships between the stronger PSOE and the PCE.[20] There are barriers on both sides, but also incentives for future cooperation. In 1978 we wrote:

> A look at the electoral map of the vote for the PCE and the PSOE separately and for the added vote of the left, shows the enormous advantage for the control of many municipalities in Andalucía, Catalonia, Valencia and Asturias of cooperation between the parties to gain control of the mayoralty, the key office in a Spanish town or village. To what extent in the proletarian villages of southern Spain will the base, following directives of the leadership in Madrid, reject offers of cooperation against bourgeois domination?

In April 1979 the leaders of the PSOE and PCE agreed on working together in the municipal government and to support for mayor the candidate of the party with the largest plurality. In this way the PSOE gained 1,116 mayoralities and the PCE 238 of 7,826 on which information is available. According to *El Socialista,* the PSOE gained 325 with communist support and the communists 150 with PSOE council member votes.[21] Pressures for similar collaboration exist in the provincial administrations — the *Diputaciones* — and probably in a number of regional governments. In this respect there is room in Spanish politics for a sphere of control for the left and for cooperation of the left. There are also, given the divided labour movement and the strength of CCOO, powerful pressures for cooperation in the trade union field.[22]

The strong anti-communist affect of a large sector of the exile leadership of the Socialist Party as a result of the bitter experiences during the Civil War, is not relevant for new generations of leaders and militants. A PSOE that rejects social democracy in principle even when probably not in practice, that has defined itself constantly as a Marxist party, that favours the neutralist position, that has welcomed communist representatives from other countries at its party congress, ultimately would have few arguments against a communist party that abandons Leninism, emphasizes its democratic commitments and even publicly criticizes the Soviet Union. It is hard to see what would be the basis for a campaign against the communists on the part of the PSOE. However, we should not ignore the tensions between the two socialist-Marxist parties that result from their competition for a similar electorate, competition between their respective trade union federations in the process of growth, and the strong feeling in the PSOE of being the larger party with ambition to be an alternative government.[23]

In fact, the moderation and desire to gain respectability of the PCE that led it to deny its support to more radical demands of the PSOE, was one of the sources of criticism and distrust of the socialists. On their part, the communists did not hide their contempt for the youthful radicalism of the PSOE which they considered tactically inadequate to the situation. Nor can one ignore the social democratic tendencies within the PSOE that would prefer to collaborate with parties in the centre, perhaps with a factional split of the UCD or see the UCD reduced in electoral strength and forced to become a minor partner in a PSOE dominated coalition. The electoral returns until now make those dreams unlikely, but they are an obstacle to compromise themselves with a better understanding with the PCE. What we can expect is collaboration of both parties in the municipal government of some cities and many villages and perhaps in some regional governments as part of a larger coalition, particularly in Catalonia. Those experiences are likely to decide the future relations between Marxist-socialists and non-Leninist communists.

In analyzing the role of the PCE, we should never forget that in no province in 1977 did it have the hegemonic position the PCP has achieved in certain parts of southern Portugal and the PCI in north-central Italy. Its greatest strength was in the province of Barcelona with 20 percent of the vote for its Catalan wing the PSUC. Even in Andalucía where it has some areas of great strength, its maximum was 15.2 percent in Córdoba, followed by Sevilla with 13.0 percent.[24] The comparison of the 10.6 percent in Madrid with the 21.9 percent of the PCP in Lisbon tells much of the story. The Italian PCI could gain 41.4 percent of the vote in central Italy and 33.5 percent in the north, and even in the islands it had 29.5 percent in 1976.

The relationship between a Eurocommunist party like the PCE and its competition on the left, the ORT and the PTE (fused in 1979), and other groups, particularly the regional nationalist left, deserves attention since those parties in some provinces of Spain have had considerably more strength than equivalent groups in any province or city of Italy, and the strength of the trade unions linked with them is probably also greater in Spain than in Italy. The Italian Communist Party has been able to hold out very well against the competition of dissidents because it was so well installed in the centres of social power in the control of municipal and regional governments with their patronage. Without enjoying that advantageous position and with the Eurocommunist line open to criticism from the left, the Spanish Communist Party finds itself in a quite different situation, even though it shows no signs of being concerned about any possible competition.

3. Extreme Left

At the time that the European party systems consolidated themselves after World War II, the Stalinist communist parties were practically the only relevant alternative on the far left. Anarcho-syndicalism had not been able to survive the ravages of fascism, having been already weak in most of central and western Europe except in Spain before the thirties. At that time, the communist movement in the world was still a single-minded Moscow-led movement.

By the 1970s things have changed remarkably. The bitter feud between Soviet and Chinese communism has divided the movement. The disillusion of the left with communism has given new impetus to Trotskyism and other independent leftist movements. The events of May 1968 in Paris and the student movement generated a new left critical of communist parties. The fusion between extreme left and minority nationalisms have generated new political forces. The radicalization after Vatican II of minorities in the Catholic Church and in the Christian labour movement have contributed to the emergence of new radical groups. It is in this quite different world context that Spain has initiated its march toward democratic politics. And it is therefore no accident that the variety of parties and groupuscules on the left of the PC should have made their appearance, and some of them should have gained some electoral support.

It could be said that the insignificance of the overall vote gained in 1977 by those groups and their lack of parliamentary representation — if one ignored the lonely deputy of the Euskadiko Ezkerra and the one elected jointly by the Esquerra Catalana and Frente Democrático de Izquierdas (FDI), the electoral coalition sponsored by the Partido del Trabajo — were proof of the irrelevance of these groups. This might well be the case in the long run, but it seems unwarranted to ignore the relative strength of the far left in comparison to the Communist Party, particularly if we look at the Spanish election returns in comparison with those of other countries, especially Italy.[25]

In the 15 June 1977 election, the three slates (FDI, AET, FUT) competing for the radical left vote (leaving now aside the supporters of regional parties within the same sector) were able to gain 1.34 percent of the total vote — 243,678 votes.[26] In 1979 the PTE was able to gain 192,440 votes (1.07 percent) and the ORT 138,364 (0.77 percent) (including its vote on the UNAI list) compared to 80,121 of the AET in 1977. If we add the 84,605 (0.47 percent) of the Movimiento Comunista-Organización de Izquierda Comunista (MC-OIC) which is of some importance in the industrial north, the three main groups represent 415,679 votes (2.31 percent of the vote). (See Table 15.)

These figures compare favorably with the 555,980 votes (1.54 percent) the Democrazia Proletaria — a coalition of similar parties — obtained in the 1976 parliamentary election in Italy. More significant than the respective share in the electorate is the fact that those groups in Italy represented only 4.41 percent of the PCI electorate, while their equivalent in Spain would represent in 1977 14.72 percent of the PCE-PSUC electorate, and in 1979, 20.87 percent. There can be little doubt that the groups to the left of the PC in Italy do not constitute a significant competitor for the PCI, but that similar groups in Spain cannot be ignored by the PCE. It remains to be seen if the fusion of

TABLE 15
Competition between the PCE and the Parties to its Left in 1979 and 1977
Votes for FDI-PTE, AET-ORT, FUT, MC-OIC and PCE

	1979 ORT + PTE %	1979 PTE %	1979 ORT %	1979 MC-OIC %	1979 PCE %	1977 FDI %	1977 AET %	1977 FUT %	1977 PCE %
Sevilla	5.44	3.89	1.55	0.15	15.76	2.86	0.27	0.09	12.98
Zaragoza	5.16	4.60	0.56	0.64	7.86	1.98	0.38	—	5.07
Navarra	4.27	—	4.27	1.15	2.19	2.54	4.98	0.31	2.41
Cádiz	3.20	3.20	—	0.25	12.63	2.62	—	0.07	9.90
Huelva	2.91	0.59	2.91	0.27	6.92	0.51	1.68	—	5.38
Santander	2.75	1.52	1.23	0.33	6.48	0.62	1.17	—	5.34
Burgos	2.46	1.21	1.25	0.62	3.92	1.67	1.19	—	2.49
Badajoz	1.96	1.44	0.52	0.11	9.30	—	1.02	—	6.87
Málaga	1.79	1.65	0.14	0.34	12.63	1.31	0.56	—	11.96
Valladolid	1.54	1.05	1.54	0.73	7.62	1.05	0.49	0.34	6.22
Cáceres	1.39	0.71	0.68	0.46	5.12	1.05	—	—	3.21
Córdoba	1.23	1.09	0.12	0.29	18.87	1.11	—	—	15.20
Granada	0.95	0.87	0.08	0.29	12.44	1.19	—	0.39	9.56
Orense	0.92	0.50	0.42	0.28	2.61	1.54	—	—	1.65
Guipúzcoa	0.83	—	0.83	1.42	3.01	0.46	0.72	1.16	3.62

Only those provinces in which either FDI or AET gained more than one percent of the vote and Guipúzcoa where in 1979 the EMK-OIC (The Basque MC-OIC) obtained 1.42 percent. The list is ordered by the added strength of PTE-ORT in 1979.

the PTE and the ORT shortly after the March 1979 election — and the parallel process in their respective trade union affiliates — will lead to the emergence of a stronger party on the left of the PCE. To this challenge one would have to add the one represented by Herri Batasuna (HB) in 1979 in the Basque country with its three deputies and 178,110 votes (0.96 percent) and the Bloque Nacional Popular Galego (BNPG) in Galicia with 84,505 (0.47 percent of the vote).

This difference between Spain and Italy becomes even more apparent when we look at some regional data. Concretely, in 1977 the Organización Revolucionaria de Trabajadores (ORT), standing behind the candidacy presented as Agrupación Electoral de los Trabajadores (AET) since the party at that time was still illegal, obtained in the province of Navarra 4.98 percent of the vote, and in the same province the candidacy running as Frente Democrático de Izquierdas (FDI) sponsored by the PTE, obtained 2.54 percent of the vote, while the PCE could only gain 6,252 votes, (2.41 percent). In 1979 the PCE was reduced to 5,629 votes (2.19 percent) while the Unión Navarra de Izquierdas (UNAI), the name under which the ORT ran, obtained 10,970 votes (4.27 percent) and the EMK-OIC 2,962 (1,15 percent). In no province of Italy has there been a similar disproportion between the vote for the PCI and the DP. But Navarra does not stand alone. In two Castilian provinces, Burgos and Logroño, the added vote for PTE and ORT (respectively 2.46 percent and 1.90 in 1979), comes very close to that of the PCE (3.92 percent and 3.53). In some Andalusian provinces with a radical tradition, like Cádiz and Málaga, these parties, particularly the PTE, also represent a serious challenge to a relatively weak PCE, with 2.62 percent (for FDI in 1977) compared to 9.90 of the PCE in Cádiz, and 1.31 for the FDI and 0.56 for the AET in Málaga, compared to 11.96 for the PC. While the ratio was more favourable to the PCE in Sevilla, the PTE sponsored candidacy in 1977 could obtain 2.86 percent of the vote in that large electorate compared to 12.98 percent of the PCE — a strength mainly due to the appeal of the PTE to some sectors of the rural electorate. This is particularly noticeable in some of the agro-towns of the province of Cádiz. In another Andalusian province, Huelva, the ORT was able (1977) to challenge the PCE by obtaining 1.68 percent of the vote compared to 5.38 for the PCE — a strength that was confirmed in the recent trade union elections in which the Sindicato Unitario, linked with the ORT, could obtain 23 percent of the seats in this traditionally mining and now heavy chemical industry centre of the southwest.

In 1979 the picture has not changed in the western Andalusian provinces where the extreme left could hold on to its votes and even improve its relative position. In addition, in Zaragoza, the demographic and economic centre of Aragón, the PTE could gain 4.60 percent of the vote, compared to 7.86 for the PCE. There are some indications that the radical movements to the left have been more successful in some of the more traditional areas of Spain, like Navarra, northern Castile, the newly industrialized Valladolid, Zaragoza (the old CNT stronghold) — a rapidly growing industrial centre, and perhaps in areas with an Anarchosindicalist tradition in western Andalucía.

One would be tempted to attribute this relative strength of the parties to the left of the PCE to the Eurocommunist position that the party has taken, but there is an alternative explanation which we think is more valid: the broader political-historical context in which the Spanish party system is born. Indirect evidence for this interpretation is provided by the data on the 1976 Portuguese elections. With the Portuguese Communist Party taking a more radical revolutionary position, disapproved by the Spanish PCE, the parties to its left also have considerable successes to their account. In 1976, the União Democrática Popular was able to obtain 91,364 votes, which in the smaller Portuguese electorate represent 1.7 percent. This Marxist-Leninist party obtained a disproportionate share of the vote in Lisbon, but also in the strongholds of the PCP — Setubal, Evora, and Beja. The other small parties of the left, the LCI, PCP/ML, AOC, PRT, MRPP, MES, and FSP in 1976 managed to get 3.1 percent of the vote. Similarly to Spain, the groupuscules sometimes are stronger or come very close to the PCP strength in areas where the Communist Party is extremely weak, particularly in some of the more conservative districts of the Portuguese interior and the islands.

4. The Extreme Right

The extreme right in 1977 ran under different labels: Alianza Nacional del 18 de Julio — a name that reminded of the date of the 1936 uprising against the Republic; Falange Espanola de las JONS — the name of the official Falangist party (dropping the addition of Traditionalist) of the Franco-period; and in a few places as Fuerza Nueva — the militant and violent neofascist organization led by Blas

Piñar (that had been born under Franco to oppose the liberalizing tendencies of the Regime).[27] These labels were not attractive, and no deputy was elected under them, the votes 94,948 (0.52 percent) were even smaller than anyone would have expected in view of the crowds that Fuerza Nueva (FN) could bring out to its rallies. In 1979 these forces regrouped for the election under a more neutral label: Unión Nacional. Their posters were more discreet in their appeal and colours, and UN was able to present candidates in practically all the provinces and gather 379,560 votes (2.11 percent). Electorally it scored the success to gain a lonely seat for Blas Piñar in Madrid where its vote went from the 13,587 (0.59 percent) for FE de las JONS in 1977 to 110,730 (4.96 percent) in 1979, a gain that even assuming (wrongly) that the 40,914 votes lost by CD compared to AP (respectively, 10.39 percent in 1977 and in 1979 8.88) would have gone to UN, would not account for its gains. The appeal of FN (within UN) to the youthful bourgeois voters and the polarization of other voters must have accounted for it. In many parts of Spain the crisis in AP when it became CD must have contributed some voters to UN (but less than it lost), as the low gains of UN in those areas where CD held its own suggest. As the map of the *No* vote in the Constitutional referendum of December 1978 already showed (and even the earlier one on the Law for Political Reform in 1976) the rural and provincial central Spain south of Madrid is the area of strongest rightwing influence (an average of 4 provinces of 5.92 percent). Its presence in the Old Castilian heartland is also noticeable. The extreme right is still very weak but the excesses of peripheral nationalisms, terrorism, the discontent of peasant-owner conservative-rural areas, the influence of conservative clergy, might have contributed to its continuing presence as an isolated minority. The disintegration of AP/CD or its centripetal move might benefit UCD, but also release some of its following for UN, an antidemocratic force.

Unión Nacional represents the continuity with the Franco regime and its authoritarian mixture of conservatism with fascist symbolism. However, a minority of ideological fascists felt betrayed by his regime and already in his lifetime advocated a return to the original fascist programme with a leftist component.[28] In 1977 they presented lists as Falange Española (*auténtica*) that obtained 40,978 votes (0.22 percent). Recriminations between the leaders and factional fights among the falangists led them in 1979 to run under four labels: Falange Española (*auténtica*) (FE (a)) 8,983 (0.05 percent);

Falange Española Independiente-Alianza del Trabajo (FEI-AT); Falange Española-Unidad Falangista (FE-UF) 2,468 (0.01 percent); and Falange Española de las Juntas de Ofensiva Nacional-Sindicalista *(auténtica)* (FE de las JONS *(auténtica)*) 22,497 votes (0.13 percent). The 34,312 votes (0.19 percent) could only prove that fascism as an ideological force, always weak in Spain, was even more something of the past than Francoism.

5. Nationalist and Regional Parties in the Periphery

In the 1977 election, only 22 of the 350 seats were gained by regionalist and peripheral nationalist parties. However, their share in votes was larger than the 6 percent in seats.[29] The underrepresentation of the highly populated provinces and the fractionalization of some of the regional movements accounts for apparent weakness of regional parties. Yet in the national legislature elected in 1979, those parties obtained 28 of the 350 seats, 8 percent of the lower house, between 9 parties. With stronger majorities for the large parties, the UCD and the PSOE, or the viability of an alternation between a popular front and a right coalition, those parties at the parliamentary level, at least, would not be part of the national party system since they would not count, according to Sartori's rules for formation of governments. This is not the case in Spain where the three larger regional parties could play a decisive role in the making of coalitions.

It would be a great mistake to ignore in any analysis of the party system that Spain today is a multilingual society, a regionalized state according to its constitution, and to some extent a multinational state.[30] The issues posed by peripheral nationalisms against the central state, and by the possible different coalitions governing in Madrid and in the different regions, are and will be central to Spanish politics. Moreover, the non-regional parties in the context of the politics of the periphery have to respond to the demands posted by those parties. Even numerically weak regional nationalist extremists, like the ETA (Euskadi ta Askatasuna), have the capacity to create serious tensions for the new Spanish democracy.

Spain for most Spaniards has been a nation-state, but particularly in the Catalan and Basque peripheries a dual national conscience and allegiance has emerged since the late nineteenth century and small, but often militant, minorities reject the idea of a Spanish nation and

even of the persistence of a Spanish state. Spain is a multilingual
country in which in addition to Castilian — normally called Spanish
— Catalan, Basque, and Galician, are also spoken to which one
could add Valencian if one accepted the claim that it is different from
Catalan.[31] The multilingualism poses special problems due to the
fact that the population in the linguistic periphery is bilingual in
Spanish and the vernacular, and that the resulting diglossia between
the universal language and less powerful one creates special problems
for the maintenence of bilingualism. In addition, the
industrialization, urbanization and wealth of Catalonia and the
Basque country has attracted large numbers of immigrants from the
Castilian speaking Spain that constitute minorities in those regions,
and in some of the metropolitan areas and industrial towns are even
immigrant majorities. The electoral results in those regions reflect
the cleavages between the speakers of the vernacular and those more
assimilated to the Spanish national culture, between natives and
immigrants.

The centralism of the Spanish state, its relative ineffectiveness, the
hostilities aroused by the authoritarian regime, the sympathy with
the more active protest movement in the Basque country and
Catalonia, produced at the end of the Franco regime and in the
transition to democracy a wave of support, particularly on the left,
for autonomy and even self-determination demands. They arose not
only in the traditional autonomous regions but, for a variety of
reasons, in the Canary Islands and even Andalucía. The extension of
the principle of autonomy to those other parts of Spain was perceived
by part of the elites as a way to make the privileges that would go with
autonomy of Catalonia and the Basque country more acceptable to
the rest of Spain. Once that dynamic was started expectations, both
of aspiring politicians and of the population frustrated by economic
underdevelopment and actual or perceived inequities in the
government action, led to further autonomist demands, and the
creation of autonomous institutions. The limitations in the
performance of those institutions, the disjunction between the
rhetoric of the support for autonomy and the growing awareness of
the costs and complications, have led to a slowdown of the process
but at the same time to further mobilization against that slow-down,
particularly in the case of Andalucía where the Partido Socialista de
Andalucía (PSA) emerged in 1979 as a significant political force.

The territorially based nationalist and regionalist parties, while
unable to gain a very significant representation at the national level,

are likely to have a decisive role in the regional parliaments and the formation of regional governments as well as in municipal politics. The fact that both the Basque country and Catalonia are highly industrialized regions, in contrast to other European areas of peripheral nationalism, leads to a class and ideological division within the autonomy movements, and the fact that in the Basque country the desire for independence of a Basque nation (constituted by part of Spain and of France) is a real concern of a minority, leads to the multiplication of regional parties and with it to an extremely complicated party system in those regions.

The Basque nationalist vote in 1977 was divided between the PNV, that before the Civil War had been practically the only representative of the aspirations of the region, and Euskadiko Ezkerra (EE) a coalition that attracted the support of the *abertzale*-nationalist left. In 1979 this electorate split between the moderate PNV, the Marxist EE, and a new surprisingly successful coalition, Herri Batasuna (HB) that combined radical nationalism with left radicalism and was suspect of ties to ETA. The PNV had advocated abstention on the Constitutional referendum while HB supported the *No* vote, but less than a year later the PNV and EE would support the autonomy statute (derived from the Constitution) and, HB advocate abstention on the referendum to approve it. In Navarra the opposition to the integration into Euskadi would be expressed by the Unión del Pueblo Navarro. If we add the presence of the statewide parties, UCD, PSOE and PCE, and their different strength in the four provinces where they compete with the Basque nationalists we get an idea of the fragmentation and complexity of Basque politics.[32]

In Catalonia the assumption of the autonomy demands by the PSUC — the Catalan wing of Spanish communism — the PSC-PSOE — a fusion of the Spanish and Catalan socialists — and even by the UCD — which fused with some minor Catalan parties still running in 1977 particularly part of the Christian democratic Unió Democràtica de Catalunya (UDC), reduced the political space for the regional parties. Even so in 1979 the Convergencia i Unió (CiU) gained 16.5 percent of the regional vote; it ran in 1977 under the label Pacte Democràtic per Catalunya (in which the Convergència Democràtica de Catalunya played a dominant role) and gained 16.9 percent of the Catalan vote. The Esquerra Republicana de Catalunya (with 4.1 percent of the regional vote), heir to a great tradition before 1936, could still gain one seat in the national parliament, and more extreme nationalist groups like the Bloc d'Esquerra d'Alliberament Nacional (BEAN) gained some minority votes.[33]

Galician nationalism that in 1977 suffered a relative defeat, in 1979 made a significant showing with 5.9 percent of the regional vote going to the far left Bloque Nacional Popular Galego (BNPG), and another 5.3 percent to the Unidade Galega.[34] In two bilingual regions, Valencia and the Balearic Islands, the regional parties have been basically unsuccessful.[35]

However, in three Castilian speaking areas, for quite different reasons, regional parties have been able to gain parliamentary representation: in Andalucía the Partido Socialista de Andalucía-Partido Andaluz (PSA) (11.0 percent of the Andalusian vote) as a party of an underdeveloped region protesting against the centre, in Aragón the Partido Aragonés Regionalista (PAR) with 5.9 percent of the regional vote, and the Unión del Pueblo Canario (UPC) (with 10.7 percent of the regional vote) expressing the grievances of faraway Canary Islands with a leftist and even secessionist appeal.[36] One of the most confusing recent developments is the threat of the PSA to compete in Catalonia with the parties of the left for the Andalusian immigrant vote.

The analysis presented of politics at the national level is only part of the total picture and it would be a great mistake to take the part for the whole. Some of the most serious problems for the consolidation of Spanish democracy are the result of the Basque problem complicated by the competition of three major parties and coalitions and the presence of an effective terrorist organization, Euskadi Ta Askatasuna (ETA), that to some extent enjoys the sympathies of one of the party coalitions, Herri Batasuna, in its struggle for independence and revolutionary change in Basque society.

Regional politics in Spain, like in Italy and Germany, will serve as a basis of power for parties not represented in the central government, and their support for regional aspirations is as much a function of this as of the strength of their regionalist commitments. Whoever is in power, the outs are likely to be stronger advocates of regionalism than the ins at the central government. One consequence of this is that the outs are more likely to make coalitions with, and support the aspirations of, the nationalist and regionalist parties.

IV. THE SOCIAL BASIS OF POLITICAL PARTIES

It goes beyond the scope of this chapter to analyze in depth the relationship between the social structure and the political behaviour in the new democracy, particularly since we would have to take into account not only nationwide but regional parties in view of the competition between national and regional parties to present the complete picture.[37] Here we shall point only to some basic patterns which in many ways parallel those found in other European countries and particularly southern Europe. The tables included should be largely self-explanatory and our comments will only highlight some of the facts.

As to the age composition, the left has been more successful among the youngest voters, those 21 to 24, while the centre and the right have been more attractive to the older age groups. Those over 55, that is the Civil War and immediate post-Civil War generations, give very few of their votes to the communists and almost all of the votes for the left went to the PSOE. (See Table 16.)

The majority of communist and socialist voters, when asked which social class they would identify themselves and their families with, say working class; supporters of UCD on the other hand are spread over the whole spectrum from upper-middle to working class with almost the same proportion saying lower-middle and working . CD receives only a quarter of its vote from the working class and the remainder is almost equally divided between the upper-middle and the lower-middle class. Non-voters, like in other countries, are disproportionately working class in their identification. (See Table 17.)

If we turn to the population of wage earners and salaried we obtain a more refined picture of the appeal of different parties to various sectors of the population. (See Table 18.) Industrial workers give their votes disproportionately to the two great parties of the left, around 50 percent, while the UCD receives only 38 percent from them, still more than CD that receives only 19 percent. Not surprisingly given the economic development and industrialization of Catalonia and the Basque country the working class vote for regional nationalist parties comes mainly from skilled workers while the unskilled workers, who in those regions are mostly immigrants, give their support to the PSOE and to a lesser extent to the

TABLE 16
Age Composition of the Electorate of Parties in the 1979
Legislative Election

Age	Total %	Extreme left %	PC/ PSUC %	PSC- PSOE %	UCD %	CD %	Extreme right %	Regional parties %	Other parties %	Did not vote %	n.a. %
18-20	7	13	7	6	3	4	11	8	8	13	6
21-24	9	26	13	11	4	6	—	11	25	15	4
25-29	10	26	16	9	6	9	14	13	8	14	6
30-34	9	15	8	12	7	2	5	9	8	10	9
35-39	10	4	10	11	11	12	16	8	8	9	10
40-44	10	7	9	12	12	9	8	12	8	6	11
45-49	9	—	8	10	10	14	8	11	17	6	11
50-54	7	4	5	7	9	10	8	7	—	6	9
55-59	7	—	9	7	9	5	8	6	17	5	8
60-64	7	—	9	5	10	7	8	5	—	4	6
65 and over	14	7	6	11	20	21	11	9	—	13	20
	(5499)	(46)	(394)	(1300)	(1486)	(162)	(37)	(369)	(12)	(1089)	(606)

TABLE 17
Subjective Class Identification and Voting, 1979

	Extreme left %	PCE/ PSUC %	PSOE %	UCD %	CD %	Extreme right %	Regional parties %	Non-voters %	d.k. n.a. %
Upper class	—	—	—	1	2	—	—	1	—
Upper middle and middle-middle class	7	8	10	17	34	40	19	16	11
Lower-middle class	52	32	32	42	35	30	39	32	30
Working class	41	60	57	39	25	32	41	51	56
n.a.	—	1	2	1	4	—	1	1	4
	(46)	(394)	(1300)	(1486)	(162)	(37)	(369)	(1089)	(606)

TABLE 18
Occupation of the Voters
of Different Parties in the 1979 Legislative Election

Occupation:	PCE PSUC	PSOE	UCD	CD	Regional parties	Did not vote	Total*
	%	%	%	%	%	%	%
Farm labourers	10	6	9	2	2	10	7
Unskilled workers	18	18	15	14	9	20	17
Skilled workers	32	33	23	5	29	24	27
Lower white-collar and supervisory	15	18	11	25	25	12	16
Middle level white-collar and technicians	15	17	20	14	19	17	17
Middle level civil servants	2	6	11	14	10	9	8
Higher civil servants	2	1	5	16	2	5	3
Entrepreneurial and managerial	1	—	5	8	2	—	3
No information	3	1	1	4	1	4	2
	(214)	(638)	(498)	(57)	(163)	(401)	(2231)

* Includes extreme left, extreme right and other parties.

communists. White collar employees and civil servants constitute one third of the employed in the electorate of the communists, more than half of that of the PSOE, and almost the same proportion in that of the UCD. The PSOE in contrast to the PCE receives a considerable number of its votes from civil servants, particularly lower civil servants, and the same is even more true for the UCD, although a larger number are higher civil servants, a group that is particularly well represented among the voters of CD. Managers, naturally, are not important in the electorate of any party but their vote is most important relatively speaking for CD.

We have already noted how the centre-right and the right are more dependent on the self-employed. The minority of self-employed voting for the left is mainly composed by artisans and shopkeepers without any employees and a few of the smaller entrepreneurs are found in the communist electorate. The left also receives the vote of some self-employed in agriculture but that sector is particularly important for UCD and contrary to what many might have thought less so for CD, much more dependent on urban self-employed than the centre party. CD surprisingly receives more of its votes among the self-employed from the middle level professionals than other parties, particularly the

UCD. Professionals compared to other self-employed in agriculture or business are also important for the PSOE. The so-called cultural workers to which the PCE directs so much of its efforts, at least to the extent that they are self-employed and even those that are employed, have apparently not responded.

A monographic study by Víctor Pérez Díaz[38] based on a large survey among industrial workers, white collar employees, and technicians allows a comparison of their political behaviour in 1977. Around one-fifth of foremen and workers at different levels gave their votes to the UCD. Fewer foremen than other workers supported the communists and slightly more of the skilled workers gave them their support. The PCE-PSUC had its greatest success among skilled workers but the difference with the less skilled and the unskilled workers was not too marked. White collar employees at the upper and the lower levels gave around one-third of their votes to the UCD, slightly less among the lower than upper level employees. A little over 1 in 10 voted for the communists and among the lower white collar employees, the PSOE was the strongest party while among the upper white collar employees it received somewhat over one-fifth of the votes. AP was gaining support only among the upper level technicians, 9 percent.

The data on the standard of living of the voters of different parties do not differentiate them very clearly, practically every one has a refrigerator, around 90 percent of the supporters of all parties own a television set, close to 85 percent have baths or a shower, with only the less urban UCD slightly below. (See Table 19.) Home ownership is somewhat higher among the CD voters and those of UCD (perhaps because of the rural component of its electorate) and among the voters of regional parties whose standard of living tends to be the highest among all the parties. Some of the other consumer durables start differentiating the electorate not necessarily in the direction we would have expected. More CD voters have an automatic washing machine and a car than those of UCD, but more communist and socialist than UCD voters have those items. The PCE-PSUC electorate in terms of car ownership ranked above the national average. Two items of the consumption society distinguish the party electorate: record player and the tape recorder are found more often among the extremists of the left and the right, perhaps because both are youthful electorates; but also communists and to a lesser extent the socialists participate in the consumer society to a slightly higher degree than the UCD. Once more age and rural and small town life

TABLE 19
Standard of Living of Supporters of Different Parties in 1979

Households owning:	Extreme left %	PCE PSUC %	PSOE %	UCD %	CD %	Extreme right %	Regional parties %	None %	d.k. n.a. %	Total %
Refrigerator	91	92	93	90	94	95	96	85	81	92
TV	89	89	91	90	91	100	94	86	88	90
Bath or shower	87	87	84	83	87	89	94	85	81	85
Homeowners	57	65	64	69	80	59	83	58	65	65
Automatic washing machine	70	63	64	61	78	81	80	64	54	64
Car	65	39	34	31	49	65	59	40	25	36
Record player	59	35	29	27	43	57	50	33	23	31
Tape recorder	59	30	26	22	26	59	40	31	17	27
	(46)	(394)	(1300)	(1486)	(162)	(37)	(369)	(1089)	(606)	(5499)

TABLE 20

Educational Level Attained by the Voters of Different Parties in 1979

Educational level	Extreme left %	PCE PSUC %	PSOE %	Regional nationalists %	UCD %	CD %	Extreme right %	None %	d.k. n.a. %	Total %
Less than primary	—	17	14	4	13	10	3	13	24	14
Primary	26	36	44	36	46	34	24	34	47	41
Vocational and lower professional	13	16	12	19	13	11	6	14	10	13
Secondary academic elementary	9	7	9	11	7	7	8	10	6	8
completed	24	10	8	10	7	13	22	12	5	9
Middle level professional	18	10	6	9	6	12	14	5	1	7
University or higher technical	11	5	4	9	4	9	16	9	2	6
No information	—	2	2	1	1	2	3	1	1	2
	(46)	(394)	(1300)	(369)	(1486)	(162)	(37)	(1089)	(606)	(5499)

are reflected in these differences. Again, on these items, the supporters of the regional parties stand out for the high level of living. Obviously, the quality, date and make of the consumer durables would differentiate the electorate but the overall picture is one of an advanced industrial society in which most of the population has acquired some of the amenities and symbols of consumer society irrespective of ideology.[39]

The two parties with the largest number of voters have also the largest proportion of those with only primary or less than primary education, the PSOE thanks to its working class following and the UCD to its rural and female electorates. (See Table 20). The PCE-PSUC seems to receive a slightly larger share of its votes from those in the middle levels, particularly vocational and middle level professional education, than the PSOE. It is, however, the extreme left that seems to be most dependent on those groups. The electorates of UCD and CD differ in the number of those with higher levels of education, a fact that in part can be accounted for by the more feminine electorate of UCD. If we are to trust our data the extreme right finds its supporters in the educationally most privileged. The economic development of Catalonia and the Basque country is reflected in the larger proportion of those with middle and higher levels of education in the electorate of regional nationalist parties. Similarly to other countries those not reporting the party for which they voted are found disproportionately among those without or only primary education.

Spain is a multilingual society even when practically the whole population with the exception of some peasants and fishermen speaks Spanish, whatever other language they might speak. Those fluent in one of the languages of the periphery, Basque, Catalan, Valencian and Galician, particularly the Basque speakers but also the Catalans, give considerable support to regional parties, one of whose vindications has been the official recognition of those languages. (See Table 21.) The left in Catalonia has given considerable support to the autonomy aspirations and the linguistic rights, and the same has been true in other regions. But on the other side, the immigrant Castilian speaking population in the two advanced industrial regions Catalonia and the Basque country has given much of its support to the parties of the left, particularly the PSOE. UCD has until now been the hegemonic party in Galicia

TABLE 21
Languages Spoken by the Voters of Different Parties (1979)

	Extreme left %	PCE PSUC %	PSOE %	Regional-nationalist %	UCD %	CD %	Extreme right %	None %	n.a. %	Total %
Catalan	11	27	17	30	14	6	8	16	20	18
Valencian	7	12	11	7	8	3	3	9	12	9
Basque	9	1	1	18	1	1	—	2	1	2
Galician	9	4	7	6	11	12	8	11	8	9
Speaking a non-Castilian language*	36	44	36	61	34	22	19	38	41	38
	(46)	(394)	(1300)	(396)	(1486)	(162)	(37)	(1089)	(606)	(5499)

* There are regionalist parties in Castilian-speaking parts of Spain and not all the voters of nationalist parties in the periphery speak the vernacular language.

Note: There may be some duplication of languages spoken, since for example, Galician immigrants in Catalonia might also speak Catalan.

sharing their vote with AP and now CD, and therefore it should not come as a surprise that those two parties should have the largest proportion of speakers of Galician in their electorate. The extreme right has been the most decided advocate of unity understood as centralism and therefore it is no surprise that few of its voters should speak anything but Castilian.

All the parties, except those with only a regional appeal, depend for the majority of votes on Castilian speakers rather than on those speaking one of the four other languages. The strength of the PSUC in Catalonia and particularly among Catalan speaking population and the relative success of the PCE in the region of Valencia account for the importance of those speaking languages other than Castilian in the communist electorate by comparison with the socialist constituency.

Spanish parties with the exception of the extreme right, and to some extent of CD, have a multilingual electorate, including UCD due to the importance of the Galician and the Catalan speaking vote in Catalonia and the Balearic Islands for the party. Contrary to the image that the claims of the nationalist linguistic-minority parties might create, the major national parties receive between 44 and 22 percent of their vote from those speaking languages other than Castilian. The support for regional autonomy of PCE, PSOE and UCD therefore is not incongruent with the composition of the electorate. The greater initial commitment of the PCE-PSUC to the recognition of the multi-national character of Spanish society has paid off.

The small proportion of Basques in the electorate and even the smaller one of Basque speakers means that none of the major parties depends heavily on their vote and even the PSOE that has some strength among the working class of the Basque country, gains most of its votes there among the non-Basque-speaking immigrant population. Language is one factor differentiating the major parties but it only is central to the understanding of the regional party systems.

V. MEDITERRANEAN COMPARISONS

1. Portugal

There are fundamental differences between the Portuguese and the Spanish party system.[40] No Spanish party has been able until now to obtain the 37.9 percent vote that the Portuguese Socialists obtained in 1975, since the UCD had in 1979 only 35.07 percent, even though those votes assured 48 percent of the seats. Both the Spanish and the Portuguese are multiparty systems, but in Spain there are regional parties with over 5 percent of the vote (some 10 percent in 1979), and 19 of the 350 seats in the lower house in 1977 and 28 in 1979, while there are no such parties in Portugal. This fact reflects one fundamental difference: Spain is for some Spaniards, a multinational state, but for a large majority it is closer to being a nation-state, while Portugal is one of the oldest nation-states of Europe without ethic or linguistic minorities. Many of the problems that confront Spanish democracy derive from that basic fact, compounding problems that also exist in Portugal.

The Communist Party of Portugal (PCP), obtained in 1975 12.5 percent of the vote to which one might add the 4.1 percent of the Movimento Democràtico Português (MDP), a fellow travelling party, while in 1976 it obtained 14.6 percent, even after the disintegration of the MDP. The Spanish communists were less successful with 9.3 percent of the vote in 1977 and 10.8 in 1979. However, those electoral returns do not tell us much about the role that both parties play in their respective societies. The semi-revolutionary period preceding the elections allowed the Portuguese communists to assume a controlling position in the Intersindical, the trade union federation, while their Spanish brethren have to compete with other trade union organizations. The initial period of Portuguese democracy allowed the PCP to consolidate what is called in Portugal *poder social,* something that might be more than the Italian communist *presenza.* In addition, there are extensive areas of Portugal in which the PCP gained the largest plurality — the industrial province of Setubal south of Lisbon, and two agricultural provinces: Evora and Beja where they obtained over 40 percent of the vote and made considerable gains between the two elections. There are no comparable communist strongholds in any Spanish province. On the other hand, the PCP finds itself much more isolated than the PCE. Its implication in a military coup in December 1975, from which it backed away just in time, and its whole bid for hegemony in the course of 1975, has created widespread distrust, not only right of centre, but in the Portuguese Socialist Party. And it seems doubtful that they would be *koalitions-fähig* in the near future.

The PCE has increasingly made credible its extreme Eurocommunist position, renouncing Leninism and many of the symbols of the past, and following a policy aimed at the consolidation of the institutions even if it might represent the consolidation of Suárez in power. The communist strategy in Spain might not pay that much in votes, but it certainly makes old fashioned anti-communism more difficult. And although there is bitter competition between the socialists and the communists in the trade union field, between the CCOO, whose vote in recent trade union elections is around 35 percent, if not more, and the UGT that according to the non-final and non-official figures ranges between 31 and 22 percent, there is more room for cooperation on specific issues among the left in Spain than in Portugal. As we predicted the electoral geography presented the parties of the left with the dilemma of either conceding to the UCD a number of mayor seats or to move toward a popular front type of cooperation to add the vote of socialists and communists that together constituted a majority in the municipal councils in many Spanish cities and towns after the municipal elections in 1979. The electoral geography of Portugal does not impose so often the opportunity and need for such a cooperation of the left.[41]

Another major difference between the two party systems is that after the initial outlawing (after the ouster of Spinola) of emerging right-wing parties, no Portuguese party claims continuity and loyalty to the past, like the AP did. The Portuguese party system is less centrifugal and fits less the model of extreme polarized multiparty system of Sartori. In fact, as long as the PCP remains isolated, the Portuguese Socialist Party (PS) with 35 percent of the vote, the Social Democratic Party (PPD) at 24 percent and the Centro Democrático Social (CDS) close to being a Christian democratic party with its 15.9 percent, should have been able to operate closer to the model of limited multiparty systems like those of northern and central European countries. However, Portuguese parties have shown great reluctance to play such a game and the PS has preferred to force other parties to accept a minority socialist government, (even though CDS entered it indirectly). It is difficult to conceive that in

Spain, the two dominant parties in the centre of the spectrum, the PSOE and the UCD, will limit themselves to competing with each other rather than to attract votes or bypass those on their flanks at the right and the left, as we would expect from the Sartori model of extreme polarized multipartism. There was a moment in which it seemed as if some PSOE leaders were thinking of attempting to bypass the PCE on the left.

It is hard to say if the hegemonic position of the moderate parties in Portugal north of the Tejo, the most populated parts of the country, and the concentration of the communist strength in a few districts south of Lisbon, is a source of stability or instability. Certainly the weakness of the left extremists north of Lisbon in the crucial year 1975, made it impossible to think of a grab at power without the risk of civil war and a commune in Lisbon. The geographic distribution of the strength of parties in Portugal however, can produce a polarization in the country and provides the right with a strong demographic base in the north. The greater urbanization of Spain, the presence of industrial centres in almost all the regions of the country, and the more even spread of the leftist vote, excludes a confrontation with well-defined geographic boundaries. It forces all parties in the future regional governments to work closer together and perhaps a greater national political integration, if we leave aside the strong position of the Basque nationalist parties in two of the three Basque provinces.

2. Italy

The party systems of Italy and Spain show many points of similarity and potential convergence, despite two important differences; the absence of a Christian democratic party and the presence of regional-autonomist and nationalist parties in Spain.[42] We should compare the Spanish party system today with the Italian in the period of consolidation of democracy. One could obviously object to such a diachronic comparison by noting that the context created by the cold war is absent today, that the PCE has adopted positions that the PCI only developed in the course of time, and that the social and economic development of Spain today is considerably higher than that of Italy in the late forties and early fifties. Against a synchronic comparison, one could argue that the PCE has not had the chance in the time since its legalization to display its organizational capacity, its

TABLE 22
Vote in Recent Elections in Southern Europe and Seats Gained by Different Parties

Ideological Tendency:	Italy June 1976			Greece November 1977			Portugal May 1976			Spain June 1977			France March 1978		
	Party	Vote %	Seats	Party	Vote %	Seats	Party	Vote %	Seats	Party	Vote %	Seats	Party	Vote %	Seats
Extreme left	DP	1.5	6				Eight Parties	5.6	1	FDI(PTE)	1.46		(1st ballot)		
										AET(ORT)	0.44				
										Other	1.15	1		3.3	
											3.05				
Communists	PCI	34.4	228	KKE (Ex)	9.4	11	PPC	15.3	40	PCE-PSUC	9.28	20	PCF	20.6	86
				C.Party of Interior	2.7	2									
Socialists	PSI	9.6	57	PASOK	25.3	92	PS	36.7	106	PSP(US)	4.49	6	PS	22.6	104
										PSOE	29.38	118			
Other left	PR	1.1	4										MRG	2.1	10
Centre left	PSDI	3.4	15				PPD	25.2	71	ASD	0.75				
	PRI	3.1	14												
Regional and Nationalist parties	Svp	0.5	2							EE	0.34	1			
	Valle d'Aosta	0.2	1							PNV	1.70	8			
										EC	0.74	1			
										PDC	3.73	11			
										UDC-CC	0.92	2			
										Galician parties	0.28				

TABLE 2 (continued)

Ideological Tendency:	Italy June 1976		Greece November 1977		Portugal May 1976		Spain June 1977		France March 1978	
	Vote %	Seats	Vote %	Seats	Vote %	Seats	Vote %	Seats	Vote %	Seats
Centre Christian democrats	DC 38.7	262			CDS 16.7	41	FDC 1.41			
Other			Centre Union 12.0	15			UCD 34.8	167	Soutien du Pres. Rep. 2.4	4
			Nea-Democratia 41.9	173					UDF 21.5	137
Right	PLI 1.3	5			PPM 0.5		AP 8.4	16	RPR 22.6	149
Extreme right	MSI-DN 6.1	35	EDE 6.8	5			3 groups 0.61		0.9	
Other parties									Ecologists 2.1	
									Other 1.2	
Total 100% of vote		629		300		259		350		491

ability to build broad alliances, its skill in penetrating a wide range of institutions and social structures, and that important factors like the regionalization of Spanish government have not yet had all the consequences for the party system that have already manifested themselves in Italy.

If we take the elections to the Constituent Assembly in 1946, a few important differences with Spain stand out. The Italian communists were able to start with twice as many votes as in Spain: 18.9 percent. Should the PCE grow over the next 30 years at the same rate as the PCI, it would reach 16.9 percent. But such an extrapolation is unwarranted given the different historical and political context. We should not forget that the PCI grew very slowly in the beginning, but made a major stride between 1972 and 1976, and that therefore the period of expansion of the PCE might be reduced. It could be argued that the PSOE with its 29.4 percent of the vote has started more auspiciously than the PSI, with 20.7 percent in 1946, and that it might avoid the costly split between PSI and PSDI in 1953 that reduced the combined vote of the socialist parties to 16.2 percent, which the reunited the PSU would not attain in 1968 with 14.5 percent and in 1976 was reduced to 13 percent. It is unlikely, but it cannot be excluded, that the PSOE, which shows many similarities with the PSI in its origins and past history, would suffer thè same fate.

If we turn to the other side of the political spectrum, the democratic parties writing a new Italian constitution in the Constituente faced an opposition on the right of similar proportions to the strength of AP, even when divided between monarchists, 2.8 percent, and Uomo Qualanque with 5.2 percent. However, AP has been more a system party than either of those rightist opposition parties in Italy. The neofacists in Spain could only obtain 0.6 percent of the vote, but in Italy in 1948 obtained 2 percent and reached a maximum of 5.8 in 1953. Today the rightwing opposition, the Destra Nazionale, obtains 6.1 percent of the vote. Were Spain to follow the Italian model, the challenge to the system from the extreme right would not be very significant (even after its vote rose to 2.1 percent in 1979). But perhaps we should learn not to be over optimistic since for many sectors of society, the Franco period is associated with economic development and order while fascism and even the monarchy were associated with war and defeat. In addition, the problems created by the peripheral nationalisms might fuel the fires of the extreme right.

In the middle of the political spectrum, the initial situation in Italy shows considerable dispersion with the presence of a left liberal democratic tradition, represented by the PRI (Partito Repubblicano Italiano) with 4.4 percent and the rightwing liberalism represented by the PLI (Partito Liberale Italiano), led by prominent personalities, among them the first president of the republic, Luigi Einaudi, with 6.8 percent. These two political formations are absent from the Spanish scene and integrated to some extent into the UCD, that as a secular party could encompass those tendencies. Rightwing liberalism in Italy has almost continuously lost support, being reduced today to 1.3 percent of the electorate. One difference in the Italian situation was the prominent role played by these minor parties, among them the small but illustrious Partito d'Azione, with their personalities in the constitution-making process. In a sense, their absence in the Spanish constituent Cortes might have been a loss, but on the other hand, it might well represent an advantage for the stability of governments compared to Italy where their particular demands and issues have often been a cause of government crisis.

In 1946 the DC started with the largest plurality, 35.2 percent of the vote, and came to play a dominant role in the Italian political system. In many respects, the UCD with a comparable vote, 34.8 percent in 1977 and 35.0 in 1979, is playing a similar role. It could be argued that the UCD is the functional equivalent to the DC in the building of Spanish democracy, but we would rather argue that it is a functional alternative. The two parties are comparable in many respects, but quite different in a crucial one. The UCD in contrast to the DC, in spite of the Christian democratic component in the founding group of leaders, is not defined as a religiously oriented party. It is not a party that has to act fully in accordance with the Church and its interests, even though the large Catholic section of its electorate inevitably will force it to take into account the position of the Church. Many UCD leaders do not have a background in Catholic Action organizations and therefore the ties with the hierarchy that most Christian democratic leaders in Italy had. The UCD cannot rely on the institutional support of the Church in the way that the DC could, but it does not produce either the negative reaction among the secularized bourgeoisie that the DC aroused and that were reflected in the vote for the laic bourgeois parties in Italy.

It would be difficult to estimate the benefits and costs of the fact that UCD does not appear as a Christian party and even less as a clerical party. Among the costs we might note that the network of Catholic organizations existing in Italy and nurtured by the Vatican during the fascist years provided the DC with a ready-made cadre of leaders at the level of each parish, many potential party members, and gave it the advantage of the direct or indirect support of the Church in the elections. It also provided it with a working class base and a trade union organization. We should not forget the enormous impact of the Comitati Civici of Gedda in the 1948 elections in which the DC gained 48.5 percent of the vote, its maximum strength. This comparison should not lead anyone to think that today the Spanish Catholic Church could get out the vote for a Christian democratic party like the Italian was able to do in 1948. Since Vatican II, times have radically changed, nor is the position of the Spanish Church in the society and polity comparable to the one occupied by the Italian after fascism. If we were to look at the DC over time, it could be argued that the future might be quite bright for the UCD since 12 years after the first election the DC had increased its vote to 42.4 percent, and even in 1976 could hold on after 30 years of sharing the responsibilities of government, (and in the opinions of many Italians, mis-government) to 38.7 percent of the vote. However, such an extrapolation from the Italian experience might be misleading since the DC had largely, thanks to its Catholic connection, an organizational density that the UCD could today not even dream of, and the long years in power had allowed it to establish clientelistic relations with many organizations and sectors of society that assured its success. It seems doubtful that the UCD would enjoy so many years of hegemony as the DC did in the late forties and early fifties. The DC enjoyed an advantage that the UCD might not have — the possibility of establishing fairly early a coalition with other parties, with their own distinctive electorate on the basis of opposition to the Fronte Democratico Populare that united communists and socialists in 1948, and a left that could be defined as anti-system in the early fifties, in addition to the social democratic split from the PSI, the PSDI of Saragat. UCD will find it much more difficult to find permanent coalition partners if we ignore the Catalan minority in parliament which, however, could exact a heavy price for its cooperation and might demand that the UCD gave up competition with it in Catalonia. There is obviously the possibility that UCD and the Convergència Democràtica de Catalunya (now Convergència i Unió) would establish a federative pattern somewhat like the CSU in Bavaria has established with the

CDU. However, there seem to be many obstacles to such a development, not the least personality conflicts within Catalan politics and a potential resistance of Catalanist voters to following their party into such a policy.

If we look at the Italian party system over time, we can see the continuous process of growth of the left and within it, of the PCI, the weakening of the laic parties in the centre, the persistence of the DC as the core of the centre, forced to accept the *apertura a sinistra* to a weakened socialist party to assure the centre option the capacity to govern. It is important to realize that the cooperation between the DC and the socialists of the PSI was only reached after the socialists had been considerably weakened, and that they did not enter the coalition as equal partners. This was often forgotten when there was talk of an *apertura a sinistra* of President Suárez under the assumption that the PSOE would make gains in the 1979 election. The comment of Giuseppe di Palma about a DC-PCI government would also be applicable at least today to a UCD-PSOE government:

> a syncretic leadership à deux is unthinkable. It is intuitive that the core of the coalition cannot be occupied at the same time and for long by two forces of approximately equal strength and clear governing ambitions. Thus, the issue of syncretic leadership is zero sum and non-negotiable.[43]

Going beyond the comparison of the party system and party alignment in the elections over 30 years in the Italian republic, there are some other potential similarities in the Italian and Spanish situation. A fundamental one is the implausibility in both cases of a real alternation in power, with cohesive and strong majorities. In both countries the reality or the perception of the anti-system parties on the extremes and the need of those parties of prior legitimation, possible in the case of the PCI and practically excluded in the case of the MSI, make an alternation between right and left (a DC dominated conservative coalition and a PCI dominated popular front) still unlikely. It could be argued that in the Spanish case such an alternation might be closer, given the fact that the left could be led by the PSOE, the stronger of the Marxist parties. But this ignores the fact that probably the PCE has achieved less legitimacy than the PCI and might be equally or more reluctant to enter into a purely leftist government. Even though AP/CD has been more successful than the MSI in acting as a responsible participant in the political system, a homogeneous coalition of the centre-right under the leadership of

UCD might still be objectionable to large sectors of the electorate that would see in it a continuation of the past. It is this impossibility of transforming a bi-polar system into a uni-polar system that characterizes both Italy and Spain.

A common consequence might well be the searching for syncretic and transformistic politics, a disjunction between visible and invisible politics, an emphasis on consensus or pseudo-consensus rather than clear definition of responsibilities, and a policy of agreements between government and opposition like those we have seen in recent times in Italy between the DC and the PCI to assure the survival of the government, often at the cost of not governing. Certainly, the PCE would favour such a development, and this explains its decided support for the pacts of La Moncloa and the reluctance of the PSOE toward that pattern. It remains to be seen if the tendencies in this direction that have been attributed on the one side to the difficult economic situation, and on the other to the need to reach a consensually approved constitution, and particularly the institutionalization of the monarchy, will persist in the future. President Suárez in the speech in the Cortes after the approval of the pacts of La Moncloa emphasized the temporary character of the policy trend initiated, but there are signs that this style of politics is congenial to his personality. The long years without partisan strife, the Catholic conception of a *bonum comune*, even the fascist ideal of the conflictless society, have left a legacy to the new democratic institutions, in addition to the deep fear underneath all the parliamentary pleasantries of real conflict, particularly in view of the memories of the Civil War.

The highly ideological character of Spanish politics makes it unlikely that an overt debate about interests and an adequate representation by the parties of the variety of social and economic interests in the society would provide the fuel for democratic politics. Parties are conceived in this rationalistic and intellectual dominated culture to represent conceptions of the world rather than specific interests. In such a context, invisible bargaining about interests and confrontation on the ideological plane is a likely pattern of politics. Under the circumstances, it is not unlikely that clientelistic relations and *sottogoverno* will also develop in Spain, to some extent facilitated by the existence of autonomist regions, to cement the system under the surface of conflict encouraging syncretic tendencies. However, the topic of the similarities and differences between the political culture of Spain and Italy exceeds the limits of this paper.

3. Greece

A Greek foreign policy crisis about Cyprus led the military-civilian coalition to recall an established party leader of the right and brought to an end a relatively short-lived dictatorship. This has contributed to a party system very different to the Spanish.[44] At his return from exile in France, this conservative leader, Karamanlis, was able to build an electoral following that assured his Nea Democratia 54.5 percent of the vote in 1974, and thanks to an electoral law favouring larger parties, 220 of 292 seats. This allowed him to govern alone and without confining compromises with the opposition in the period of institutionalization of the regime, including a referendum that solved the constitutional question in favour of a republic. Although his party suffered a setback in 1977 with a reduction of its vote to 41.9 percent, Karamanlis still was able to retain 173 seats of the 300 member assembly. In addition, he could count on the support of the remanent of the Centre Union, a moderate party. This position of strength has allowed him to pursue a model of politics closer in its political style to De Gaulle than the continuous searching for consensus that has been the success and also the weakness of Suárez.

The leftist parties were kept at bay without significant concessions. This was possible because of the weakness of the Communist Party as part of the United Left, that obtained 9.3 percent of the vote in 1974, and the split between the KKE (Es) (Communist Party of the Interior), and the KKE (Ex) (Communist Party of the Exterior), between a more Eurocommunist and a Stalinist Communist Party, the first with 2.7 percent of the vote and the second with 9.3 percent in 1977. The more orthodox than Eurocommunist position of the dominant faction of the Communist Party, places it in a position that was quite different from the PCI and the PCE, and in some respects, similar to the PCP.

The main opposition force is the Panhellenic Socialist Movement (PASOK) under the leadership of Papandreou that started in 1974 with 13.6 percent of the vote, but in a short period was able to make considerable gains reaching 25.3 percent. These electoral gains, thanks to the electoral system, meant a gain in seats from 12 to 92. PASOK is a populist radical party that wants to stand for Mediterranean socialism, rejecting the social democratic model. Electorally, however, it depends on clientelistic ties given the lower level of urbanization and industrialization of Greece. One of its strengths is its capacity to exploit the difficult international problems of Greece particularly the Cyprus question, the relationship with Turkey, and, by implication, with NATO, the EEC and the United States. Its interpretation of the Greek situation links with the underdevelopment and the *dependencia* themes. These issues provide a basis for appeal to nationalism, particularly in an international crisis situation and represent a serious challenge to the initial dominance of Nea Democratia. The ideological stance of PASOK had a certain similarity with the now defunct Partido Socialista Popular of Tierno in Spain.

The Greek situation approaches more the model of uni-polar opposition, even though the left is divided in its party allegiances. Papandreou has the opportunity to engage in a frontal campaign against Karamanlis' domestic and foreign policies, and the remanents of the Junta rule. The leader of Nea Democratia, on the other hand, has no need to search for an understanding with the opposition of the type that Suárez was forced and eager to find in the constitution making period to consolidate the regime. However, the returns of the 1977 election, (in spite of his success in the referendum establishing the republic with 70 percent voting against the monarchy), with the growth of the support of PASOK, the KKE (Ex) and of EDE, the extreme-right National Front, the long-run trend in Greece might also be in the direction of extreme polarized multi-partism. However, leaving out international complications, particularly the conflict with Turkey, the regime founding leadership has a chance to create the institutions of the new democracy.

To account for the dominant position of Nea Democratia, we should not forget that in Greece the colonels' regime displaced not only the left, but a prominent leader of the right, and that their rule did not last long and did not gain widespread support. In this respect, the transition was rather smooth and responded more to a Gaullist strategy that differs from developments both in Spain and Portugal. But, it has the risk of potentially leading to a confrontation without the coalitional buffers that exist in other Mediterranean countries. In some respects, the Greek situation resembles the French.

CONCLUDING COMMENTS

After the death of Franco in November 1975, in the course of a complex process of transition from authoritarianism to democracy a new party system has emerged in Spain as a result of three main components: 1) the traditions of party politics initiated in the constitutional monarchy and strengthened in the Republic and Civil War; 2) the changes in the social structure and the climate of opinion, and the emerging opposition forces in the last decade and a half of the rule of Franco; 3) the political processes of the *reforma* rather than *ruptura* and the emerging leadership of Prime Minister Suárez. The first of these historical legacies is reflected in the continuity of the PSOE, the PCE and the PNV, as well as a number of minor historical relics. The second, in addition to strengthening the PCE has led together with the internal crisis of the PCE to the emergence of a number of groupings to the left of the communists (ORT-PTE), and new nationalist and regionalist parties particularly *abertzale*, Galician, Canary Islands, and Andalusian left. In 1976 it seemed that, like in other European countries after fascism, a powerful Christian democratic party would emerge but a number of factors we have discussed frustrated that attempt. It is remarkable that forty years of partly successful Franco rule have left only a die-hard minority claiming enthusiastically that heritage, and only a minority on the right linking explicitly with its last attempts of liberalization or transformation of the regime but incorporating itself into the new democratic order (AP). Undoubtedly, the experience and memory of the Civil War and the politics in the opposition in the last years of his rule have left their mark on all parties including those like the PSOE and the PCE that can claim a continuous identity.

Thirdly, the unique process of the *reforma,* democratization from above rather than by revolution, together with a crisis of Christian democracy and the weakness of conservative opposition, has led to the emergence of a new laic centre-right party under the personal leadership of Suárez that sociologically is the functional equivalent to many Christian democratic parties in other European countries but also the parties on the right in the Fifth Republic.

The UCD is a unique party in that it brings together men of the younger generations raised to positions of power in the late years of the Franco regime who decided to make possible the peaceful transition, within formal legality, from an authoritarian regime to democracy and those who in different groups, largely Christian democratic, had opposed the regime.

In this complex process of emergence of the party system many parties and political traditions practically disappeared. There is nothing left of bourgeois-republican and radical parties. The proud and powerful anarcho-syndicalist labour movement, the CNT, that led a significant number of Spanish voters to abstain in the thirties is no longer significant. The Lliga, the party of the Catalan bourgeoisie and perhaps the best organized of all Spanish parties before 1936, is no longer there. The leader of the once powerful CEDA could not get a seat in the new legislature.

Looking at the party system in terms of social and ecological continuities the novelty and the discontinuities we have just noted at the level of organizations and leadership are considerably smaller. If we were to look at the electoral maps of 1933, 1936, 1977, and 1979 we would recognize the areas of strength of the main political tendencies and even of parties, sometimes with the same name, others with a different name and identity. But the extension of the areas of influence and the intensity of their presence would be somewhat different. In this Spain does not differ from other European countries after the authoritarian interlude in spite of all the changes in the social structure and the political spectrum.

More than in the stable democracies of Europe, West Germany and Austria, the first elections in forty years have shown a considerable shift of the Spanish electorate toward the left with the appearance of a stronger communist party, a major socialist party that has taken to a large extent the place of the bourgeois left, and the appearance of leftist peripheral nationalist parties. Catalan nationalism has undergone a crisis and a transformation with its issues having largely been taken over by the regional organizations of the communists and socialists and the renewed presence of a Spanish statewide party largely absent since the turn of the century. On the contrary, Basque nationalism has gained appeal but also become bitterly divided along class and ideological lines. Left nationalism has made its appearance in Galicia and the Canary Islands and a new regionalist sentiment has found expression in Andalucía and even Aragón. This presence of nationalist — even secessionist — parties, the renewed consciousness of the multilingualism, and the far-reaching institutionalization of autonomy in the Constitution, that will give continuity and strength to those parties, differentiates Spain from many European democracies with the exception of Belgium and to a lesser extent the United Kingdom. It is this presence of peripheral nationalisms that distinguishes most decisively the Spanish party system from those of Portugal, Greece, and Italy (if we disregard less than one percent of the vote). There is some similarity with France and Quebec in that those primordial nationalisms have a strong extreme-left component but there is none in their strength electorally in France.

While there has been a growth of the left there has been also a significant change on the right; it is today much less clerical, less reactionary, and instead of bitterly rejecting autonomy aspirations of nationalities and regions has supported a Constitution and legislation that has given them more rights than they had under the Second Republic. This fundamental change represented by the UCD and the capacity until now and probably in the immediate future of the PSOE to hold on a centre-left course without a split of its maximalist wing or the bitterness of struggle within the party in the thirties, are both a reflection of the desire of the electorate to place itself on the centre of the left-right dimension with a leaning toward the left and the probable reduction compared to 1936 of those placing themselves on the right and extreme right. There is in the Spanish like the other southern European electorates and that of France a considerable potential for polarization on the left-right dimension but the bulk of the electorate tries to escape from those tendencies and the political leadership conscious of the risk involved has made, under sometimes trying circumstances, an effort to pursue a centripetal rather than centrifugal policy. Without the formal institutional mechanisms of consociationalism in Austria in the post-war years, the Spanish Constitution-making process in 1977-1978 has had elements of consociationalism. This tendency, positive as it has been, also reflects the difficulty of turning toward real alternation like in other European democracies and might lead to patterns of overt and covert political behaviour not unknown to the students of Italian politics.

The location of the parties on the left-right dimension by the electorate and, to a lesser extent, the self-placement of the voters on that axis places Spain among the extreme polarized multi-party systems of Sartori, close to Italy, Finland and Chile before Pinochet. The presence of the Communist Party accounts for this "Latin" pattern, and the decided Eurocommunism of the PCE makes the similarity with Italy even more obvious. There is, however, a fundamental difference between Italy and Spain — the presence of an electorally strong and single socialist party. It is the strength of the PSOE that could lead to a party system dynamics closer to the French than the Italian and in some respects could lead one to think of a greater similarity between Spain and Portugal and Greece than with Italy. The future of Spanish politics depends largely on the options that will be made in the coming years by the PSOE leadership and its capacity to hold its own against the strong competition of the PCE and in some cases the nationalist left on the periphery. On the other hand, the ideological self-definition of the PSOE together with the presence of the PCE makes it unlikely that the Spanish party system would ever evolve in the direction of the European democracies in which a social democratic party has been a dominant or governing alternative. In view of the very different ideological cement and organizational structure of the UCD from the great Christian democratic parties, in spite of the great similarity in the composition of its electorate and its function in the political system, it is still an open question if it will play the role that the Democrazia Cristiana has held over thirty years in Italy.

It is the indeterminacy of the future electoral strength, ideological and programmatic positions, and organizational articulation as mass parties of the PSOE and the UCD that makes it so difficult to advance any solid prediction about the future dynamics of Spanish democratic politics. If we add to these the uncertainties created by Basque nationalism in its multiple manifestations, from the PNV to the terrorists of the ETA, the difficulties of articulating a central government with regional governments of different colour, and the demands of developed and underdeveloped regions in a semi-federalized state, the uncertainties of Spanish politics are evident. Against those uncertainties stands the will of a political elite that has learned much from the breakdown of democracy in the thirties in Spain, and in the case of the communists perhaps in Chile, to pursue policies towards the consolidation of democracy in unfortunately difficult times. In that endeavour the political class finds ready support in the basic attitudes of the electorate since the death of Franco and even before. It is up to the leadership of the new democracy to maximize the tendencies towards consolidation of democracy since there are also in the electorate potential tendencies towards polarization, fragmentation and alienation from the new regime that they could mobilize. The social cleavage lines of attitudinal predispositions are the materials with which the parties and their leaders can either destroy or create a stable democracy.

ABBREVIATIONS

AET	Agrupación Electoral de los Trabajadores
AP	Alianza Popular
ASD	Alianza Socialista Democrática

BEAN	Bloc d'Esquerra d'Alliberament Nacional
BNPG	Bloque Nacional Popular Galego
CD	Coalición Democrática
CDC	Convergència Democràtica de Catalunya
CEDA	Confederación Española de Derechas Autónomas
CiU	Convergència i Unió
CNT	Confederación Nacional del Trabajo
EE	Euskadiko Ezkerra
EMK-OIC	Movimiento Comunista de Euskadi-Organización de Izquierda Comunista
ETA	Euskadi ta Askatasuna
FDC	Federación Demócrata Cristiana
FDI	Frente Democrático de Izquierdas
FE(a)	Falange Española (auténtica)
Fe de las JONS (a)	Falange Española de las Juntas de Ofensiva Nacional-Sindicalista (auténtica)
FEI-AT	Falange Española Independiente-Alianza del Trabajo
FE-UF	Falange Española-Unidad Falangista
FN	Fuerza Nueva
FUT	Frente por la Unidad de los Trabajadores
HB	Herri Batasuna
MC-OIC	Movimiento Comunista-Organización de Izquierda Comunista
ORT	Organización Revolucionaria de Trabajadores
PAR	Partido Aragonés Regionalista
PCE	Partido Comunista de España
PDC	Partido Demócrata Cristiano
PNV	Partido Nacionalista Vasco
PSA	Partido Socialista de Andalucía-Partido Andaluz
PSOE	Partido Socialista Obrero Español
PSP	Partido Socialista Popular
PSP/US	Partido Socialista Popular/Unidad Socialista
PTE	Partido del Trabajo de España
UCD	Unión de Centro Democrático
UDC	Unió Democràtica de Catalunya
UN	Unión Nacional
UNAI	Unión Navarra de Izquierdas
UPC	Unión del Pueblo Canario

NOTES

A version of this paper was presented at a session organized by the Committee of Political Sociology at the Ninth World Congress of Sociology, Uppsala, 1978. The text has been left largely unchanged, but some sections, tables and data have been added to update it to the legislative election of 1979.

This paper was written while the author was holding a German Marshall Fund of the United States Fellowship that is gratefully acknowledged. I benefited from the help of colleagues at DATA, Madrid, and the assistance of Rocío de Terán.

The surveys used were designed and planned by Francisco Andrés Orizo, Manuel Gómez Reino, Juan J. Linz, and Darío Vila Carro of DATA and executed by DATA (except the fieldwork of the 1979 study executed by Consulta). The 1977 study was realized with the support of the Adenauer Foundation, the 1978 survey was commissioned by the Fundación Democracia y Humanismo, and the 1979 study by the Centro de Investigaciones Sociológicas. The 1977 study of Madrid voters was made possible by the grant of the German Marshall Fund of the United States. Their support is gratefully acknowledged. With the support of the Fundación FOESSA we plan to publish a book based on these studies.

---

1. On the parties before the Civil War, see J.J. Linz "The Party System of Spain: Past and Future", in S.M. Lipset and S. Rokkan (eds.), *Party Systems and Voter Alignments* (New York: The Free Press 1967): 197-282; M. Artola, *Partidos y programas politicos, 1808-1936,* 2 vols., (Madrid: Aguilar, 1974-75).

2. The number of publications on political parties and electoral sociology has been growing, for bibliographic references, see: Jesús de Miguel and Melissa G. Moyer, Sociology in Spain, *Current Sociology,* 27, 1, (Spring 1979): 109-112; J.J. Linz and J. de Miguel "Hacia un análisis regional de las elecciones de 1936 en España", in *Revista Española de la Opinión Pública,* XXXXVIII, (1977): 27-68; M. Martínez Cuadrado, "El retorno a la democracia," *Historia 16,* II (1977): 145-155. Some useful information on parties before the 1977 election can be found in a special issue of *Posible,* May 1977. On party programs, see: J.F. Pastora Herrero (ed.), *Partidos políticos y educación* (S.L. Minón, 1978). On the legal status of parties in the period 1975-1977 and the manoeuvres for the legalization of the PCE see Francisco Rubio and Manuel Aragón, "La Legalización del PCE y su incidencia en el estatuto jurídico de los partidos políticos en España," in Pedro de Vega, (ed.), *Teoría y práctica de los partidos políticos* (Madrid; Edicusa, 1977): 219-37. For the official list of candidates and electoral coalitions see: *Boletín Oficial del Estado,* 20, 20 May 1977 and for a list of those elected ib. n.1, 12 July 1977.

For the election legislation, see: *Elecciones Generales,* Madrid, Separatas del Boletín Oficial del Estado. Gaceta de Madrid. Ley 39/1978, July 17, de elecciones locales, Boletín Oficial del Estado, num. 173, 21 de julio 1978. On the 1977 campaign see Pedro J. Ramírez, *Asi se ganaron las elecciones* (Barcelona: Planeta, 1977); and on the posters Sylvie and Gérard I Martí, *Los discursos de la calle, Semiologia de una campaña electoral* (Paris-Barcelona: Ruedo Ibérico — Ibérica de Ediciones y Publicaciones, 1978).

3. On the continuity between postfascist and prefascist legislatures, see J. Linz, "Continuidad y discontinuidad en la elite política española: de la Restauración al Régimen actual", in *Homenaje al Profesor Carlos Ollero* (Madrid: Carlavilla, 1972): 361-423.

4. The two parties claiming the Republican heritage, Izquierda Republicana (IR) and Acción Republicana Democrática de España (ARDE) in 1979 could respectively gain only 54,887 (0.3 percent) and 707 votes. Of the centre-left parties of the thirties only Esquerra Republicana de Cataluña could gain a lonely seat with 123,266 (0.7 percent) votes, compared with the 36 seats it held in 1936 (7.6 percent of the 475 deputies).

5. On the geographical continuity of areas of strength of Italian parties, see Vittorio Capecchi, Vittoria Cioni Polacchini, Giorgio Galli and Giordano Sivini, *Il comportamento elettorale in Italia* (Bologna: Il Mulino, 1968) 44-47, fig. 3 and 4.

6. On Carlism today, see José María Zavala, *PC. Partido Carlista* (Barcelona: Avance, 1976).

7. On Alianza Popular See: Manuel Fraga Iribarne, *Alianza Popular* (Bilbao: Albia, 1977).

8. On the stillborn attempt to channel political participation through political associations within the Movimiento, see: Jesús Conte Barrera, *Las asociaciones políticas,* (Barcelona,: ATE, 1976).

9. The scholarly literature on the transition to democracy in Spain is not very significant and by now largely dated since it focussed mainly on the crisis of the Franco regime, the internal politics of the opposition groups in their struggle for recognition, the shifting coalitions of illegality and legality.   See: Lothar Maier, *Spaniens Weg zur Demokratie,* (Meisenheim am Glan; Anton Hain, 1977); Paul Preston, (ed.), *Spain in Crisis. The Evolution and Decline of the Franco Regime* (Hassocks, Sussex: Harvester, 1976); Juan J. Linz, "Spain and Portugal: Critical Choices" in David S. Landes, (ed.), *Western Europe: The Trials of Partnership* (Lexington, Mass: D.C. Heath Co.): 237-96. For an even earlier period, Juan J. Linz, "Opposition in and under an Authoritarian Regime: The Case of Spain" in Robert Dahl, (ed), *Regimes and Oppositions* (New Haven: Yale University Press, 1972): 171-259. For an overview of the process, see John F. Coverdale, *The Political Transformation of Spain after Franco* (New York: Praeger, 1979), and José Ramón Saiz, *Los mil días del Presidente (Claves históricas de una transición, 1976-1979)* (Madrid, n.p., 1979).

10. Giuseppe di Palma, "Left, Right, Left, Right-or Center. On the Legitimation of Parties and Coalitions in Southern Europe", at the Conference on The Politics of Mediterranean Europe, IPSA, Athens, May-June, 1978.

11. Giovanni Sartori, *Parties and Party Systems. A Framework for Analysis* (Cambridge, UK: Cambridge University Press, 1978), chapters 5 and 6, "Rivisitando il pluralismo polarizzato" in Fabio Luca Cavazza, Stephen R. Graubard (eds.), *Il Caso Italiano* (Milan: Garzanti, 1974).

12. There is no official publication of the 1977 and 1979 returns on elections and referenda. The Ministerio de la Gobernación has made available computer printouts of the returns by province and municipalities, which we have used in our analysis. These data do not always coincide exactly with those reported in the press and those calculated by the parties on the basis of the reports from the polling places. All sources of information have gaps and errors, sometimes caused by the computer. The figures for participation and the total votes cast often do not add exactly. In our analysis we have generally calculated the percentages of votes cast, including blank and void ballots, rather than valid votes (respectively 0.28 and 1.45 percent in 1977 and 0.32 and 1.47 in 1979), since in some cases they have a political significance. This sometimes leads to small differences with those using valid votes as a base. For 1979 the data at the provincial level have been taken from *El País,* 2 and 3 May 1979. DATA is in the process of computerizing at the municipal level the information on the elections of 1933, 1936, 1977 and 1979, and the referenda of 1976, 1978 and 1979.

13. José M. Maravall, "The Socialist Alternative. The politics and the Electoral Support of the PSOE," in Penniman (ed.), *The Polls in Spain,* (Washington: American Enterprise Institute, forthcoming). This provides interesting evidence,

based on survey data, of the more left orientation of the party militants than the voters. For example while 57 percent of the former favour an alliance with the PCE only 37 percent of the latter do so; 43 percent of the militants and 26 percent of the themselves in a leftwing of the party.

14. For a stimulating review of the debates on the spatial models of party systems and the use of the left-right dimension, see Hans Daalder, "In Search of the Centre: Some Preliminary Notes", Colloquium on Recent Changes in European Party Systems. European University Institute: Florence, December 1978.

15. The question we asked was: "Many people when they think of politics, use the words *left* and *right*. Here you have a scale with boxes that go from "left" to "right." According to your political opinions, in which box would you place yourself? Depending on if you place yourself more at the left or more to the right, choose the box that corresponds better to your position. (Give card.) (By using an equal number of boxes instead of an unequal number, we tried to reduce the well-known temptation of giving a central answer (i.e. there is no explicit midpoint in the scale). However, a few respondents insisted on saying "in the middle." Additional data on the left-right dimension in the electorate have been published in Juan J. Linz "Il sistema partitico spagnolo," *Rivista Italiana di Scienza Politica,* 8, 3 (December 1978): 363-414 (an earlier version of this paper). See, Table 3 self-placement, ideological preference and rejection of Francoism and communism as a possible vote; Table 4, on self-placement of voters of different parties in Madrid and distance between parties, Table 5 on self-placement of youth; pp. 376-377. Instituto de la Juventud, Ministerio de Cultura, Dirección General de la Juventud, *Informe de la encuesta sobre la juventud 1977* (Cuadernos de Documentación No.1. Madrid, Instituto de la Juventud, 1978). Another study making use of the left-right scale — of seven rather than ten points — is Francisco Alvira, Katharina Horter, Marina Peña and Ludgerio Espinosa, *Partidos políticos e ideologías en España* (Madrid: Centro de Investigaciones Sociológicas, 1978).

16. The data on the "distance" between parties can be found in Samuel H. Barnes, "Left, Right, and the Italian Voter", *Comparative Political Studies,* 4, 2, (1971): 157-75. Giacomo Sani, "A Test of the Least-Distance Model of Voting Choice. Italy, 1972", *Comparative Political Studies,* 7, 2 (1974): 193-208.

17. On the history of Christian Democracy in Spain, see Javier Tusell, *Historia de la Democracia Cristiana en España.* I: *La CEDA y la II República.* II: *Los nacionalismos Vasco y Catalán. Los solitarios* (Madrid: Edicusa, 1974). Also José R. Montero, *La CEDA, El catolicismo social y político en la II República* (Madrid: Ediciones de la Revista de Trabajo, 1977). For the history and programmatic positions of the parties emerging in the opposition to Franco, see Joaquín Antuña, Carlos Bru, Jaime Cortezo and Eugenio Nasarre *ID. Izquierda Democrática* (Barcelona: Avance, 1976); Jaime Gil-Robles, *FPD. Federación Popular Democrática* (Barcelona: Avance, 1976); and Anton Canyelles, *La meva proposta a Catalunya: L'alternativa Demòcrata-Cristiana* (Barcelona: Nova Terra, 1977). For an analysis of the reasons of the electoral defeat by a leader, see José María Gil-Robles, *Análisis de una derrota* (Madrid: private printing, 1977).

18. For further analysis see: Juan J. Linz, "Religion and Politics in Spain: From conflict to consensus above cleavage". Paper presented at the International Conference of Religious Sociology, Venice, 1979.

19. There are no sociological analyses of the PCE or PSUC comparable to the research on Italian and French communism. Useful for the PCE before Franco's death is Guy Hermet, *The Communists in Spain, Study of an Underground Political*

Movement, (London: Saxon House, 1974), and Eusebio M. Mujal-León, "Spanish Communism in the 1970s", *Problems of Communism,* 24 (March-April, 1975). For the present debate on Eurocommunism, Santiago Carrillo, *"Eurocomunismo" y Estado. El "eurocomunismo" como el modelo revolucionario idóneo en los paises capitalistas desarrollados* (Barcelona: Crítica, 1977), represents the Spanish contribution, that should be read in conjunct on with the documents of the IX Congress, 19 April 1978, reported in *Mundo Obrero* and *Nuestra Bandera,* no. 93. For a collection of earlier "Eurocommunist" documents, see Mariangela Bosi and Hugues Portelli, (eds.), *Les P.C. espagnol, français et italien face au pouvoir* (Paris: Christian Bourgois, 1976). For the debate within the party in 1964, see Fernando Claudín, *Documentos de una divergencia comunista. Los textos del debate que provocó la exclusión de Claudín y Jorge Semprún del PCE* (Barcelona: El Viejo Topo, 1978), and Jorge Semprún, *The Autobiography of Federico Sánchez* (New York: Karz, 1979). Useful for the "genealogy" of the splits within the communist camp is Antonio Sala and Eduardo Durán, *Crítica de la izquierda autoritaria en Cataluña 1967-1974* (n.p. Ruedo Ibérico, 1975) p. XIII. Gianfranco Pasquino, "Organizational Models of Southern European Communist Parties: A Preliminary Approach", paper presented at the Woodrow Wilson International Center for Scholars, Washington DC, is an outstanding comparative analysis of institutional norms and ideological debates. Richard S. Fischer, *The Spanish Left. Resurgence After Four Decades of Franco* (Ithaca, NY Cornell University, Western Societies Program, Occasional Papers, 1978). Jonathan Story, "El pacto para la libertad: The Spanish Communist Party", in Paolo Filo della Torre, Edward Mortimer and Jonathan Story (eds.), *Eurocommunism. Myth or Reality?* (Harmondsworth, Middlesex: Penguin, 1979): 149-88. Víctor Alba, *El partido comunista en España* (Barcelona: Planeta, 1979) On the PCE within the communist movement, see Lilly Marcou, *L'Internationale après Staline* (Paris: Bernard Grasset, 1979), passim. On Eurocommunism in general see Giuseppe Di Palma, "Eurocommunism?", Review Article, *Comparative Politics,* 9, 3 (April 1977): 357-75. And Kevin Devlin, "The Challenge of Eurocommunism", *Problems of Communism,* 26 (January-February 1977).

20. On the PSOE, see Fundación Pablo Iglesias, *Cien años de Socialismo en España (Bibliografía)* (Madrid: Editorial Pablo Iglesias, 1979). Felipe González et al., *Socialismo es Libertad. Escuela de Verano del P.S.O.E. 1976* (Madrid: Edicusa, 1976). Francisco Bustelo, Gregorio Peces-Barba, Ciriaco de Vicente and Virgilio Zapatero, *PSOE. Partido Socialista Obrero Espanol* (Barcelona: Avance, 1976). Most interesting for the history of Spanish socialism in the underground is: Elías Díaz, "Sobre los orígenes de la fragmentación actual del socialismo español (Autocritica para la unidad), *Sistema* 15 (1976): 125-137. On the PSP, see the numerous writings of its leader the distinguished intellectual Enrique Tierno Galván. The little book: Francisco Bobillo, *PSP. Partido Socialista Popular* (Barcelona: Avance, 1976). This series on parties is informative. See also the biographies of Tierno Galván and Raúl Morodo. For a bibliography of recent studies in Spanish socialism, re-edition of classic works, magazines, etc. see: Enrique Moral, "Estudios sobre el socialismo en España," *Sistema,* 15 (1976): 139-197, with bibliography for the period 1951-1976 between 150-156. An outstanding sociological monograph to understand the Spanish Left based on interviews with working class and student leaders is José Maravall, *Dictatorship and Political Dissent. Workers and Students in Franco's Spain* (London: Tavistock, 1978), and his unpublished paper, "Spain, Eurocommunism and Socialism".

21. *El Socialista,* no. 104, 15 April 1979. A calculation based on the 1977 returns gave the PSOE the absolute majority of votes in 230 municipalities (and therefore the mayoralty) and in 9 to the PC, but the added vote of PSOE, PSP and PCE assured the left that office in 823 cities and villages. The difference is the result not only of the PSOE-PCE pact, but also of other coalitions and the leftward shift in the municipal elections of 1979.

22. For the history and programmatic positions of the main trade union federations see: Marco Calamai, *Storia del movimento operaio spagnolo dal 1960 al 1975, con un saggio introduttivo di Nicolas Sartorius* (Bari: De Donato, 1975). Colectivo Sindicalista de la UGT, *UGT. Unión General de Trabajadores* (Barcelona: Avance, 1976). Julián Ariza, *CCOO Comisiones Obreras* (Barcelona: Avance, 1976). Reyes Mate, *Una interpretación histórica de la USO (por un socialismo autogestionario)* (Madrid: Carlos Oya, 1977). Very interesting collection of historical and ideological documents. José María Zufiaur, *USO. Unión Sindical Obrera* (Barcelona: Avance, 1976). Fernando Almendros Morcillo, Enrique Jiménez Asenjo, Francisco Pérez Amorós, and Eduardo Rojo Torrecilla, *El sindicalismo de clase en España (1939-1977)* (Barcelona: Península, 1978), is the most informative work. For a table showing the correlation between the vote in the 1977 legislative elections and in the trade union elections in 1978 at the provincial level, see J. Linz, "Il sistema partitico spagnolo", op. cit., Table 14, p. 411. For further analysis of those elections see Robert Fishman, forthcoming.

23. In fact, among PSOE party members 57 percent were in favour of an alliance with the PCE, while among the PSOE voters only 37 percent favoured it, José M. Maravall, "The Socialist Alternative. Politics..." op. cit.

24. For an ecological analysis in this southern agricultural province, Enrique Soria Medina, *Sevilla: Elecciones 1936 y 1977* (Sevilla: Diputación Provincial de Sevilla, 1978).

25. Roberto Leonardi, "The Smaller Parties in the 1976 Italian Elections," in H.R. Penniman, *Italy at the Polls. The Parliamentry Elections of 1976* (Washington DC: American Enterprise Institute for Public Policy Research, 1977): 229-57, see esp. 248-57

26. On the parties to the left of the PCE there are no scholarly analyses, but a large number of pamphlets, some biographies of leaders, journalistic collections of party platforms, etc. See among others Fernando Ruiz and Joaquín Romero (eds.), *Los partidos marxistas. Sus dirigentes — Sus programas* (Barcelona: Anagrama, 1977); *Saida,* "Candidaturas malditas", 8 June 1977. On the ORT see the biography by Pedro Calvo Hernando, *Camarada Intxausti. Retrato político de José Sanromá Aldea* (Madrid: Emiliano Escolar, 1977).

27. There is no scholarly or even journalistic study. For the ideology: Blas Piñar, *Combate por España* (Madrid: Fuerza Nueva, 1975), the journal *Fuerza Nueva* and the newspaper *El Alcázar.*

28. Pedro Conde, *FE de las Jons (auténtica)* (Bilbao: Albia, 1977).

29. The author discussed the regional party systems in the Uppsala Congress version of this paper and in his contribution to the Colloquium on Recent Changes in European Party Systems, European University Institute, Florence, December 1978, to be published under the editorship of Hans Daalder.

30. For a detailed analysis of the historical and sociological background of the regional problem in comparative perspective (with bibliographic references) see Juan J. Linz, "Early State-Building and Later Peripheral Nationalisms Against the State:

The Case of Spain", in S.N. Eisenstadt and Stein Rokkan (eds.), *Building States and Nations* (Beverly Hills, Sage, 1973): 32-116; and on Spain as a multilingual society, Juan J. Linz, "Politics in a Multi-Lingual Society with a Dominant World Language: The Case of Spain," in Jean-Guy Savard and Richard Vigneault (eds.), *Les états multilingues, problèmes et solutions. Multilingual Political Systems, Problems and Solutions* (Quebec: Les presses de l'Université Laval, 1975): 367-444. For the voting patterns by region, see J. Linz, "The Party System of Spain: Past and Future", in Seymour M. Lipset and Stein Rokkan (eds.), *Party Systems and Voter Alignments* (New York: Free Press, 1967): 197-282; and J. Linz and Jesús de Miguel, "Hacia un análisis regional de las elecciones de 1936 en España", *Revista Espanola de la Opinión Pública*, 48 (April-June 1977): 27-68. Two recent studies of political attitudes on the regional question are: Salustiano del Campo, Manuel Navarro and J. Félix Tezanos, *La cuestión regional española* (Madrid: Edicusa, 1977) and José Jiménez Blanco, Manuel García Ferrando, Eduardo López Aranguren and Miguel Beltrán Villalva, *La conciencia regional en España* (Madrid: Centro de Investigaciones Sociológicas, 1977).

31. On the multilingualism see Rafael Ninyoles, *Cuatro ídiomas para un Estado* (Madrid: Cambio 16, 1977).

32. Of the growing literature on Basque politics and society we will mention only Stanley G. Payne, *Basque Nationalism* (Reno, Nevada: University of Nevada Press, 1975). The survey of Basque parties by Alberto Pérez Calvo, *Los partidos políticos en el País Vasco. (Aproxìmación a su estudio)* (San Sebastián-Madrid: Haranburu-Tucar, 1977). And the synthesis on the socio-economic structure of the region by Luis C-Nunez, *Clases sociales en Euskadi* (San Sebastian: Tertoa, 1977).

33. Catalan parties, elites and elections before the Civil War have been the object of research that can serve as a point of departure for comparisons with the present. Isidre Molas, *El sistema de partits polítics a Catalunya (1931-1936)* (Barcelona: Ed. 62, 1972), and his outstanding monograph *Lliga Catalana* (Barcelona, Ed. 62, 1972), two vols. On the elites: Ismael E. Pitarch, *Sociologia des polítics de la Generalitata (1931-1939)* (Barcelona: Curial, 1977). On Catalan parties today see Jaume Colomer et al., *El grups polítics a Catalunya. Partits i programes* I: *De la dreta al centre-esquerra.* 2: *Esquerra, extrema esquerra i organisimes unitaris* (Barcelona: Avance, 1976); a well organized and documented collection of materials on each of the parties. On the Catalan Christian democrats, see H. Raguer, *La Unió Democràtica de Catalunya i el seu temps* (Montserrat Publicacions de l'Abadia de Montserrat, 1976), in addition to Tusell, op. cit. PSUC, with introduction by Gregori López Raimundo, *PSUC: Per Catalunya la democràcia i el socialism* (Barcelona: Avance, 1976). Pere Ardiaca (ed.), *PSUC: Una proposta democràtica i socialista per a Catalunya* (Barcelona: Avance, 1976). PSC Partit Socialista de Catalunya, *PSC. Documents aprovats en el seu congrés constituent, celebrat l'1 de novembre de 1976* (Barcelona: 7 × 7, 1977). For the PSAN see Jaume Colomer et al., *Els grups polítics a Catalunya,* op. cit., Vol. II, pp. 107-118. See also pp. 53-65 on another party arguing for the "liberation of the Países Catalans" the Front Nacional de Catalunya. On the PSAN in Valencia see Amadeu Fabregat, *Partits polítics al País Valencià* (Valencia: Eliseo Climent (Sèrie Unitat, no. 28, 1976), see Vol. 2: 11-42. For the positions of leaders of parties integrated in the electoral coalition Pacto Democràtic per Catalunya, see Ramón Trías Fargas, *Solucions per a Catalunya* (Barcelona: Pòrtic, 1977), and *El precio de la libertad* (Barcelona: Destino, 1976). Also Jordi Pujol, *Una política per Catalunya* (Barcelona: Nova Terra, 1976), and *La immigració, problema i esperanca de Catalunya* (Barcelona: Nova Terra, 1976).

Electoral Participation

34. While there is a growing literature on Galician society and politics before 1936, there is a dearth of scholarly monographs on the present. For an informative overview see José Luis Prada Fernández, "El sistema de partidos políticos en Galicia. Una aproximación descriptiva", in Pedro de Vega (ed.), *Teoría y práctica de los partidos políticos,* (Madrid: Edicusa, 1977): 193-218, which deals mainly with the efforts of the parties to coordinate their activities as an opposition at the regional level during the transition. Also Manuel Rivas and X. Taibo, *Os partidos politicos na Galiza* (La Coruna: Rueiro, 1977). Cesar Díaz is writing a study of elections, parties and political elites in Galicia.

35. For the parties of the País Valencià and the statewide parties in Valencia, see Amadeu Fabregat, *Partits polítics al País Valencià,* op. cit., based on a questionnaire addressed to the leaders of each party, with brief biographies.

36. Oscar Bergasa and Antonio González Viétez, *Desarrollo y subdesarrollo en la economía canaria* (Madrid: Guadiana, 1969). José A. Alemán, *Canarias hoy. Apuntes a un proceso histórico* (Madrid: Biblioteca Popular Canaria, (Taller de Ediciones J.B. 1977).

37. On the social bases of political parties there are a number of analyses by Spanish sociologists: José Félix Tezanos, "Análisis sociopolítico del voto socialista en las elecciones de 1979", *Sistema* 31 (1979): 105-121, and "El espacio político y sociológico del socialismo español", *Sistema* 32 (1979): 51-76; Mónica Threlfall, "El socialismo y el electorado femenino", *Sistema* 32 (1979): 19-34; Enrique Gomariz, "El espacio electoral del PSOE", *Leviatán,* II Epoca, 1 (1978): 99-115.

38. Víctor M. Pérez Díaz, "Clase obrera y organizaciones obreras en la España de hoy; política y vida sindical", *Sistema* 32 (1979): 3-18.

39. On the social bases and attitudes of the PCE-PSUC electorate and that of the PSOE, see a forthcoming essay by the author, presented at a Conference on Eurocommunism held at the City University of New York.

40. On the Portuguese party system and elections see the excellent ecological-statistical study and factorial analysis of party language, by Jorge Gaspar and Nuno Vitorino, *As Eleiçoes de 25 de Abril. Geografia e Imagem dos Partidos* (Lisboa: Horizonte, 1976). Instituto Superior Económico e Social, "Eleiços 1976. Assembleia da República", *Economia e Sociologia (Estudos Eborenses),* 21-22 (1976). *Eleições '75 (Primeras Eleiçoes Livres). O Programa do M.F.A. e dos Partidos Politicos* (Lisbon; Acropole, 1975). Maria Emilia Arroz et al., *Elceições Legislativas -algunos aspectos regionais* (Lisbon: Horizonte, 1977).

41. Preliminary evidence for the much closer competition in terms of the geographical location of their respective electorates in Spain than in Portugal of communists and socialists can be found in the fact that the correlation between the PS and the PCP vote was only 0.40 (in 1976) and that between the PSOE and the PCE vote, at the provincial level (in 1977) was 0.55. For the Portuguese data see Gaspar and Vitorino, op.cit.

42. On Italian elections see Howard R. Penniman (ed.), *Italy at the Polls,* op.cit., and Arturo Parisi and Gianfranco Pasquino (ed.), *Continuità e mutamento elettorale in Italia,* (Bologna: Il Mulino, 1977).

43. Giuseppe di Palma, "Italia Portogallo, Spagna: ipotesi su tre regimi alla prova", *Prospettive Settanta* (January-March 1977): 42-61; and his unpublished papers: "Italy: Transitions" presented at the panel on Mediterranean Politics: Transitions, sponsored by the Conference Group on Italian Politics, The Modern Greek Studies Association, the Society for Spanish and Portuguese Historical Studies,

at the American Political Science Association Meeting, September 1977.

44. Nicos Nouzelis, "On the Greek Elections," *New Left Review* 108 (March-April 1978): 59-74. Antonio Agosta, "Le Elezioni del 1977 e le prospettive della nuova democrazia in Grecia", *Rivista Italiana di Scienza Política* I (1979): 97-135.

5
Israel: Electoral Cleavages in a Nation in the Making

Ofira Seliktar
University of Haifa, Israel

INTRODUCTION

Israel provides a particularly interesting case for the study of electoral behaviour. In some respects the Israeli society is Western and modern. Although the dominant socialist-Zionist ideology reflected the pecularities of Jewish existence in the diaspora it was firmly rooted in Western political culture and expressed the cleavages of nineteenth century Europe. Since the fundamental social divisions of the society have by and large originated in the pre-independence period, we might expect Israel to show characteristics of electoral behaviour common in Western democracies. In other respects Israel is a developing country which has many problems in common with other new states. Because of its immigrant origin it is extremely heterogeneous socially, with immigrants from traditional Moslem countries and strong religious subcultures.

HISTORICAL BACKGROUND

The contemporary political system of Israel has been shaped most by the different waves of Jewish immigrants. In order to understand Israeli political behaviour it is necessary to follow the interaction of immigrant traditions with changing conditions in Palestine leading to the institutional crystallization of the "Yishuv" (i.e. the pre-independence Jewish community in Palestine).

It is commonplace to use 1882 as the starting point of modern Israeli politics. It was in this year that the first wave of Jewish immigrants (the First "Aliyah") established farming communities in pursuit of an independent national existence.

They adhered to a Zionist ideology which sought to solve the Jewish problem in Europe by creating a national state in the Ottoman-ruled Palestine. When the First Aliyah ended in 1903, the political and social structure of the Jewish settlement had all the trappings of a typical colonial culture. The 20,000-30,000 immigrants along with the 25,000 Jews of the Old Yishuv (these who lived in Palestine prior to the First Aliyah), who were highly orthodox and predominantly urban, formed self-administered communities, socially homogenous and politically undifferentiated. The Jewish society was thoroughly traditional. It combined elements of Ottoman authoritarianism with traditional community councils of the diaspora, i.e. the *kehillah* which was headed by a group of lay notables chosen indirectly by the community members. Together with the rabbinical leaders, they represented community interests.

This traditional structure was radically transformed during the next and most important period of the Yishuv (1904-1924). The changes were generated by a number of immigration waves of which the Second Aliyah (1904-1915) was the most influential. Although only 35,000-40,000 strong, they initiated new forms of land settlement and urban development. In this process a progressive division was created between the socialist-Zionists immigrants and their land-owning colonist predecessors in Palestine. But the roots of this division go back to the industrial tensions of nineteenth century Europe. The young, mostly Russian immigrants were influenced by the revolutionary movements in Tsarist Russia; they first adopted the socialist creed in their struggle against the Jewish middle classes and traditional oligarchy. In the relative political vacuum of the Yishuv they could construct an essentially socialist-agrarian society which stressed collectivism, a fair division of labour and relative economic equality. This line was continued by the 35,000 immigrants of the Third Aliyah (1919-1923).

Yet the influence of the Second Aliyah, which has become a political concept rather than a specific group, was enhanced above all by its elaborate social organization. It conformed more than European labour movements to what was described by Duverger as "total" parties (Akzin, 1955). The socialist movement of the Second Aliyah represented a way of life rather than an attempt to express particular political principles. Its socialist-Zionist ideology came to symbolize the legitimacy of the political system (Arian, 1968) and became the dominant national belief system. Its reach has extended beyond the particular Yishuv period to shape the contour of the state in the making. (Horowitz and Lissak, 1977: 130-218).

The other major cleavage stemmed from the immigrants' secularism. This division originated in the *Haskala* (Enlightenment) movement in Germany and Eastern Europe which aimed at secularizing and modernizing Jewish life in the diaspora. Not unlike the clerical-anticlerical dispute in Christian Europe, many of the socialist-Zionists questioned the legitimacy of organized religious values to control the Jewish society.

The later waves of immigrants helped to deepen these cleavages. Most notably the Fourth and Fifth Aliyah (1924-1944) brought a large number of middle class immigrants. Shaken by the economic crisis in Europe and the rise of Nazism, they sought refuge in Palestine but were not prepared to accept the socialist pioneering style of the Second and Third Aliyah.

One immediate consequence of the later immigrations was the alteration of the rural-urban balance of the Yishuv. In the earliest census carried out in 1922 by the British Mandatory Government in Palestine, a total of 83,794 Jewish residents were recorded. By 1948 there were about 650,000. This spectacular growth occured in urban settlements. In 1945 85 percent of the Jewish population was urban and this pattern of settlement has not changed significantly since independence (Matras, 1965: 20ff). The inflow of private capital, mostly of the German immigrants, laid the foundation of private owned industry and commerce.

The dominant pioneering ideology of the "founding fathers," which emphasized the supremacy of collective goals over individual needs clashed with the liberal-bourgeois outlook which preached the primacy of individual rights and freedom of economic enterprise. The most serious challenge to the dominance of the socialists came with the political crystallization of the liberal forces known as the *Ezrachim* (civilian) group (Horowitz and Lissak, 1971). There political existence has sustained the left-right cleavage in Israeli politics.

The demographic changes caused by the later immigrations also aggravated religious tension, for a substantial number of the latter arrivals were orthodox Jews who actively opposed the secular character of the evolving society, as promoted by the socialist parties (Schiff, 1977: 38-49).

The waves of immigration also changed the ethnic balance of the Jewish community. In the diaspora, there were three distinctive communities: the *Ashkenazi, Sephardi* and Oriental Jews. The former were predominantly European; either Anglo-Saxon and German-assimilated, or *shtetl*-oriented Jews from the Tsarist domain. The *Sephardim* were descendants of the medivial Spanish Jewry but they became progressively identified with the Oriental Jews who came from the Islamic countries of Asia and Africa. Whereas in the pre-independence period, Jews of European-American origin constituted 54.8 percent of the population as compared to 9.8 percent of Africa-Asia born, their proportion decreased to 31.9 percent after two decades of independence. The figure for Oriental (including *Sephardi*) Jews increased to more than 45 percent of the population (excluding Arabs) (Matras, 1965: 35ff). The high concentration of the Oriental Jews in the lower manual sector and their low integration have prompted Eisenstadt (1967: 31) to compare their situation to that of a "backward" people in a modern and economically advanced society.

Yet in spite of this, ethnic tensions have not given rise to any durable ethnic parties. The few attempts to organize ethnically based parties failed because the Oriental Jews lacked the skills and resources to compete against the established parties (Safran, 1978: 195). It is also plausible that they did not want to divide the community in the face of the Arab threat.

The existence of the bitter and continuous "supra-national" cleavage between Arabs and Jews has tempered internal divisions of the Yishuv society. Faced with the necessity to create a nation without a firm basis of sovereignty, the dominant labour movement legalized its authority by mobilizing the various groups into building the Yishuv. Although the British Mandatory Government granted the Jewish community only religious and communal autonomy within Palestine, Zionists turned it into a proto-state, with its own parliament *Asefat Nivharim* (Elected Assembly) and executive organ *Va'ad Leumi* (National Council), with universal suffrage for elections to these bodies. To ensure the voluntary cooperation of the varied political forces in the community, a pattern closely resembling what became known in Austria and Germany as the *proportz* system, was adopted (Engelmann, 1966). Proportionality became the basis for representation as well as allocation of resources and services. Although the system was fragmented in terms of parties, the need for unity in the struggle against both the British and the Arabs, facilitated the coalescing of subcultures who accepted the legitimacy of the *Mapai*-led national institutions, most notably, the centre-liberal and part of the religious bloc (Paltiel, 1974).

The one case in which uncompromising resistance to the organized Yishuv occured was that of the rightwing Revisionist Party (later *Herut*). As well as rejecting the socialist value system of the Yishuv, the Revisionists made maximalist territorial demands, claiming the right to the whole *Eretz Israel* (Land of Israel) including Transjordan. Their withdrawal from the Zionist organization and the governing bodies of the Yishuv gave raise to a centre-periphery cleavage (Horowitz and Lissak, 1971). The Revisionists offered an alternative to the dominant value system of the Yishuv; a vague but highly emotional identification with national symbols and goals and a greater emphasis on Jewish tradition and religion. Much of *Herut's* recruitment came from the Oriental immigrants, outside the European tradition of the modernizing socialist-Zionist ideology.

At the founding of the state, in 1948 there were three main cleavages which cut across the political structure: the socialist-bourgeois (cf., Scandinavia) the religious-secular (cf., Netherlands) and the established-maximalist tradition (not unlike the rift between the governing parties and Sinn Fein-IRA in Ireland). The changing patterns of immigration since 1948 have strengthened the religious and maximalist tradition through the influx of Oriental voters. Concurrently, the growing intensity of the external Arab-Jewish cleavage has tended to reduce the salience of these three main divisions.

THE PARTY SYSTEM TODAY

By and large, the contemporary political parties represent the divisions of the pre-independence society. Taking mergers, splits and changes of name into account, their lineage can be usually traced to the historical parties of the Yishuv. They are conventionally grouped into socialist, liberal, rightist and religious parties.

Socialist Parties

Labour Party (Mifleget Avoda) — The party was established in 1968 by a merger of three parties: *Mapai, Ahdut-ha-Avoda* and *Rafi*.

Mapai, acronym for *Mifleget Poalei Eretz Israel* (Workers Party of the Land of Israel), led by Ben-Gurion, was since its formation in 1930 the most important party in the Yishuv. Regressing on its militant socialism, it has turned, together with the leftist *Ahdut-ha-Avoda* and its former splinter *Rafi* (led by Dayan), the Labour into a moderate left-of-centre party. *Mapam,* acronym for *Mifleget Poalim Meuhedet* (United Workers Party), was formed in 1948 by the *Ahdut-ha-Avoda* group which split from *Mapai* in 1944, *Poalei Zion* and a youth movement *Hashomer Hatzair.* In 1954 *Ahdut-ha-Avoda* left *Mapam* and in 1968 joined *Mapai* to form the Labour Party.

Alignment (*Ma'arach*) — a parliamentary bloc formed by Labour and *Mapam* in 1969.

The Communist Party of Israel (*Miflaga Hakommunistit Haisraelit*) — The party was formed in 1949. Following the 1965 split, the New Communist List (*Rakah,* acronym for *Reshima Kommunistit Hadasha*) a pro-Arab Communist Party was established. In 1973 the parent party and a number of leftist groups formed *Moked* (Focus) — For Peace and Social Change. Shortly before the 1977 elections, the party was renamed *Shelli,* acronym for *Shalom le'Israel Shivion le'Israel* (Peace for Israel, Equality for Israel).

The Centre Parties

The Liberal Party (*Hamiflaga Haliberalit*) was established during the fifth Knesset (1961-1965) by a merger between the General Zionist Party (*Hatzionim Haklalim*) deriving from liberal groups in the World Zionist Organization and the Progressive Party (*Hamiflaga Haprogressivit*), a smaller group of liberal, mostly Central European immigrants.

ILP Independent Liberal Party (*Haliberalim Ha'atzmaim*). Before the 1965 elections, the Progressive faction in the Liberal Party left to establish this small party.

CRM The Civil Rights Movement (*Hatnuah Lezhuiot Ha'ezrach*). A civil-rights oriented party, founded in 1973.

DMC The Democratic Movement for Change (*Hatnuah Hademocratit Leshinui*) was formed in 1976. Supported mainly by middle class liberals it made significant inroads into the strength of the Labour and Liberal parties in the 1977 elections.

Rightist Parties

Likud (Unity). Formed in 1973 as a parliamentary block, it grew out of several liberal, conservative and nationalistic parties. It is dominated by the *Herut* (Freedom) party which, under the leadership of Begin, evolved from the Revisionist Party, the underground military organizations *Irgun Zvai Leumi* and the "Stern group." In 1965 it was joined by the former General Zionists in the Liberal Party in forming the parliamentary bloc *Gahal*, acronym for *Gush Herut-Liberalim* (Block of *Herut* and Liberals). A much smaller faction in the *Likud* is the *La'am* (Towards the People) group which is a merger of three different groups: the remnants of the *Merkaz Hahofshi* (The Free Centre), *Reshima Mamlachtit* (the State List), a former *Rafi* splinter and the Movement For Greater Israel *(Hatnuah LeEretz Israel Hashlemah)*.

The Religious Parties

NRP National Religious Party *(Miflaga Datit Leumit)*. Founded in 1956 by the *Hamizrachi* (Spiritual Centre) and the *Hapoel Hamizrachi* (Workers of the Spiritual Centre) it seeks to combine orthodox principles with a moderate Socialist orientation in socio-economic matters.

AI *Agudat Israel* (Association of Israel). An ultra-orthodox party which demands that the state should be based on the *Torah* and Code of Jewish Law.

PAI *Poalei Agudat Israel* (Workers of the Association of Israel) is an ultra-religious labour movement. For most of the time, the AI and PAI operated within the parliamentary *Torah* Religious Front.

Finally, there have been a number of smaller parties whose durability was short. Some of the *Landmannschaft* parties, (i.e., parties based on ethnic or linguistic background) like the *Sephardi* or *Yemenite* lists merged with *Mapai*. Others, like the Black Panthers did not survive electoral defeat. In addition, there were a number of small lists such as the *Wizo* (Women's International Zionist Organization), *Ha'olam Hazeh* (New Force), Women's Party *(Mifleget Hanashim)*, *Mifleget Hador Hahadash* (The Young Generation Party). Generally, such lists have articulated highly particularist interests, but did not muster enough support to implement them.

By any numerical criterion, Israel has a multiparty system. The number of parties which participated at any one time in the Knesset is considerably high (see Table 1; for earlier data see Mackie and Rose, 1974: 200-207). The Israeli party system corresponds to what Sartori has described as polarized pluralism (Sartori, 1966). Thus, for example in the election to the first Knesset, 24 parties and lists competed, and 16 managed to obtain one or more seats. A decade later, in the election to the fifth Knesset, 23 parties and groups competed and eleven succeeded in returning at least one candidate. The same number of parties competed in the elections to the ninth Knesset, and the number of successful parties went up to thirteen. This was greatly facilitated by the system of proportional representation that guarantees a seat for any party that can poll as little as one percent of the vote nationwide.

But if we adopt the criterion of competitiveness, i.e., the size of the margin of votes between the largest party and the runner up, Israel had from 1948 to 1973 a dominant party system (Arian and Barnes, 1974). The gap between *Mapai* and the next largest party has been particularly large in the first decade after independence, when *Mapai* led by an average of 21.3 percent. Since *Mapai* was alone capable of forming a viable coalition government, gains made by one party at the expense of another have resulted only in the displacement of one coalition partner by another; the dominant *Mapai* could not be dislodged.

However, since the mid-1960s the party system has become increasingly competitive. The left-wing Alignment, due to a leadership crisis and voters' dissatisfaction, was returned to power by an ever smaller majority, whereas the main opposition bloc *Likud* (*Herut* and Liberals) increased its strength considerably. In the eighth Knesset, the marginal lead of the Alignment (Labour and *Mapam*) over the *Likud* declined to 10 percent and in the following election of 1977 *Likud* won the election by getting 8.8 percent of the vote more than Alignment. The break down of the dominant party system has led to a government vs. opposition arrangement. In the eighth Knesset an unofficial "shadow cabinet" was formed by *Likud* as an alternative to the Alignment dominated coalition. Accordingly, the two major parties have considerably increased their share of seats in the Knesset. The two-party share of votes ranged from as low as 44.8 percent in the fourth Knesset to as high as 75 percent in the eighth Knesset.

Still, there is little chance that the two main parliamentary blocs, the Alignment and *Likud,* should approach a duopoly of seats under the present PR system. There remain well organized third groups, most notably the religious parties and some of the centre parties. Nevertheless, the emergence of the Alignment and the *Likud,* matched by the disappearance of many small parties, have decreased the fractionalization of the party system, as measured by Rae's fractionalization index (Rae, 1967: 53-58). While Israel has a higher fractionalization score that the 0.73 mean index for proportional representation electoral systems, excessive fragmentation has declined during the last decade (1949-0.82; 1951-0.81; 1966-0.84; 1959-0.81; 1961-0.82; 1965-0.80; 1969-0.73; 1973-0.74; 1977-0.72).

There is little doubt that this particular pattern of political culture is perpetuated and even magnified by the working of the electoral system. Although the Bader-Offer PR system (see above p. 205) tends to give a slightly disproportional bonus of seats to the larger parties (Table 1), the one percent threshold still leaves enough incentive to a splinter group to compete in elections. The system has been often utilized by disgruntled factions or even individuals to improve their bargaining position. In some cases they left their respective parties, only to rejoin later as an official faction. For instance, prior to the 1969 elections a number of leaders left *Herut* to establish the Free Centre, which later rejoined *Likud* as an independent faction. A more prominent example was the 1965 split of *Rafi* from *Mapai*; it subsequently joined *Mapai* to establish the Labour party, where it became one of the most influential factions. Also, the small parties which join the cabinet coalition can often exercise political leverage far beyond their electoral strength. This is particularly the case with the religious parties (Don Yehia, 1975); the Independent Liberals have also benefited over the years.

The endemic tendency to split and regroup is sometimes traced to the political culture of Israel. It was argued that the pattern of "dogmatism and argumentativeness" is behind the execessive fractionalization (Akzin, 1955). Neither is the stability helped by the low level of tolerance in intra-party relations (Fein, 1967: 92-93). Since the late sixties the party system has become more stable. A major point in this process was the progressive coalescence of the socialist parties. *Mapai,* which dominated the system for over two decades lost its dominance due to a number of factors: weakening leadership, the loss of identification with the state and demographic changes increasing the Oriental and young Israel-born groups which

TABLE 1
The Relationship of Seats to Votes in Israel,
Eighth Knesset, 1973

	Candi-dates	MPs	MPS	Votes	Votes	Votes per MP
			%		%	
Alignment (Labour + *Mapam)*	113	51	42.5	621,183	39.6	12,180
National-Religious Party	102	10	8.3	130,349	8.3	13,035
Religious Front (Agudat Israel + Poalei Agudat Israel)	91	5	4.2	60,012	3.8	12,002
Likud	120	39	32.5	473,309	30.2	12,136
Independent Liberals	120	4	3.3	56,560	3.6	14,140
Civil Rights Movement	8	3	2.5	35,023	2.2	11,674
Moked	120	1	0.8	22,147	1.4	22,147
Rakah	120	4	3.3	53,353	3.4	13,338
Minority Lists	94	3	2.5	52,230	3.3	17,410
Others*	227	0	0	62,689	4.0	—

* Ad-hoc local or ethnic movements.
Source: Central Bureau of Statistics, 1974: (Gov.) Publications Portfolio, 1973.

favoured *Likud*. To avert its electoral slide, *Mapai* proceeded to establish the Labour Party, which later joined *Mapam* in forming the parliamentary bloc Alignment. It was in order to counteract the specter of socialist unity, that *Herut,* the Liberals and some minor rightwing groups formed the rival bloc *Likud*. Although the factional tension within the blocs did not subside, factionalism became legitimized. Instead of splitting, factions could now compete for power in a manner not disimilar to the rival wings in the British or American parties.

The change in the party system has affected the parties' platforms. The main *tendances* have been previously described as leftist, liberal-bourgeois, religious, secular and nationalist. Their various combinations produced three major dimensions of cleavage: the socio-economic, the secular-religious and the national-security domain.

First, socio-economic matters pitted those committed to social equality, collective ownership and welfare system against the adherents of the basic tenets of a free economy. The division line runs between the five leftist parties — the Communists, *Mapam,* Labour, *Hapoel Hamizrahi* and *Poali Agudat Israel* and the five liberal or rightist parties — the ILP, CRM, DMC, the Liberals and *Herut.*

Second, religion separates secular parties, adhering in varying degrees to the principle of separation between the state and religion from religious parties who seek to establish in Israel a state founded on the law of the *Torah.* The Communists are the most militant secular party, followed by *Mapam,* the Labour Party and the ILP. *Likud* is only mildly anti-clerical. At the other end of the continuum is the ultra-theocratic *Agudat Israel* and the socialist-clerical *Poali Agudat Israel.* A more moderate stance was adopted by the National Religious Party, which is generally dominated by lay leaders as opposed to the rabbinical leadership of AI and PAI.

Third, the definition of the territorial claims of Zionism and the State of Israel confront the "minimalists" with the "maximalists." The dispute, which weakened considerably after independence, has become progressively divisive after the Six Day War of 1967. Among the "minimalists" are the Communists who denounce Israel's retention of the administered territories and support the foundation of a Palestinian state. *Mapam* whose antecedent, the *Shomer Hatzair* advocated a bi-national Jewish-Arab state, has considerably moderated its position. It is only a few shades more "minimalist" than Labour who seeks to combine territorial concession in all the territories with some sort of solution to the Palestinian problem. Quite a similar position was adopted by the Liberal parties, most notably the ILP and the DMC. On the other hand the Liberals had adopted a maximalist stand by joining *Herut,* which has all along been pressing for greater militancy in securing the historical frontiers of the ancient Jewish state. The position of *Agudat Israel* is unclear. Being essentially a non-Zionist party, it has been known to hold a minimalist position. However, its participation in the 1977 *Likud*-led coalition, indicates a movement towards "maximalist" stand. A most consistent "maximalist" position has been expounded by *Herut* and later *Likud.* The party's insistence on the annexation of Judea and Samaria is combined with a rejection of a national solution for the Palestinians. *Likud's* hard-line policy is supported by the NRP which has become increasingly "maximalist" in recent years.

What emerges is a very complex cleavage structure. Some parties which agree on socio-economic matters are divided by their religious views; others which share similar religious sentiments do not necessarily agree on socio-economic or national matters. The spatial model of Israeli parties is difficult to model because of its relatively low stability through time (Stokes, 1966). The location of some parties has changed on one or more axes. For instance, in joining the Labour Party *Mapam* moved nearer the centre in all dimensions. The present maximalist stand of the NRP is another example of a pronounced change in a party's location. But undoubtedly, the bulk of the changes were caused by the two major parties, *Mapai* and *Herut*. The policy of *Mapai* has undergone an evolutionary development since 1948. Having perceptibly shifted from its pronounced leftwing ideology to a slight left-of-centre position, the party was able to expand beyond its core group support and attract a broad following (Medding, 1972: 299-307).

The problem of attracting new supporters has been more acute for *Herut* than *Mapai*. Initially it was a small, hard-core opposition party with no clearly defined electoral basis. In order to compete with *Mapai* over the Oriental immigrant vote, it had to modify in the fifties its rightist socio-economic position. However, the disproportionally high appeal of *Likud* to the lower-class ethnic vote has been only marginally related to socio-economic considerations. In fact, Arian and Barnes (1974) claim that its appeal has been mainly nationalistic, enabling *Herut* to adhere to hard-line security policies. But in order to reach the largely traditional Oriental immigrants *Herut* has progressively supported the clerical parties. *Herut* has been closely supported by its Liberal partners in *Likud* who moved to the right in security and religious matters.

The complexity of all this is staggering, but the coalitional exigency has produced some relatively stable patterns of cooperation. The *Mapai*-led governments normally included *Mapam* and *Ahadut-ha-Avoda*, the NRP and Independent Liberals. (Seliktar, forthcoming). *Likud's* 1977 cabinet was based on a coalition with *Agudat Israel*, NRP and the Democratic Movement for Change.

The majority of the approximately 160,000 Arabs who remained in Israel after 1948, whether Muslim, Druz or Christian, were organized along kin-controlled traditional lines. This gave rise to the form of paternalistic political participation in which voting went little beyond personal loyalty to traditional leaders, whose status was based on economic wealth and prestige within a kinship group. A number of political lists designed to capture this vote have been affiliated with *Mapai* and the National Religious Party.

However, the steady rise in the socio-economic standards of the Arabs with the concomitant differentiation of the class structure created a sizeable urban middle-class and intellectual elite. It made for a growing tension between the custom-hallowed leadership and the young modernizing elements in the community. This rift was profitable for the leftwing Israeli parties such as *Mapam* and the Communists, which made substantial efforts to integrate Arabs by placing Arab candidates in safe places on its lists (Landau, 1969: 154).

After the 1967 war the traditional-modernizing cleavage became increasingly submerged by the tensions stemming from the rise of nationalism among the Arabs. The alienation between the Arabs and Jews which was due in some measure to the minority status of the Arabs was greatly influenced by the persistent Middle Eastern conflict. The party which benefited from the nationalist vote was *Rakah*. After it split from the pro-Jewish faction in the Communist Party, *Rakah* came increasingly to identify itself with the Arab interests. Although including a number of dissident Jews, its image as a pro-Arab party was aided by its pronounced anti-Zionism and a sizeable representation of Arabs among its leaders (Nahas, 1976: 55-64).

ELECTORAL SYSTEM SINCE THE YISHUV PERIOD

Preparatory committees met between 1917 and 1919 in order to arrange for a Constituent Assembly to be elected by the Jewish community in Palestine. The proposal that it should be elected by direct, equal, secret ballot and universal suffrage for both men and women was hotly contested by the orthodox elements in the Yishuv, which were strongly opposed on religious-*Torah* grounds to giving women the right to vote. But these objections were overruled and the Elected Assembly (*Assefat Ha-Nivharim*) was elected through proportional representation (Schiff, 1977: 22-23). The age requirement for voting in elections from 1920 to 1948 was twenty. Only Jews who had resided in Palestine for at least three months were eligible to vote. The franchise laws created an electorate of 28,765 in the first elections. The actual number of eligible voters was actually higher but since membership in the Jewish community was voluntary, not all the Jews registered for the election. The subsequent waves of immigration increased the number of eligible and registered voters, in 1944 reaching 300,018.

In principle elections were to be held every three years, but in practice the elections were frequently postponed because of the clashes between Arabs and Jews, the disputes with the British mandatory authorities and the difficulties in reconciling the feuding factions within the *Assefat Ha-Nivharim*. There were altogether four elections during the mandatory period, in 1920, 1925, 1931, and 1944. In order to ease the ethnic conflicts among the parties, it was decided, prior to the elections to the third Assembly, to deviate from the principles of universal and proportional voting. The election was held on a curia basis; every voter could vote only in his own curia, *Ashkenazi, Sephardi* or *Yemenite*. The number of candidates for each curia was determined by the relative strength of the respective communities: 53 Ashkenazi, 15 Sephardi and 3 Yemenite. However, in the fourth Assembly voting by curiae was only partially adhered to and it was dropped altogether after independence.

The number of seats in the Elected Assembly fluctuated widely, because the basis of representation was not fixed. In the first election, each list received one delegate for every 80 votes polled bringing the number of members in the Elected Assembly to 314. In the second election the ratio of votes to members was 164, the size of the Elected Assembly was 221 members. In the third Assembly there were only 71 members, one for every 710 votes polled. In the fourth Assembly there were 171 members, each elected by 1,183 votes.

During the Yishuv period, the Assembly did not hold regular sessions. Its legislative functions were limited to the approval of the budget and debates on some organizational and political matters. In order to fill the void in its work, the *Assefat-ha-Nivharim* elected an intermediate body, the *Va'ad Leumi* (National Council) which met several times a year. Its membership which varied from 23 to 43, represented closely the parties of the Elected Assembly. The National Council elected the Executive of 6 to 14 members who acted in a capacity quite similar to that of cabinet ministers.

When the state of Israel emerged in 1948 as a parliamentary democracy, it vested authority in the Knesset, a unicameral legislature of 120 members. Like its predecessor, the Knesset is elected by universal nationwide, direct, equal, secret and proportional votes. The minimum voting age was lowered to eighteen. The Knesset limited the maximum term of its office to four years from the date of its election. Usually elections have been held every four years;

but there were a number of contingencies which led to a premature dissolution of the Knesset.

Israel's post-1948 electoral system is modeled after the list system of proportional representation in an extremely pure form. The entire country forms a single 120-member constituency. Any party represented in the outgoing Knesset and other groups may submit a party list for election. The new groups must secure the signatures of 750 eligible voters and post a deposit of 45,000 Israeli pounds before the Central Election Committee, which validates the lists. The deposit is forfeited if the party fails to pass the threshold fixed in 1951 at one percent of the total of valid votes cast in each election. In the period following independence the actual number of votes which constituted the parliamentary threshold was very small; in the first Knesset it amounted to 3,622 votes. Since the expansion of the electorate in the last decade this number has gone up steadily. In the 1977 election it reached approximately 17,717 votes.

In distributing votes among the party lists a simple quotient is used. After deducting the votes polled by the parties that have failed to overcome the one percent threshold and invalid votes, the rest of the votes are divided by the number of seats in the Knesset. The remnants of the votes are allocated by the Hagenbach-Bishoff system (known in Israel as the Bader-Offer system) which follows closely d'Hondt's greatest average technique. The Hagenbach-Bishoff system was used in the first Knesset, but it was dropped in 1951 in favour of the Hare system (the division of mandates and the technique of the largest list quotient for the distribution of the remaining votes). The number of seats of each party was computed by dividing the total number of valid votes cast divided by 121. Seats that remained after the primary computation were distributed by assigning a list quotient, computed by dividing the total number of votes polled by a party by the number of seats of the party plus one. Seats were awarded to parties in descending magnitude of the list quotients until the total number of seats to be filled was distributed among the parties. Before the 1969 election the Hagenbach-Bishoff system was adopted again, in spite of the objections of the smaller parties which were hurt by the bias of the system towards larger parties (Brichta, 1977: 30 ff).

Voters have the choice between rival lists of candidates. Every party has an accepted alphabetical symbol which is made known during the campaign. At the polling booth the voter chooses between ballot slips which bear the alphabetic characters that represent the various parties. The name of the party appears in smaller print beneath the bold letter symbols. The voter is not free to choose individual candidates or make any changes in the order or precedence in the list for which he casts his vote.

The nominating of candidates is left entirely to the discretion of the parties. Since members are declared elected in the numerical order in which they appear on the list, according to the number of votes polled by each party, the placement on the list is crucial. Most parties submit a 120-member list for elections, but only candidates placed near the top of the list are normally assured of election. The candidates that are placed in safe places are known as "realistic candidates" (*mu'amadim re'aliyim*). Candidates placed next to them are "doubtful candidates" and the lists are closed by honorary candidates, i.e., either retired politicians or public figures who want to express support for a party. The list system makes by-elections unnecessary; in the case of a vacancy the first unelected candidate on the list of the party to which the previous member belonged is automatically coopted by the Knesset.

In the list system of proportional representation, there is no competition between individual candidates of the respective parties. It is the parties that count and their top leaders are expected to attract voters. However, the selection of candidates is motivated by electoral competition. The larger parties which appeal to a heterogenous electorate strive to produce a balanced ticket by employing group-oriented representation and symbolic representation. The former "are candidates who have been formally elected or otherwise designated by an organized group for the inclusion on the list of a given party". The latter are representatives of groups "selected by a party in order to gain the support of specific demographic, cultural, regional and occupational groups" (Czudnowski, 1970; see also Brichta, 1972).

Throughout the years there have been numerous suggestions for an electoral reform. The larger parties and in particular *Mapai* have wished to adopt the majority system as used in Britain or one of its variants. They are hampered by the smaller parties, which firmly opposed any change in the proportional representation system. The compromise suggestion put forward by *Mapai* included the division of the country into a number of constituencies while retaining PR, the introduction of a single transferable vote to reduce the rigidity of PR or different combinations of majority representation with proportional representation.

However, the issue was submerged because of coalition consideration. The smaller parties whose political existence would be gravely imperilled by reform have normally conditioned their participation in the *Mapai* (later Labour) led cabinets, upon a strict adherence to the PR system. Since *Likud* is equally dependent on the small parties, the future of the electoral reform is by no means clear.

VOTING AND ITS STUDY

The only nationwide election in Israel is the choice of the members of the Knesset. In addition, citizens participate in elections to local authorities. Local elections do not differ much from parliamentary contests; they have been normally held on the same day as the Knesset elections with the same parties competing (Weiss, 1972). In 1976 the Knesset passed a law which provides for the direct election of mayors, and local elections were separated from the Knesset ballot.

Establishing and maintaining the register of qualified voters is the responsibility of the Ministry of Interior. Registration is automatic: the Ministry of Interior compiles the Voters Registry from the records used for issuing identity cards. Before each election, the Registry is displayed for ten days in local communities. Persons whose names are absent from the lists can file an appeal with the Ministry of Interior. Surveys of the Central Election Committee, a bureau within the Ministry of Interior in charge of elections, indicate that the register is not fully updated; in the 1977 elections, 74,000 eligible voters were omitted from the Registry, 2.3 percent of the total electorate. This excluded consist mostly of new immigrants, and individuals recently arrived at voting age.

Participation is made easy by the large number of polling stations. In 1977 there were 3,880 polling stations, averaging 576 electors per polling station. Election day is a legal holiday. The polls are open from 7 a.m. until 10 p.m. There are no absentee ballots. Only servicemen and merchant seamen are permitted to cast their vote outside the locality in which they reside.

Any measurement of electoral turnout is complicated by a number of factors. One of them, common to any country which holds general elections, pertains to the difficulty in keeping the register accurate because of death of voters, holidays and changes in residence. Another factor is more specific to Israel: a large number of Israeli emmigrants who retain their citizenship (it is very difficult to give up an Israeli citizenship) are included in the Voters Registry. Governmental sources have estimated that anything up to 200,000 Israelis who live permanently abroad are registered voters.

Voter turnout has been as high as 86.9 percent in 1949; the median is 81.6 percent. The high level of participation is stimulated by interest and involvement in politics, even though at least half of the respondents believed that their vote was of little importance or influence (Arian, 1973: 27-31). The high turnout rate is influenced by social norms and the widespread efforts of the parties to get as many of their potential supporters as possible to the polls (Kies, 1971). A 1973 survey found that non-voting was not caused by conscientious abstention but rather by objective obstacles. The social characteristics of the non-voters are comparable to those of non-voters in other countries; women vote less than men, uneducated less than educated and immigrants less than veterans and Israeli-born, (Avner, 1975).

Academic research on voting and its measurement in Israel has developed only recently. Following the tradition of general elections studies of Nuffield College, a study of the 1969 and 1973 elections has been prepared at Tel-Aviv University, initiated and edited by A. Arian (1972a; 1975a). Ecological analysis is relatively easy to carry out because election results are published by polling stations which fit well with the units used by the Israel Census of Population and Housing. This ecological technique was, however, used only once, in analyzing the 1961 elections (Matras, 1965).

Sample surveys of voting preference have been occasionally carried out by private opinion research centres. The largest single collection of public opinion data about Israel, dating from the mid-sixties is held by the Institute of Applied Social Research in Jerusalem. Private organizations, like *Dahaf* Poll, *Pori* Poll and the Civil Information have periodically published polls in the newspapers. The practice became widespread in the 1973 election and culminated in the 1977 elections.

The earliest University-based survey of voting was conducted by Antonovsky but it was limited to a number of socio-economic indicators (Antonovsky, 1963). The most comprehensive nationwide survey to date has been undertaken by Tel-Aviv University, directed by A. Arian with repeated surveying in 1969, 1973, and 1977. Results were published in *The Choosing People* (Arian, 1973). The data of the 1969 survey is deposited in the Inter-University Consortium for Political Research, Ann Arbor, Michigan. Other studies related to voting include the extensive research on ideological considerations of Israelis. The main publications are by Arian (1958) and Antonovsky (1964, 1972). Most recently a study of political culture based on a secondary analysis of the available survey data was published (Etzioni-Halevy with Shapiro, 1977). A more structured study based on the original outline of the *Civic Culture* by Almond and Verba was carried out in Haifa University (Golan, 1977). A number of sociological studies deal with social stratification and status perceptions among Israelis (Lissak, 1969, 1970; Bar-Yosef and Padan, 1964; Matras, 1965).

The Israeli surveys measure partisan voting by asking an individual how he voted at the last election and how he intends to vote at the forthcoming election. About 30 percent of the respondents refuse to state their party preference. This figure is higher than the 21 percent refusal rate in Italy but somewhat lower than the 33 percent in Belgium (Hill, 1974). Israel also shares with Belgium the problem of social conformism, which results in over-reporting preference for the dominant party. The reported vote for the then dominant Labour Party exceeded by 5.0 percent, its actual parliamentary strength. It was suggested that this systematic bias reflects a certain trait of the political culture whereby many people consider a vote for Labour to be a "correct" answer in a survey (Arian, 1973; 40-41).

In the 1969 Arian survey some of the parties were under-reported. *Likud* is under-reported by 9.3 percent and some supporters of the smaller parties, especially the communists, are also reluctant to reveal their true party preference. This should change after the Alignment lost in the 1977 elections.

One strategy available for coping with this problem is to employ questions which deal with party identification in general. Doing this lowers the rate of the refusal to about 10 percent, but 15 percent have no identification.

It has been customary to regard the Israeli electorate as fairly stable, especially in view of the extreme demographic changes of the country. Frequent cabinet crises, some of which led to parliamentary elections, did not cause significant realignment of power until the early 1970s. Of course, aggregate data is a poor indicator of voters stability. When the respondent's vote in the 1965 elections and their intended vote in the 1969 election was compared, it was found that the floating vote has not been extensive. Out of the sample of 1,095 only 20 percent changed their vote. As far as the stability of the three major party groups is concerned, the religious parties were most stable, having lost only 9.3 percent of their 1965 supporters. The Alignment was slightly less stable, with a loss of 15.8 percent of its 1965 voters. It is followed by *Likud,* 26.6 percent of the 1965 voters shifted to other parties in 1969. The group of the smaller parties who account for about 10 percent of the electorate are sustained mainly by floating voters.

This study is based on a survey conducted before and during the 1969 election. It was chosen in preference to the survey conducted in 1973 because the November 1969 election qualifies better as a "normal election". The 1969 election was the last of a series of normal elections in Israel which *Mapai* (Labour) won most decisively. The 1973 election following in the wake of the Yom Kippur War, introduced chance elements into voting. Although the 1973 election did not represent a full deviation from "normal" elections, it indicated a turning point in the process which brought the 1977 shift of power between Alignment and *Likud* (Arian, 1975).

The data used in the study is based on the third phase of the interviews, which were conducted during October, November and December 1969 and included 1,825 respondents. The sample covers the urban Jewish population of Israel. A subsequent comparison of the survey population with census data reveals that the survey is representative of the population with respect to such parameters as sex, ethnic origin, year of immigration, and education. The survey leaves out the rural settlements and the Arab voters. The former include about four percent of the population. Most of the *kibbutzim* and *moshavim* (cooperative settlement) movement belong to the Alignment; *Ihud ha-kvutzot ve Kibbutzim* (The Unity of Groups and *Kibbutzim*) is linked with *Mapai, Kibbutz haMeuahad* (the United *Kibbutz*) follows *Ahdut-ha-Avoda* and the *Kibbutz Ha'artzi* (The Land *Kibbutz*) is associated with *Mapam.* The NRP commands the much smaller *Kibbutz ha-Dati* (The Religious *Kibbutz* Movement). Aggregate data indicates that the *kibbutz* and *moshav* members vote overwhelmingly for their respective parties, no matter what their individual socio-economic characteristics may be.

The problem of the Arab vote is more complex. The number of eligible Arab voters in the 1969 election was quite high; approximately 151,000 persons out of a total of 1,748,710 voters. The actual weight of the Arab vote is even higher because of the extremely high rate of participation (Landau, 1969: 253). No survey analysis of Arab voting behaviour has been carried out to date.

SOCIAL STRUCTURE AND VOTING

The following section will discuss a number of social structural variables that can explain voting preference. To measure voting preference, the respondents were asked to report their party vote. After excluding those who refused to state a party preference, the respondents were placed in four categories, the alignment, *Likud,* Religious Parties and others. The Alignment group includes Labour and *Mapam* (46.2 percent in the 1969 elections); *Likud* includes Gahal, i.e. *Herut* and Liberals (21.7 percent); State List (3.1 percent) and Free Centre (1.2 percent); the Religious Parties group includes the National Religious Party (9.7 percent), *Agudat Israel* (3.3 percent) and *Poalei Agudat Israel* (1.8 percent); the supporters of the small parties not linked to the major groupings who were too few to consider separately, constitute the "Other" category. It includes the Independent Liberals (3.2 percent) the two Communist Parties (1.8 percent and 2.8 percent), *Havlam Hazeh* (1.2 percent) and minority lists (3.5 percent). Among the 1,182 respondents who had party preferences, 58 percent favoured the Alignment, 20 percent the *Likud,* 13 percent the religious parties, and 9 percent the other parties.

Occupational Class

Given the importance of the socialist-labour bloc in the formation of the state we shall start by examining the impact of social class. In its founding phase, the egalitarian socialist-Zionist ideology bestowed considerable prestige upon manual and especially agricultural occupations. At the bottom of the ladder were placed occupations which were not related to the collective national mission; for instance, free professions and merchants had a particularly low prestige. However, the continuous economic and social differentiation of the post-independence period has considerably undermined this pattern. Surveys now show that the public ranking of occupational prestige is quite comparable with the occupational hierarchy in the West (Lissak, 1970).

Using the occupation of the head of the household in which a respondent lives as the indicator of class the Arian study develops a nine-fold schema:

A. Professional, higher managerial and technical workers
B. Lower managers, administrators and clerks
C. Businessmen and merchants
D. Farmers
E. Transport and communication workers
F. Industrial and building workers
G. Artisans
H. Service workers
I. Unemployed

But even the most straightforward listing of occupations holds certain ambiguities in the category of businessmen and merchants (C). Because they differ significantly in income, education and party preference from other non-manual groups, the middle class is subdivided into two subcategories: the self-employed middle class (group C) and the salaried middle class (groups A and B). The farmers pose another difficulty. Although engaged in manual work, in the Israeli context they belong with the self-employed middle class. The manual group (E-I) present no problems in classification.

Table 2 confirms previous findings that there is no consistent pattern of class voting in Israel (Arian, 1973: 45-47).

TABLE 2
Occupational Class and Partisanship, in Percentages

	Alignment	Likud	Religious Parties	Others	Percentage of Total
Self-employed middle class	42	30	17	11	7
Salaried middle class	60	18	10	12	41
Working class	61	20	13	6	52

N = 1182

In this and the following tables: Alignment includes the Labour Party and *Mapam*; *Likud* includes *Gahal (Herut* and Liberal Party), the Free Centre and State List; Religious Parties include the National Religious Party, *Agudat Israel* and *Poalei Agudat Israel.* Others include all the remaining small parties.

The dominance of Alignment in all categories is the most important aspect of the distribution. This reflects the position of *Mapai* in the Israeli political system. Such class voting as there is occurs among self-employed middle class; support for the Alignment declines in favour of the non-socialist parties. The working class distributes its vote among all the major parties. Thus, the Alignment draws 52.8 percent of its vote from this category, the *Likud* 52.7 percent, and the religious parties 61.1 percent.

Subjective Class Assessment

In view of the poor correlation between occupational class and party preference, we sought to interpret the class system in terms of shared beliefs and life styles which underlies subjective class perception (cf. Cohen, 1968: Lissak, 1969). In the Arian survey, respondents were asked to place themselves in a number of hierarchally arranged class categories, which are here collapsed into upper-middle, middle, and working classes (Antonovsky, 1963).

The bulk of the respondents (70.7 percent) described themselves as middle class, 5.8 percent and 4.6 percent as upper-middle class; objectively, however, only 49.1 percent of the respondents had middle class occupations. Notwithstanding the socialist ideology of the country, only 15 percent of the respondents regarded themselves as working class. Within each occupational group (Table 3), voting for Alignment rises sharply with descent in the subjective status ladder. Among the *Likud* supporters; the higher the self-rating of a person, the more likely he is to favour the non-socialist party. In the case of religious parties, they are more likely to gain votes from those who identify with the middle or upper-middle class.

TABLE 3
Self-Perceived Class, Occupational Class, and Partisanship, in Percentages

Objective	Subjective	Alignment	Likud	Religious parties	Others	Percentage of Total
Self-employed middle class	Upper middle	—	—	—	—	0.4*
	Middle class	38	32	18	12	6
	Working class	58	17	17	8	1
Salaried middle class	Upper middle	51	31	14	4	5
	Middle class	58	17	10	15	33
	Working class	85	6	7	2	5
Working class	Upper middle	46	30	12	12	3
	Middle class	59	20	15	6	36
	Working class	74	15	7	4	10

N = 1111

* Percentage distribution of the upper middle class was not recorded because it constitutes less than 1 percent of the sample.

Israeli society has been associated with socialism and egalitarianism and yet only a minority of the people perceive themselves as working class. Moreover, only a fraction of the Alignment following (22.2 percent) regard themselves as working class. Labour is a left of centre party of middle class voters (Arian and Barnes, 1974).

Trade Union Membership

It is doubtful whether the Israeli labour movement, *Histadrut* is an equivalent to trade unions in other countries. With a membership of about 1.3 million, it is the largest organization in the country, combining trade unionism with a wide variety of activities in the fields of economy, health service, services, education and culture. About half of this membership is affiliated with the *Histadrut* through the trade unions. Other members come from the cooperative settlements, the *kibbutzim* and *moshavim* and there are also self-employed members from the free professions, businessmen and artisans. A major avenue for membership recruitment is the *Kupat Holim, Histadrut*-owned and the largest Sick Fund in Israel. Thus, union membership may mean many things. To some, it may have class connotations, while others may join because of the health insurance extended to members. Moreover, the *Histadrut,* both as a large-scale employer on its own and through its close association with the governing Labour Party, has quite often supported policies which were hardly commensurable with working class interests (Zweig, 1970).

   Histadrut membership appears to be a major influence upon party preference (Table 4). Within each occupational category, membership leads to a higher vote for Alignment and a lower vote for *Likud*. Non-members are much more likely to vote for the religious parties and the *Likud*. At least part of this relationship may be explained by the traditional role of the *Histadrut* in the Labour Party's organization and its penetration of society (Medding, 1972: 195).

Education

In Israel schooling is compulsory until the age of fourteen. In 1968 it was extended to fifteen, but the reform has not been fully implemented. The students have a choice between a secular school *(Beit*

TABLE 4
Union Histadrut Membership, Occupational Class,
and Partisanship, in Percentages

		Alignment	Likud	Religious parties	Others	Percentage of Total
Self-employed middle class	Member, Histadrut	67	12	15	6	3
	Non-member	26	41	18	15	5
Salaried middle class	Member	73	12	4	11	28
	Non-member	34	28	24	14	13
Working class	Member	73	14	8	5	33
	Non-member	39	33	21	7	18

N = 1180

Sefer Mamlachti) or a religious one *(Beit Sefer Mamlachti Dati)*. Eight or nine years of schooling would operationally define a minimum education. Upon leaving primary school, about 30 percent of youth proceed to a secondary school for an intermediate education. Beyond the first year, which was compulsory and free, the additional three years of secondary schooling were not free until 1977, when awarded to needy students. Students who pass the matriculation examinations held by the Ministry of Education at the last grade of the secondary school may proceed to higher education. The number of persons who continue into university is relatively large, about 18 percent. However, the university-educated are not prominent in elite politics, and their over-representation in the Knesset is modest compared with some Western countries (Brichta, 1972).

In an immigrant society, education is not as good an indicator as in a stable society. There are a sizeable number of literate immigrants who have not mastered the Hebrew language and about 60 percent of Oriental Jews who arrived in Israel after 1948 were illiterate. Notwithstanding these difficulties, Table 5 makes it clear that education has some independent influence upon partisanship. In each occupational category the less educated are more likely to vote Alignment, though within the working class the difference is minimal. More interesting is the fact that the religious parties draw a disproportionate share of votes from those with minimum education, regardless of class. A low level of education is positively correlated with ethnic origin and traditional outlook, reinforced by the religious elementary schools

TABLE 5
Education, Occupational Class,
and Partisanship, in Percentages

		Alignment	Likud	Religious parties	Others	Percentage of Total
Self-employed middle class	Further	25	25	8	41	1
	Intermediate	39	30	19	12	4
	Minimum	52	30	18	0	3
Salaried middle class	Further	57	17	11	15	13
	Intermediate	60	20	9	11	22
	Minimum	67	10	13	10	6
Working class	Further	59	13	11	17	4
	Intermediate	61	22	10	7	23
	Minimum	61	20	16	3	24

N = 1179

which attract a disproportionate number of Orientals. Yet because fewer Orientals continue in high school, religious commitment declines with higher education (Schiff, 1977: 109). Further education increases support for the smaller parties, especially in the salaried middle and working class.

Income

Data on income in Israel is difficult to analyze for several reasons. First, income is a delicate subject to raise in an interview because of the suspicion of the respondents that the information may be used against them in some formal capacity. Questions relating to income have a higher refusal rate and the income level may be deliberately downgraded. Second, income questions tend to ignore additional sources of family revenue such as dividends or reparations as well as the stability of income. Third, rapid wage increases and the severe inflation make income measures defined in current money terms difficult to adopt. One way to overcome these problems is to classify the respondents according to broad income categories. The monthly income levels of the 1969 survey measured in Israeli *Lirah* were collapsed into three ordinal categories: low income (up to 599 IL), medium income (600-1,249 IL) and high income (1,250-1,750 IL).

The conclusion derived from Table 6 is that there is a small but

TABLE 6
Income, Occupational Class, and Partisanship, in Percentages

	Income	Alignment	Likud	Religious parties	Others	Percentage of Total
Self-employed middle class	High	42	42	0	16	2
	Medium	42	27	16	15	5
	Low	35	30	35	0	1
Salaried middle class	High	57	24	8	11	4
	Medium	62	17	10	11	24
	Low	59	10	16	15	13
Working class	High	61	21	9	9	19
	Medium	63	22	9	6	28
	Low	58	18	18	6	4

N = 1153

steady tendency within each class for *Likud* vote to decline with income and for support for religious parties to rise as income declines within a class. For Alignment, within each class, lowest income groups are least likely to support it. Since the lowest income voters are overwhelmingly Oriental and religious, they are inclined to favour the religious parties to the detriment of the secular ones.

Religion

While there are ten recognized denominations in Israel, in terms of nominal identification the country is overwhelmingly Jewish. The Muslims, Druzes and various Christian sects form only small religious communities. Because Judaism is a state religion, for some people Jewishness is only nominal. The degree of religious orthodoxy is more indicative of religious commitment. But among Jews there are no universal standards of observance with regard to the commands and prohibitions of the rabbinical code of norms known as the *halacha*. Hence, religiosity is subjective; each respondent was asked to state the extent to which he or she observes religious tradition.

Such a question, customarily used in surveys in Israel, divides the correspondents into four categories: the orthodox Jews who observe all of the *halacha* rules, the semi-orthodox Jews who observe the most important rules (i.e., Dietary Laws, Sabbath, and synagogue attendance), the traditional Jews who observe some *halacha* principles such as Sabbath and visits to the synagogue on high holidays and those who are completely non-observant. Since the distinction between the semi-orthodox and traditional is tenuous, they were collapsed into one, traditional category. The distribution in the 1969 survey resembles the results obtained in the early surveys: about 11 percent of the respondents reported that they are highly orthodox, 59 percent claimed that they are either semi-orthodox or traditional, while 29 percent were completely non-observant. Religiosity sharply differentiates the choice between religious and secular parties; 63 percent of orthodox voters support religious parties. In a complementary manner, the less observant an Israeli is the more likely he is to vote Alignment. *Likud* too gets a disproportionate share from orthodox-traditional Jews, but not in a linear manner. Controlling for class does not transfer this relationship in any meaningful way, a clear indicator that religion is a more powerful influence.

TABLE 7
Religiosity and Partisanship, in Percentages

	Alignment	Likud	Religious parties	Others	Percentage of Total
Orthodox Jews	21	10	63	6	12
Traditional Jews	61	23	8	8	59
Nonobservant Jews	70	17	0	13	29

N = 1201

It is natural for sectarian believers to vote en block for a political party which is subordinated to their religious views, especially as Alignment and *Likud* are basically secular. Yet the religious parties seem to be less successful in attracting the middle-of-the-road traditional voters. One possible explanation arises from the special position of the Jewish religion in Israel. Unlike Christian denominations, Judaism is not a universal but a national religion. Many of its elements have been customarily perceived as a part of the common national heritage (Liebman, 1975). The prevailing positive attitudes towards essentially religious national values may have hurt the claim of the religious parties solely to represent religious interest. While the ultra-orthodox AI and PAI could count on the hard-core orthodox followers, the more moderate and non-fundamentalist NRP was much less successful in attracting the traditional vote.

Ethnicity

Formally, the Jewish community is relatively homogeneous. But in terms of ethnocultural groups, the Jewish society is extremely hetero-geneous, being divided into *Ashkenazi, Sephardi* and Oriental groups. Each group is further differentiated along country of origin, thus creating *landsmanshaften* of Polish, Russian, Rumanian, German and English-speaking Jews within the *Ashkenazi* category. The *Sephardi* and Oriental groups are equally diverse, as they include Jews from a variety of Asian and African countries.

Numerous studies have focused on the high salience of ethnic ties in Israel (Shuval, 1962; Weller, 1974; Eisendstadt, 1970; Ben David, 1970; Lissak, 1969; Inbar and Adler, 1977: 13-21). The major divide runs between the Europeans *(Ashkenazi)* and the Orientals, inclusive of the *Sephardi* (Peres, 1971). Politically, the cleavage between the Europeans and the Orientals who are commonly perceived as lower classes has been quite persistent. It was even suggested that this division amounts to having two "nations" among the Israeli Jews, with the Orientals becoming the "Second Israel" *(Israel ha Shnia)* (Greenberg and Nadler, 1977: 72). At times, this cleavage triggered violence; in the Haifa slum *Vadi Salib* in the early sixties, demands for better housing for poor Orientals deteriorated into ethnic riots. More recently, a group of young Orientals called Black Panthers (modelled on the American Black Panthers) used violence in publicizing their demands for better housing, education and job opportunities (Cohen, 1972).

The 1969 Israeli Election Study lists 25 percent of the sample as born in Asia or Africa and 50 percent in Europe-America. The remaining 25 percent are Israeli-born. Compared to the distribution in the population (37 percent Orientals, 46 percent Westerners and 16 percent Israeli born) the Orientals are under-represented, whereas the Westerners and Israeli born are slightly over-sampled.

Since ethnic differences were found to persist even among Israeli-born children of European and Oriental parentage (Weingrod, 1962), ethnicity in Israel is commonly determined by father's origin. Adopting this criterion in our study created a residual category of non-classifiables, which include second-generation Israelis and border cases, i.e., Bulgarians, Greeks, Yugoslavs etc. Although it caused a drop in the number of respondents (Table 8, 9 and 10) their inclusion would obscure the subject under discussion, especially as no consistent pattern of voting was manifest in this category.

TABLE 8
Ethnicity, Religiosity, and Partisanship, in Percentages

		Alignment	Likud	Religious parties	Others	Percentages of Total
Orthodox	Oriental	10	3	80	7	3
Jews	European	18	7	72	3	7
Traditional	Oriental	43	34	9	14	19
Jews	European	70	17	7	6	37
Non-observant Jews	Oriental	57	21	0	22	12
	European	79	13	0	8	22

N = 895

Ethnic origin influences the relationship between religiosity and partisanship. (See Table 8.) European Jews are more likely to support Alignment, in all three categories. There is no consistent pattern for *Likud,* as it appears to do better with Orientals in the traditional and the non-observant group but not among the orthodox. Religious parties do slightly better among Oriental than European Jews, but the difference is not very important.

Ethnic differences are also significant among occupational groups. In the salaried middle class and working class *Likud* is preferred by Orientals; in the self-employed middle class the pattern is reversed but the small number of self-employed Orientals does not warrant generalizations. There is a consistent tendency for Europeans to prefer Alignment.

TABLE 9
Ethnicity, Occupation, and Partisanship, in Percentages

		Alignment	Likud	Religious parties	Others	Percentages of Total
Self-employed middle class	Oriental	35	16	17	32	2
	European	41	33	30	6	5
Salaried middle class	Oriental	48	29	10	13	16
	European	63	15	10	12	30
Working class	Oriental	50	28	10	12	17
	European	72	12	12	4	30

N = 885

Originating from traditional Middle East societies whose socio-economic organization and value system differed from Israel's

Westernized structure, Orientals have tended to gravitate towards low-status manual occupations. A popular argument advanced to explain this phenomenon suggests that the Oriental vote is a form of protest vote. Since the Labour party *(Mapai)* has been in power for nearly three decades the left has apparently become associated with the establishment, thus detracting from the traditional appeal of the left among the less privileged (Zloczower, 1972). It is also suggested that Labour has been traditionally concerned more with the theoretical constructs of inequality of workers vis-a-vis employers than with problems of ethnic discrimination and poverty (Etzioni-Halevy with Shapira, 1976: 56). *Likud* may be perceived by the Orientals as a party of protest, because of its long history of opposition. Likewise, the fact that the economic ideology of the right is hardly responsive to the underprivileged ethnic groups is less relevant than that Alignment is seen as the party of the better-to-do *Ashkenazi* Israelis. *Likud's* appeal to the Oriental voter is also influenced by its image of integral nationalism. The essentially Western concept of a left-right political division had held little meaning for the Oriental community in the Yishuv (Etzioni-Halevy with Shapira, 1976: 39). *Likud* has always combined an appeal to broad national values with populist politics which stood above particular social cleavages. Rather than seeking to redress their grievances through the socialist establishment, the Oriental voters choose to elevate their periphal status by identifying with radical national symbols (Horowitz, 1977). The tendency of under-privileged social or ethnic groups to support rightist parties is not unique to Israel. In other modernizing societies, rightwing parties which generate traditional and national sentiment often attract the least modernized and deprived segments of the society (Apter, 1965: 340-1).

Recency of Immigration

Israel is virtually unique among modern nations in absorbing a mass immigration within a short period of time and important sources of heterogeneity of the Jewish population can be traced to the date of arrival of the various immigration waves (Matras, 1970). There are common aspects in the periods in which each immigrant generation formed its political allegiance. Most notable is the difference between the veterans who arrived before 1948 and the more recent post-

independence immigrants. Antonovsky found that old-timers have a
more leftist political orientation than the newer immigrants (1963).
Arian's survey in 1969 lends further support to this relationship
(Arian, 1973: 45) and a similar trend is reported in the political
culture study in Israel (Etzioni-Halevy with Shapiro, 1977: 58).

TABLE 10
Recency of Immigration, Ethnicity, and
Partisanship, in Percentages

		Alignment	Likud	Religious parties	Others	Percentage of Total
Israeli-born	Oriental	46	26	12	16	17
	European	39	20	10	31	4
Veterans	Oriental	35	29	16	20	3
	European	67	18	8	7	29
Immigrants	Oriental	45	20	25	10	10
	European	67	12	14	7	37

N = 885

The hypothesis that there is an immigrant generation seems to get
some confirmation in Table 10. The three categories follow the
common distinction in Israel between the Israeli-born *(sabras)*; the
veterans *(vatikim)* who arrived up to 1948 and the immigrants *(olim)*
who came after. Although the differences are not dramatic, veteran
and immigrant voters tend to support Alignment more than the Israeli-
born. This is normally attributed to the fact that in the Yishuv period
and in the first decade after independence, *Mapai* was the focal point
of the political system. Some of the veterans and many immigrants
who arrived during the big immigration waves of 1948-59 have often
become clients of *Mapai,* because the dominant party was best in
distributing patronage (Gitelman, 1973).

Yet a theory of "immigrant generations" is not adequate to describe
the ethnic vote. There is a consistent tendency within each category for
Orientals to favour the right. Even the Oriental veterans and immigrants from the period when *Mapai* was dominant and socialist norms
widely prevalent, are more likely to support *Likud* than the
Europeans. In other words the influence of ethnicity goes beyond a
common experience created by different stages of immigration.

The behaviour of the Israeli-born, who least favour the Alignment is
more of a puzzle. The question of why these voters, some of whom
came to maturity during the dominance of *Mapai,* should prefer *Likud*
is quite complicated. It is undoubtedly true, as Arian suggested, that

the Israeli-born have been always less dependent on the patronage of *Mapai*. Paradoxically, for those who were born in the country *Mapai* may have had less messianic appeal (1973: 45). But it would also seem that the behaviour of the Israeli born and other categories is influenced by age distribution within the respective groups. While the veteran group has a high percent of older people, the recent immigrants are younger. The percent of young people is particularly high among the Israeli-born.

Age

The generational effect of coming to political maturity has not been yet satisfactorily separated from the life cycle effect (Glenn, 1977: 13-14), although it is customary to regard the generational influence as the stronger one. The evaluation of generational behaviour in Israel is further complicated by the immigrant nature of the society. Since cohort analysis assumes that the successive generations lived in *one* country, it leaves the question of new arrivals open to speculations. We would expect that coming of age is less meaningful when applied to people who were socialized in different countries.

Indeed, Table 11 which presents the relationship between age and party while recency of arrival is held constant, reveals that the generational impact is most visible in the native-born group. Significant differences between the age groups are also noticeable in the veteran category. This is not surprising if we take into account that these voters have lived in Israel for at least fifteen years prior to the 1969 elections; often they arrived young enough to qualify for common generational experience. The least structured is the vote of the immigrants, which confirms the impression that cohort analysis is difficult to apply in a strongly heterogeneous setting.

When the direction of voting by age group is inspected, the Alignment vote is shown to be ageing. It does least well with the young under 35s and best with the 50+ group. *Likud* shows a reversed trend; although it has a much smaller following, it is most consistently supported by the 18-34 group in every category. As the age goes up, *Likud* supports declines. The vote for the religious parties is not linear; they enjoy an advantage in the young and old groups but not among the middle aged.

There is no doubt that the pattern of age voting works against the common belief that younger people are "naturally" more leftist than

TABLE 11
Age, Immigration, and Partisanship, in Percentages

		Alignment	Likud	Religious parties	Others	Percentage of Total
Israeli-born	18-34	44	25	14	17	15
	35-49	54	33	2	11	5
	50+	55	15	15	15	2
Veterans	18-34	45	30	15	10	2
	35-49	61	22	7	10	10
	50+	66	18	11	5	20
Immigrants	18-34	55	26	12	7	17
	35-49	68	16	11	5	17
	50+	62	9	21	8	12

N = 1180

their seniors. Although no consistent pattern of voting differences by age was found in Western democracies (Rose, 1974) it is still true that Israel is different from a number of countries where socialists have disproportionally attracted the younger generation as opposed to the older following of the conservative parties. The rightist orientation of the younger Israelis is often explained by what may be termed the "reaction syndrome." Since the government was historically socialist, the anti-establishment drive of the young took a rightist direction (Halevy-Etzioni with Shapiro, 1977: 54). Alternatively, it is claimed that the younger generation which participated most actively in the Arab-Israeli conflict became highly nationalistic and thus, most responsive to the claims of *Likud* (Area Handbook For Israel, 1970: 153-162).

Although both explanations are undoubtedly reasonable, they are only partially based on assumptions of cohort analysis. What seems to matter more is the fact that the younger groups formed partisan allegiance at a time where a variety of social and political factors moved the country away from *Mapai;* it was during the late fifties and sixties that the right emerged as one of the major parties. Seen in this way, the switch from left to right is not an aberration of the cohort theory. Rather, it calls for a broad concept of cohort-induced electoral movements; the direction of the new alignment being determined by conditions specific to each society. It is augmented by the ethnic factor; ethnic differences in a family size work for *Likud* which is supported by the larger-than-average Oriental families.

Generational differences offer an opportunity to test the hypothesis about the seculariztion of modern societies. The first point in any test for secularization is whether the younger generation is getting less observant in religious terms. Table 12 provides limited support for the secularization hypothesis. The over 50s age group has the highest percentage of orthodox people, but orthodoxy, though dropping, is almost the same in the middle age and younger group. Traditionalism shows no clear pattern; contrary to expectations, it is lowest in the older age category and higher in the two other groups.

TABLE 12
Age, Religiosity, and Partisanship, in Percentages

		Alignment	Likud	Religious parties	Others	Percentage of Total
	Orthodox Jews	5	6	86	3	3
18-34	Traditional Jews	50	30	9	11	20
	Non-observant Jews	61	23	0	16	11
	Orthodox Jews	34	15	47	4	3
35-49	Traditional Jews	61	21	12	6	22
	Non-observant Jews	69	18	0	13	8
	Orthodox Jews	26	6	65	3	5
50 +	Traditional Jews	65	18	9	8	18
	Non-observant Jews	83	8	0	9	10

N = 1190

When the party preference of the age groups is examined with control for secularization, religiosity is still the stronger indication; in all age groups, the orthodox provide most of the religious vote. (See Table 12.) Religious support amoung the traditionals does not exceed 10 percent and it disappears completely among the non-observant. However, age is a factor of some importance in the relative distribution of the religious votes in the orthodox category. Religious parties are least successful in the 35-49 group and best in the young and old groups. The middle age decline is apparently related to the circulatory way in which the fortunes of the religious parties have evolved. In the Yishuv and immediate post-independence period, the religious parties, as indeed other political groupings were overshadowed by the secular socialist norms. The coming of age of the younger people coincided with a period when greater legitimacy was accorded to religious values (Liebman, 1975; Don-Yehiya, 1975). Since the young orthodox comprise only 2.9 percent of the sample, this trend is negligible in electoral terms. Religiosity also affects the support for secular parties. Alignment is disproportionally favoured by the non-observant, but its following increases with age. *Likud* has a slight advantage among the traditionals, especially in the young group.

Sex

The greater proclivity of women to vote for conservative and religious parties has been commonly attributed to their greater religiosity. However, these findings do not receive confirmation in Table 13, which measures sex and partisanship by introducing religiosity as an intervening variable. While there is a correlation between sex and voting, its direction is reversed: women are more likely than men to vote for the "modern" Alignment bloc within every category of religiosity. The apparent success of the socialists among women is at least partially caused by the age factor. Because women live longer, they are dominant among the older age groups which disproportionally support the socialists.

TABLE 13
Sex, Religiosity, and Party Preference, in Percentages

		Alighment	Likud	Religious parties	Other	Percentage of Total
Orthodox	Men	20	6	70	4	6
Jews	Women	27	11	60	2	5
Traditional	Men	60	24	8	8	29
Jews	Women	61	23	8	8	31
Non-observant	Men	66	22	0	12	16
Jews	Women	76	11	0	13	13

N = 1193

Another reason for the discrepancy between the Western countries and Israel can be traced to the way Christianity and Judaism relate to both sexes. Christian denominations have historically held a broad appeal to women, while Judaism has been very much a "man's" religion. There are more orthodox and traditionalists among Jewish men than among women (12.5 percent vs. 9.5 percent), whereas in Christian societies women are normally more observant than men.

Moreover, under the rabbinical legal system, men have more prerogatives than women (Bar Yosef and Shelach, 1970).

Political Orientation

Political orientation is important in Israel because the political system has been historically differentiated along a left-right continuum. A large number of studies have probed the political orientation of Israelis and found that people tend to identify with left, centre and right (Arian, 1968; Antonovsky, 1964; Etzioni-Halevy with Shapiro, 1977: 25-33). We would expect that political orientation will explain fairly well voting choices, all the more so, given the instability of party labels. The broad political trends in Israeli politics are derived from the left-right cross-national continuum, collapsed into four categories: left, moderate left, centre and right. More difficult to classify in terms of the conventional left-right economic dimension is religious orientation. Since the religious parties are non-economic in a sense, while displaying a rightist position in confessional and national matters, the religious orientation may be, by courtesy, classified as right/religious.

TABLE 14
Political Orientation and Partisanship, in Percentages

	Alignment	Likud	Religious parties	Others	Percentage of Total
Left	74	11	1	14	7
Moderate left	88	4	2	6	29
Centre	56	25	6	13	29
Right	39	47	5	9	23
Right-religious	3	4	88	5	12

N = 971

Table 14 does not indicate a consistent relationship between political orientation and electoral choice. Only the right/religious support overwhelmingly the religious parties. On the other hand, Alignment is not strongest among the left, neither is *Likud* weakest on the left. In other words, the centre-right corresponds to conventional expectations, but not the left-moderate left. This pattern reflects quite faithfully Israeli politics and is theoretically important.

It shows (as the previous data indicated) that simple ideological stereotypes drawn from class politics do not really fit Israeli realities.

Conjoint Social Influence

An analysis of Western party systems suggests that cleavage lines have evolved from the conflict between four paired clusters of groups: church-state; employers-workers; urban-rural and centre-periphery as defined by race, region, linguistics or national identity (Lipset and Rokkan, 1967). In applying this thereoretical model to the Israeli Jews some qualifications should be made. The tension between agrarian and urban interests could hardly arise in a society with no inherent peasantry. The very smallness of the country and its highly centralized structure prevented the development of any regional tension. The Jewish society is also largely unilingual; while immigrants have a variety of languages, none has impinged the legitimacy of Hebrew. The cleavage generated by the bitter dispute over religious issues, is wholly comparable to the church-state division in Europe. The middle class vs. working class dichotomy has its Israeli equivalent. The centre-periphery cleavage is evident in the ethnic tension between the dominant European culture of the *Ashkenazi* Jews and the peripheral Orientals. Empirically, the number of dimensions will be confined to three: religion vs. class, Europeans vs. Orientals, the middle class vs. working class. The religious variable is trichotomized into orthodox, traditional, and non-observant Jews. The ethnic variable does not include the non-classifiables. The combination of one trichotomized and two dichotomized categories provides twelve social subgrouping.

By using a matrix analysis, it is possible to present their relative distribution among the population as well as the level of support that the subgroupings accord the parties. The matrix in Table 15 makes it clear that the Jewish society is quite fragmented. The largest group (21.2 percent of the sample) is traditional, European and working class, and 17.5 percent has the same religious and ethnic characteristics but is middle class. The traditional, Oriental Jews are next in size; with 10.6 percent working class and 7.7 percent middle class. Non-observant Europeans form another sizeable group, with 11.2 percent manual workers and 4.6 percent middle class. The remaining six subgroups are smaller but collectively account for nearly a quarter of the Israeli electorate.

TABLE 15
Size and Partisanship of Major Social Groups
in Percentages

	Oriental		European	
Orthodox Jews	**Middle class**	**Working class**	**Middle class**	**Working class**
Alignment	12	12	14	20
Likud	2	6	6	7
Religious parties	86	82	80	73
Total	(1.6)	(1.5)	(3.6)	(5.8)
Traditional Jews				
Alignment	52	49	77	73
Likud	40	40	18	18
Religious parties	8	11	5	9
Total	(7.7)	(10.6)	(17.5)	(21.2)
Non-observant Jews				
Alignment	72	73	84	87
Likud	28	27	16	13
Religious parties	0	0	0	0
Total	(4.9)	(5.6)	(4.6)	(11.2)

N = 798

Percentages in parentheses refer to the proportion that each cell contributes to the total vote for the three party blocs. Total party strength: Alignment, 58.4 percent; Likud, 20.6 percent; Religious parties, 12.4 percent.

When the distribution of party strength with regard to all the subgrouping is examined, Table 15 confirms that religiosity and ethnicity are dividing the electorate to a much greater extent than class. Most noteworthy is the non-observant category, which gives no support to the religious parties. By contrast the orthodox overwhelmingly vote for the religious parties. The ethnic factor, though less divisive, is most evident in the support pattern for the secular parties. Regardless of class, the strength of Alignment consistently declines amoung the Oriental voters in the traditional and nonobservant category.

The alternative way of exploring aggregate influences of socioeconomic variables can be based upon tree analysis, i.e., the Automatic Interaction Detector (AID) program (Sonquist and Morgan, 1964) which provides the total amount of variance in partisanship explained by different socio-economic characteristics. The predictor variables used in AID were those treated in the preceding discussion: occupational class, income, education, *Histadrut* membership, religiosity, ethnicity, age, sex and recency of immigration. The choice of the independent variable requires that partisan preference be dichotomized; in the Israeli context the only meaningful way is to separate the Alignment voters from the followers of the *Likud*, the religious parties and all the others.

The tree analyses displayed in Figure 1 reveals that Israeli electoral behaviour is structed to a very limited extent. Its openness is demonstrated by the fact that only 9.2 percent of variance in party preference is explained, lower than 15 out of 16 other political systems in which similar analyses have been conducted (Rose, 1974a: 17). Social structure does not explain partisanship nearly as well as in the Netherlands, the Scandinavian countries or even Britain. Only Ireland shows less relation between social structure and party preference. This is not altogether surprising; Israel is at least partially a developing country in which "value politics" transgress the traditional dividing lines based on class and other social attributes. Occupational class, which in most countries is an important influence upon party preference, appears very low in the tree.

When the contribution of the individual variables is examined Figure 1 shows the particular importance of the organizational factor. The first level split divides the sample on the basis of *Histadrut* membership into members and non-members. The portion of the total variance explained by this bifurcation is 5.3 percent. The second-level split shows the importance of religiosity, as it divides *Histadrut* members and non-members into observant and non-observant. The pair of divisions by religious observance explains another 3.5 percent of the total variance. At the next stage it became impossible to split the non-observant *Histadrut* members in any meaningful way, but the observant *Histadrut* members can be split by age.

Voting preferences in Israel are influenced by both organizational and subcultural ties. Combinations of the two major networks give rise to four blocs: the *Histadrut* — non-observant; the *Histadrut* — observant; the non-*Histadrut* — observant; and the non-*Histadrut* — non-observant (Arian, 1973: 54-55). The largest single bloc is the *Histadrut* — non-observant which comprises more than a half of the respondents. It does not split into subgroups, which suggest the relative political cohesion of the bloc. Much smaller are the other blocs; the non-*Histadrut* — non-observant includes about 25 percent, with the remaining respondents split about equally between the last two blocs.

FIGURE 1
A Tree Analysis of Israeli Voting

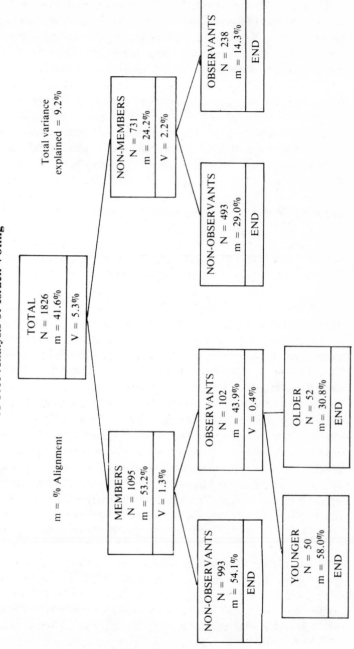

m = % Alignment

Total variance
explained = 9.2%

TOTAL
N = 1826
m = 41.6%
V = 5.3%

NON-MEMBERS
N = 731
m = 24.2%
V = 2.2%

OBSERVANTS
N = 238
m = 14.3%
END

NON-OBSERVANTS
N = 493
m = 29.0%
END

MEMBERS
N = 1095
m = 53.2%
V = 1.3%

NON-OBSERVANTS
N = 993
m = 54.1%
END

OBSERVANTS
N = 102
m = 43.9%
V = 0.4%

OLDER
N = 52
m = 30.8%
END

YOUNGER
N = 50
m = 58.0%
END

The tree analysis confirms the degree of importance of influence commiting an individual to a particular bloc. Historically, the socialist parties have buttressed their power by intensive and massive organization of numerous elements in the society. The individual was called upon to manifest his organizational commitment by becoming a *Histadrut* member. The strength of *Mapai* was closely associated with the trade-union influence on its members. Yet trade-union membership in Israel goes beyond mere organizational behaviour. Since the *Histadrut* was among the most important networks through which *Mapai* was able to disseminate and maintain the socialist-Zionist ideology, it resembles religiosity in also being a subcultural variable. Should the impact of the *Histadrut* subculture weaken — and there are indications that the socialist-Zionist ideology has become less relevant — the dominant network may disintegrate.

THE CHANGES IN THE POLITICAL
SYSTEM: 1973-1977

The Yom Kippur War of October 1973 accelerated the decade long decline in the dominance of the Labour Party. In addition to the growing dissatisfaction of the electorate with social and economic conditions, the Alignment was held responsible for military failures. The 31 December 1973 election, though decreasing Alignment's lead over *Likud* (see Table 1) still left it in a position to form a cabinet. However, a bitterly divisive leadership crisis in the Labour Party and the shift of the National Religious Party towards the "hawkish" stand of the *Likud* made coalescing difficult; the three ensuing coalition cabinets were highly fragile. (Seliktar, 1976). Moreover, the possibility of a religious-right alliance substantiated *Likud's* image as an alternative to the Alignment. The former could also capitalize on the leadership crisis of Labour, which nearly paralyzed the party; its inability to control the runaway inflation; and charges of corruption involving some of its top leaders, including Prime Minister Rabin.

When, after a series of cabinet reshuffles, the Alignment government finally collapsed in December 1976, the outcome of the May 1977 elections, led to a transition from a dominant to a competitive party system. The magnitude of the political realignment was best reflected in the decline of Alignment's share of votes from 39.6 percent in 1973 to 24.6 percent. *Likud* increased its electoral holding from 30.2 percent to 33.4 percent, becoming the strongest bloc in the Knesset. The collective gains of the religious parties amounted to 2.4 percent, giving them 14.5 percent of the total vote. The most spectacular showing was made by the Centre Democratic Movement for Change, a new party established only six months prior to the elections. By gaining an unprecedented 11.6 percent of the vote, this "flash party" became the fourth largest group in the Knesset. A fraction of the DMC vote came from the Independent Liberals and the Civil Rights Movement, but the bulk of its support was provided from Alignment. To a much lesser degree, Alignment losses fed into the *Likud*. The 1977 realignment, while causing some minor splits and factional deflections left the major party groups in the same framework. Nevertheless, the shift in aggregate vote led to a new pattern of cooperation among the parties. Led by *Likud*, the 1977 coalition was based on the NRP, *Agudat Israel* and the DMC.

The voting pattern which brought *Likud* to power was undoubtedly affected by the upheavals of the Yom Kippur War. But from a relatively short perspective, it would seem that it only accelerated the process of changes in voting behaviour. The ethnic and generational influences worked for *Likud* even during Labour's dominance. Demographic factors, making for an increased proportion of the Oriental and the younger groups in the population, may continue to benefit *Likud* in the future, while sustaining the ethnic cleavage. It is also plausible to assume that the drive of the religious parties in the coalition to impose the *Torah* rules would enhance the influence of religiosity upon voting behaviour.

Less clear are the possible changes in the impact of social status on partisanship. The election poll data showed that social class still overlapped with ethnicity; the working class Orientals disproportionally prefering the *Likud*, whereas the middle class Europeans voted for either the Alignment or the Democratic Movement For Change, which attracted a large number of the better educated (Arian, 1977). Yet, neither the Alignment nor the *Likud* attained a sufficient degree of social homogeneity to qualify as a "class party." Paradoxically, the economic policy of the *Likud*, influenced by its Liberal faction, increased the inflation rate and depressed the standard of living of the largely Oriental working class.

ISRAEL IN COMPARATIVE PERSPECTIVE

The Israeli electoral system is comparable to other multiparty systems with proportional representtion. In particular, it can be compared to the Netherlands and Italy, which has also a tradition of a fragmented multiparty system and coalition cabinets. In both countries the extreme PR system encourages the proliferation of small and splinter parties. In neither country, however, are the small parties politically weighty; taken together their electoral strength amounts to a small percentage of the total vote.

The nature of the political parties is more difficult to describe in cross-national terms, but the difficulties hardly confirm Sartori's assertion that Israel "defies any generalization" (1976: 136ff). The extreme left is relatively easy to compare; the pro-Jewish and the pro-Arab Communist Parties are quite similar to the small communist parties in Western Europe. The moderately socialist Labour has its ideological equivalent in the German Social Democrats, British Labour and the Dutch Labour Parties. Likewise, it reveals some interesting parallels with the Congress Party of India, because both are nation-building types. The historical liberal parties, i.e., the General Zionists and the Progressive Party and their inheritors, the Independent Liberal Party, the Civil Rights Movement and the Democratic Movement For Change may be likened to the small liberal parties of continental Europe, most notably the Dutch VVD, the Italian PLI, and the FDP in Germany.

More difficult to classify are the religious parties. Although they hold some common ground with the Christian Democrats in Germany and Italy, their smaller following and fragmentation makes them most comparable to the religious parties in the Netherlands. The National Religious Party, which is moderately clerical and represents the religious establishment in Israel, is closest to the ARP and CHU. The ultra-orthodox *Augdat Israel* and *Poalei Agudat Israel* resemble the two smaller Calvinist parties (SGP and GPV); both are bent on fundamentalism and almost complete subcultural isolation. The rightwing *Likud* is hard to put into cross-national perspectives because its factions are politically heterogeneous. The old *Herut* party was most similar to the Irish Fianna Fail, but its more recent association with the Liberals and the electoral success of 1977 would make the *Likud* bloc somewhat comparable to the British Conservatives and American Republicans.

While the Israeli parties are comparable to other Western

countries, the impact of the socio-economic structure on electoral choice is much more difficult to match. In its fairly low level of structured voting behaviour, Israel resembles many nations in the making, for class cleavages were overcast by the struggle for independence. In such countries, most notably Ireland and India, it was customary for one party, either socialist or national-conservative, to establish dominance by cross-cutting class, ethnic and religious lines. The parallels between Israel and India are most instructuve; both Labour *(Mapai)* and the Congress Party have lost their broad electoral support when the societies emerged from the crucial nation-building period in their history.

Nevertheless, the similarities should not be pushed too far. More than in the Indian Congress Party, *Mapai* made enormous efforts to socialize the society into its ideology through an extensive organizational network. Israel was also less successful than Ireland in solving the state-religion tension. The importance of trade unionism and religiosity in voting behaviour demonstrates the existence of distinctive ideological and religious subcultures. In this respect, a case might be made for comparison with the "segmented pluralist" societies in continental Europe.

In sharing the phenomenon of *Verzuiling,* Israel is closest to the Dutch case; in both countries vertical cross-class compartmentalization has an important impact on political behaviour. This is especially evident in the prominance of the religious-secular cleavage, the fractionalization of the party system and its emphasized ideological bent. Perhaps the most interesting finding, though, is that Israel like the Netherlands has witnessed a gradual disintegration of the traditional socio-political blocs. There is little doubt that the process of realignment is comprehensive.

REFERENCES

AKZIN, B. (1955), "The Role of Parties in Israeli Democracy," *The Journal of Politics,* 17 (November): 507-545.

ANTONOVSKY, A. (1963), "Emdot Politiot Socialist B'Israel" ("Israel Social-Poltical Attitudes"), *Amot,* 1 (June-July): 11-22.

— — (1964), "Ideologiot Politiot Shel haIsraelim" ("Israel Ideologies of Israelis"), *Amot,* 2 (August-September): 21-28.

— — (1966), "Classification of Forms, Political Ideologies and the Man in the Street," *Public Opinion Quarterly,* 30 (Spring): 109-119.

ANTONOVSKY, A. (1972), *Hopes and Fears of Israelis; Consensus in a New Society.* Jerusalem: Jerusalem Academic Press.

APTER, D.E.. (1965), *The Politics of Modernization.* Chicago: University of Chicago Press.

ARIAN, A. (1966), "Voting and Ideology in Israel," *Midwest Journal of Political Science* 10 (August): 265-287.

— — (1968), *Ideological Change in Israel.* Cleveland: The Press of Case Western University.

— — (1970), "Consensus and Community in Israel," *Jewish Journal of Sociology,* 12 (June): 39-54.

— — (ed.) (1972a), *The Elections in Israel – 1969.* Jerusalem: Jerusalem Academic Press.

— — (1972b), "Electoral Choice in a Dominant Party System," in A. Arian (ed.), 1972a.

— — (1973), *Ha'am Haboher. (The Choosing People)* Tel Aviv: Massada.

— — (ed.) (1975a), *The Elections in Israel – 1973.* Jerusalem: Jerusalem Academic Press.

— — (1975b), "Were the 1973 Elections Critical?" in A. Arian (ed.), 1975a.

— — (1977), "The Passing of Dominance," *The Jerusalem Quarterly,* 5 (November): 33-52.

— — and S.H. BARNES (1974), "The Dominant Party System: A Neglected Model of Democratic Stability," *The Journal of Politics,* 36 (August): 592-614.

AVNER, U. (1975), "Voter Participation in the 1973 Elections," in A. Arian (ed.), 1975a.

BAR-YOSEF, R. and D. PADAN (1964), "Hakehilot haEtniot haMizrahiot ba Mivne haHevrati beIsrael" ("Eastern Ethnic Communities in the Class Structure of Israel"), *Molad,* 22 (November): 504-516.

— — and I. SHELACH (1970), "The Position of Women in Israel," in S.N. Eisenstadt, R. Bar-Yosef and C. Adler (eds.), 1970.

BARNES, S.H. (1974), "Italy: Religion and Class in Electoral Behavior," in R. Rose (ed.), 1974a.

BEN DAVID, J. (1970), "Ethnic Differences or Social Change," in S.N. Eisenstadt, R. Bar-Yosef and C. Adler (eds.), 1970.

BRICHTA, A. (1972), 'The Social and Political Characteristics of Members of the Seventh Knesset," in A. Arian (ed.), 1972.

— — (1977), *Demokratia ve Bhirot: Al Shinui Shitat haBhirot beIsrael (Democracy and Elections: On Changing the Electoral and Nomination System in Israel).* Tel Aviv: Am Oved.

COHEN, E. (1968), "Social Images in an Israeli Development Town," *Human Relations,* 21 (May): 163-176.

— — (1972), "The Black Panthers and Israeli Society," *Jewish Journal of Sociology,* 14 (July): 93-110.

CZUDNOWSKI, M.M. (1970), "Legislative Recruitment Under Proportional Representation in Israel: A Model and a Case Study," *Midwest Journal of Political Science,* 14 (May): 216-248.

DERBER, M. (1970), "Israel's Wage Differential: A Persistent Problem," in S.N. Eisenstadt, R. Bar-Yosef and C. Adler (eds.), 1970.

DON-YEHIYA, E. (1975), "Religion and Coalition: The National Religious Party and Coalition Formation in Israel," in A. Arian (ed.), 1975a.

EISENSTADT, S.N. (1970a), *Israeli Society*. London: Weidenfield and Nicolson.
— — (1970b), "The Process of Absorption of New Immigrants in Israel," in S.N. Eisenstadt, R. Bar-Yosef and C. Adler (eds.), 1970.
— — R. BAR-YOSEF and C. ADLER (eds.) (1970), *Integration and Development in Israel*. New York: Praeger.
ENGELMANN, F.C. (1966), "Austria: The Pooling of Opposition" in R. Dahl, (ed.) *Political Opposition in Western Democracies*. New Haven: Yale University Press.
ETZIONI-HALEVY, E. and R. SHAPIRO (1977), *Political Culture in Israel: Cleavage and Integration Among Israeli Jews*. New York & London: Praeger.
FEIN, L.J. (1967), *Politics in Israel*. Boston: Little Brown & Co.
FOREIGN AREA STUDIES OF THE AMERICAN UNIVERSITY (1970), *Area Handbook for Israel*. Washington, DC: US Government Printing Office.
GITELMAN, Z. (1973), "Absorption of Soviet Immigrants," in M. Curtis and M. Chertoff (eds.), *Israel: Social Structure and Change*. New Brunswick, NJ: Transaction Books.
GLENN, N.D. (1977), *Cohort Analysis*. Beverly Hills: Sage Publications.
GOLAN, E. (1977), *Tarbut Politit beIsrael: Heker Mikre (Political Culture in Israel. A Case Study)*, MA Dissertation. Haifa: University of Haifa.
GRENBERG, H and S. NADLER (1977) *Poverty in Israel: Economic Realities and the Promise of Social Justice*. New York. Praeger.
HILL, K. (1974), "Belgium: Political Change in a Segmented Society," in R. Rose (ed.), 1974a.
HOROWITZ, D. (1977), "More than a Change in Government," *The Jerusalem Quarterly* 5 (November) 3: 19.
— — and M. LISSAK (1971), "Authority with Sovereignty," in M. Lissak and E. Gutmann (eds.), *Political Institutions and Processes in Israel*, Jerusalem: Academon.
— — (1977), *MeHesuv leMedina. Yehude: Eretz Israel beTkufat haMadat haBriti keKechilla Politit. (The Origins of the Israeli Polity. The Political System of the Jewish Community in Palestine Under the Mandate)* Tel-Aviv: Am Uved (Hebrew).
INBAR, M. and Ch. ADLER (1977), *Ethnic Integration in Israel. A Comparative Case Study of Moroccan Brothers Who Settled in France and Israel*. New Brunswick, New Jersey: Transaction Books.
KIES, N.E. (1971), "Elections and Campaigning in Jerusalem," in M. Lissak and E. Gutmann (eds.), *Political Institutions and Processes in Israel*. Jerusalem: Academon.
LANDAU, J.M. (1969), *The Arabs in Israel*. London, New York, Toronto: Oxford University Press.
LIEBMAN, C.S. (1975), "Religion and Political Integration in Israel," *The Jewish Journal of Sociology*, 17 (June): 17-28.
LIJPHART, A. (1974), "The Netherlands: Continuity and Change in Voting Behavior," in R. Rose (ed.), 1974.
LIPSET, S.M. (1970), "Political Cleavages in 'Developed' and 'Emerging' Polities," in E. Allardt and Stein Rokkan (eds.), *Mass Politics: Studies in Political Sociology*.
— — and S. ROKKAN, (1967) "Introduction" in S.M. Lipset and S Rokkan (eds.), *Party Systems and Voters Alignments*. New York: Free Press.

LISSAK, M. (1969), *Social Mobility in Israeli Society.* Jerusalem: Israel University Press.

— — (1970), "Patterns of Changes in Ideology and Class Structure in Israel," in S.N. Eisenstadt, R. Bar-Yosef, C. Adler (eds.), 1970.

MACKIE, T. and R. ROSE (1974), *The International Almanac of Electoral History.* London: Macmillan.

MATRAS, J. (1965), *Social Change in Israel.* Chicago: Aldine Publishing Co.

— — (1970) "Some Data on Integrational Occupational Mobility in Israel," in S.N. Eisenstadt, R. Bar-Yosef and C. Adler (eds.), 1970.

MEDDING, P.Y. (1972), *Mapai in Israel: Political Organization and Government in a New Society.* Cambridge: University Press.

NAHAS, D.H. (1976), *The Israeli Communist Party,* London: Portico Publications.

PALTIEL, K.L. (1974), "The Israeli Coalition System," *Government and Opposition,* 10 (October): 397-414.

PERES, Y. (1971), "Ethnic Relations in Israel," *American Journal of Sociology* 76 (May): 1021-1047.

RAE, D. (1967), *The Political Consequences of Electoral Laws.* New Haven: Yale University Press.

ROSE, R. (ed.) (1974a), *Electoral Behavior: A Comparative Handbook.* NY: The Free Press.

— — (1974b), "Britain: Simple Abstractions and Complex Realities," in R. Rose (ed.), 1974a.

— — (1974c), "Comparability in Electoral Studies," in R. Rose (ed.), 1974.

SAFRAN, N. (1978), *Israel. The Embattled Ally.* Cambridge, Mass. and London: The Belknap Press of Harvard University Press.

SARTORI, G. (1966), "European Political Parties: The Case of Polarized Pluralism," in M. Weiner and J. Lapalombara (eds.), *Political Parties and Political Development.* Princeton, NJ: Princeton University Press.

— — (1976), *Political Parties and Party Systems,* Cambridge: Cambridge University Press.

SCHIFF, G.S. (1977), *Tradition and Politics: The Religious Parties in Israel.* Detroit: Wayne State University Press.

SELIKTAR, O. (1976), "Hebetim al Harkavat kaKoalicjia Ahrei Milhemet Yom kuKippurim" ("Aspects of Coalition Formation After the Yom Kippur War") in A. Cohen (ed.) *BeZel Milhemet Yom huKippurim (The Aftermath of the Yom Kippur War)* Haifa: Haifa University Press.

— — (forthcoming), "Coalition Behavior in Israel: Fragile Coalitions in a New Nation," in E. Brown and J. Dreijmanins (eds.), *Coalition Governments in Western Democracies.* New Haven: Yale University Press.

SHUVAL, J.T. (1962), "Emerging Patterns of Ethnic Strain," *Social Forces,* 40 (May): 323-328.

— — (1963), *Immigrants on the Threshold.* NY: Atherton Press.

SONQUIST, J.A.T. and J.N. MORGAN (1964), *The Detection of Interaction Effects.* Ann Arbor: Monograph No. 35, Survey Research Centre.

STOKES, D. (1966), "Spatial Models of Party Competition," in A. Campbell, P. Converse, W. Miller and D. Stokes, *Elections and the Political Order.* NY: Wiley.

WEINGROD, A. (1962) *Group Relations in a New Society.* New York: Praeger.

WEISS, S. (1972), "Results of Local Elections," in A. Arian (ed.), 1972a.

WELLER, L. (1974), *Sociology in Israel*. London, Westport, Conn.: Greenwood Press.

ZLOCZOWER, A. (1972), "Occupation, Mobility and Social Class." *Social Science Information* 11: 329-357.

ZWEIG, F. (1970), "The Jewish Trade Union Movement in Israel," in S.N. Eisenstadt, R. Bar-Yosef, and C. Adler (eds.), 1970.

6

The Social Bases of Danish Electoral Behaviour

Ole Borre
University of Aarhus, Denmark

1. HISTORY OF THE PARTY SYSTEM

In a brief outline of the history of the Danish party system one may pick out seven phases distinguished by important discontinuities or periods of rapid transformation.

1784-1849. The development of the social bases of the party system preceded the Danish constitution of 1849 and may be traced back at least to structural changes associated with the international economic upswing in the closing decades of the eighteenth century (Hansen, 1974). The results were land and school reforms gradually raising political consciousness in the peasant class. In the new European order created by the Treaty of Vienna, Denmark was reduced to a small power through the ending of Norway's century-old union with Denmark. In 1834 four consultative diets were introduced in East Denmark, West Denmark, Schleswig, and Holstein. They were required by the Treaty of Vienna for members of the German Federation, to which the southern province of Holstein belonged. The diet elections in 1834, in effect the first political election in Denmark, showed that the peasants tended to vote for representatives of their own class. The diets spurred a liberal movement, and during the 1840s several blueprints for a constitution were in circulation. The decisive moment came when a rebellion broke out in Holstein and Schleswig prompted by the 1848 revolution in Paris. In a march to the royal castle the citizens of Copenhagen pressed the unambitious King Frederick VII to announce an election for a convention to draft a constitution.

1849-1870. The second phase of the party system is characterized by the interplay of three parliamentary groups in the bicameral Danish legislature: Conservatives *(Konservative)* consisting mainly of landlords and top administrators appointed by the King; the National Liberals *(Nationalliberale)* constituting the centre group, elected mainly from the intelligentsia and the leading commercial class; and the Peasants' Friends *(Bondevennerne),* representing the farmers and elected in large numbers as a consequence of a determined grass-roots mobilization. The main political driving force was the National Liberals, who formed most of the governments. However, the disastrous war in 1864, which resulted in the loss of both Holstein and Schleswig, thereby reducing the area and population of the monarchy by 40 percent, precipitated the dissolution of the National Liberal movement, which was blamed for that war. The resulting revision of the constitution restricted the franchise to the upper house *(Landstinget)* sufficiently to ensure a conservative majority there, and since the lower house *(Folketinget)* was not recognized as dominant it was possible to rule with support from the upper house only.

1870-1901. The third phase of the development of the party system was dominated by a political struggle between two parties, the liberal forces uniting in 1871 in the Left *(Venstre)* Party and the conservative forces, forming the Right *(Højre)* Party in 1881. Grass-roots organizations and a partisan press grew up in every town. Throughout the whole period the government was in the hands of the Right, and the king selected his prime ministers from among the aristocratic landlords. At the level of the voter the Right dominated the towns, while the Left dominated the countryside. The electoral system until 1915 was a simple plurality rule. In Denmark proper there were 100 constituencies until 1894, when the number was extended to 113, as newly populated quarters in the large cities were subdivided. Most provincial constituencies consisted of a town together with its surrounding rural area. Farmers surged in on election day, often constituting a solid majority over the townspeople. After an initial show of hands the weaker candidate(s) could withdraw, and if only one candidate remained the votes were not necessarily counted. It was not until the end of the century that a record of votes was made in almost all constituencies. Concurrently, voting turnout rose steadily. Where vote recording was demanded by at least one of the candidates, the electors line up to have their votes assigned to their names on the election list. In effect this was an election in two rounds, making partisan manoeuvres possible between the rounds. The vote was not secret until an electoral reform in 1900 (Høgh, 1972; Elklit, 1973a and b; Borre, 1975).

The struggle between the urban Right and the rural Left gradually led to an overwhelming majority for the Left in the lower house, but the Right continued to govern because of their support in the upper house. Opposition against the ruling landlords began to emerge also in the urban middle class, whose economic interests suffered from the legislative deadlock; for example, in the session of 1883/84 only one bill was passed, dealing with an insane asylum!

After an early attempt to organize a socialist movement had been suppressed by the police and the courts in the 1870s, the Social Democratic Party (Socialdemokratiet) made its appearance in 1882. From 1885 the new party gained significance in parliament, electing representatives in particular from the fast-growing suburbs of Copenhagen (Dybdahl, 1969). The Social Democrats were a threat to Right strongholds in the cities, and also won support among small-holders and farm workers. The appearance of the third party was an important factor in inducing a moderate wing of the Left party toward a policy of negotiation with the Right. This policy failed when the Right refused to give up their power, and the result was an over-whelming public support for the opposition Reforming Left (Reformvenstre). But it was not until 1901, when the government's support in the lower house had been brought down to seven percent of the seats and dissident Right candidates threatened the government's majority even in the upper house, that the Left Party came to power.

1901-1920. During the period 1901-20 the party system acquired the basic structure which was to last almost to the present time (see Table 1). The Reforming Left Party split when its radical fraction, mainly consisting of intellectuals in Copenhagen and other major towns, in 1905 formed the Radical Liberal Party *(Radikale Venstre),* being joined by smallholders who resented the tendency of the new income tax system to favour large farms over small farms. In 1910 the Reforming Left merged with the Moderate Left *(Moderate Venstre)* in a party which was simply called the Left *(Venstre).* Finally, the Right Party in 1915 changed its name to the Conservative People's Party *(Konservative Folkeparty)* and assumed a programme with a supposedly broader appeal than that of the old Right. With the addition of the Social Democratic Party a four-party system had emerged, which on most important issues presented a clear ranking from left to right: Social Democrats, Radical Liberals, Left (henceforward called Agrarian Liberals), and Conservatives. However, the simple plurality system was not ideally suited to represent these divisions. In some elections Social Democrats and Radical Liberals succeeded in unseating an Agrarian Liberal or Conservative candidate by agreeing to run only one candidate between them in the constituency. Furthermore, the Conservatives were grossly underrepresented and the Agrarian Liberals grossly over-represented in seats relative to their voting strength. Pressures to change the electoral law toward proportional representation merged with desires to extend the franchise to women (Dahlerup, 1977), servants, and younger persons in the first decade of the century. The result was a constitutional revision in 1915, bringing proportional representation into operation in Copenhagen at the 1918 election and in the provincial constitutencies in April 1920.

TABLE 1
Electoral Support for the Parties at General Elections 1906-71, by Period

Period	No. of elections	Average Support in Percent of Valid Votes					Total
		Social Democrats	Radical Liberals	Agrarian Liberals	Conservatives	Other parties	
1906-20	8	29.0	15.9	33.4	19.8	1.9	100.0
1924-43	7	41.7	10.2	23.5	18.8	5.8	100.0
1945-57	6	38.9	7.9	23.8	16.5	12.9	100.0
1960-71	5	38.7	9.5	19.1	18.8	13.9	100.0

Besides constitutional issues, the defence issues were prominent in the first two decades of the century. Anti-militarism was, for example, a major cause for the split-off of the radical Liberals from the Left and the stagnation of the Left, whose stand on defence issues was less clearly positive than was the stand of Conservatives. Economic and social issues had had increasing importance since the 1890s, first dealing with the early social welfare programmes and later, during World War I, with crisis management. But it was not until the period 1920-40 that the interventionist role of the state became the dominant divisive issue.

1920-1960. The period from 1920 to 1960 is characterized by the expansion of the Danish welfare state, promoted by Social

Democratic dominance in a stable four-party system. The 1924 election established the Social Democrats as the largest party in the system, and it took over the government. This moment had been dreaded by the bourgeois middle class for more than a generation. But the government in reality had to rely on support from the radical Liberals in the lower house and even from the Agrarian Liberals in the upper house, and if this were not enough to ensure a cautious policy, the desire of the leading Social Democrats to create an image of respectability did the rest. In comparison with the Agrarian Liberal government, with which the Social Democratic government alternated throughout the 1920s, and which adhered to an extreme laissez-faire policy, the Social Democrats appeared moderate. They succeeded in capturing the political centre, paving the way for a generation of Social Democratic dominance in Danish politics. The support of the Social Democratic Party reached a peak in 1935; in fifteen years it increased its voter support by 17 percent of the electorate, while the Agrarian Liberals lost a similar share of the voters (Svensson, 1974: 142).

The strength of the major parties did not change noticeably from the 1930s to the end of the 1950s. Even the German occupation, 1940-45, and its aftermath entailed only a temporary disturbance of the strength pattern. When the German forces, to everyone's surprise, permitted an election in 1943 the occasion was used as a national manifestation to reinforce the normal pattern. Most of the time the government was a coalition of Social Democrats and Radical Liberals. Only in 1945-47 and in 1950-53 did Agrarian Liberals come to power, the latter period in coalition with the Conservatives. Besides these two broad coalitions only two more parties were regularly in parliament, namely the Communist Party and the Justice or Single-Tax Party (Retsforbundet) based on the ideas of the economist Henry George. Roll-call analysis has shown that the legislative positions of major parties were relatively stable during the period from World War II up to 1960 (Damgaard and Rusk, 1976). So far as constitutional reform goes, the major event of the period was the revision of the constitution in 1953, when the upper house was abolished, the lower house broadened from 149 seats to the present number of 179 seats, and a two percent threshold of representation introduced. The revised constitution also incorporated Greenland as a regular part of Denmark.

Since 1960. This period has been marked by increasing political instability and challenges to the established party system, leading to the downfall of the four-party system in 1973. The same four parties no longer control the legislature and monopolize the cabinet with highly predictable coalitions, long duration governments, and high chances of bills passing the legislature (Damgaard, 1974). The downfall was occasioned by the growth of other, socialist and non-socialist, parties (see Table 2). Mogens Pedersen, in analyzing the characteristics of politicians of the four-party system, has shown that from 1900 to 1920 an important change took place from a relatively open toward a relatively closed political elite (Pedersen, 1967, 1976). The possibility that this elite was becoming too closed and self-contained to respond to public pressure is raised in a communications study of the 1971 election (Siune and Borre, 1975).

TABLE 2
Vote Division at Folketing Elections, 1960-79

	Percent of Votes Cast								
	1960	1964	1966	1968	1971	1973	1975	1977	1979
Social Democrats	42.1	41.9	38.2	34.2	37.3	25.7	30.0	37.0	38.3
Socialist People's Party	6.1	5.8	10.9	6.1	9.1	6.0	4.9	3.9	5.9
Communists	1.1	1.2	0.8	1.0	1.4	3.6	4.2	3.7	1.9
Left Socialists	—	—	—	2.0	1.6	1.5	2.1	2.7	3.6
Total Socialist parties	(49.3)	(48.9)	(49.9)	(43.3)	(49.4)	(36.8)	(41.2)	(47.3)	(49.7)
Radical Liberals	5.8	5.3	7.3	15.0	14.4	11.2	7.1	3.6	5.4
Agrarian Liberals	21.1	20.8	19.3	18.6	15.6	12.3	23.3	12.0	12.5
Conservatives	17.9	20.1	18.7	20.4	16.7	9.1	5.5	8.5	12.5
Justice Party (Single-Tax)	2.2	1.3	0.7	0.7	1.7	2.9	1.8	3.3	2.6
Independent Party	3.3	2.5	1.6	0.5	—	—	—	—	—
Liberal Centre	—	—	2.5	1.3	—	—	—	—	—
Christian People's Party	—	—	—	—	2.0	4.0	5.3	3.4	2.6
Progressive Party	—	—	—	—	—	15.9	13.6	14.6	11.0
Centre Deocrats	—	—	—	—	—	7.8	2.2	6.5	3.2
Total non-socialist parties	(50.3)	(50.0)	(50.1)	(56.5)	(50.4)	(63.2)	(58.8)	(51.9)	(49.8)
Remaining small parties	0.4	1.2	—	0.2	0.2	—	—	0.9	0.4
Total	100.0	100.1	100.0	100.0	100.0	100.0	100.0	100.1	99.9
Voting turnout	85.8	85.5	88.6	89.3	87.2	89.0	88.2	89.0	85.5

The first serious threat to the four-party system came in 1960 from the left, when the new Socialist People's Party *(Socialistisk Folkeparti)* entered parliament. Apparently the New Left fed on several sources including the ending of the Cold War, rising prosperity, and the advent of mass education. Two other additions to the party system, the Independents *(Uafhængige)* on the right and the Liberal Centre *(Liberalt Centrum)* in the middle, proved short-lived. But when the Socialist People's Party in 1966 grew to the status of a regular fifth member of the party system, a two-bloc system with a clear socialist – non-socialist cleavage resulted. The Social Democrats governed in 1966-68 and 1971-73, whereas the Radical Liberals joined the Conservative and Agrarian Liberal forces in a coalition that governed in 1968-71.

The year 1973 became a turning point in Danish politics. The appearance of the new anti-tax party, the Progressive Party *(Fremskridspartiet)*, led to a general instability of party support in the polls, and the election in December brought four additional parties into parliament: Communists, Single-Taxers, the Christian People's Party *(Kristeligt Folkeparti)*, which had been formed in 1970 in protest against secularized politics, and the Centre Democrats *(Centrum-Demokraterne)*, which split away from the right side of the Social Democratic Party. With the addition of the Left Socialists *(Venstresocialisterne)*, a split-off from the left side of the Socialist People's Party in 1967, the party system from 1973 onwards includes eleven parties. All except the Left Socialists were represented in parliament in the election period 1973-75, all except the Single-Taxers were represented in 1975-77, all eleven were represented in 1977-79, and all except the Communists are represented after the election of October, 1979. An Agrarian Liberal government took over in 1973 and was succeeded by a Social Democratic government in 1975. This government has remained in power since then, although it was broadened to a coalition with Agrarian Liberal ministers from August 1978 to October 1979. These cabinets have generally sought to build parliamentary majorities from an "inner circle" of parties consisting of the four old parties, the Centre Democrats, and the Christian People's Party. The three left-wing parties, the Progressives, and the Single-Taxers are normally not participants in these shifting coalitions. At the present time, the party system seems to have crystallized into five groups of parties:

Leftwing	Left-of-centre	Centre	Right-of-centre	Rightwing
Communist	Social Dem.	Radical Lib.	Agrarian Lib.	Progress.
Left Soc.		Single-Tax	Conservative	
People's Soc.			Centre Dem.	
			Christian Peo.	

This structure roughly applies to legislative behaviour as well as to voter sympathies and vote shifts. The large majority of vote shifts occur either within the two multiparty blocs (in particular among the four parties right-of-centre) or between neighbouring blocs, thus indicating a certain predictability of the behavioural pattern underlying the apparent fragmentation and fluency.

2. THE INSTITUTIONAL FRAMEWORK OF ELECTORAL BEHAVIOUR

Earlier Arrangements

A wide suffrage was given to the male population in the 1849 constitution, both with respect to the direct "Folketing" (lower house) election and the first stage of the indirect "Landsting" (upper house) election (Elklit, 1974). The electorate consisted of all men over 30 years who were not in the personal service of others. The same persons were eligible for the Folketing; the age limit was 40 for candidates to the Landsting. During later revisions of the constitution, the principle of broad suffrage at Folketing elections was never seriously challenged. Instead, conservative efforts were directed toward limiting the electorate for the Landsting and undermining the competence of the Folketing. Debate about this partial return to absolutism continued until 1863 when the government declared the federal constitution abolished, an act which led to the second Schleswig war in 1864. The government and its conservative supporters in 1866 enacted a revision by which 12 of the 66 Landsting members were appointed by the king (in practice by the government), while the remaining members were elected indirectly by an assembly consisting of 400 members, strongly biased in favour of the largest landlords and upper-level urban taxpayers. This system of representation was in force until the constitutional revision in 1915. From 1915 to 1953, one quarter of the Landsting was elected by the previous Landsting while three-quarters was elected by universal suffrage of those above the age of 35. The Landsting was abolished at the constitutional revision in 1953.

The most important extension of the suffrage was made in 1915, when women obtained the vote and the age limit was lowered from 30 to 25 years. By means of referenda, the age limit was further lowered to 23 years in 1953, 21 years in 1964, 20 years in 1972, and 18 years in 1978.

Present Method of Representation

Since the constitutional reform in 1953 the Folketing has consisted of 179 members, of whom two represent the Faroes, two Greenland, and 175 Denmark proper. Seats are allotted to parties (or independent candidates) according to the following procedure, which stems from 1970 when the counties and communes were re-structured. Basically the same procedure was used during the period 1953-70.

1. The country is divided into three main areas: Copenhagen, the Islands, and Jutland. These areas are subdivided into a total of 17 constituencies of which 3 are in Copenhagen, 7 in the Islands, and 7 in Jutland. The 14 provincial constituencies correspond to the county divisions.

Of the 175 seats, 135 are directly attached to multi-member constituencies *(kredsmandater)* while the remaining 40 seats float between constituencies in the same main area *(tillægsmandater)*. These 40 seats are used to make up for the lack of proportionality in the distribution of directly won seats. However, the 135 directly elected seats and the total of 175 seats are divided between the main areas according to a formula which over-represents thinly populated areas, mostly in Jutland. The result is the distribution shown in Table 3.

2. After each election, the division of the 135 direct seats between the parties in each constituency is the first step. For this purpose the number of votes for each party in the constituency is divided by the divisors 1.4, 3, 5, 7, and successive odd figures, i.e., a modified version of the St. Lagüe formula. The resulting coefficients are arranged in descending order across parties, and direct seats are assigned to the parties associated with these figures until the number of direct seats in the constituency is exhausted.

3. Parties obtain shares in the distribution of floating seats if they

TABLE 3

**Allocation of Folketing Seats to the Three Main Areas, and
its Deviation from Proportional Representation, by 1970**

Main Area	Direct seats	Floating seats	Total	No. of seats if distribution were proportional	Deviation between actual and proportional representation
Copenhagen	19	5	24	31	−7
Islands	54	16	70	69	1
Jutland	62	19	81	75	6
Denmark proper	135	40	175		
Greenland	2		2		
Faroes	2		2		
Total	139	40	179		

(a) have obtained at least one direct seat, or (b) have won more than two percent of all valid votes cast, or (c) in two of the three main areas obtain as many votes as the average "price" of a direct seat in that area, measured in terms of votes. Among parties thus qualified, a complete proportional distribution of all 175 seats is made, and by subtracting the number of direct seats already allotted one arrives at the residual number of floating seats to be allotted to each party.

4. The next problem is to calculated *where* the party's floating seats will be located. This is done in two stages, one to assign the seats to main areas and the second to assign them to constituencies in that area. On the first stage the party's vote in the area is divided by the series 1, 3, 5, 7 . . . discarding as many initial divisors as the number of direct seats the party has already won in that area. For example, if the party has won two direct seats, the first divisor will be 5. Across parties and main areas the resulting quotients are then arranged in descending order, and seats are assigned from the top of this array. On the second state the party's vote in the different constituencies in the main area are compared and divided by 1, 4, 7, 10 . . . again discarding initial divisors where the party has obtained direct seats.

This process ensures that parties that pass one or more of the thresholds become proportionally represented in the Folketing, although its representation in some cases may come from a constituency in another main area than that where its highest vote is located. The next steps in the process, often postponed until two or three days after election night, have to do with the determination of *who* is elected. The procedure here varies according to the type of nomination which the party has chosen for the constituency.

5. The 17 constituencies are subdivided into 103 nomination districts of roughly equal size. In nominating candidates the party organizations decide between several type of slate. In any case all the party's candidates in a given constituency appear on the slate of every nomination district in the constituency, and a voter has a choice between checking a particular candidate or the party as such with his cross. But the way in which the votes for the party as such are to be ascribed to the candidates varies with the type of the slate. In one type of slate votes are even transferred from one candidate to other candidates according to complicated accounting procedures.

Effect of Personal Voting

The votes cast for a particular candidate constitute around half the number of votes cast at recent elections, with a tendency for the rate of personal voting to increase. However, personal voting does not always affect the various candidates' chances of getting elected (Pedersen, 1966). Votes given to top candidates in slates where only one candidate is nominated are not different from votes for the party as such and should be classified as ineffective. Pedersen shows that the rate of effective personal voting on average has been increasing within all four old parties since 1920, and that female candidates and candidates that are already members of Folketing tend to benefit by drawing personal votes from other nomination districts and restricting effective personal voting for other candidates in their own nomination district. The type of slate also exerts considerable influence on the distribution of personal votes between candidates. Above all, the nominated candidate or candidates receive a disproportional share of the personal votes in their nomination district.

3. SOCIAL CLASS AND VOTING BEHAVIOUR

In spite of the comparative homogeneity of the Danish population, it will emerge from the following sections that most parties and partisan blocs have their support unevenly distributed among social groupings, and that in particular social class cleavages are a pervasive phenomenon of Danish voting behaviour. Systematic surveys of the social forces underlying individual voting behaviour has only been available from 1971 onward. Thus, surveys span the period during which the present multiparty system evolved but not the period of the preceding four or five party system.

Social class, defined either in terms of objective occupational groups or subjective identification with the working or the middle class, constitutes the most important cleavage in the Danish party system, even though the effect of class position is less clear-cut in the present party system than previously.

Occupational Class

Of the parties already established around 1920, the three largest seem to have been fairly unambiguous in their social bases: the Social Democratic Party was the party of the working class, the Conservative Party the party of the urban middle class, and the Agrarian Liberal Party the party of the rural middle class. In the 1960s two new political tendencies made inroads in the political spectrum: the ideological New Left and the de-ideologized New Centre. These movements found their political expression in the emergence of the Socialist People's Party and the growth of the Radical Liberal Party, respectively. Table 4 shows the preference of occupational groups around the 1971 election. The farmers were solidly behind the Agrarian Liberal Party and the workers almost as solidly behind the Social Democratic Party, whereas the urban middle classes and especially the salaried employees had become the primary battleground between all four or five parties. Among the self-employed in urban industries the Conservatives apparently where losing ground to the Radical Liberals, headed by prime minister Baunsgaard.

This pattern of preferences naturally was upset in 1973. The thin data base used in the survey of the 1973 election does not permit a detailed breakdown into occupational groups. Table 5 shows the results of a pooling of ten commercial polls. The three leftwing parties — Socialist People's Party, Communist Party, and Left Socialist Party — have here been combined into one group, and five minor parties of the political centre-right orientation — Radical Liberal Party, Conservative Party, Centre Democrats, Christian People's Party, and Justice Party — into another group. With regard to the occupational groups, pensioners have been singled out as a separate group rather than being referred to their previous

TABLE 4
Occupation and Party Choice, 1971

Occupational Group	Parties						Total	No. of
	Soc. Peop. %	Soc. Dem. %	Rad. Lib. %	Agr. Lib. %	Cons. %	Other %	%	respondents %
Farmers	0	6	14	70	3	7	100	111
Self-employed in urban occupations	1	23	26	13	34	3	100	86
Higher salaried employees	6	26	18	20	26	4	100	125
Lower salaried employees	8	35	22	12	19	4	100	204
Workers	10	65	10	8	4	3	100	506

Source: Ole Borre, Hans Jørgen Nielsen, Steen Sauerberg, and Torben Worre, *Vælgere i 70'erne* (Voters in the '70s), Copenhagen: Akademisk Forlag, 1976: 51.

TABLE 5
Occupation and Party Choice, 1974

Occupational Group	Parties					Total	No. of
	Left-wing %	Soc. Dem. %	Minor Centre-right %	Agr. Lib. %	Pro-gress %	%	respondents
Farmers	1	2	24	61	12	100	298
Self-employed in urban occupations	5	10	36	22	27	100	520
Higher salaried employees	11	15	39	23	12	100	526
Lower salaried employees	14	30	33	12	11	100	1020
Skilled workers	19	42	19	7	13	100	819
Unskilled workers	15	55	13	5	12	100	673
Pensioners (elderly or disabled)	4	45	27	19	5	100	1161
Students, other unoccupied	42	19	22	12	5	100	275

Source: Vælgernes veje (The Voter's Ways), Copenhagen: Børsen, 1974, consolidated from several tables in the book.

occupation. The coding probably differs between the two tables in other ways too, so that they may be compared only with some caution.

Of the three new bourgeois parties emerging at the 1973 election, the Progressive Party established a particularly strong voter base among the self-employed in urban industries, that is, in those occupations where traditionally the Conservative Party gathered support until the middle 1960s. Its support among higher and lower salaried employees is probably somewhat weaker than was the Conservative strength in these groups a decade earlier, but on the other hand the Progressive Party has captured a much stronger share of the working-class vote than the Conservatives have ever enjoyed. Only among pensioners and students has the Progressive Party a definitely weak standing, whereas it is likely that the Conservative Party used to be fairly strongly represented in these groups. The Centre Democrats and the Christian People's Party are also primarily middle-class based but have some following in the working-class.

The elections of 1975 and 1977 confirmed the broad contours of the cleavage between the occupational categories with regard to their partisan preferences. Though every new election entails massive exchange of voters and change in party fortunes, it seems fairly clear from Table 6 that the social bases established at the 1973 election in the main have been working throughout the 1975 and 1977 elections. Among *workers* the vote for the four socialist parties combined has fluctuated around two-thirds at all three elections. Since it was higher than three-quarters in 1971 and probably also at many previous elections under the four-party and five-party systems, a permanent shift of working-class allegiance away from the socialist parties appears to be a fact. The Social Democratic gains at the 1977 election were largely offset by leftwing losses, contrary to what happened in the other occupational groups. Among *lower salaried employees* the socialist parties altogether suffered almost no setback in 1973, because the leftwing advanced from around 10 percent to 14 percent, and the Social Democratic gains in 1977 in this group suggest that the lower white collar population in the process of becoming a socialist stronghold during the 1970s. By contrast, the *higher salaried employees* left the Social Democratic Party in large numbers in 1973, reducing the combined socialist vote in this group from around one third to around one fourth. The 1977 election, however, has advanced the leftwing vote from 8 to 13 percent and the Social Democratic vote from 16 to 24 percent and thereby brought the total socialist vote among the upper white collar voters to a higher point than it has probably ever been.

It is interesting to see that both wings of the party system, the three leftwing parties on one side and the Progressive Party on the other, are represented in each of the employee groups in the proportion which these wings have in the population on the whole. The leftwing receives 12 to 13 percent in the three groups while the Progressive Party receives 17 percent among workers and 13 to 14 percent among salaried employees. Only when it comes to the choice between the Social Democratic Party and the various parties of the centre-right category, do the three voter groups disagree widely, and large fluctuations occur from one election to the next. For example, the Agrarian Liberal Party, after acquiring 20 percent of the upper white collar vote in 1971, 23 percent in 1973, and 29 percent in 1975, went down to 8 percent in 1977. And in the same group of voters, the Centre Democrats suddenly emerged at the 1977 election as the second largest party, going up from 3 to 15 percent.

The *self-employed* part of the population, whether in urban industries or in farming, shows very little sympathy with the leftwing. The Social Democratic Party which traditionally had a foothold among small entrepreneurs, lost most of it in the 1973 debacle, but has recovered since. The Agrarian Liberal Party during the period 1971 to 1975 rapidly expanded its voter base among urban entrepeneurs, going up from 13 percent in 1971 to 22 percent in 1973 and to 32 percent in 1975, but it suffered a violent setback to 11 percent in 1977. The Progressive Party appears to have established a much more secure base in this group, polling between 27 and 30 percent at the last three elections. Among the farmers, the Agrarian Liberal Party is still the dominant party, but its support has been reduced from 70 percent in 1971 to 52 percent in 1977. The opposite movement can be noticed with regard to the Progressive Party, which by 1977 polled 20 percent of the farm population.

The *students* differ from all the other groups because of the strong and consistent leftwing preference at between 42 and 46 percent at all three elections under the new party system. Their sympathy switches between the three parties from one election to the next, but the Left Socialists appear more than the other two parties to have specialized in attracting the students' votes. Of the remaining parties the Social Democratic Party polls a significant number of student votes, producing a total socialist vote between 60 and 70 percent at each election; a rising trend for the Progressive Party is also observed.

The *pensioners* (old-age or disabled) divide their vote almost evenly between the socialist and non-socialist parties at every election. Both wings of the party system have a conspicuously weak standing in this group: the leftwing polls 4 to 6 percent and the

TABLE 6
Occupation and Party Choice, 1975 and 1977

Party	Year	Workers %	Lower salaried employees %	Higher salaried employees %	Occupational Group[1] Urban self-employed %	Farmers %	Students %	Pensioners %
Communist	1975	8	4	1	1	0	11	3
	1977	6	5	2	0	1	3	3
Left Socialist	1975	2	3	3	1	0	14	1
	1977	2	2	6	1	0	24	1
Socialist People's	1975	7	7	4	1	0	21	2
	1977	4	6	5	2	0	18	1
Total, leftwing parties	1975	(17)	(14)	(8)	(3)	(0)	(46)	(6)
	1977	(12)	(13)	(13)	(3)	(1)	(45)	(5)
Social Democratic	1975	47	28	16	9	2	14	41
	1977	55	38	24	16	2	24	47
Total, socialist parties	1975	(64)	(42)	(24)	(12)	(2)	(60)	(47)
	1977	(67)	(51)	(37)	(19)	(3)	(69)	(52)
Radical Liberal	1975	4	8	12	7	9	9	6
	1977	2	3	5	5	8	0	4
Justice (Single-Tax)	1975	1	2	2	2	1	4	2
	1977	3	5	5	5	1	2	2
Centre Democratic	1975	2	4	3	1	2	2	1
	1977	4	8	15	9	4	6	3
Christian People's	1975	3	5	5	6	9	2	8
	1977	2	3	5	3	5	2	4

TABLE 6 (continued)

Party	Year	Workers %	Lower salaried employees %	Higher salaried employees %	Urban self-employed %	Farmers %	Students %	Pensioners %
						Occupational Group[1]		
Agrarian Liberal	1975	10	21	29	32	63	13	21
	1977	4	9	8	11	52	4	12
Conservative	1975	1	6	12	10	2	2	7
	1977	1	7	12	19	7	4	14
Total, centre-right parties	1975	(21)	(46)	(63)	(58)	(86)	(32)	(45)
	1977	(16)	(35)	(50)	(52)	(77)	(18)	(39)
Progressive	1975	15	12	13	30	12	8	8
	1977	17	14	13	28	20	13	6
Pensionist Party	1975	—	—	—	—	—	—	—
	1977	0	1	0	1	0	0	3
Total, non-socialist parties	1975	(36)	(58)	(76)	(88)	(98)	(40)	(53)
	1977	(33)	(50)	(63)	(81)	(97)	(31)	(48)
No. of respondents (= 100%)	1975	3014	2354	1101	1023	1006	390	2281
	1977	917	732	412	318	360	110	805

1. Housewives are classified under their husbands' occupations.

Source: Gallup data published by Ingemar Glans in the daily newspaper *Information*, 22 April 1977.

Progressive Party 5 to 8 percent. As seems natural, it is particularly the old Social Democratic, Agrarian Liberal, and Conservative parties that command the pensioners' support.

Class Voting and Class Identification

The previous tables suggest that Denmark, along with Britain and the other Scandinavian countries, bases its political system heavily on class cleavages. Yet these tables also reveal that developments through the 1970s have entailed a decrease of the correlation between social class and political preference. Table 7 sums up this development in terms of the coefficient of class voting proposed by Robert Alford. In 1971, among skilled and unskilled workers together, the combined vote for the socialist parties was 77 percent, whereas among salaried employees and self-employed the socialist vote was 31 percent. The difference, which is the coefficient of class voting, was therefore 46 percent. The transition to the new multi-party system in 1973 implied a drop in class voting to the level of 37 to 39 percent. This sizeable decrease has been the result of the emergence of the Progressive party as a bourgeois, or at least a non-socialist, party with a fairly balanced support in all classes (see Table 6).

TABLE 7
Change in Class Voting 1971-77

Occupational Class	Strength of Socialist Parties (percent)			
	1971	1974	1975	1977
Working class	77	65	64	67
Middle class	31	28	25	33
Difference (= coefficient of class voting)	46	37	39	34

The 1977 election diminished the distance between the two main social classes with respect to their partisan preferences even further. The dimension of class differences this time took the form of Social Democratic gains, in particular among salaried employees.

A recurrent theme in political sociology has been the "embourge-oisement" hypothesis, according to which a decrease in the inclination toward class voting would be expected as the workers gradually acquired the life style of the middle classes. The above figures may be seen to conform to this broad hypothesis. In its crude

TABLE 8
Social Class Identification and Party Choice 1971 and 1977

Party or party bloc	Respondents with		
	Working class identification %	No class identification %	Middle class identification %
1971 Election:			
Three Leftwing parties	15	6	6
Social Democratic	75	42	27
Total socialist parties	(90)	(48)	(33)
Agrarian Liberal	2	21	22
Conservative	1	13	21
Radical Liberal	4	16	20
Other non-socialist parties	3	2	4
Total non-socialist parties	(10)	(52)	(67)
No. of respondents	222	620	281
Distribution of respondents	20%	55%	25%
1977 Election:			
Three Leftwing parties	17	8	8
Social Democratic	66	39	32
Total socialist	(83)	(47)	(40)
Agrarian Liberal	4	17	15
Conservative	2	8	12
Progressive	4	11	12
Other non-socialist parties	7	17	21
Total non-socialist parties	(17)	(53)	(60)
No. of respondents	320	550	348
Distribution of respondents	26%	45%	29%

form, however, the embourgeoisement hypothesis does not include two reservations which are important in the light of the previous tables, (1) that class voting decreases in the young generation not only as a consequence of bourgeois preferences among young workers, but just as much as a consequence of socialist voting in the middle-class youth, and (2) that the Social Democratic parties may be expected to counter bourgeois infiltration by seeking compromises with bourgeois parties, and where possible, to play on disagreements and competition among bourgeois parties.

The decreasing importance of social class as determinant of the choice between socialist and non-socialist parties may be the result either of a lack of class consciousness or of a decrease in the extent to which the class-conscious part of the voters perceives the parties as representing class interests. Table 8 permits a comparison between responses to very similar questions on class identification in the 1971 and the 1977 election surveys. Common to both surveys is the fact that working class identification is accompanied by a high probability of socialist voting (90 percent in 1973, 83 percent in 1977) whereas middle class identification is accompanied by a less strong tendency toward non-socialist voting (67 percent in 1971, 60 percent in 1977).

Within each of these social psychological groups, however, parties of the opposite class have gained ground from 1971 to 1977. Notably, the Social Democratic Party has lost support among working-class identifiers but gained support among middle-class identifiers. There is no evidence of a waning of class consciousness. Instead, the drop in class voting has been caused by a reduction of the correlation between subjective class and partisan preference.

Level of Education

Since an important function of education is to assign occupational role and status to the individuals, one might expect social class differences in voting behaviour to be anticipated in educational differences. Table 9 presents a breakdown of the 1977 election survey into four levels of education.

Primary schooling for seven years is by far the most common in the Danish electorate, even though the last decade has entailed an expansion of the compulsory school education to ten years. Still, a large proportion of the middle class and in particular the self-employed and farmers have received only primary education. Since we know from previous tables that the self-employed constitute the most important stronghold for the bourgeois parties, the relationship between low education and socialist preference becomes rather weak. Another factor which disturbs the simple relationship between level of education and bourgeois party preference is the socialism of many intellectuals. Altogether these two tendencies generate a weak and non-linear relationship between level of education and bourgeois preference. However, within each of the two main blocs of parties, there are clear educational differences in partisan preferences. The support for the Social Democrats varies negatively with level of education, from 51 percent at the lowest end to 22 percent at the highest end of the educational ladder, while the Socialist People's and Left Socialist parties have higher support

TABLE 9
Level of Education and Party Choice 1977

Party	Primary, 7 yrs. or less %	Primary, over 7 yrs. %	Secondary, 9-10 yrs. %	Gymnasium 12 yrs. %
Communist	2	4	1	4
Left Socialist	0	2	5	7
Socialist People's	3	7	6	21
Social Democratic	51	47	33	22
Total socialist	(56)	(60)	(45)	(54)
Radical Liberal	4	3	1	8
Justice (Single-Tax)	4	4	3	2
Centre Democratic	3	8	12	1
Christian People's	2	1	5	4
Conservative	6	1	14	11
Agrarian Liberal	15	8	12	8
Progressive	9	14	8	9
Other	1	1	0	3
Total non-socialist	(44)	(40)	(55)	(46)
No. of respondents	694	151	269	113
Distribution of respondents (%)	57	12	22	9

among the more educated. Among the bourgeois parties, the Agrarian Liberal Party is the most important party for those with only 7 years primary education (to which the majority of the farm population belongs), while the Progressive Party is the most important for those who stayed in school longer without taking secondary education. Those with secondary education are primarily divided among Conservative, Agrarian Liberal, and Centre Democrats, while the Conservative Party is relatively stronger among those with a *gymnasium* education. Also the Christian People's Party appears to have its largest following among people with more than primary schooling.

4. GENERATIONAL DIFFERENCES

Age and Party Preference

The voter's age has come to play an increasing role in Danish voting behaviour during the last fifteen years. Studies carried out in the 1950s did not generally find any important monotonic relationship between age of voter and support for a particular party or category of parties (Svalastoga, 1959). Surveys from the late 1960s or the 1970s,

by contrast, display regular relationships. Table 10 presents the result
of an age breakdown of 1977 voters.

TABLE 10
Age of Respondent and Party Choice, 1977

| Party | Age of Respondent | | | | | |
| | 20-24 | 25-29 | 30-39 | 40-49 | 50-66 | 67+ |
	%	%	%	%	%	%
Communist	5	5	4	1	1	2
Left Socialist	5	5	2	4	0	0
Socialist People's	18	18	4	4	4	1
Social Democratic	38	29	46	49	44	52
Total socialist	(66)	(57)	(56)	(58)	(49)	(55)
Radical Liberal	3	2	1	2	4	5
Justice (Single-Tax)	1	7	3	3	3	4
Centre Democratic	1	7	9	9	3	3
Christian People's	2	2	3	1	4	2
Conservative	1	3	5	7	10	12
Agrarian Liberal	8	9	12	12	16	14
Progressive	18	11	11	8	9	3
Other	0	2	0	1	2	2
Total non-socialist	(34)	(43)	(44)	(43)	(51)	(45)
No. of respondents	133	146	217	180	376	235

It is seen that all three leftwing parties have a disproportionately
strong standing in the young generation, while the Social Democratic
Party largely increases its support with increasing age. These two
tendencies roughly offset one another, leaving only a slight tendency
for the youngest category (20-24 years old) to vote socialist to a larger
extent than other age groups.

Of the bourgeois parties, the Agrarian Liberal Party tends to
receive more support from the older than from the younger voters,
and this tendency is more outspoken with regard to the Conservative
Party, which does not seem to appeal to people under thirty. The
opposite tendency is observed with regard to the Progressive Party,
which is by far the strongest of the bourgeois parties among the
youngest voters but fades away to insignificance in the oldest generation. The Centre Democrats present a curvilinear relationship,
getting most support in the age brackets between 30 and 50.

A classification of the parties into three major categories brings
out more clearly an important tendency underlying generational
differences in party support. In Table 13 the three leftwing parties
have been combined into one group; the three new non-socialist

TABLE 11
Age of Respondent and Choice between Leftwing, New Bourgeois, and Four Old Parties, 1971-77

Party group[3]	Age of Respondent					
	20-24	25-29	30-39	40-49	50-64[1]	65 +[1]
	%	%	%	%	%	%
Leftwing parties						
1973[2]	30	11	12	9	6	2
1975	25	21	9	7	6	3
1977	28	28	10	9	5	3
New bourgeois parties						
1973[2]	41	33	31	26	14	16
1975	33	15	24	20	18	18
1977	21	20	23	18	16	8
Four old parties						
1973[2]	29	56	57	65	80	82
1975	42	64	67	73	76	78
1977	50	59	64	70	74	83

1. The age intervals are in 1977 50-66 years, and 67 years and more.

2. Age reported in 1971-73 survey. In 1973 these respondents were two years older than indicated in the age brackets.

3. Leftwing parties = Communist, Left Socialist, and Socialist People's Party; New bourgeois parties = Progressives, Centre Democrats, and Christian People's Party; Four old parties = Social Democrats, Agrarian Liberal, Radical Liberal, and Conservative Party.

parties entering the Folketing in 1973 (Progressives, Centre Democrats, and Christian People's Party) into another; and the four old parties (Social Democrats, Agrarian Liberals, Conservatives, and Radical Liberals) into a third group, while remaining minor parties are excluded. Data from 1973 and 1975 have been added to the 1977 data even though the age brackets are not strictly comparable in all cases. It is clear, however, that the strong relationship between youth and leftwing support goes back at least to 1973 in a largely unchanged form, except that the strong leftwing preference has remained as the 20-24 years old voters grew into the next group of 25-29 years old. Concerning the three new bourgeois parties as a whole, again one finds a strong negative relation between age and support. It was most outspoken in 1973, where it varied from 41 percent among the youngest to 16 percent among the oldest voters. In 1975 the difference was mostly between the youngest voters, who gave the three parties 33 percent of their votes, and the other age groups, who gave them between 24 and 15 percent. In 1977 it was the

oldest age group which created the relationship by giving these
parties only 8 percent of their votes as against the 23 to 16 percent
support in the other age groups. It appears that with the waning of the
"newness" of the three parties, support has become evenly
distributed over the age groups.

The compensating positive relation between party support and age
comes from the four old parties. In 1973 it was particularly the
youngest voters who reacted against the established parties, giving
them only 29 percent of the vote, while of those over fifty, 80 percent
or more remained loyal to the old parties. The difference between
young and old voters diminished at the next election, at which the old
parties regained territory among those below fifty while losing
ground among those over fifty. By 1977 most of those originally
20-24 years old had grown into the next age group, presumably
taking their disillusionment with the old parties with them, whereas
the next cohorts have not reacted quite as negatively toward the old
parties.

Most of these tendencies repeat themselves within individual
occupational groups, though the level of partisan support varies
strongly from one group to the next. The ability of the leftwing
parties to capture the young voters is visible in the working-class
population. In 1971 17 percent of those aged 21-39 voted for one of
the three parties concerned, as against 12 percent of those aged 40-64
and only 7 percent of those over 64 years. This pattern had become
even more pronounced by 1975; in addition the Progressive Party
had established a surprising following among young workers: 37
percent amoung those aged 21-25 (though based on only 43 cases), as
against 14 percent of those aged 25-50 and 7 percent of those over 50.
An inverse relationship is found with respect to the Social Democratic strength, but totalling the socialist strength one still finds a
rather impressive "embourgeoisement" of the young workers: of
those aged 21-25 only 40 percent voted socialist, while 59 percent of
those between 25 and 50, and 69 percent of those over fifty did so.

In terms of the coefficient of class voting in Table 7, one finds a
very marked tendency for the new generations to discard class differences in their political choice. In 1975 the socialist vote was 52 percent
among workers in their twenties, only 11 percentage points higher
than the 41 percent given to the four socialist parties by self-
employed and salaried employees in their twenties. Among voters in
their thirties and forties, the socialist vote in 1975 was 58 percent
among workers as against 25 percent among self-employed and sala-

ried employees, a class voting coefficient of 33 percent, or three times higher than for younger voters. Finally, among voters aged fifty or more, the socialist vote was 68 percent in the working class as against only 22 percent in the two middle-class categories combined, a class voting coefficient of 48 percent.

Age and Party Identification

It is a common finding in voting research that new parties with growing support are disproportionately preferred by the young voters. Yet the dramatic generational cleavages visible in Table 11 give rise to some vital questions concerning both causes and long-range effects. A study of party identification around the 1971 election (Borre and Katz, 1973) established the well-known tendency for young voters to have weaker party ties than older voters. Among voters in their twenties, only 34 percent called themselves "adherents" of one party or another, while the figure rose steadily with each ten-year group, ending up with 70 percent among those aged 60 or more. On average, party identification rose 8 percentage points for every ten years age difference.

It is still a little too early to assess to what extent the new parties have profited from a short-term dissatisfaction with the older party system and to what extent they have succeeded in establishing loyalties of an enduring nature. The proportion of party identifiers went down from 57 percent just after the 1971 election to 48 percent after the 1973 election, but has since then recovered to 52 percent after the 1975 election and rose to 60 percent in 1977. Lasting sympathies have been established by a significant share of the electors for such new parties as the Progressive Party and the Christian People's Party, and for the leftwing parties as a group, though perhaps not for any particular one of the three parties. Comparatively speaking, the new components of the party system exhibit as much stability as the older components.

5. FAMILY STRUCTURE AND LIFE STYLE

Both social class and age differences give rise to important partisan cleavages in the Danish voting public. In addition there are several life style factors which may be presumed to reflect cleavages in the political system, although sometimes these cleavages amount to no more than an inclination toward or taste for two different but ideologically neighbouring parties. An example would be the three leftwing parties. As we have already seen, the working-class radicals prefer the Communist Party, the white-collar group incline toward the Socialist People's Party, and the students embrace the Left Socialist Party. With the change from a five-party, two-bloc system to a more erratic multiparty system in 1973 it is likely that the political heterogeneity and diversity has increased to such an extent that slight differences in style between population groups are matched by equally slight differences in the image and style of the parties.

Sex Differences

Sex differences in the partisan choice are slight, and to the extent that a pattern is at all discernible, women tend to be underrepresented among votes for parties on both wings of the system (the three leftwing parties and the Progressive Party). Aside from this, the Christian People's Party and the Conservative Party have a majority of female voters, the Agrarian Liberals probably a majority of male voters, though some of the differences reported may be due to sample errors.

Type of Residence

Of the various indicators of consumption pattern, perhaps none is as important as the distinction between house-owners and apartment-dwellers (see Table 12). Perhaps as a consequence of Danish housing policy throughout a generation, the parties have forced one another into taking sides in the perennial dispute over government support and tax relief to one-family house-owners and apartment-dwellers. Buying a house requires capital, usually in the form of borrowing long-range credit corresponding to several years' income of a young couple, and consequently abstention from more immediate consumption, but with a promise of rapidly rising value of the house. Apartment-dwelling is congenial with socialist voting. In particular the Socialist People's Party and the Communist Party recruit their support overwhelmingly among apartment-dwellers, while the

Conservative Party is three times as strongly supported among house-owners as among apartment-dwellers and the Agrarian Liberal Party more than twice as strongly. The latter party can also count on strong support from the farm-dwelling population. The new bourgeois parties, on the other hand, receive only slightly more support from the house-owners than from the apartment-renters, and this applies even to the Centre Democrats, who appear more than any other party to favor house-owners in their policy. The institution of owned apartments dates back only a few years, and the number of apartment-owners is consequently small (though rapidly growing), but it is anyway remarkable to find a strong leftist orientation in this group, considering the party constellation that advocates the extension of opportunities for this type of residence.

TABLE 12
Type of Residence and Party Choice, 1977

Party	Type of Residence			
	Owned house %	Owned apartment %	Farm %	Rented apartment %
Communist	1	13	0	5
Left Socialist	2	22	0	2
Socialist People's	2	9	2	11
Social Democratic	45	39	5	54
Total socialist	(50)	(83)	(7)	(72)
Radical Liberal	4	0	7	2
Justice (Single-Tax)	4	0	1	3
Centre Democratic	6	9	3	4
Christian People's	3	0	1	2
Conservative	12	0	4	4
Agrarian Liberal	9	0	65	4
Progressive	11	9	11	8
Other	1	0	1	1
Total non-socialist	(50)	(18)	(93)	(28)
Total	100	101	100	100
No. of respondents	583	23	132	503

Religious Activity

The huge majority of the population belongs to the official Lutheran church which is supported by the state and membership of which is automatic. According to the 1971 election survey 96.5 percent of the electorate were members of the official church although only 75 percent declared that they would be members if one had to enroll in order to become a member of the church. Divergent views within the official church mean little to the general public, since only 7 percent of the electors declared that they were attached to a particular branch of the church.

Religious issues have not traditionally been prominent in Danish politics on a national scale. Yet bourgeois parties generally take a more positive stand on and a greater interest in such issues. This difference is apparently felt in the electorate, since 43 percent answered yes to a question of whether they thought there were differences between the political parties with regard to religious issues.

The Christian People's Party emerged in 1971 as the first and only political party with explicitly positive views on religious matters. It may be regarded as a protest party against the liberalization of the abortion laws and laws prohibiting pornography, against curbing religious teaching in the schools, and against other signs of secularization. It was the leader of the Conservative Party, who as general attorney in the bourgeois government 1968-71 executed the liberal pornography laws, and this fact may have triggered the emergence of the new party. Its general moral-religious appeal, as opposed to an appeal to a specific religious denomination, may be illuminated by the fact that the leader since 1973 is a Catholic. Both the general bourgeous inclination toward religious activity and the particular appeal of the Christian People's Party to the religiously active may be gathered from Table 13. For 1971 the socialist vote varies from 20 percent among regular churchgoers, of whom 13 percent voted for this party.

Nationality, Ethnicity, and Language

Compared with most nations, Denmark has an extremely homogeneous population containing only a few and numerically unimportant ethnic or national minorities. In North Schleswig, which belonged to Germany from 1864 to 1920, the German Minority Party ran candidates until and including the 1971 election, but its 6,700 votes at that election fell far below any of the three thresholds of representation. In the elections of 1975 and 1977 their candidates ran on the list of the Centre Democrats. The situation of the German minority has been investigated by a community study in the 1950s (Svalastoga and Wolf, 1965), and a recent, more comprehensive

TABLE 13
Relation between Frequency of Churchgoing 1971 and Partisan Choice, 1971 and 1973

| | Goes to Church | | | |
	At least once a month %	More seldom %	Only at celebrations %	Never %
Party choice 1971:				
Leftwing	1	5	8	26
Social Democratic	19	34	50	40
Total socialist	(20)	(39)	(58)	(66)
Radical Liberal	13	19	15	8
Agrarian Liberal	39	24	14	9
Conservative	11	15	12	16
Christian People's	13	0	0	0
Single-Tax	4	3	1	1
Total non-socialist	(80)	(61)	(42)	(34)
Total	100	100	100	100
No. of respondents	126	156	760	99
Party choice 1973:				
Leftwing	4	6	8	32
Social Democratic	13	20	35	22
Total socialist	(17)	(26)	(43)	(54)
Radical Liberal	23	20	10	10
Agrarian Liberal	27	20	15	7
Conservative	2	4	6	10
Christian People's	17	4	2	0
Single-Tax	3	6	1	2
Centre Democratic	6	11	7	5
Progressive	6	9	16	12
Total non-socialist	(84)	(74)	(57)	(46)
Total	101	100	100	100
No. of respondents	52	70	24	41

survey (Elklit, Noack, and Tonsgaard, 1976). In Greenland the independence movement has been gaining strength during the 1970s and since 1971 it has occupied one of the two seats in the Folketing, usually siding with the socialist parties. Non-Scandinavian foreign workers numbered 36,000 in 1973, but unlike Sweden, are not incorporated in the electorate.

6. REGIONAL AND URBAN/RURAL
CLEAVAGES

Whereas nineteenth century politics was initially a struggle between
an urban right and a rural left, the emergence of the Social Democratic and Radical Liberal parties introduced cleavage lines cutting
across the urban/rural division. Even so, regional and community
differences remain some of the most important determinants of
partisan choice.

Ecological studies can be made on the basis of the accounts
appearing in *Statistiske Efterretninger* produced by the census
bureau (Danmarks Statistik) a few weeks after each election, which
use nomination districts as the ecological units, or by means of the
more detailed *Statistiske Meddelelser* produced by the same bureau
six to eight months after the election. For the period 1960-68 two
comprehensive studies of electoral statistics are available. The first of
these (Borre and Stehouwer, 1968) mainly contains commune-level
breakdowns (in Copenhagen, breakdowns into 22 nomination districts) of the support for the parties in 1960 by level of urbanization,
predominant occupational structure, growth rate of population, and
level of average income. It is shown that for almost every party these
dimensions separately exert effects on electoral strength. Residual
variation in party strength is shown to constitute a characteristic
pattern of political regions.

The second study (Borre and Stehouwer, 1970) traces the development of support for the various parties over the four elections from
1960 to 1968, using alternatively communes and electoral districts as
ecological units. Across various types of communes and districts, the
analysis bears out the fact that changes in support for a party often
depend primarily on the party's own previous strength and on the
strength of other parties and major groups of parties. An overall
tendency for the ecological variation to decrease, and thus for the
strength of each party in various ecological units to converge upon a
national average, is noted.

A comprehensive restructuring of commune borders and borders
of electoral districts in 1970 makes it difficult subsequently to follow
ecological changes in detail. In the following, the ecological pattern
of party·support in 1975 and its changes from 1971 to 1975 will be
discussed.

Ecological Pattern in 1975

The evidence of electoral statistics points toward an interaction of regional factors and urbanization in determining the strength of several of the parties. Table 14 contains a classification of the 103 nomination districts according to their location, level of urbanization, and, in the case of Copenhagen, their social class composition.

The strength of the socialist bloc is seen to vary from a maximum of 68.4 percent of the votes cast in working-class districts of Copenhagen to a minimum of 25.7 percent in rural districts of North and West Jutland. Among the semi-urban districts in rows 5 to 7, the socialist strength falls off from about 44 to about 31 percent as one moves from the Island region to North and West Jutland. Among the predominantly rural districts in rows 8 to 10, it falls off from about 36 to about 26 percent as one moves in this fashion. The same pattern is repeated for the four socialist parties individually. They are stronger in the urban than in the rural areas and stronger in the eastern region closest to Copenhagen than in western regions. Relatively speaking the smaller leftwing parties vary much more than the Social Democrats between their weak and their strong types of district.

Turning to the non-socialist parties, the small Justice Party shows an almost uniform strength across all district types. The Radical Liberal Party's strength shows little variation with level of urbanization, but one observes that it is somewhat higher in the Island area (rows 5 and 8) than in Jutland. The Centre Democrats do not display great variation in their strength either, though it is particularly weak in Copenhagen's working-class districts. Of all the non-socialist parties it is the Agrarian Liberal Party which shows the strongest variation in strength, from 9 percent in Copenhagen's working-class districts to 35 percent in North and West Jutland's rural districts. By comparing rows 5 to 10 with one another, one finds that both level of urbanization and geographical region influence the strength of the Agrarian Liberals. With regard to the Conservative Party, Copenhagen's middle-class districts and suburban districts stand out as the stronghold. In the provincial districts the Conservative support decreases both with decreasing level of urbanization and with increasing distance from the capital. Finally, the Progressive Party shows a fairly uniform strength across district types. It is weakest in Copenhagen's working-class districts and in the other highly urbanized districts with the exception of the suburban belt; among the remaining less urbanized districts in rows 5 to 10, there is a slight

TABLE 14

Party Division in Nomination Districts Classified by Region and Level of Urbanization 1975, in Percent of Valid Votes

Type of nomination district	Parties													Total	Dis-tricts	No. of Electors
	Com-munist	Left Soc.	Soc. Peop. Dem.	Social Demo.	Total socia-list	Just-ice	Rad. Lib.	Chr. Peop. Dem.	Cen. Dem.	Agr. Lib.	Con-servat.	Pro-gress-ive	Total non-social.			
1. Copenhagen, working-class districts	11.5	3.9	10.2	42.8	(68.4)	1.6	4.6	2.6	1.2	8.9	3.8	8.9	(31.6)	100.0	10	267,632
2. Copenhagen, middle-class districts	7.2	4.3	8.2	31.2	(50.9)	1.8	6.4	3.6	1.6	16.1	8.6	11.0	(49.1)	100.0	9	242,056
3. Copenhagen, suburban zone	5.1	3.0	7.4	26.8	(42.3)	2.1	7.4	3.3	3.3	19.0	8.1	14.5	(57.7)	100.0	10	474,489
4. Three largest provincial cities	5.2	2.7	6.2	34.8	(48.9)	1.9	6.6	4.7	1.9	18.8	5.8	11.4	(51.1)	100.0	10	411,584
5. Semi-urban districts in Island region	3.8	1.7	4.7	33.6	(43.8)	1.5	8.1	4.3	2.2	21.7	5.2	13.2	(56.2)	100.0	12	443,633
6. Semi-urban districts in East and South Jutland	2.9	1.1	3.4	33.1	(40.5)	1.8	5.9	5.9	2.8	23.4	5.1	14.5	(59.4)	99.9	9	330,832
7. Semi-urban districts in North and West Jutland	2.3	1.0	2.5	25.0	(30.8)	1.8	5.4	9.5	2.1	29.3	4.9	16.2	(69.2)	100.0	7	293,099
8. Rural districts in Island region	2.5	1.3	3.2	29.1	(36.1)	1.4	9.5	4.9	1.9	27.5	5.0	13.7	(63.9)	100.0	14	400,234
9. Rural districts in East and South Jutland	1.6	1.0	2.1	25.4	(30.1)	1.8	7.1	6.9	3.1	30.0	4.7	16.3	(69.9)	100.0	10	257,433

TABLE 14 (continued)

Type of nomination district	Parties													Total	Dis-tricts	No. of Electors
	Com-munist	Left Soc.	Soc. Peop.	Social Demo.	Total socia-list	Just-ice	Rad. Lib.	Chr. Peop.	Cen. Dem.	Agr. Lib.	Con-servat.	Pro-gress-ive	Total non-social.			
10. Rural districts in North and West Jutland	1.5	0.9	1.7	21.6	(25.7)	1.5	7.4	9.1	1.7	34.9	3.5	16.2	(74.3)	100.0	12	356,629
Whole country	4.2	2.0	4.9	30.0	(41.2)	1.8	7.1	5.3	2.2	23.3	5.5	13.6	(58.8)	100.0	103	3,477,621

Source: Danmarks Statistik, 1975. The classification of the nomination districts by region and level of urbanization is as follows:

1. Copenhagen, working-class districts: Christianshavn, Blågård, Amagerbro, Husum, Nørrebro, Bispebjerg, Valby, Vesterbro, Enghave.
2. Copenhagen, middle-class districts: Rådhus, Sundby, Ryvang, Østbane, Østerbro, Brønshøj, Frederiksberg, Gl. Kongevej, Frederiksberg Slot, Falkoner.
3. Copenhagen, suburban zone: All nine districts in Københavns amtskreds, plus Fredensborg.
4. Three largest provincial cities: Odense Øst, Odense Vest, Odense Syd, Århus Øst, Århus Nord, Århus Syd, Århus Vest, Ålborg Nord, Ålborg Vest, Ålborg Øst.
5. Semi-urban districts in Island region: Helsingør, Hillerød, Roskilde, Køge, Holbæk, Slagelse, Næstved, Nakskov, Nykøbing Falster, Rønne, Nyborg, Svendborg.
6. Semi-urban districts in East and South Jutland: Haderslev, Åbenrå, Sønderborg, Fredericia, Kolding, Vejle, Horsens, Randers, Silkeborg.
7. Semi-urban districts in North and West Jutland: Esbjerg, Holstebro, Herning, Thisted, Viborg, Frederikshavn, Hjørring.
8. Rural districts in Island region: Frederiksværk, Lejre, Nykøbing (Zealand), Kalundborg, Ringsted, Sorø, Præstø, Vordingborg, Maribo, Åkirkeby, Kerteminde, Middelfart, Otterup, Fåborg.
9. Rural districts in East and South Jutland: Augustenborg, Tønder, Løgumkloster, Rødding, Give, Juelsminde, Mariager, Hammel, Grenå, Skanderborg.
10. Rural districts in North and West Jutland: Varde, Ribe, Grindsted, Ringkøbing, Skjern, Morsø, Skive, Kjellerup, Sæby, Fjerritslev, Hobro, Års.

tendency for the party to be stronger in the periphery than toward the centre. Its maximum is reached in North and West Jutland and in the rural parts of East and South Jutland.

Broadly speaking, the parties which have their strength concentrated in the urban and eastern regions of the country are the four socialist parties and the Conservative Party. Those having their main strength in the less urban and western regions are the Agrarian Liberal Party, the Christian People's Party and the Progressive Party, although the pattern is not very distinct in the case of the latter two parties.

Change 1971-75

In many countries ecological differences of the type shown in Table 14 have been proved to persist for generations; in fact this kind of stability may be the oldest discovery in the study of voting behaviour (Siegfried, 1913). In view of the recent upheavals in the Danish party system one might wonder, however, to what extent the ecological pattern has been affected by the addition of some parties and the drastic reduction of others. In order to assess the stability of the pattern shown in Table 14, the voting strength in these ten community types was correlated with the voting strength in 1971 for those parties or party groups which were in existence at both elections. For the combined socialist vote the product-moment correlation was 0.99 and for the four individual socialist parties it varied between 0.94 and 0.99. On the bourgeois side a similar stability was observed. The Conservative, Agrarian Liberals, and Christian People's Party all showed correlation coefficients of around 0.99 between their 1971 and 1975 strength. The fact that the Conservative Party had decreased to one-third of its former size and that the Agrarian Liberal Party had varied between 12 and 23 percent of the votes cast (see Table 2) did *not* affect that ecological pattern. For the Radical Liberal Party the 1971/75 correlation sags to 0.90 mainly because of the bad performance of this party in North and West Jutland in 1975. Finally, for the Justice or Single-Tax Party, which shows little ecological variation, the correlation was only 0.31.

This analysis shows that strong realignments in the party system accompanied by the introduction of sizeable new parties may occur without affecting the ecological pattern very much: regions and community types that constitute strong holds for a given party at one time remain so at a later time even though the overall support for the party may undergo drastic changes.

The Progressive Party and the Centre Democrats appeared for the first time at the 1973 election, and consequently the stability of the ecological pattern of their support cannot yet be assessed across several election periods. But the 1975 Progressive vote in the ten community types can be closely predicted from the 1971 combined non-socialist vote. The correlation is 0.95 and the regression line $Y = 0.026 + 0.217X$, indicating that the Progressive vote in 1975 amounted to an average of 21.7 percent of that share of the 1971 non-socialist vote which exceeded 2.6 percent. When looked at from this angle, the Progressive Party does not represent the periphery any more than do the non-socialist parties as a whole.

7. INTERACTION OF SOCIAL CLEAVAGES: A TREE ANALYSIS

The preceding three sections have shown that partisan preferences of Danish voters to a large extent depend on the place of residence, social class position, and age of the voter. By way of concluding we therefore feel it necessary to respond to the changing scenario of class conflict. A method that appears appropriate for this purpose is the AID or tree analysis in which the respondents are subdivided into relatively homogeneous electoral groups. Originally, three dependent variables were selected on grounds of their presumed relevance for describing the political orientation of the respondents:

(1) Voting for one of the three leftwing parties (Communist Party, Socialist People's Party, or Left Socialist Party),

(2) Voting for the socialist parties (the Social Democratic Party or one of the leftwing parties), and

(3) Voting for the Progressive Party.

It will be observed that these cutpoints in the political spectrum are consistent with the four-bloc party system that appears to be one of the more enduring outcomes of the 1973 election. The political orientation of respondents is dichotomized at three different points in the political spectrum.

To explain group differences in these variables the following six independent variables were selected:

(1) Respondent's occupation, categorized into manual worker, salaried employee, self-employed, and not employed. Housewives were coded according to the occupations of their husbands, and in general persons who were not employed, where possible, were coded according to the occupation of the head of the household.

(2) Type of residence: House-owners vs. tenants. 'House-owners' include almost all farmers and a few persons owning their apartments.

(3) Education: Primary education only, or more than primary education.

(4) Household income: Below 40,000 D.kr., 40,000-79,000 D.kr., or 80,000 D.kr. and over.

(5) Age of respondent: 20-29 years, 30-49 years, or 50 years or more.

(6) Whether head of household is publicly or privately employed.

The data used for analysis was a survey conducted just after the election in January 1975. In addition to about 1,000 respondents being interviewed more intensively, about 1,500 respondents came from the regular Gallup survey in February 1975. The 2,475 respondents from these two surveys were pooled for the AID analysis. This procedure restricted the number of social background variables available, but it was judged more important to include as many cases as possible in the analysis.

In the case of the vote for the Progressive Party the AID analysis resulted in a mere dichotomy between self-employed and other persons, yielding a between sum-of-squares of only 1.1 percent of the total sum of squares. Results of the two other analyses are presented in Figures 1 and 2 in the form of diagrams. The rectangles indicate groups of respondents and contain information on the number of cases (N), the percent voting for the party group in question (Y), and the label of the group, resulting from dichotomizing one of the independent variables. V indicates the variance reduction obtained by this dichotomy. They contain information on the independent variable being dichotomized, and the between sum-of-squares (BSS) obtained by this dichotomization.

By far the most successful breakdown, appearing in Figure 2, occurred in the case of the combined socialist vote. The first distinction here follows the Marxian framework of pitting capitalists against proletarians. Only 6.2 percent of the self-employed vote

FIGURE 1
Tree Analysis of the Socialist Vote
(Leftwing plus Social Democrats), 1975

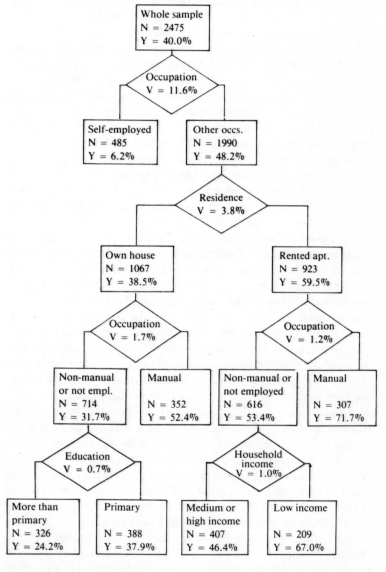

Total variance explained: 19.7%.

socialist as against 48.2 percent of the wage-earners and those not employed. The second group is subdivided into house-owners, among whom 38.5 percent vote socialist, and apartment-dwellers, among whom the socialist parties receive 59.5 percent. Both of these groups are then further divided on the same criterion, namely manual workers vs. salaried workers and persons who are not employed. In the four groups obtained by cross-classifying the workers by type of residence and whether or not they are manual workers, the socialist vote varies from 71.7 percent among blue-collar workers living in apartments to 31.7 among white-collar workers having a house of their own. This latter group is subdivided once more, the program finding that those with only primary school education have a socialist vote of 37.9 percent while of those with more than primary school only 24.2 percent vote socialist. With respect to white-collar workers living in apartments, the program finally distinguished between those with low income, among whom 67.0 percent vote socialist, and those with medium or higher income, among whom it is only 46.4 percent. Together, these various dichotomies account for 19.7 percent of the variance of the socialist vote.

The leftwing vote is analyzed in Figure 2. The most important variable is here the age of respondent: among the young voters in the ages 20-29 years the leftwing vote is 24.2 percent whereas it is 6.6 percent for those aged 30 or more. Second in importance is the cleavage between house-owners and apartment-dwellers. Both for the young voters and for the rest, apartment-dwellers display considerably more leftwing preference than do those with a house of their own, so that the leftwing vote varies from 37.3 percent among young people living in rented apartments to 3.3 percent among middle-aged or older people living in their own houses. These two extreme groups are further subdivided by the AID programme: among the young apartment-dwellers a distinction is drawn between those actively employed, having a leftwing vote of 32.3 percent, and the small group of those not employed, among whom the leftwing vote rises to 61.8 percent; the opposite group of house-owners aged 30 or more is divided into a major group of people in private employment, among whom the leftwing vote shrinks to 2.1 percent, and a minority of people in public employment, among whom it is 11.6 percent.

The moderate success of the programme in accounting for the leftwing vote is shown in the figure below the diagram. Of the total variance of the leftwing vote, 11.5 percent is explained by these breakdowns into homogeneous groups. Almost half of this variance

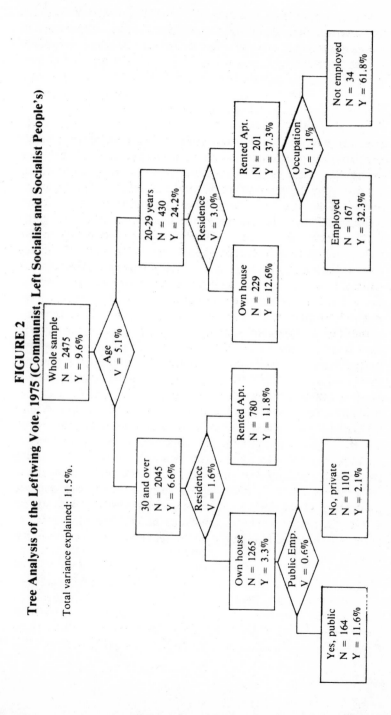

FIGURE 2

Tree Analysis of the Leftwing Vote, 1975 (Communist, Left Socialist and Socialist People's)

Total variance explained: 11.5%.

reduction stems from the initial division at the age of 30. It is characteristic that the leftwing vote appears to be concentrated in small groups, while leftwing voting is rare in the large majority of the Danish population.

8. CONCLUSION

The history of the Danish party system and contemporary accounts of partisan support show the major parties and party groups to have a strong class base. The cross-cutting class cleavage is, however, intertwined with persisting urban/rural and regional variation in the ecology of the vote. In the face of the importance of such permanent factors, one may wonder how massive changes, as experienced at the 1973 election, are possible. There are several elements in the preceding analysis which point toward an answer. In the first place the new generations of voters are less inclined to express their class or regional location in their vote than are older voters. Secondly, protest parties and one-issue parties without a clear class appeal have emerged, profiting from the high rate of participation, the stalemate of the older party system, and the low threshold of representation in the Danish parliament. It is possible that in this analysis we have caught the party system in the middle of a leap; in the last few years no new significant political force has emerged, and the party system seems to gravitate toward a more predictable and one-dimensional structure. The recovery of the voting strength of the Social Democratic Party (to 38.3 percent at the election in October 1979) and the fragmentation of the balance of the electorate into many minor parties makes for a normal political order under which a Social Democratic minority government compromises with as many of its adjacent parties as is necessary to form a coalition around a particular packet of bills. Socio-economic cleavages may be as strong as ever, in a party system of this type, though these cleavages are more differentiated than in the earlier versions of the Danish party system.

REFERENCES

BORRE, O. (1975), "A Latent Structure Approach to Voting Behavior", paper read at the Nordic conference of political science in Århus.

— — and D. KATZ (1973), "Party Identification and Its Motivational Base in a Multiparty System: A Study of the Danish General Election of 1971", *Scandinavian Political Studies*, 8.

— — H. J. NIELSEN, S. SAUERBERG, and T. WORRE (1976), *Vaelgere i 70'erne* (Voters in the 1970s) Copenhagen: Akademisk Forlag.

— — and J. STEHOUWER (1968), *Partistyrke og social struktur 1960* (Party strength and social structure 1960). Århus: Akademisk Boghandel.

— — (1970), *Fire folketingsvalg 1960-68* (Four general elections 1960-68). Århus: Akademisk Boghandel.

DAHLERUP, D. (1977), "Women's Representation in the First Local and General Elections in Denmark After the Vote was Won", paper presented at the workshop on women in politics, ECPR Joint Session, Berlin.

DAMGAARD, E. (1974), "Stability and Change in the Danish Party System over Half a Century", *Scandinavian Political Studies*, 9.

— — and J. G. RUSK (1976), "Cleavage Structures and Representational Linkages: A Longitudinal Analysis of Danish Legislative Behavior", in I. Budge, I. Crewe, and D. Farlie (eds.), *Party Identification and Beyond*. London: John Wiley & Sons.

DANMARKS STATISTIK (1975), *Statistiske Efterretninger*, 67 (6).

DYBDAHL, V. (1969), *Partier og Erhverv: Studier i partiorganisation og byerhvervenes politiske aktivitet ca. 1880-ca. 1913*, 1-2 (Parties and trades. Studies in party organization and the political activity of the urban trades ca. 1880-ca. 1913, vol. 1-2). Århus: Universitetsforlaget.

ELKLIT, J. (1973a), "Udforskning af vaelgeradfaerd i Danmark i det 19. århundrede" (Research in voting behaviour in Denmark in the 19th century), *Historie, Jyske Samlinger*, Ny raekke, X (2).

— — (1973b), "Valg- or stemmelister vedr. folketingsvalg 1849-98 i Landsarkivet for Nørrejylland" (Electoral and voting lists regarding Folketing elections 1849-98 in the regional archive for North Jutland), *Tidsskrift for Arkivforskning*, 4 (4).

— — (1974), "Udviklingen af den danske lovgivning vedr. valg til Folketinget (udkast)" (The development of the Danish legislation with regard to elections for the Folketing (Draft)). Århus: Institute of Political Science.

— — J. P. NOACK, and O. TONSGAARD (1976), "Germans and Danes in North Schleswig", paper presented for publication in A. Verdoodt (ed.), *Language and National Identity*, and presented at the ECPR Joint Session, Louvain.

PEDERSEN, M. N. (1976), *Political Development and Eite Transformation in Denmark*. London & Beverly Hills: Sage Publications, Professional Paper in Contemporary Political Sociology 06-018.

SIUNE, K., and O. BORRE (1975), "Setting the Agenda for a Danish Election", *Journal of Communication*, 25:1.

SVALSTOGA, K. (1959), *Prestige, Class, and Mobility*. Copenhagen: Gyldendal.

SVALASTOGA, K., and P. WOLF (1965), *En by ved graensen* (A town at the border). Copenhagen: Gyldendal.
SVENSSON, P. (1974), "Support for the Social Democratic Party 1924-39: Growth and Response", *Scandinavian Political Studies,* 9.

7

Language, Religion, Class and Party Choice: Belgium, Canada, Switzerland and South Africa Compared

Arend Lijphart
University of California, San Diego

I. INTRODUCTION

The comparative analysis of the social and demographic bases of voting behaviour has made great progress during the past decade — culminating in the comparative handbook on *Electoral Behavior* edited by Rose (1974a). As a result, there is now a substantial body of evidence in support of the overall conclusion that there are two especially important determinants of party choice: social class and religion. The influence of other social and demographic variables tends to be much weaker.

The purpose of this study is to investigate a third potentially powerful variable — language — and to compare its influence with that of religion and class. Linguistic cleavages are relatively rare in Western democracies; most of these states are completely or almost completely homogeneous in this respect. In fact, a shared language is regarded as one of the principal building-blocks of nationalism in the traditional literature on this subject, and even in Deutsch's (1953) more refined concept of a nation as an intensive network of communication, language obviously plays a crucial role. Conversely, because language is an important differentiator between nations, we can expect it to be a major cleavage and a strong source of partisan differences in 'nations' that are not linguistically homogeneous. The hypothesis that language should be a strong determinant of party choice also follows logically from the developmental theory of cleavage structures and party systems expounded by Lipset and Rokkan (1967): cultural-territorial conflicts are one of the four basic sources of party system cleavages that they distinguish.

There are several Western countries with small linguistic minorities, but only three that can really be said to be linquistically divided: Belgium, Canada, and Switzerland. Hence these three countries are obvious candidates for comparison with regard to the impact of linguistic divisions on voting. An interesting fourth case that can be added is the Republic of South Africa. It fits all three of the theoretical criteria used by Rose (1974b: 5-6) to demarcate the universe of countries suitable for inclusion in his *Electoral Behavior:* the persistence of competitive free elections since 1945, a high rank on the conventional socio-economic indicators of industrialization, and Christian cultural origins. Although the South African electorate is severely restricted and excludes all non-whites, the elections have been both free and competitive. South Africa's socio-economic ranking is somewhat less high than that of Belgium, Canada, and Switzerland (see Taylor and Hudson, 1972: 306-343). The theoretical reason for using this criterion is that it "avoids problems of the comparability of literate and illiterate electors, or the validity of national elections without national media of communication", but these problems do not affect the white South African electorate. The third criterion — cultural origins in Christendom — which excludes developed and democratic countries like Israel and Japan, clearly includes the white population of South Africa. In practice, Rose's criteria entail an emphasis on Western Europe, but he does not use a geographic criterion and his volume also embraces the United States, Canada, and Australia: "Bridging the Atlantic and Pacific oceans is important in order to reduce the Eurocentrism of some comparative scholars." By crossing the Indian ocean and including South Africa, Eurocentrism can be reduced further.

Another reason why these four countries are especially interesting cases is that they present an outstanding opportunity for a comparative analysis of the *relative* weights of the linguistic, religious, and class variables, since all four countries are divided along all of these dimensions. In addition to their linguistic cleavages and the socio-economic or class differences present in all industrialized societies, there is a Protestant-Catholic division in Canada, South Africa, and

Switzerland, and a religious-secular split in homogeneously Catholic Belgium. The latter cleavage is at least as important as the denominational difference in the other three countries. The analysis of Belgian social and political structure in terms of the three cleavages of religiosity, class, and language is the standard approach (Lorwin, 1966; Van den Brande, 1967; Claeys van Haegendoren, 1967; Urwin, 1970; Hill, 1974; Huyse, 1974 and 1975; Frognier, 1976). This article will take into consideration church affiliation in Canada, South Africa, and Switzerland, and religiosity — operationally defined as the frequency of church attendance — in all four countries.

Belgium, Canada, Switzerland and South Africa also deserve to be analyzed comparatively because they have been relatively neglected by students of comparative voting behaviour. Sample surveys of voting have been fewer and there have sometimes been problems in undertaking multivariate statistical analysis.[1] Hill's (1974) treatment of Belgian voting behaviour faithfully adheres to the comparative format, but it is seriously flawed by the absence of a question on language in the 1968 national election survey (Delruelle, Evalenko, and Fraeys, 1970).[2] Region can be used as an approximation of language because Flanders and Wallonia are linguistically homogeneous, but bilingual Brussels presents an insuperable problem. As Hill (1974: 96) readily admits himself, language is likely to be as important as the religious and class variables and may even be "the dominant influence in electoral choice" for certain groups and areas, of which he mentions Brussels as the prime example.

This study will use survey data collected in the 1970s for a systematic comparison of the influence of language, religion, and class on party choice in Belgium, Canada, South Africa, and Switzerland. It is explicitly designed to build upon such prior research achievements in comparative voting behaviour as Rose's (1974a) handbook and Alford's (1963) analysis of class voting in the Anglo-American democracies. The methods and indices that have proved valuable in these earlier studies will be used here again: in particular, the AID (automatic interaction detector) technique, also known as tree analysis, which is the major multivariate statistical method employed in the Rose volume; and Alford's well-known index of class voting and similar indices for measuring linguistic and religious voting.

II. FINDINGS CONCERNING THE RELATIVE INFLUENCE OF CLASS, RELIGION, AND LANGUAGE ON PARTY CHOICE: AN APPRAISAL AND AN ALTERNATIVE STRATEGY

Religion and social class have been recognized as prime determinants of party choice from the very beginning of voting behaviour research: in the first American voting study, Lazarsfeld et al. (1944) used these two variables, in combination with rural-urban residence, to construct the famous "Index of Political Predisposition," which could serve as a highly accurate predictor of voting. Similar findings have emanated from comparative studies, but no consensus has emerged about which of the two variables is the better predictor.

The earliest cross-national analyses reached diametrically opposite conclusions. Lipset (1960: 220, 223-224) found that although religious differences could also contribute to party support, "on a world scale, the principal generalization which can be made is that parties are primarily based on either the lower classes or the middle and upper classes." And he added: "More than anything else the party struggle is a conflict among classes, and the most impressive single fact about political party support is that in virtually every economically developed country the lower-income groups vote mainly for parties of the left, while the higher-income groups vote mainly for parties of the right." In line with these conclusions, the chapter of *Political Man* in which they are stated is entitled "Elections: The Expression of the Democratic Class Struggle." Similarly, Berelson and Steiner (1964: 427) included the following proposition in their inventory of established scientific findings concerning human behaviour: "Class is the single most important differentiator of political preferences across societies." But De Jong (1956: 160) — in which was probably the very first broadly comparative analysis of voting behaviour, based on survey results from eleven European countries — concluded that religion was of primary significance and that class, although important, occupied only a secondary place in the hierarchy of voting determinants: "for the explanation of electoral behaviour both in our own country [the Netherlands] and abroad, we always have to pay attention first to the religious factor."

The evidence on which these early generalizations were based was fragmentary and of uneven quality. Later and more systematic cross-national analyses that could benefit from more and better survey findings, have not been able to resolve the disagreement although they have tended to be considerably more cautious in stating their conclusions. In his in-depth study of four Anglo-American democracies, Alford (1963) found that class voting was stronger than religious voting in Great Britain and Australia, but that religious voting was the stronger tendency in Canada; no clear pattern appeared in the United States. Because class turns out to be the "winner" by only a narrow margin and because only four countries are taken into consideration, this does not constitute convincing evidence. It prompts Sartori (1969: 76) to comment that "a reviewer could well subtitle Alford's book as bearing on *non-class voting* in the Anglo-American democracies." A recent study of eight countries by Budge and Farlie (1976: 120-121; see also Budge and Farlie, 1977) also yields the conclusion that class is a better predictor than religion — but by only a narrow margin. These authors rank the predictive power of fourteen social and demographic variables and calculate the average ranks for their eight countries. Occupation attains the highest average rank: 4.60. It is followed closely by a few other class characteristics, but also by religion and church attendance with average ranks of only about one unit lower than occupation: 5.57 and 5.86.

Conversely, religion emerges as the more important dimension of party cohesion in Rose and Urwin's (1969: 12) study of 76 parties in seventeen countries: "religious divisions, not class, are the main social basis of parties in the Western world today." Religion is a common factor in 54 percent of the parties examined by Rose and Urwin, and class in only 42 percent. Using indices similar to Alford's but extending his analysis to ten countries, Lijphart (1971: 7-8) found that religious voting was higher than class voting in six of the ten countries. Moreover, the indices of religious voting generally reached higher values than the indices of class voting. Finally, a fifth attempt to compare the relative influence of class and religion on party choice is Lancelot's (1975) review of the major findings in the handbook on voting behaviour by Rose (1974a). Lancelot divides the twelve countries covered in the handbook in three groups: countries in which religion is the most discriminant explanatory variable, countries where class is the best discriminator, and a third residual category in which neither variable is of great importance. The first two groups are of exactly equal size, each consisting of five countries.

Are there any general conclusions that can be drawn from these divergent findings? Because the differences in the predictive power of religion and class are limited — two studies pointing to class and two to religion as the strongest determinant of party choice — it is tempting to hypothesize that the truth must lie somewhere in the middle. But at least five other potential explanations come to mind: the differences may be attributed to the different measures of association that were used, the different times in which the surveys were conducted, whether or not controls were established, the different units of analysis, and the different countries sampled. As will be shown, only the last of these explanations is of decisive importance.

The first explanation is based on the fact that different measures are used to express the strengths of the relationship between class and religion on the one hand and party choice on the other. Unfortunately, the findings cannot easily be made comparable by converting the different measures into a single one, but the fact that the two studies using basically the same measure — Alford's indices of class and religious voting used both by Alford himself and by Lijphart — reach opposite conclusions, suggests that this explanation cannot account for the substantive differences that were found.

A second possible explanation is that the divergent findings may simply reflect changes in voting behaviour over time. For instance, all five studies cover Great Britain, but they all use different British survey data collected at different times. Longitudinal analyses show that there may indeed be significant shifts in class and religious voting in the same country (Alford, 1963: 101-104; Alford, 1967; Books and Reynolds, 1975), but cross-national differences tend to be greater than intra-national diachronic differences. Alford (1963: 103-104) comments that as far as the four countries analyzed by him are concerned, "what is striking . . . is not the variation within the countries, but that, regardless of that variation, the differences in class voting between the countries are so sharp and consistent."

Thirdly, the differences might be caused by the fact that the measures of association sometimes reflect controlled and sometimes uncontrolled relationships. The rankings by Budge and Farlie are adjusted for the influence of all other variables, and Lancelot's classification is based on tree analyses in which the second and lower explanatory variables are controlled in the sense that their strength is expressed in terms of the *residual* variance that they explain. In the latter case, an examination of the materials in the Rose (1974a) handbook on which Lancelot bases his categorization of countries, reveals that his conclusions would not be different if he had used uncontrolled relationships. Lijphart's (1971: 7-8, 21-22) conclusions are based on uncontrolled indices of class and religious voting, but he also presents adjusted voting indices for four of his countries: this introduction of controls does not change the relative ranking of class and religious influences.

Nor, fourthly, do differences in the units of analysis used in the different studies provide a valid explanation. Rose and Urwin's approach differs from that of the others in that their analysis is in terms of parties instead of party systems or countries. However, their findings can be converted from parties to countries as units of counting without difficulty: instead of examining whether individual parties have class and/or religion as a basis of cohesion, we can classify countries in terms of how many times class and religion appear as cohesive factors for their political parties. Using only the fourteen countries for which full information on both dimensions is available, we arrive at the following result: religion is the most important factor in seven countries, class in four, and the two dimensions are of equal importance in three countries.[3] In other words, Rose and Urwin's original conclusion that religion surpasses social class remains valid whether expressed in terms of individual parties or in terms of party systems.

It is the fifth explanation that hits upon the critically important difference among the five studies: the different samples of countries that provide the empirical bases for the conclusions. The religious factor is especially strong in the Continental European countries with the exception of Scandinavia, but the proportion of these core Continental European states in the different samples is highly unequal, ranging from nil in Alford's study to 60 percent in Lijphart's. These differences correspond perfectly with the conclusions of the five studies. What are the reasons for this wide variation in the composition of the sample? Alford (1963: 4) chose his four countries, all of them outside Continental Europe, because they are comparable cases: "The common political culture of the Anglo-American countries means that a comparative study of political cleavage is not complicated by widely varying political values and traditions." The other authors applied a looser standard of comparability and tried to maximize the size of their samples by including all Western countries with Christian traditions on which appropriate data were available; Budge and Farlie also included Japan.[4]

In order to arrive at a definite conclusion about the relative influence of class and religion on party choice, two alternative approaches present themselves. One would be to attempt to maximize the sample to such an extent that it would closely approximate or, ideally, coincide with the universe of countries with free electoral competition. The disadvantage of this strategy is that, while it appears to be impartial, it actually gives social class a better chance to emerge as the more significant predictor: class cleavages are present and potentially salient everywhere, whereas denominational differences may be absent and differences in religiosity, though in principle present everywhere, are politically relevant mainly in the Continental European countries with their traditions of religious-anticlerical conflict.

The logical alternative is to focus the analysis on those countries where the forces of class and religion actually compete with each other. These cases may be labeled "comparable," not in the usual sense of being similar in a large number of background characteristics and dissimilar with respect to the operative variables (see Lijphart, 1975), but in the sense that all of the variables which the researcher tries to relate to each other are present — and hence truly operative — in all cases. This strategy resembles what Naroll (1966: 336) calls a "crucial experiment," in which cases are chosen for their special nature, for instance, "because certain variables happen to be present together." As Converse states: "the general rule seems to be that religious differentiation intrudes on partisan political alignments in unexpectedly powerful degree *wherever it conceivably can.*" (1974: 734, emphasis added; see also Converse, 1964: 247-248). Similarly, Sartori argues that class may be the principal determinant of voting only when there is no other salient cleavage, and that therefore "the correct formulation of the problem is: *Given a multiplicity of cleavages,* can it be shown that there is a hierarchy of cleavages according to which the class cleavage tends to prevail?" (1969: 76, emphasis added).

The contrast between the two approaches is more striking when language is added as a possible predictor of party choice, because linguistic differences are relatively rare. Rose and Urwin (1969: 14) exemplify the first approach when they conclude that "linguistic or ethnic communalism is not today a major source of social cohesion for parties in Western countries."[5] This conclusion is entirely legitimate and empirically correct for the universe of countries with free elections. But although linguistic and ethnic heterogeneity is rather infrequent, "where it occurs . . . it seems to become expressed in partisan cleavages as persistently and vigorously as religious differentiation'' (Converse, 1974: 735). This study adopts the perspective exemplified by the latter statement. It is a ''crucial experiment'' of the relative impact of language, religion, and class on party choice in the four countries where all of these variables are simultaneously present.

FIGURE 1
Dimensions of Differentiation in Social Structure

	Must Differentiate	May Differentiate
Spatial	Region Trading areas Urban/rural	None
Status	*Industrial classes* Farm/industry	*Language Religion* Identity Race

Source: Adapted from Rose and Urwin (1975: 10).

The alternative approach also finds support in Rose and Urwin's (1975: 10) distinction between necessary and contingent sources of social and partisan differentiation: ''some *must* differentiate individuals or groups within a society, whereas another *may be a constant* or a *variable.*'' They further distinguish between spatial and status differences, and thus arrive at the fourfold typology shown in Figure 1. The dimensions that are of special importance to this analysis are italicized. They are all status differences, but the class division is present in all Western industrialized societies, whereas both linguistic and religious divisions are present and potentially salient only in the four countries under consideration here. Language and religion are distinguished from spatial factors, all of which are necessary sources of differentiation. However, language and religion may be closely related to region in the sense that linguistic and religious groups may be geographically concentrated, affecting the degree to which religion and language have become sources of partisan differentiation.

III. SURVEY DATA, METHODS, AND
INDICES

It is necessary to turn first to a few methodological considerations: the comparability of the survey data, the sample sizes, and the characteristics of the indices in which the relationships among the variables will be expressed.

(a) The Data

This four-country comparison relies on a secondary analysis of data from separate and independent national surveys. Comparability and equivalence are always difficult objectives in cross-national survey research, but for the purposes of the present study this drawback does not cause any serious problems, because the questions that were used are quite simple and straightforward.

Another favourable factor is that the different surveys were conducted at approximately the same time: the Belgian surveys in 1970 and 1973, the Swiss survey in 1972, and the Canadian and South African surveys in 1974. The Canadian and the Swiss surveys were election studies, although the Swiss survey was not held until several months after the elections. The South African data were collected in an election year but not in connection with explicit electoral research. The only major Belgian election study done so far, in 1968, could not be used because it did not include any question about the respondents' language; instead, two more recent socio-political, non-election surveys had to be used. Only in Canada have election surveys been conducted across time; in addition to the 1974 study, some results of the 1968 survey will therefore also be presented.

The multivariate nature of the AID analysis required that the sizes of the national samples be relatively large to allow a sequential division into progressively smaller subgroups. Only those respondents willing to indicate their party choice *and* their occupation, religion, church attendance, and language could be included in the analysis. Missing information on any one of these variables entailed the elimination of a respondent, resulting in a considerable reduction in the size of the usable sample. Moreover, some of respondents had to be excluded because they could not be classified in the categories of one or more of the variables: for instance, individuals who do not fit the categories of manual or non-manual workers (such as farmers), persons not belonging to any church, and persons belonging to a minor linguistic community.

The size of the samples ranges from about 1,300 respondents in the Belgian and South African studies to approximately 1,900 in the Swiss survey and more than 2,500 in the 1974 Canadian survey. In the Belgian case, two similar surveys conducted in 1970 and 1973 could be combined in order to make a larger sample of about 2,600 respondents.[6] However, no additional data were available to increase the size of the South African sample which consists of two weighted separate sub-samples of about equal size (a sample of Afrikaners and one of English-speaking white South Africans to whom similar questionnaires were administered).[7] The South African data were collected in cities, towns, and villages, and exclude the rural, mainly farming, population, but this does not affect comparability here because of the exclusion of farmers from the other samples, too. All four samples can therefore be regarded as comparable representative samples of the national voting populations.

(b) Indices of Voting

Two measures will be used to express the relationships between the independent and the dependent variables: indices of class, religious, and linguistic voting and, on the basis of AID analysis, the proportions of the variance in the dependent variable that are explained by independent variables. The index of class voting devised by Alford (1963: 79-86; see also Chandler and Chandler, 1974: 35-40) is computed as follows: "Subtract the percentage of persons in non-manual occupations voting for Left parties from the percentage of persons in manual occupations voting for Left parties" (Alford, 1963: 79-80). The index of class voting is a measure of association in 2 x 2 contingency tables. A very important characteristic of the index is that it is also the regression coefficient for the regression of party choice on class if these dichotomized variables are given the numerical values of 0 and 1 (Särlvik, 1969: 132; Korpi, 1972: 631; Alker, 1965: 84-85). The index can vary from -100 to $+100$. An index of 0 indicates that the variables are not related at all.

Similar indices may be developed to measure the strength of language or religion by dichotomizing the independent variable and party choice and calculating the difference between the percentages. Alford (1963: 91) uses an index of religious voting which he defines as "the percentage-point difference in Left voting between religious groups (mainly Protestant and Catholic) within a given class." He also gives the index of religious voting for the whole sample (Alford, 1963: 136, 202-203, 242-243, 274-276). In addition to a denominational index of religious voting, based on Catholic vs. Protestant church affiliation, the second index of religious voting (church attendance), dichotomizes between frequent church attendance (at least twice per month) and infrequent or no attendance. The index for language uses the dichotomy of the two major language groups in each country. A positive index of class voting indicates that manual workers have a greater tendency to vote for left parties than non-manual workers; the plus or minus sign is based on the expected correlation between lower-class membership and left voting. The signs of the other indices are based on similar expected correlations between church affiliation, attendance, and language on the one hand and preference for dichotomized groups of parties on the other hand.

(c) AID Analysis

The automatic interaction detector or tree analysis is a multivariate statistical technique that can be used for many different purposes (see Sonquist, Baker, and Morgan, 1971; Stouthard, 1971). It has been especially useful, however, in comparative research on voting behaviour (Liepelt, 1971; Rose, 1974a). In one of the pioneering applications of tree analysis to electoral behaviour, Särlvik (1969: 104) succinctly describes its objective and procedure in the following words:

> [It seeks] to explain as much as possible of the variance in the dependent variable [e.g., party choice] by partitioning the sample into a series of categories which are defined by the explanatory variables [e.g., class, religion, and language]. The program arrives at that end through a sequence of binary splits, starting with the division of the sample into two parts. In each step, it constructs a new pair of mutually exclusive combinations of characteristics specifying the two groups to be formed. Before a split, all existing groups and the entire predictor battery are screened in order to find the group division that will contribute most to reduce the proportion of unexplained variance in the dependent variable . . . The further division of a group comes to a stop when none of the predictors can exceed certain minimal criteria for splitting: these are defined in terms of the relative increase in the proportion of explained variance and the group size.

Tree analysis can thus show which social factors are important determinants of party choice, and it can show how much of the variance is explained by each of these social predictors and by all of them together. This can also be done, of course, by more traditional techniques like multiple regression, but the advantage of AID is that it does not assume additivity and that it is able to reveal any interaction effects that may be present among the independent variables. Moreover, the terminal groups in the tree are of special interest: as Rose (1974b: 12) states, "the size and exclusiveness of political partisanship of these end groups is itself important in characterizing the aggregate balance of social and political forces within a society."

A disadvantage of both Alford's voting indices and the AID method appears to be that they either require dichotomized variables as inputs or transform the variables into dichotomies. Dichotomization necessarily entails at least some loss of information in two ways: subtle distinctions may be lost when small categories are combined into two broader classes, and there may be a residual group of cases that do not fit the dichotomous classification and that must therefore be ignored altogether in the analysis. This disadvantage should not be exaggerated, however. One variable, language, is almost a natural dichotomy because of the dominance of two major languages in the four countries in question, and the other dichotomies can be formed in such a way as to highlight their interrelations as much as possible.

Furthermore, dichotomization has two important countervailing advantages. In the first place, it can improve the comparability of the data. Even when in different surveys the same question is asked, the response categories are often different. The best example is provided by occupational categories, which tend to vary widely in different surveys but which can usually be rearranged without much difficulty into the two larger categories of manual and non-manual workers. The same advantage applies to the dichotomization of church affiliation and church attendance. Secondly, because Alford's voting indices are based on dichotomized variables and can be interpreted as regression coefficients, it is possible to use multiple regression analysis in order to calculate controlled indices of voting. This means, for instance, that in addition to the regular index of class voting, a "pure" index of class voting can be computed from which the influence of religion and language has been removed.

IV. THE VARIABLES: OPERATIONAL
DEFINITIONS AND DICHOTOMIES

The independent variables (social class, church affiliation, church attendance, and language) present relatively few problems in operationalization. More difficult is the question of how party choice should be dichotomized.

(a) Social Class

Class will be operationally defined in terms of the occupation of the head of the respondent's household. Occupations are assigned to the manual and non-manual strata according to the criteria of Alford (1963: 70-71). Farmers are the only significant group that cannot be accommodated in this dichotomous classification.

The selection of occupation as the indicator of class position can be defended on both practical and theoretical grounds. The most important consideration is that, as Broom (1976: 10) states, "in industrialized societies occupation is the best single indicator of a person's social level because it summarizes the interplay of education, opportunity, performance and reward." Occupation is included in most surveys, and it is usually fairly easy to reclassify varying occupational categories into the manual- non-manual dichotomy. It has also been found to be the best objective class-related predictor of party choice. For instance, the authors of *The American Voter* (Campbell et al., 1960: 344) conclude that of the principal objective criteria of social class — occupation, income, and education — "occupation tends to predict political attitudes and voting most efficiently." A comparison of the relative utility of the same indicators in four countries — the United States, Great Britain, Germany, and Italy — also found that indices of class voting reached the highest level when class was defined in terms of occupation, and considerably lower levels when education and income were used to define social class and to compute the indices (Lijphart, 1971: 13).[8]

(b) Religion

The two religious variables that will be considered are church affiliation and church attendance. The former will be dichotomized into Protestant and Catholic categories with all respondents of other faiths and without religious affiliation left out of consideration. This is the most meaningful and obvious classification for the Canadian and Swiss cases. It may be argued that the more significant dividing line in South Africa lies between the adherents of the Dutch Reformed churches on the one hand and Anglicans, Methodists, Catholics, and Jews on the other hand. Such a dichotomy coincides so closely with the linguistic-ethnic difference between Afrikaners and English-speakers, however, that it turns church affiliation into a virtual replica of the linguistic variable (see Peele and Morse, 1974: 1526). For the sake of comparative consistency, too, it makes more sense to use the Catholic-Protestant dichotomy in all three countries.

The dichotomization of church attendance presents slightly more serious problems because the categories in the different surveys were not always the same. Moreover, even with exactly the same categories, the problem of equivalence is not solved, because, as Linz (1967: 318) points out, the obligation of church attendance has a different meaning for Protestants and Catholics. In order to keep the dichotomy as simple and straightforward as possible, the dividing line will be drawn between frequent churchgoers (at least twice a month) and those attending church only infrequently or never.

(c) Language

The linguistic variable is operationally defined as the language usually spoken at home or the mother tongue. A question about the home language was asked in the Belgian, Canadian, and South African surveys, but the Swiss survey only inquired into the mother tongue of the respondents. It is a reasonable assumption, however, that the mother tongue and the usual language spoken at home coincide in the vast majority of cases. Dichotomizing this variable presents few problems because there is a natural English-French dichotomy in Canada, a Dutch-French dichotomy in Belgium, and an Afrikaans-English dichotomy in South Africa. Switzerland is officially multilingual rather than bilingual, but among the Swiss voting population the Italian-speakers and Romansh-speakers constitute a minority of only about five percent; it is therefore permissible to focus exclusively on the German-French dichotomy.

(d) Party Choice

The respondent's choice of political party may be elicited by means of several different questions. The principal possibilities are: the respondent's last vote (or his vote in more than one previous election), intended vote (if an election will take place in the near future), probable vote (in answer to the hypothetical question about how he would vote if an election were held at the time of the survey), and general party preference or party identification. In American voting behaviour research a clear conceptual distinction is usually drawn between these variants, especially between party identification and actual voting choice. In other countries, there tends to be such a close relationship between the two that they are virtually indistinguishable. As Budge and Farlie (1976: 123; see also Zuckerman and Lichbach, 1977) point out, party identification in non-American political contexts predicts actual voting so well that one must "suspect its empirical independence of voting choice, its conceptual antecedence and its explanatory capacity." Because the data of the present study were collected partly in election surveys and partly in non-election surveys, the best method to maximize comparability on this dimension is to avoid the intended or most recent votes as indicators of party choice and to use party preference (Canada and Switzerland), the probable vote (South Africa), or a combination of the two (Belgium).

The dichotomization of the political parties presents two problems. One is that all four countries have multiparty systems including a number of very small parties. These are sometimes coded separately but often lumped together as "other parties." All minor parties receiving less than roughly three percent of the votes in the elections of the early 1970s will be disregarded, and the analysis restricted to the more important parties, numbering from four to seven, in the countries under consideration. In Canada, four parties will be considered — in line with Laponce and Uhler's (1974: 3) description of the system as a "four-party system" and Meisel's (1975: 18) characterization of it as a "multiparty, one-party dominated configuration" of the large Liberal Party, the medium-sized Conservatives, and the smaller New Democratic Party (NDP) and Social Credit (SC). Six parties will be considered in Belgium: the traditional Christian Social Party (the Flemish name of which has the initials CVP), Socialists, and Liberals, and the newer and smaller Flemish party (*Volksunie,* VU), Brussels Francophone Party (FDF), and Walloon Rally (RW). From the highly complex Swiss configuration of parties (see Steiner, 1969; Steiner, 1974: 17-32), seven parties will be included in the analysis: the large parties that are of nation-wide importance — the closely allied Christian Conservatives (CC) and Christian Social Party (CS), the Socialists, and the Radicals — and three smaller and more regionally concentrated parties — the Liberals, who are particularly strong in French Switzerland, the Farmers (PAB) with special strength in Berne, and the mainly Zurich-based Independents. At the time of the 1974 survey, the four important South African parties were the large National (NP) and United (UP) parties, and the smaller Progressive (PP), and Reconstituted National (HNP) parties.[9]

The second problem is how to dichotomize these larger parties. Our interest in class, religion, and language points to four dimensions of party differentiation and conflict: the left-right, Catholic-Protestant, religious-secular, and majority vs. minority language dimensions. Many parties can be classified easily on the basis of their programmes and traditions. For instance, the socialist parties and the Canadian NDP clearly belong to the left, and the Belgian Liberals, the Swiss Liberals and Radicals, and the Canadian Conservatives to the right; the Belgian and the two Swiss Christian parties obviously fit the Catholic and religious categories; and the Flemish and Walloon parties in Belgium as well as the South African Nationalists and HNP are parties of linguistic-ethnic defense. In more doubtful cases, the criterion is the maximization of the correlation between the independent variables and party choice. This means, for example, that the Belgian Christian Social Party which has both Flemish and Walloon wings and which is not a linguistic party in the programmatic sense, is still classified as a party of the Dutch-speaking majority, and that the South African United Party which is religiously neutral, is placed in the "Catholic" category.

The classifications are summarized in Table 1. A few further comments are in order. As far as the first dimension is concerned, the Belgian and Swiss dichotomies correspond with the relationships that have been found between the respondents' left-right self-placement and party choice in these countries (Kerr, 1974: 9-10; Sidjanski et al., 1975: 96-109; Inglehart and Sidjanski, 1976: 230-235; Inglehart and Klingemann, 1976: 252-254). The Canadian dichotomy is in accord with both scholarly judgment and the voters' opinions that the NDP should be located on the left, the Liberals in the centre, and the Conservatives on the right, but whereas most

TABLE 1
Classification of 21 Parties in Four Countries According to
Four Dimensions of Cleavage

	Class dimension		Religious dimension I		Religious dimension II		Linguistic dimension*	
	Left	Right	Prot.	Cath.	Sec.	Rel.	Maj.	Min.
Belgium	Soc.	CVP	—	—	Soc.	CVP	CVP	Soc.
		Lib.			Lib.	VU	VU	Lib.
		VU			RW			RW
		RW			FDF			FDF
		FDF						
Canada	NDP	Lib.	Cons.	Lib.	Cons.	Lib.	Cons.	Lib.
	SC	Cons.	NDP	SC	NDP	SC	NDP	SC
S. Africa	NP	UP	NP	UP	UP	NP	NP	UP
	HNP	PP	HNP	PP	PP	HNP	HNP	PP
Switzerland	Soc.	CC	Soc.	CC	Soc.	CC	CC	Soc.
		CS	Rad.	CS	Rad.	CS	CS	Rad.
		Rad.	Lib.		Lib.		PAB	Lib.
		Lib.	PAB		PAB		Ind.	
		PAB	Ind.		Ind.			
		Ind.						

* Note: The majority and minority languages are respectively: Dutch and French (Belgium), English and French (Canada), Afrikaans and English (South Africa), and German and French (Switzerland).

scholars place Social Credit on the extreme right, the voters show considerable uncertainty on this question (Elkins, 1974: 502-511; Laponce, 1970: 483-485). The criterion of maximizing the correlation between social class and party choice leads to the assignment of the Social Credit to the left together with the NDP and to the grouping of the Liberals with the Conservatives on the right. It should be pointed out that this dichotomy is radically different from Alford's (1963; 1967) left-right classification of Liberals and NDP vs. Conservatives and Social Credit. For South Africa, the placement of the Nationalists and HNP on the left and the United and Progressive parties on the right reverses the usual classification of these parties on the liberalism-conservatism scale, but the latter classification is based on attitudes toward ethnic and racial issues rather than class issues (Peele and Morse, 1974: 1532-1534). In terms of class-based support, the Nationalists have traditionally received more lower-class votes than their opponents (see Van der Merwe and Buitendag, 1973: 201-204).

With regard to the party dichotomies on the two religious dimensions, it should be noted that the dividing lines coincide in all three countries in which both a Catholic-Protestant and a religious-secular split occurs, but that the descriptive labels differ: "Catholic" parties are also the "religious" parties in Canada and Switzerland, but they are the "secular" parties in South Africa. As indicated earlier, the split between the Dutch Reformed churches and the other South African religions may be regarded as a much more fundamental division than the Protestant-Catholic dichotomy. The political parties should then be classified as "Reformed" and "other" parties. Section VII will explore this alternative approach.

As far as the linguistic dichotomies are concerned, it may be argued that the distinctive language parties in Belgium should be contrasted instead of combined with the cross-language parties. However, this would result in a considerable decrease in the index of linguistic voting. Compared with the index of +46 based on the classification of Table 1, the index based on the dichotomy of the *Volksunie* vs. all other parties is only +19, the index for the Brussels Francophone and Walloon parties vs. all others +20, and the index of these three language parties together contrasted with the three cross-language parties a completely insignificant +1. Finally, it should be pointed out that the linguistic dichotomies in Table 1 are identical with the religious dichotomies in all countries except Switzerland.

V. CLASS VOTING, RELIGIOUS VOTING, AND LINGUISTIC VOTING

The indices of class, religious, and linguistic voting for the four countries are presented in Table 2. The top half of the table contains the unadjusted (uncontrolled) indices that are basically the same measures as are used by Alford (1963). The adjusted indices of voting in the lower half are the equivalents of the regression coefficients in a multiple regression equation; they represent the voting index for a particular independent variable when the other independent variables are controlled.

The most striking result that emerges from the array of indices is the weakness of class voting. It finishes last in all four countries in the unadjusted indices of religious and linguistic voting.[10] The only relatively high index of class voting is the Swiss index of +21, but the

TABLE 2
Unadjusted and Adjusted Indices of Class, Religious, and Linguistic Voting in Four Countries

	Class	Church affiliation	Church attendance	Language
Unadjusted Indices				
Belgium	+ 10	—	+ 49	+ 46
Canada	+ 7	+ 33	+ 14	+ 33
S. Africa	+ 9	+ 27	+ 23	+ 66
Switzerland	+ 21	+ 49	+ 46	+ 25
Adjusted Indices				
Belgium	+ 9	—	+ 39	+ 37
Canada	+ 6	+ 23	+ 5	+ 15
S. Africa	+ 4	− 10	+ 3	+ 67
Switzerland	+ 21	+ 37	+ 27	+ 27

other indices are higher still; church affiliation is + 49 percent.[11] The lowest index of class voting is the Canadian one of only + 7. It would have been even lower (+ 4) if Alford's dichotomy of Liberals and NDP vs. Conservatives and Social Credit had been used. When the indices of class voting are adjusted for the influence of church affiliation, church attendance, and language, they remain weak. Language is always stronger than class and religion usually so.

Whereas it is easy to identify class as the weakest variable, it is much more difficult to say which is the strongest of the independent variables. Three different patterns appear among the unadjusted indices: religion as the strongest factor (Switzerland), language as the strongest factor (South Africa), and religion and language with approximately equal strength (Belgium and Canada). The Belgian and Canadian patterns fit the third category; language is strong, but the strong religious variable is church attendance in Catholic vs. secular Belgium and church affiliation in Protestant/Catholic Canada.

The adjusted indices of religious and linguistic voting differ from the unadjusted indices, but the overall patterns remain the same for three of the four countries. The Belgian indices both decrease in value but by about equal amounts. The predominance of language in South Africa is accentuated by the introduction of controls: the index of linguistic voting stays at its very high level whereas the other indices are reduced to insignificance. This finding for South Africa as a whole confirms the earlier conclusion by Peele and Morse (1974: 1537), based on a voting study of three Cape Town constituencies, that "ethnicity [or language] is the major determinant of party vote ... Party vote also varies with other demographic categories (SES, religion, place of origin), but this is largely because these factors covary with ethnicity. When ethnicity is held constant, therefore, all these variables lose their predictive power." In Switzerland, church affiliation remains the most potent variable, but the difference with the linguistic voting index has narrowed. Also, church attendance and language are now at the same level. In Canada, finally, the pattern of equal religious and linguistic indices is changed by the introduction of controls. In line with the findings of most other Canadian studies of voting (see Irvine, 1974), church affiliation now emerges as the strongest factor. The difference between the adjusted indices of religious voting (church affiliation) and linguistic voting — + 23 and + 15 respectively — in the 1974 survey is not as great, however, as the differences found in other surveys. For instance, the 1968 election study data yield similar unadjusted indices of + 29 and + 25 respectively but sharply divergent adjusted indices of + 28 and + 6.

Since religious and linguistic influences appear to be closely interrelated, a further examination of the patterns of their effect on party choice is needed. The first step is to take a closer look at the religious factors. Table 3 presents the percentages of support for the "religious" parties among the respondents classified by four frequencies of church attendance and by church affiliation. Switzerland and Catholic Belgium, the two countries with the highest indices of religious voting (church attendance), show very strong monotonic relationships between the frequency of churchgoing and party choice. The differences are smaller and also somewhat uneven in the other two countries. The percentages in the top third of Table 3 also suggest that higher voting indices — but also quantitatively unbalanced dichotomies — could have been attained by dichotomizing at different levels of church attendance. Dividing between the very frequent churchgoers and all others yields an index of + 16 instead of the + 14 of Table 2 for Canada and an index of + 53 instead of + 46 for Switzerland. A division between those never attending church and all others gives an index of + 32 instead of + 23 for South Africa.

The further division into Catholics and Protestants in Table 3 shows that frequency of church attendance is an especially important factor only for either the Catholics or the Protestants in each country: for the Catholics in Switzerland and, albeit less strongly, in Canada, and for the Protestants in South Africa. For the other religious groups in these three countries, it is of negligible importance.

TABLE 3

Percentage Support for the "Religious" Parties Among Respondents with Different Frequencies of Church Attendance in Four Countries

Church affiliation	Church attendance	% Supporting the "religious" parties in			
		Belgium	Canada	S. Africa	Switzerl.
Cath. & Prot.	Very freq.	—	72	73	72
	Frequent	—	61	76	42
	Infrequent	—	56	62	15
	Never	—	57	38	9
Catholic	Very freq.	95	84	41*	86
	Frequent	75	82		63
	Infrequent	43	74	36*	36
	Never	16	74		10
Protestant	Very freq.	—	42	77	5
	Frequent	—	52	78	13
	Infrequent	—	45	63	8
	Never	—	49	40	9

*Note: These categories had to be combined, because there were not enough cases to present reliable percentages for each of the four categories separately.

TABLE 4

Percentage Support for the Liberals and Créditistes among Respondents with Different Frequencies of Church Attendance in Canada (1968)

Church attendance	Church affiliation		
	Cath. & Prot. %	Catholic %	Protestant %
Very frequent	66	76	34
Frequent	52	69	43
Infrequent	50	72	47
Never	58	61	58

Table 4 shows that in the Canadian election survey of 1968 there was a clear and almost monotonic relationship between frequency of church attendance and party choice for both Catholics and Protestants but in opposite directions: for the non-practicing Catholics and Protestants, the percentages of support for the Liberals and Créditistes are virtually identical, but they increase with increasing frequencies of churchgoing among Catholics, and decrease with increasing church attendance among Protestants.

Table 3 also makes clear where the main lines of cleavage appear when church affiliation and church attendance are considered together. In Canada, there are differences in party support *within* both the Protestant and the Catholic communities, but the far greater difference is that *between* Protestants and Catholics. In South Africa, non-churchgoing Protestants have about the same kind of party choice as the Catholics, and the most obvious cleavage here is between churchgoing Protestants and all others. A similar pattern emerges in the Swiss case: non-practicing Catholics behave very much like Protestants and unlike their more faithful co-religionists.

These distinctions can be used to compare the relative impact of religion and language on party choice. This is done in Table 5 which presents the percentages of support for the "religious" parties cross-tabulated according to religion, as classified in the previous paragraph, and language. The "religious" parties are also the parties representing linguistic majorities or minorities except in Switzerland where the two dichotomies do not coincide; for this reason, two matrices are given for the Swiss case.

Religion and language are mutually reinforcing determinants of party choice in Belgium, Canada, and Switzerland. In terms of their relative strength, religion has a slight edge over language in Belgium: the indices of religious voting within the Dutch and French linguistic communities are +38 and +44 respectively, whereas the indices of linguistic voting within the frequent church-attending group and the less frequently and non-practicing group are a somewhat lower +32 and +38 respectively. The Canadian percentages are more difficult to interpret because there are hardly any French-speaking Protestants in the country. Nevertheless, religion emerges as the more important variable because there is relatively less difference between Francophone and Anglophone Catholics than between Catholic and Protestant Anglophones. In Switzerland, religion is clearly the more powerful predictor in Table 5d, but this is not surprising since the parties are here dichotomized in such a way as to accentuate the religious differences. It is therefore of decisive importance that in Table 5e, where the party system dichotomization has the opposite bias in favour of linguistic differences, religion remains the stronger determinant: the two indices of religious voting within the linguistic groups are +36 and +43 compared with the lower indices of linguistic voting of +23 and +30 within the two religious categories.

TABLE 5
Percentage Support for the "Religious" Parties Among Religious and Linguistic Groups in Four Countries (and Support for the "German Majority" Parties in Switzerland)

a. Belgium	% Dutch	% French
(Very) frequent churchgoers	84	52
Infrequent & non-churchgoers	46	8
b. Canada	**French**	**English**
Catholics	85	70
Protestants	*	46
c. South Africa	**Afrikaans**	**English**
Practicing Protestants	94	24
Catholics & non-pract. Prot.	91	31
d. Switzerland (support for the "religious" parties)	**German**	**French**
Practicing Catholics	64	52
Protestants & non-pract. Cath.	9	8
e. Switzerland (support for the "German majority" parties)	**German**	**French**
Practicing Catholics	76	53
Protestants & non-pract. Cath.	40	10

*Note: Insufficient number of cases.

In South Africa, language and religion do not reinforce each other. In the Afrikaner community, there is a slightly weaker tendency to support the two nationalist parties among Catholics and non-practicing Protestants than among practicing Protestants, whereas in the Anglophone group the pattern is reversed. The more important conclusion from Table 5c, however, is that language is the overwhelmingly powerful determinant of party support among white South Africans.

The overall pattern of the relative strength of religion and language in the four countries in Table 5 reinforces the earlier conclusions based on the adjusted voting indices of Table 2. Religion is the better predictor in two countries (Canada and Switzerland); language is stronger in one country (South Africa); and the two factors have approximately the same strength in one of the countries (Belgium). In this group of four countries, religion therefore emerges as the more important determinant.

FIGURE 2
A Tree Analysis of Party Choice in Belgium

Total variance reduced by 35.8 percent.

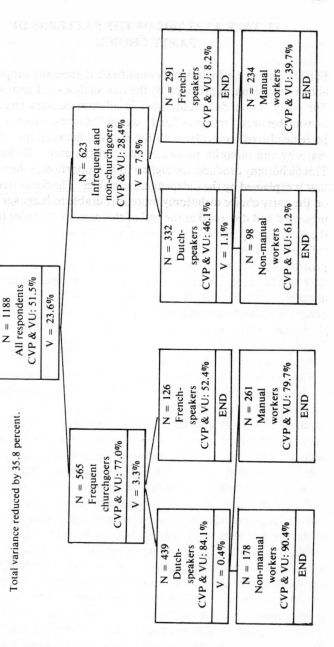

VI. TREE ANALYSIS OF THE PATTERNS OF
PARTY CHOICE

Further evidence, which slightly modifies but generally supports the above conclusion, is provided by the tree analyses in Figures 2 to 5. The party choice dichotomy used in all four country trees is the division between "religious" and "secular" parties, which, it should be remembered, coincides with the division between the linguistic majority and minority parties in all countries except Switzerland. This dichotomy produces the highest total proportion of the variance that is explained by the independent variables. The Swiss tree based on the party choice dichotomy more favourable to language will be presented and discussed at the end of this section. In order to make the results comparable with the analysis of the indices of voting, the independent variables are dichotomized in exactly the same way. The process of splitting the samples into subgroups was continued until no predictor could be found that reduced the variance by at least another 0.3 percent. This cutting-off point is lower than the 0.6 percent threshold recommended by the designers of the AID method (Sonquist, Baker, and Morgan, 1971: 10), but the lower level has been used in several voting studies (see Rose, 1974a: 214, 261, 309, 644; Liepelt, 1971: 188-189).

The results of the tree analyses are summarized in Table 6, which presents the proportion of the variance in party choice explained by each of the independent variables separately and by all of them together. The table also gives the comparable proportions of the variance explained by the stepwise multiple regression method which, unlike tree analysis, cannot detect interaction effects. It should be pointed out that for the purpose of this table the tree analysis was extended to the 0.1 percent level, since the variance explained by regression is also measured in tenths of a percent. The two sets of percentages turn out to be remarkably similar. The logic of the two methods necessarily leads to identical percentages of the variance explained by the strongest variable. As far as the other variables and the total reduction of variance are concerned, the tree analysis gives consistently but only slightly better results. This means that interaction effects play a rather small role.

Before we turn to an inspection of the individual country trees, a number of general conclusions can be stated. First, it is worth noting that three of the four tree analyses explain a high proportion of the variance in party choice. In Western countries generally the total

FIGURE 3
A Tree Analysis of Party Choice in Canada

Total variance reduced by 12.6 percent.

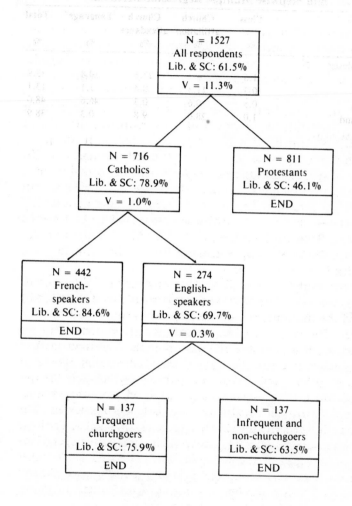

TABLE 6
Percentages of the Variance in Party Choice ("Religious" vs. "Secular" Parties) in Four Countries Explained by the Class, Religious, and Linguistic Variables According to the Tree Analysis and Stepwise Multiple Regression Methods

	Class %	Church affiliation %	Church attendance %	Language %	Total %
Tree Analysis*					
Belgium	1.6	—	23.6	10.8	35.9
Canada	0.3	11.3	0.4	1.1	13.1
S. Africa	0.5	0.6	0.3	46.6	48.0
Switzerland	1.0	28.0	9.8	0.3	38.9
Stepwise Multiple Regression					
Belgium	0.6	—	23.6	10.7	34.9
Canada	0.0	11.3	0.2	1.1	12.7
S. Africa	0.1	0.4	0.1	46.6	47.2
Switzerland	0.0	28.0	6.3	0.3	34.6

*Note: The percentages tend to be slightly higher than in Figures 1 to 4 because the analysis was continued to the 0.1 percent level of explained variance (instead of the 0.3 percent level used in the Figures).

variance explained is about 25 percent on the average (Rose, 1974a: 17; Lancelot, 1975: 419-420), and by comparison the Belgian, Swiss, and South African percentages are very high indeed. This result is especially remarkable because the present analysis considers only four independent variables (and only three in the Belgian case) in contrast with the dozens of social and demographic variables that are usually applied in tree analyses of voting. The exception is Canada where a below-average total of 13.1 percent of the variance can be explained, reflecting "the lack of social definition in the Canadian party system" (Irvine, 1976: 355). The proportion of the variance explained in a similar tree analysis of the 1968 voting study was an even lower 9.5 percent.

Secondly, the class factor once again turns out to be extremely weak. Tree analyses were also carried out with the parties dichotomized so as to highlight class differences. These trees are not presented here for reasons of space, but the results can be briefly summarized. In the three countries in which the dichotomies favourable to class differs from the dichotomies used in Table 6 — Belgium, Canada, and Switzerland — the total proportion of the variance

FIGURE 4
A Tree Analysis of Party Choice in South Africa

Total variance reduced by 47.8 percent.

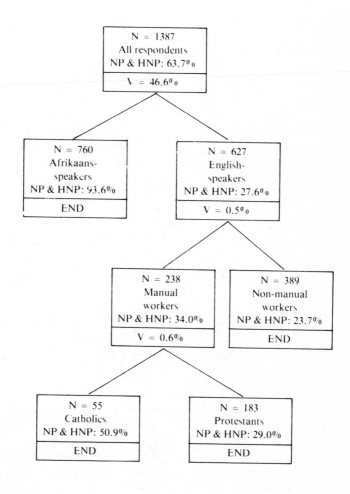

FIGURE 5
A Tree Analysis of Party Choice in Switzerland

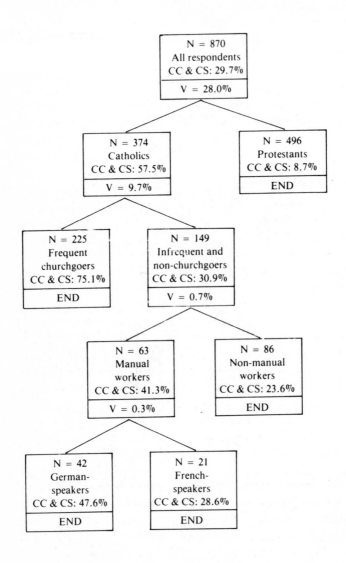

Total variance reduced by 38.6 percent.

explained is now reduced to 19.5, 3.9, and 17.3 percent respectively, and the percentage explained by class is only 1.2, 1.1, and 5.2 respectively. The religious variables remain the strongest determinants of party choice in all three cases.

Thirdly, religion now emerges more clearly as the strongest factor. Church affiliation and/or church attendance explain a much higher proportion of the variance than language not only in Canada and Switzerland, but also in Belgium. In South Africa, language remains the overwhelmingly powerful predictor.

Fourthly, all of the country trees show relatively simple patterns. With four independent variables (three in the Belgian case) it would have been theoretically possible to find as many as sixteen (or, for Belgium, eight) end groups. In fact, the trees have only from four to six end groups. This means that the high total proportions of explained variance are not the result of many small cumulative additions but of large shares of variance explained especially on the first split.

The Belgian tree in Figure 2 is, unlike the other three trees, an almost symmetrical one. Neither the order of the successive splits nor the nature of these splits contain any surprises: church attendance accounts for the first split, followed by language and class at the second and third levels of splitting, and the frequent churchgoers, Dutch-speakers, and non-manual workers are consistently the people who prefer the "religious" to the "secular" parties.[12] The Canadian, South African, and Swiss trees are all asymmetrical. In the last two of these cases, this is caused by the fact that the initial split yields a group that cannot be split further because it is highly homogeneous with regard to party choice and contains very little variance: the Swiss Protestants who overwhelmingly reject the Catholic parties, and the Afrikaners who overwhelmingly support the two Nationalist parties. Compared with the Afrikaners' political unanimity, the English-speakers can be characterized as "politically refracted" (Charton, 1975: 118; see also Lever, 1972: 24-26; Van der Merwe and Buitendag, 1973: 198). The most striking aspect of the South African tree is the great strength of the linguistic factor: close to half of the variance is explained on the first split (see Peele and Morse, 1974: 1527-1528; Lambley, 1974: 496). The asymmetry of the Canadian tree is not due to the virtual absence of variance in party choice among the Protestants. In fact, this group contains much more variance than the Catholics, but it is linguistically homo-geneous, and neither of the remaining variables emerges as a significant differentiator, whereas the Catholic group can be split further — albeit without contributing impressively to the amount of explained variance. The general pattern of the Canadian tree is similar to that of a series of trees based on surveys between 1957 and 1968 that Laponce (1972: 277) presents: religion consistently emerges on the first split, and region — which, of course, closely corresponds to language — on the second split.

It should be pointed out, finally, that the third of the conclusions presented above — the conclusion that religion is clearly the strongest predictor of party choice in the Belgian, Canadian, and Swiss trees — is not changed when the Swiss tree analysis is based on the party choice dichotomy more favourable to language instead of the religious-secular dichotomy. This tree is presented in Figure 6. Church affiliation still accounts for the first split, although it now explains only 11.2 percent of the variance instead of 28.0 percent as in Figure 5. Language does emerge as a more important predictor than in the tree of Figure 5, explaining 4.3 percent of the variance (and 4.5 percent if the analysis is continued to the 0.1 percent level of explained variance). The total variance is reduced by 20.3 percent — only slightly more than half of the 38.6 percent of the variance explained by the earlier tree of Figure 5.

VII. THE DEVIANT CASE OF SOUTH AFRICA

Before turning to an interpretation of this chapter's findings in the concluding section, it is necessary to take a second look at the deviant case of South Africa. Whereas in the other three countries religion is a stronger predictor of party choice than language, in South Africa language is not only the stronger factor, but a very much stronger one. Hence the question arises whether this deviant pattern can be explained by the fact that the church affiliation variable was dichotomized into Protestants vs. Catholics in all of the countries. In the South African context, as was pointed out earlier, the more meaningful dividing line lies between the members of the Dutch Reformed churches on the one hand, and other Protestants, Catholics, and Jews on the other. The reason why the Protestant-

FIGURE 6
Tree Analysis of Party Choice in Switzerland:
Socialists, Radicals, and Liberals vs. the Other Parties

Total variance reduced by 20.3 percent.

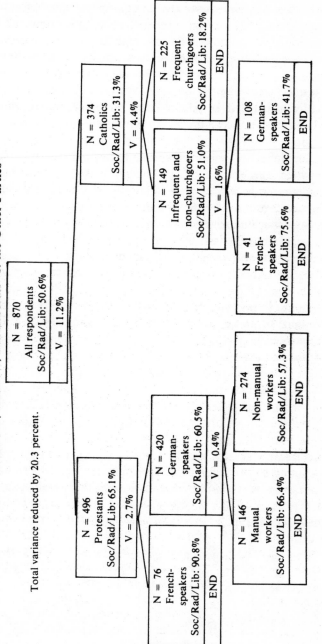

Catholic division was used for the South African case, too, was to maximize nominal cross-national equivalence in the four-country comparison. Moreover, the religious dichotomy of Dutch Reformed vs. the other religions coincides to a considerable extent with the dichotomy of Afrikaners vs. English-speakers. It is worth examining this relationship in some detail, however, and especially the question of whether the strong linguistic voting pattern in South Africa is matched, or possibly even surpassed, by religious voting when the Reformed churches are contrasted with the other religious groups.

The index of religious voting (church affiliation) that was reported earlier was +27. On the basis of the alternative dichotomy, it increases dramatically to +56. The index of linguistic voting of +65 is still higher, but the difference has become much narrower. (The slight discrepancy between this index of linguistic voting and the one reported earlier, +66, is due to the enlargement of the sample by the inclusion of Jewish respondents.) The voting index for church attendance remains unchanged at +23.

Table 7 presents the percentage of support for the two Nationalist parties among the respondents classified by four frequences of church attendance and four categories of church affiliation. Adherents of the Reformed churches are extremely loyal supporters of the National Party and the HNP, and their support decreases only very slightly as church attendance decreases. Different frequencies of religious observance do not significantly differentiate the Catholic and Jewish respondents. Among the non-Reformed Protestants, the very frequent churchgoers display considerably greater support for the nationalist parties than those attending less regularly; this is mainly due to the relatively high proportion of devoutly religious members of small sects in the former category. On the whole, Table 7 shows unambiguously that the main partisan difference is between the Reformed respondents and all others.

This religious dichotomy is used to examine the relative influence of religion and language on party choice in Table 8. The table also shows the numbers of respondents on which the percentages are based in each of the four categories, in order to emphasize that there are relatively few Reformed English-speakers and non-

TABLE 7
Percentage Support for the National Party and the HNP among Respondents with Different Frequencies of Religious Observance in South Africa

Church attendance	All %	Dutch Reformed %	Other Prot. %	Catholic %	Jewish %
Very frequent	73	93	50	41*	36*
Frequent	75	93	26	41*	36*
Infrequent	60	90	30	36*	38*
Never	40	87	28	36*	38*

*Note: These categories had to be combined, because there were not enough cases to present reliable percentages for each of the four categories separately.

TABLE 8
Percentage Support for the National Party and the HNP among the Major Religious and Linguistic Groups in South Africa

Religion	Afrikaans %	English %
Members of Reformed churches	93 (N = 662)	62 (N = 42)
Other Christians and Jews	95 (N = 98)	26 (N = 639)

Reformed Afrikaners. When the percentages are compared, it becomes clear that language is the stronger determinant of party choice. Reformed and non-Reformed Afrikaners give approximately equal and overwhelming support to the Nationalists and the HNP. Among the English-speakers, religion does emerge as a significant differentiator: the small group of Reformed English-speakers are much more likely to support the Nationalist parties than the more numerous English-speakers with different religions. But in both religious groups, language is the sharper differentiator. The relative impact of language and religion is also shown clearly when we compare the voting indices for the separate groups. The indices of linguistic voting are +31 for the Reformed respondents and a very high +69 for the non-Reformed category. The indices of religious voting are a respectable +36 for the English-speakers, but an insignificant −2 for the Afrikaners. Given these findings, it is not surprising that, when

FIGURE 7
Tree Analysis of Party Choice in South Africa, Using the Dichotomy of Reformed Church Members vs. All Other Christians and Jews

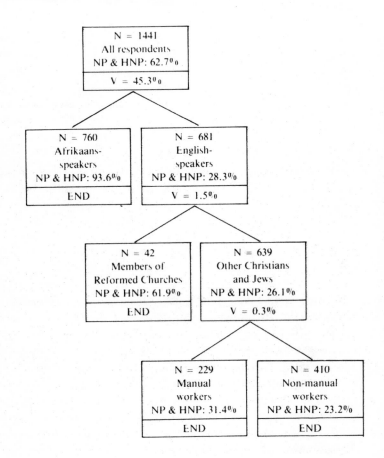

Total variance reduced by 47.1 percent.

the dichotomy of Reformed vs. other religions is used in a tree analysis of party choice in South Africa, language again turns out to be the dominant force. This tree is shown in Figure 7. Church affiliation does perform slightly better than in the earlier tree analysis of Figure 4: it now contributes 1.5 percent to the explained variance instead of only 0.6 percent. The reason for the weakness of the religious factor, of course, is that once language has been used as a predictor, religion has lost much of its explanatory power, too, because it is so closely tied to language. The politically homogeneous Afrikaner group cannot be split further, as in Figure 4. The religious differences do have an impact on the English-speakers, but the Reformed English-speakers, who are much more pro-Nationalist than the others, are a too small group to add a great deal to the amount of explained variance. But language remains the strongest predictor of party choice and, in this respect, South Africa remains a deviant case.

VIII. CONCLUSION: THE PARADOX OF RELIGIOUS VOTING

This four-country comparison was described earlier as a "crucial experiment" in Naroll's sense of the term. It may also be likened to a decisive trial of strength, in which religion turns out to be victorious, language is a strong runner-up, and class finishes as a distant third. How can these findings be explained?

The conspicuous weakness of class voting compared with religious and linguistic voting is not really surprising. Primordial communal loyalties can be extremely tenacious even in the modern world, and they constitute a formidable obstacle to the development of competing cleavages based on objective socio-economic interests (see Geertz, 1963: 109-113; Birch, 1978: 333-334). Dahl's (1978: 193) unequivocal conclusion with regard to this issue is the following:

It is possible to interpret cleavages other than those formed by social class as crumbling obstacles to class consciousness, left behind by the slow recession of traditional society and early capitalism, destined nevertheless to rapid erosion by the push of new economic relationships. Historically, however, this interpretation has led to a persistent underestimation of the continuing strength of identifications formed by subcultures centered around religion, region, ethnic group, race, and language.

Social class is clearly no more than a secondary and subsidiary influence on party choice, and it can become a factor of importance only in the absence of potent rivals such as religion and language.

The more surprising — and the theoretically more interesting and challenging — empirical finding concerns the relative strength of religious and linguistic voting: religion emerges as the more important dimension of party choice in the 1970s, whereas especially in Belgium and Canada the linguistic-ethnic cleavage has been the more salient dimension of political conflict in recent years. For instance, Meisel (1974: 9) writes that he considers religion to be "of virtually no political importance in contemporary federal politics" in Canada; the conflict between Francophone and Anglophone Canada is reckoned of the greatest political significance. Similarly, linguistic issues have in recent years been much more prominent than religious problems in Belgium (Frognier, 1978). Conversely, language has remained the paramount determinant of party choice in South Africa, although, as Van der Merwe and Buitendag (1973: 190) observe, "there is much evidence that the traditional divisions between the two language groups are tending to become muted." Switzerland is a more doubtful case. In recent years, the Jura problem has called attention to the fact that even Swiss politics is not immune from linguistic tensions, but the Jura question is primarily a regional rather than a national issue and it is also just as much a religious as a linguistic problem. At the national level, neither religious nor linguistic issues can be said to have high salience.

Two explanations of the paradox may be offered. One follows the well-known argument of Lipset and Rokkan (1967: 50-51) that party systems tend to reflect the political cleavages of the periods in which the parties came into existence, instead of the dimensions of contemporary political conflict. The conflicts of the past have structured the political parties and the differences between them, and are able to survive as entrenched atavisms in the party systems. The party systems in turn structure the electoral contests, even when other political dimensions have become more salient. Following this line of reasoning, Schwartz (1974: 589) argues that in Canada "class-based voting exists; it is consistent class-based parties that are missing." Similarly, one can say that in Belgium, Canada, and Switzerland, the potential strength of linguistic voting is suppressed by the religiously oriented structure of the party systems. The Belgian case also demonstrates, however, that the "freezing" of the party system in the 1920s was not absolute: Flemish linguistic parties already made their appearance in 1919 and have survived in the form of the *Volksunie*, but the Walloon and Francophone parties originated in the 1960s in a long and solidly established party system. The presence of these specifically linguistic parties also accounts for the considerable strength of linguistic voting in Belgium, which does not lag very far behind the strength of religious voting.

The second explanation of the paradox of strong religious voting is based on the notion that political parties are important, but not the only, vehicles for the articulation and representation of various kinds of interests. In Belgium, Canada, and Switzerland, a significant difference between the religious and linguistic communities is that the former tend to be geographically dispersed whereas the latter are regionally more concentrated. Consequently, the most suitable organs for the representation of religious interests have been the political parties, whereas the strongest organs for the representation of the linguistic interests could be the subnational governments, especially if they possessed or acquired a high degree of political autonomy: the provincial and cantonal governments in federal Canada and Switzerland and the recently established cultural councils in semi-federal Belgium (Dunn, 1972; Lijphart, 1977: 90-97, 121-124).[13] The deviant case of South Africa with its extremely strong linguistic voting patterns significantly reinforces this argument. Because South Africa has a unitary form of government and because its linguistic communities are geographically interspersed to a high extent, the linguistic interests have had to protect themselves mainly through the party system.

The greater strength of religious compared with linguistic voting in Belgium, Canada, and Switzerland is neither the result of the greater contemporary salience of religious issues in these countries (with the partial exception of Switzerland), nor exclusively the outcome of an atavistic survival of past religious conflicts. At least to some extent, it is also the effect of the presence of alternative regional-federal structures for the articulation and representation of the linguistic interests.

NOTES

I wish to thank the scholars and the organizations who made the data collected by them or tabulations based on these data available to me for the purpose of this study. The Belgian data were part of the 1970 and 1973 European Communities Studies of which Ronald Inglehart and Jacques-René Rabier were the principal investigators. The data of the 1974 Canadian national election survey were orginally collected by Harold Clarke, Jane Jenson, Lawrence LeDuc, and Jon Pammett. The 1968 Canadian election survey was conducted by John Meisel. The South African data were collected in 1974 by Market Research Africa (Pty) Ltd under the guidance of Lawrence Schlemmer. The Swiss national election study of 1972 was organized by the Department of Political Science of the University of Geneva and the Sozialforschungsstelle of the University of Zurich under the direction of Henry H. Kerr, Jr., Dusan Sidjanski, and Gerhard Schmidtchen. The Belgian data and the 1974 Canadian data were obtained from the Inter-University Consortium for Political and Social Research. Neither the original collectors of the data nor the Consortium bear any responsibility for the analyses or interpretations presented here. I should also like to express my appreciation to Ian Budge, Galen A. Irwin, David Laitin, Richard Rose, Jürg Steiner, Hendrik W. van der Merwe, and Jan Verhoef for their advice and assistance, to the Netherlands Institute for Adanced Study in the Humanities and the Social Sciences in Wassenaar, where I was a Fellow in 1974-75 and where I did part of the research for this chapter, and to the Netherlands Foundation for the Advancement of Pure Research (ZWO) for its financial support. An earlier and shorter version of this chapter was published, in Italian translation, in the *Rivista Italiana di Scienza Politica* 8 (April 1978): 77-111.

1. Switzerland and South Africa were omitted from the earlier cross-national survey analysis by Rose and Urwin (1969: 18-19, 44), but they are both included in Mackie and Rose's (1974) compilation of electoral statistics.

2. In a brief appendix, Hill (1974: 103) presents a tree analysis based on more recent data that do include the linguistic variable.

3. Three of Rose and Urwin's seventeen countries are excluded by these criteria: Denmark and Finland because of the lack of data on the religious support of their parties, and Northern Ireland because it is not a "country" on a par with the other sovereign states.

4. The following countries were included in one or more of the studies: Great Britain and the United States (all five studies); Australia and Canada (all except Lijphart); Germany, the Netherlands, and Norway (all except Alford); Belgium, Italy, and Sweden (Lancelot, Lijphart, Rose-Urwin), Austria and France (Lijphart and Rose-Urwin); Ireland (Lancelot and Rose-Urwin); Finland (Lancelot); Japan (Budge-Farlie); and New Zealand (Rose-Urwin).

5. Another interesting attempt to compare the relative importance of class, religion,

and language or ethnicity in an illustrative set of four countries (Britain, Germany, Norway, and the United States) may be found in the SETUPS publication by Asher and Richardson (1975: 40-46).

6. The key questions for the purpose of this analysis were included in both surveys, and the two samples could therefore be combined without the complicated adjustments outlined by Ithiel de Sola Pool (1963).

7. The exact numbers of respondents in the samples are as follows: Belgium (1970), N = 1296; Belgium (1973), N = 1266; Canada (1974), N = 2562, weighted N = 2445; South Africa (1974), N = 641 (Afrikaners) + 659 (English-speakers) = 1300; weighted N = 2175; Switzerland (1972), N = 1917. The Swiss data have been used by Kerr (1974), Sidjanski et al. (1975), and Inglehart and Sidjanski (1976). Secondary analyses of Belgian survey data have tended to use the 1968 election study: see Hill (1974), Frognier (1973), and Frognier (1976). For earlier studies of voting in Belgium, see De Smet and Evalenko (1956) and Dewachter (1967).

8. In Canada, where class voting tends to be low, Ogmundson (1975: 509-510) similarly compared the three indicators of class and found that they did not lead to great differences in the levels of class voting. See also the comments by Thompson (1970: 137-138).

9. In recent years, the South African United and Progressive parties have regrouped: the leftwing of the United Party has merged with the Progressives to form the Progressive Federal Party; its centre has combined with the small Democratic Party into the New Republic Party; and its rightwing continues as the South African Party.

10. The data of the 1968 Canadian election study yield the same conclusion. The unadjusted indices of class, religious (church affiliation and attendance), and linguistic voting are +9, +29, +10 and 25 respectively. The adjusted indices, in the same order, are +9, +28, -4 and +6.

11. On the basis of the same data, Kerr (1974: 7) finds class, religious (church attendance), and linguistic indices with almost identical values: +22, +21, and +23 respectively. The explanation of this discrepancy is partly that Kerr includes a few minor parties in his analysis in addition to the more important ones considered here, but mainly that he uses the dichotomy of Socialists and Communists vs. the other parties for all of his indices; this left-right dichotomy maximizes the index of class voting but not high values for the indices of religious and linguistic voting.

12. It is surprising that in the tree presented by Hill (1974: 103) language does not emerge as a differentiating factor. The most likely explanation is that Hill dichotomizes party choice as left vs. right, and that he includes region, which to a considerable extent coincides with language, among his variables.

13. Similarly, it may be argued that class interests have not been more strongly expressed through the party systems because they have been able to use the alternative political channels of labour unions and employers' organizations.

REFERENCES

ALFORD, R.R (1967) "Class voting in the Anglo-American political systems," pp. 67-93 in S.M. Lipset and S. Rokkan (eds.) *Party Systems and Voter Alignments: Cross-National Perspectives.* New York: Free Press.

— — (1963) *Party and Society: The Anglo-American Democracies.* Chicago: Rand McNally.

ALKER, H.R. (1965) *Mathematics and Politics.* New York: Macmillan

ASHER, H B. and B. RICHARDSON (1975) *Comparative Voting Behavior.* Supplementary Empirical Teaching Units in Political Science. Washington, DC: American Political Science Association.

BERELSON, B. and G.A. STEINER (1964) *Human Behavior: An Inventory of Scientific Findings.* New York: Harcourt, Brace & World.

BIRCH, A.H. (1978) "Minority nationalist movements and theories of political integration, "*World Politics* 30 (April): 325-344.

BOOKS, J.W. and J.B. REYNOLDS (1975) "A note on class voting in Great Britain and the United States," *Comparative Political Studies* 8 (October): 360-376.

BROOM, L. (1976) "Problematics in the study of social mobility: a commentary on the Coloured people," pp. 9-24 in H.W. van der Merwe and C.J. Groenewald (eds.) *Occupational and Social Change Among Coloured People in South Africa: Proceedings of a Workshop of the Centre for Intergroup Studies at the University of Cape Town.* Cape Town: Juta.

BUDGE, I. and D. FARLIE (1977) *Voting and Party Competition: A Theoretical Synthesis Based on a Critique of Existing Approaches Applied to Data from Ten Democracies.* London: Wiley.

— — (1976) "A comparative analysis of factors correlated with turnout and voting choice," pp. 103-126 in I. Budge, I. Crewe, and D. Farlie (eds.) *Party Identification and Beyond: Representations of Voting and Party Competition.* London: Wiley.

CAMPBELL, A., P.E. CONVERSE, W.E. MILLER, and D.E. STOKES (1960) *The American Voter.* New York: Wiley.

CHANDLER, W.M. and M.A. CHANDLER (1974) "The problem of indicator formation in comparative research," *Comparative Political Studies* 7 (April): 26-46.

CHARTON, N. (1975) "English-speaking white elites in South African politics," *Politikon* 2 (December): 115-128.

CLAEYS-VAN HAEGENDOREN, M. (1967) "Party and opposition formation in Belgium," *Res Publica* 9(3): 413-435.

CONVERSE, P.E. (1974) "Some priority variables in comparative electoral research," pp. 727-745 in R. Rose (ed.) *Electoral Behavior: A Comparative Handbook.* New York: Free Press.

— — (1964) "The nature of belief systems in mass publics," pp. 206-261 in D.E. Apter (ed.) *Ideology and Discontent.* New York: Free Press of Glencoe.

DAHL, R.A. (1978) "Pluralism revisited," *Comparative Politics* 10 (January): 191-203.

DE JONG, J.J. (1956) *Overheid en Onderdaan.* Wageningen: Zomer & Keunings.

DELRUELLE, N., R. EVALENKO, and W. FRAEYS (1970) *Le comportement politique des électeurs belges.* Brussels: Institut de Sociologie de l'Université Libre de Bruxelles.

DE SMET, R.E. and R. EVALENKO (1956) *Les élections belges: Explication de la repartition géographique des suffrages.* Brussels: Institut de Sociologie Solvay.

DEUTSCH, K.W. (1953) *Nationalism and Social Communication: An Inquiry into the Foundations of Nationality.* Cambridge, Mass.: Technology Press.

DEWACHTER, W. (1967) *De wetgevende verkiezingen als proces van machtsverwerving in het Belgisch politiek bestel.* Antwerp: Standaard.

DUNN, J.A., Jr. (1972) " 'Consociational democracy' and language conflict: a comparison of the Belgian and Swiss experiences," *Comparative Political Studies* 5 (April): 3-39.

ELKINS, D.J. (1974) "The perceived structure of the Canadian party systems," *Canadian Journal of Political Science* 7 (September): 502-524.

FROGNIER, A.P. (1978) "Parties and cleavages in the Belgian parliament," *Legislative Studies Quarterly* 3 (February): 109-131.

— — (1976) "Party preference spaces and voting change in Belgium," pp. 189-202 in I. Budge, I. Crewe, and D. Fairlie (eds.) *Party Identification and Beyond: Representations of Voting and Party Competition.* London: Wiley.

— — (1973) "Distances entre partis et clivages en Belgique," *Res Publica* 15(2): 291-311.

GEERTZ, C. (1963) "The integrative revolution: primordial sentiments and civil politics in the new states," pp. 105-157 in C. Geertz (ed.) *Old Societies and New States: The Quest for Modernity in Asia and Africa.* New York: Free Press.

HILL, K. (1974) "Belgium: political change in a segmented society," pp. 29-107 in R. Rose (ed.) *Electoral Behavior: A Comparative Handbook.* New York: Free Press.

HUYSE, L. (1975) "Vijftien Angelsakische auteurs over politiek, verzuiling en compromisvorming in België," *Res Publica* 17(3): 413-431.

— — (1974) "Un regard sociologique sur la question linguistique en Belgique," *Septentrion* 3 (3): 23-35.

INGLEHART, R. and H. KLINGEMANN (1976) "Party identification, ideological preference and the left-right dimension among Western mass publics," pp. 243-273 in I. Budge, I. Crewe and D. Farlie (eds.) *Party Identification and Beyond: Representations of Voting and Party Competition.* London: Wiley.

INGLEHART, R. and D. SIDJANSKI (1976) "The left, the right, the establishment and the Swiss electorate," pp. 225-242 in I. Budge, I. Crewe and D. Farlie (eds.) *Party Identification and Beyond: Representations of Voting and Party Competition.* London: Wiley.

IRVINE, W.P. (1976) "Testing models of voting choice in Canada," pp. 353-363 in I. Budge, I. Crewe, and D. Farlie (eds.) *Party Identification and Beyond: Representations of Voting and Party Competition.* London: Wiley.

— — (1974) "Explaining the religious basis of the Canadian partisan identity: success on the third try," *Canadian Journal of Political Science* 7 (September): 560-563.

KERR, H.H., Jr. (1974) *Switzerland: Social Cleavages and Partisan Conflict,* Sage Professional Papers in Contemporary Political Sociology, 1, 06-002. London and Beverly Hills: Sage.

KORPI, W. (1972) "Some problems in the measurement of class voting," *American Journal of Sociology* 78 (November): 627-642.

LAMBLEY, P. (1974) "Racial attitudes and the maintenance of segregation: a study of voting patterns of white, English-speaking South Africans," *British Journal of Sociology* 25 (December): 494-499.

LANCELOT, A. (1975) "Comparative electoral behavior," *European Journal of Political Research* 3 (December): 413-424.

LAPONCE, J.A. (1972) "Post-dicting electoral cleavages in Canadian federal elections, 1949-68: material for a footnote," *Canadian Journal of Political*

Science 5 (June); 270-286.

— — (1970) "Note on the use of the left-right dimension," *Comparative Political Studies* 2 (January): 481-502.

LAPONCE, J.A. and R.S. UHLER (1974) "Measuring electoral cleavages in a multi-party system: the Canadian case," *Comparative Political Studies* 7 (April): 3-25.

LAZARSFELD, P.F., B. BERELSON, and H. GAUDET (1944) *The People's Choice: How the Voter Makes Up His Mind in a Presidential Campaign*. New York: Duell, Sloan and Pearce.

LEVER, H. (1972) *The South African Voter: Some Aspects of Voting Behavior, With Special Reference to the General Elections of 1966 and 1970*. Cape Town: Juta.

LIEPELT, K. (1971) "The infra-structure of party support in Germany and Austria," pp. 183-202 in M. Dogan and R. Rose (eds.) *European Politics: A Reader*. Boston: Little, Brown.

LIJPHART, A. (1977) *Democracy in Plural Societies: A Comparative Exploration*. New Haven: Yale University Press.

— — (1975) "The comparable-cases strategy in comparative research," *Comparative Political Studies* 8 (July): 158-177.

— — (1971) *Class Voting and Religious Voting in the European Democracies: A Preliminary Report*, Occasional Paper No. 8, Survey Research Centre. Glasgow: Univerisity of Strathclyde.

LINZ, J.J. (1967) "Cleavage and consensus in West German politics: the early fifties," pp. 283-321 in S.M. Lipset and S. Rokkan (eds.)*Party Systems and Voter Alignments: Cross-National Perspectives*. New York: Free Press.

LIPSET, S.M. (1960) *Political Man: The Social Bases of Politics*. Garden City: Doubleday.

LIPSET, S.M. and S. ROKKAN (1967) "Cleavage structures, party systems, and voter alignments: an introduction," pp. 1-64 in S.M. Lipset and S. Rokkan (eds.) *Party Systems and Voter Alignments: Cross-National Perspectives*. New York: Free Press.

LORWIN, V.R. (1966) "Belgium: religion, class, and language in national politics," pp. 147-187 in R.A. Dahl (ed.) *Political Oppositions in Western Democracies*. New Haven: Yale University Press.

MACKIE, T.T. and R. ROSE (1974) *The International Almanac of Electoral History*. London: Macmillan.

MEISEL, J. (1975) "The party system and the 1974 election," pp. 1-28 in H.R. Penniman (ed.) *Canada at the Polls: The General Election of 1974*. Washington, DC: American Enterprise Institute for Public Policy Research.

— — (1974) *Cleavages, Parties and Values in Canada*. Sage Professional Papers in Contemporary Political Sociology, 1, 06-003. London and Beverly Hills: Sage.

NAROLL, R. (1966) "Scientific comparative politics and international relations," pp. 329-337 in R.B. Farrell (ed.) *Approaches to Comparative and International Politics*. Evanston: Northwestern University Press.

OGMUNDSON, R. (1975) "Party class images and the class vote in Canada," *American Sociological Review* 40 (August): 506-512.

PEELE, S. and S.J. MORSE (1974) "Ethnic voting and political change in South Africa," *American Political Science Review* 68 (December): 1520-1541.

POOL, I. de SOLA (1963) "Use of available sample surveys in comparative research," *Social Science Information* 2(2):16-35.

ROSE, R. (ed.) (1974a) *Electoral Behavior: A Comparative Handbook.* New York: Free Press.
—— (1974b) "Comparability in electoral studies," pp. 3-25 in R. Rose (ed.) *Electoral Behavior: A Comparative Handbook.* New York: Free Press.
ROSE, R. and D.W. URWIN (1975) *Regional Differentiation and Political Unity in Western Nations.* Sage Professional Papers in Contemporary Political Sociology, 1, 06-007. London and Beverly Hills: Sage.
—— (1969) "Social cohesion, political parties and strains in regimes," *Comparative Political Studies* 2 (April): 7-67.
SÄRLVIK, B. (1969) "Socioeconomic determinants of voting behaviour in the Swedish electorate," *Comparative Political Studies* 2 (April): 99-135.
SARTORI, G. (1969) "From the sociology of politics to political sociology," pp. 65-100 in S.M. Lipset (ed.) *Politics and the Social Sciences.* New York: Oxford University Press.
SCHWARTZ, M.A. (1974) "Canadian voting behavior," pp. 543-617 in R. Rose (ed.) *Electoral Behavior: A Comparative Handbook.* New York: Free Press.
SIDJANSKI, D., C. ROIG, H. KERR, R. INGLEHART, and J. NICOLA (1975) *Les Suisses et la Politique: Enquête sur les Attitudes d'Electeurs Suisses.* Berne: Herbert Lang.
SONQUIST, J.A., E.L. BAKER, and J.N. MORGAN (1971) *Searching for Structure (Alias-AID-III): An Approach to Analysis of Substantial Bodies of Micro-Data and Documentation for a Computer Program (Successor to the Automatic Interaction Detector Program).* Ann Arbor: Survey Research Center, Institute for Social Research, University of Michigan.
STEINER, J. (1974) *Amicable Agreement versus Majority Rule: Conflict Resolution in Switzerland.* Chapel Hill: University of North Carolina Press.
—— (1969) "Typologisierung des schweizerischen Parteiensystems," pp. 21-40 in *Annuaire Suisse de Science Politique,* vol. 9. Lausanne: Association Suisse de Science Politique.
STOUTHARD, P.C. (1971) "Analysis by means of sequential contrasting groups: a computer algorithm," *Sociologia Neerlandica* 5 (Spring): 60-73.
TAYLOR, C.L. and M.C. HUDSON (1972) *World Handbook of Political and Social Indicators.* New Haven: Yale University Press.
THOMPSON, K. (1970) *Cross-National Voting Behavior Research: An Example of Computer-Assisted Multivariate Analysis of Attribute Data.* Sage Professional Papers in Comparative Politics, 1, 01-003. Beverly Hills: Sage.
URWIN, D.W. (1970) "Social cleavages and political parties in Belgium: problems of institutionalization," *Political Studies* 18 (September): 320-340:
VAN DEN BRANDE, A. (1967) "Elements for a sociological analysis of the impact of the main conflicts on Belgian political life," *Res Publica* 9(3): 437-469.
VAN DER MERWE, H.W. and J.J. BUITENDAG (1973) "Political, ethnic and structural differences among white South Africans," pp. 106-21 in ASSA, *Sociology Southern Africa 1973.* Durban: University of Natal.
ZUCKERMAN, A.S. and M.I. LICHBACH (1977) "Stability and change in European electorates," *World Politics* 29 (July): 523-551.

8
Does Consociationalism Exist?
A Critique of the Dutch Experience

Ilja Scholten
Carleton University, Ottawa

The Dutch polity is a fascinating example of the relationship between representative government and electoral participation. In this multiparty system, only *after* an election is the political machinery set in motion to determine both the composition and colour of the new coalition government. The process has become increasingly cumbersome and lengthy. Recent cabinets have taken over half a year to form and sometimes the outcome is hardly anticipated in election results. A socialist party with a huge victory, by Dutch standards, has lost office because negotiations were wrecked, and a new coalition cabinet formed. When cabinets representing new coalitions are formed without new elections, this does not conform to an Anglo-American view of selecting government. Within this flux, there is one element of continuity. Since 1918 confessional parties have uninterruptedly been at the pinnacle of Dutch governments. After World War II especially, their intraparty politics were of importance in bringing either liberals or socialists into an alliance, (and sometimes determining whether a cabinet fell). Such a political system is undoubtedly fascinating, but is it also democratic?

In the last decade a number of influential publications dealing with the Netherlands have appeared under the label "consociationalism". We may usefully begin our discussion with a quote by Arend Lijphart (1975a:vi), from the theory's empirical cornerstone, *The Politics of Accommodation:*

consociationalism retains its theoretical value as a source of constructive amendments to pluralist theory, its empirical value as an explanation of the pattern of Dutch democracy in the 1917-1967 period, and practical value as a normative model that is more appropriate than the pluralist model for the world's many highly divided societies aspiring to democratic rule.

Daalder (1974a) notes the model's "major contribution" as a "formidable challenge to existing typologies of democratic regimes and to widely held beliefs on the conditions of effective and democratic rule".

Not only has this literature shaped the Netherlands' image abroad; domestically it has received considerable theoretical acceptance. Yet, despite the theory's appeal, some ambiguity in definition cannot be denied. The label is attached to studies ranging from efforts to offset multicultural centrifugal forces to intimate interactions between business and political elites. While a number of studies of social and political structures within several countries have been called consociational, the term should properly be reserved for those analyses which explicitly relate political stability to conciliatory elite behaviour. This can be sub-divided into a *political culture* approach which emphasizes historical traditions of compromise and another of *elite behaviour as conscious response to manifest perils of fragmentation*. The latter, forcefully expounded by Lijphart, will be the focus of our analysis because of his major contribution to the literature.

The general thrust of Lijphart's thesis is that the elites applied a "self-denying hypothesis" which led to unique institutional arrangements, behavioural rules and decision-making procedures. Meanwhile, the masses were to be kept rigidly separated, lest they would thwart the delicate interactions of the elites. Lijphart describes four aspects of this "consociationalism": the absence of subcultural civil strife; immobilism of policy output; the proliferation of "pillarization"; and elaborate socio-economic policy-making institutions.

Within consociational systems, according to Lijphart, *rules of the game* have been developed to resolve the problems caused by multiculturalism (rules are numbered and italicized). Accepting that consociationalism is an ideal model, with qualifications such as "even Britain does not follow the pure 'British model'" (Lijphart, 1977:112), in theory these practices should be present in consociational polities while *not* being part and parcel of the political process in homogeneous and/or majoritarian systems. But in fact they are, and while everywhere they may have facilitated stability by serving as lubricants between inelastic formal rules and perceived demands of practical politics, why should they acquire a halo only in multicultural polities?

To take a homogeneous polity, we learn from Stjernquist (1966:139) "compromise is traditionally considered the Swedish technique in politics." This correspondence is particularly pronounced in Rustow's (1955:71) *The Politics of Compromise,* named after the 1907 legislative pact when opposing parliamentary leaders "took a prominent part in formulating the details of the 'great compromise' — a formula that combined the Liberal demand for a more democratic franchise with tory guarantees of proportional representation and bicameralism". It formed the prototype of the standard mediation techniques of the legislative process between the parties, and between parliament and cabinet. Paraphrasing, we note their correspondence with Lijphart's consociational rules (whose numbers are in brackets). "Within these proportional (4) committees, composed of especially the elderly, seasoned politicians (3) and experts, *saklighet,* a businesslike attitude (1) is the motto. Negotiations taking place behind closed doors (6), in an atmosphere conducive to mutual understanding and appreciation of the sincerity of the opponents' position (2), there is no point for flamboyant oratory (5)" (Rustow, 1955:180-187, 197, 209).

While Lijphart metaphorically compares the Dutch rule that *"politics is serious business (1)"* to the "game of politics" in France, Almond (1956:41) argues "because (American) political culture tends to be homogeneous and pragmatic, it takes some of the atmosphere of a game", which distinguishes it from the ideological continental European political process such as in France (but see Lijphart, 1977:27). As a "direct deduction from this axiom, *'the cabinet has a right to govern'* (7)" and this rule "is of great importance" (Lijphart, 1968: 134,137). However, in a parliamentary democracy a cabinet remains in office as long as it is supported or tolerated by a majority, and if based upon several parties, then cooperative practices are probably intended to prolong the term of office rather than to stabilize the system. Split voting is not at all unusual in other polities, although more frequent in the USA than for example Great Britain precisely because the former resembles a coalition party system. This explains the formation of oversized cabinets, without any need for assumptions about *system* stabilizing efforts. Since confessional parties were socio-economically heterogeneous, oversized coalitions reduced intra-party tensions by providing cross-over elasticity which enabled functional delegates to voice dissent without the cabinet being threatened.[1] Also, joint participation of confessional parties in a cabinet can be used to wedge-in other coalition members. Finally, oversized cabinets may be formed in anticipation of things like constitutional changes requiring two-thirds majorities.

Relevant to both oversized cabinets and the "first and most important consociational element, *grand coalition*" (Lijphart, 1977:25) is *"summit diplomacy (3)"* whereby on important or sensitive issues consultations take place between the major political actors. Of course bipartisan consultations and representation on advisory committees are also featured in North America and Great Britain. This is duly noted but not incorporated, while moreover he concedes that the Belgian and Dutch cases provide weak examples (Lijphart, 1977:28, 112, 185). Moreover, if there are three or more parties there could also be a swapping of coalition partners called "diachronic grand coalition" (Lijphart, 1977:30). Dutch observers tend to refer to this confessional practice as holding other parties to ransom, or "political bedhopping". The additional varieties of grand coalitions are confusing, while later elaboration on the theory particularly demonstrates the tendency to concept-inflation. Thus while the 1977 volume deals with the "chances for democracy in severely divided or plural societies," there are also "consociational elements in nonconsociational democracies"; fair enough, but how is this worked out? The "highly homogeneous" Scandinavian countries "have moved the farthest in the direction of a depoliticized type" of democracy which has as its main characteristic that the elites practise a *glidningspolitik,* coalescent elite behaviour whereby "the rule of the parliamentary game prescribes that the top leaders of all (four) major parties do their utmost to reach a consensus" (Lijphart, 1977:111). This is widely practised in the field of socio-economic planning and administration. Similarly what Lowi (1969:78) identified as "interest-group liberalism", specifically Schlesinger's call to include the leading interest in the process of policy formation, which the latter saw as a "new consensus harnessing government, business and labour to a rational partnership" is according to Lijphart (1977:107) "strikingly similar to the typical pattern of grand coalition politics in the New Europe". The question becomes, of course, what is *not* any longer included in the grand coalition concept? All shades and forms of corporatism could be subsumed. In fact, even studies that find precisely the *absence* of tri-partitism and emphasize the collusive interactions between the state and business elites are included. Lijphart and Presthus quote each other that Canada "fits nicely", and the latter emphasizes the "precarious legitimacy" and "marginal social and political position of Labour" and its "low effectiveness ... compared with business and professional groups" (Presthus, 1973:7;154;178).

Related to the question of functional representation — never solved in corporatist theories — is the crucial *proportionality* (4) rule. Neither should its effectiveness be assumed nor its significance exaggerated. Frequently it is the only logically possible allocation criterion, but the more important question is *to whom* proportionality will be granted. This is not neutral but often selective and depends on the willingness to legitimize a particular claimant, and on whether the latter is willing to recognize the other actors and operate within the system. For example, after World War II, the Catholic, Protestant and Socialist unions stated that only membership of one of their organizations was "representative", or worthy of legitimation (Telderstichting, 1958:69). This was directed against the new, communist-inclined EVC, which was excluded from the bipartite "Organized Wage Consultations" in the Foundation of Labour and the tripartite statutory Social and Economic Council, although its membership exceeded that of another union allotted 20 percent of the union seats.

Prime Minister Schemerhorn stated that no recognition could be granted unless one abided by the rules of the game, that is the norms and values established by the traditional actors. These included the innovation that wages and labour conditions were to be nationally fixed by government mediators after having heard the Foundation of Labour, and especially that the right to strike would be de facto suspended. If they did take place all "recognized" social actors were obliged to establish a common front against them (Bank, 1978:288; Drees, 1976:196, 214). The creation of new arenas induced a new kind of game.

A final misleading implication of the theory is that in majoritarian countries public appointments are solely determined by the colour of the party in power. Leaving aside the well known difference between the USA and Great Britain in the magnitude of personnel changes after entry of a "new" administration, for *any* system to deviate from *approximate* proportionality is to invite either charges of discrimination, or resentment and ineffectiveness caused by rigid proportionality. The latter tendency appears in the EEC and Belgium, and is sometimes solved as in the Netherlands, by attaching a knowledgeable deputy-minister to a weak, arithmetically required superior. For reasons of continuity, in most countries parliamentary committees are proportionally composed and adjusted. Lastly, the combination of patronage dominance, inherent slow adjustment, and cumulative effects at different levels may cause huge disproportionality. In 1976, over 69 percent of the mayors in the Netherlands belonged to confessional parties, while their popular vote was less than 32 percent.

In addition the creation of the Social and Economic Council (SER) was another direct consequence of the corporatist tradition and the importance attached to the cooptation of members of interest organizations for parliamentary seats or ministerial posts. Romme (1962) calculated that over 50 percent of the members of the parliamentary committees on Economic Affairs, Industry, Small Business, Agriculture and Fishery, and Social Affairs performed leading functions in the related interest groups. In the House, these party-specialists would dominate debates, and *this* led to the "complicated economic arguments ... incomprehensible to most people" (Lijphart, 1968:118) rather than that these were deliberate attempts at *depolitization*(5). Instead, it was possible to work out committee agreements and present them in technical terms precisely because the actors had reached an ideological modus vivendi, dramatically illustrated by the smooth technocratic decision-making approach in the SER (and EEC) which deadlocked when political/ideological disagreements developed. This refutes the hypothesis on the establishment and success of such decision-making models.

It makes political sense to stall non-urgent problems in the hope that time will solve them, but to elevate it to a pacifying *agreement to disagree* (2) principle goes a bit far. In fact, it would scarcely be worth commenting on were it not considered a variation of the essential "minority veto" principle (Lijphart, 1977: 36-38). We fail to understand Lijphart's example. A large parliamentary majority wanted a football pool but the Calvinist party was "fundamentally opposed on religious grounds — not allowing any pragmatic compromise". However, "concessions" — a maximum on the amounts that could both be staked or won — "made it possible for the (party) to remain in the Cabinet. In this form, the agreement-to-disagree rule comes close to Calhoun's doctrine of concurrent majority" (Lijphart, 1968:125). The latter is debatable. The opposition would have happily supported the bill without concessions. To avoid a crisis the coalition *had* to formulate a proposal whereby the Calvinists could stay in the cabinet without losing too much face in the eyes of the folks back home — a common political practice.

That the political process is clouded in a lot of *secrecy* (6), often taking place in smoke-filled rooms, has been a widespread complaint, but among practitioners it is seen as unavoidable; as Disraeli observed "if you wish to keep your respect for government, like sausages, you should not look into their making". The abetting role of the free press, applying self-censorship under the guise of prudence, was already attacked by American muckrakers.

The conclusion from this section on the seven 'rules' is that these Dutch practices are hardly unique compared with the USA and Great Britain, or the homogeneous Scandinavian multiparty systems. The 'rules' reflect rational political calculation which, combined with the basic consensus on form and processes of the political system, makes the Netherlands, in Almond's terms, a "secularized" political system, which should be stable, and are scarcely distinctive enough to place them in a new, singular, analytic category. This list of practices *is* full of insight, and could be recommended as a practical primer for aspiring politicians, but the significant question is about the conditions under which they can be implemented. Moreover, Lijphart (1977:185) concedes that Belgium and the Netherlands provide a weak case on two out of the four "essential consociational elements" contained within the "rules."

Analysis of the explanatory variables is similarly hampered by the weak operationalization of concepts and faulty empirical premises which cause theoretical paralysis. First, Lijphart oscillates between a high theoretical level and particularistic examples. His examples locate elite accommodation at the levels of summit diplomacy between bloc leaders, within the cabinet and parliament; but he also takes in the Social and Economic Council, and even academics, editors and journalists become "fellow conspirators" belonging to the consociational establishment, which can thus refer to a small inner circle as well as a large group. This poses a dilemma for the theory; a narrow interpretation gives it a genuine conspiracy element, but a wider one loses conviction as a general prescription.

Secondly, Lijphart (1969b: 64-66) specifies that for consociationalism to succeed "four prerequisites must all be fulfilled". The elites must recognize the inherent dangers, be committed to system maintenance, transcend subcultural cleavages at the elite level and, most important, must develop both institutional arrangements and rules of the game. Lijphart then elucidates this with the argument that in France, a non-consociational archetype, there was "simultaneous existence of ideological (subcultural) cleavage at the mass level and the lack of ideological concerns at the elite level", with the absence of only the last prerequisite causing her instability. Here he contradicts his theory's "essential characteristic (which) is not so much any particular institutional arrangement as the deliberate joint efforts...." The existence of consociational elite perceptions, attitudes and behaviour, makes the real acid test not the elite characteristics but the country's stability.

A later reformulation presents the *problem* — the ability to achieve an accommodation of diverse subcultural interests and demands — as the first prerequisite, and hence a truism (Lijphart, 1969a:79). Yet, the fact remains that all this theoretical speculation was based on faulty empirical conjectures about the French case.[2] This objection also applied to the "classical case", Belgium, which in reality displays poor performance in terms of governmental turnover and societal stability (Jackson, 1971: 203). A definition limited to elite characteristics immunizes the theory from falsification.

If stability is included then additional conditions have to be introduced, such as those in his article in *World Politics*. We will suffice with a comment on the first, "most striking" of these eight "conducive factors", namely "external threats". Often an external enemy is perceived by certain subcultural groups as a potential ally, clearly demonstrated by the cases of Austria (World War II), Belgium (World War II), Cyprus, Lebanon, and Northern Ireland, and Slovakia (World War II).

I. A THEORETICAL PARADOX OR FALSE DILEMMA?

The fundamental question is whether the Netherlands constitutes a paradox in need of explanation. This problem can be approached in three basic ways. One, reject the theories and search for alternative explanations. Two, the consociational approach, accept the theoretical propositions but with the reservation that factors outside it have enough autonomous influence to offset the original predictions. Three, the option followed here, to re-examine the theories, particularly as they relate to pillarization and the causes of conflict.

Daalder (1974a:606) notes that consociationalism starts from the familiar proposition

> that social cleavages are moderated if different cleavages cut across one another, but become loaded with conflict if they cumulatively reinforce one another.... [Such] societies are designated as 'vertical pluralism', 'segmented pluralism', 'social fragmentation', 'ideological compartmentalization', or...pillarization...In an extreme form there would be such a hardening of cleavage lines that civil war is likely to erupt.

Lijphart also analytically equates *fragmentation* and *pillarization*, but both authors make the fundamental mistake of accepting as a premise that "pillarization" should be equated with politically salient reinforcing cleavages — as in *The Politics of Accommodation,* which characterizes the Dutch polity as contrary to the model of "sociological pluralism", and therefore prone to a variety of political ailments.

While some consensus is said to exist in the Netherlands, it was only "narrow and limited: as the Netherlands cannot be called a consensual society, not even by the most generous stretch of the imagination" (Lijphart, 1968:78). The chapter describing this consensus refers to a sense of nationalism and national symbols (royal family), but ignored are a host of much more important consensus values. While most consociational evidence is drawn from the post-1945 period, events around 1917 illustrate that already the actors accepted as legitimate the basic national political processes and structures while recognizing that the existing conditions and excesses of capitalism were unacceptable.

More important, all actors saw to a greater or lesser extent, the need for structural changes involving a special role in the economy for corporatist/functional intermediary bodies. Both Social Democrats and Confessionals, though for different reasons, were weary of too much direct state involvement. Disagreements within the pillars were sometimes larger than between factions of the different parties. Therefore, if Great Britain was generally considered a consensual society, then the Netherlands certainly should be characterized as such. "Paradoxically, stability exists in spite of the wide divergence in *substantive* values among the subcultures" (Lijphart, 1968:102 orig. emph.). However, while crucial consensus values were omitted, even less substantiated is the evidence about the *dissensus* of values; we find no trace of it, only references to pillarization.

The crucial argument that there existed a wide divergence in *substantive* values is not substantiated. Of course we do not suggest that there existed no divergence whatsoever, or that pillarization had no political impact. The latter led to stable voting patterns, and hence party configurations, but our argument is precisely that while political parties were sometimes based on different *types* of values than in say Great Britain or the USA, this neither implies nor precludes *political* value congruence.

In the light of the inadequacy of the claim about the value divergence, the weight of the thesis that the Netherlands were subjected to centrifugal forces must shift to the impact of pillarization (*verzuiling*) itself. This may be defined as organizational crystallization based on particular identification criteria leading to parallel structures performing similar functional tasks. The existence of numerous structural and non-structural linkages in the system renders the loaded term "mutually reinforcing cleavages" inappropriate; more accurate is La Palombara's term "cumulative organizational affiliation". Within the confessional pillars there existed all types of functional organizations — trade unions, employers' associations, farmers' organizations, etc. Fostered by their corporatist ideologies, various formal organizational linkages were created between them, and consequently it was precisely on this economic dimension, which had such a high conflict loading in other polities, that the Netherlands were far more integrated than, say, Britain. More importantly, despite common interests, on the criterion from which workers' movements derive their strength — organization — they were fragmented, which discouraged strikes due to the anticipation of diminished chances of success. Employers though, managed a considerable degree of coordination, and even had formal linkages since 1921 where the executives of the organizations met on a regular basis (*Kring van Werkgevers-centralen*) (Slotemaker, 1931: 160-161) and in this respect "were many years ahead of the workers organizations" (Windmuller, 1970:75). At the political system level, the religious criterion had largely lost its conflict potential with respect to both the religious-secular antithesis, and between the three confessional parties who formed the government coalition between 1918 and 1939. As Lipset and Rokkan (1967:50-51) observed, party systems may "freeze" around certain cleavage structures and remain unchanged for several generations. Therefore, a freezing of low conflict-loaded alignment promotes stability and may moderate retard or even prevent the development in salience of other identification criteria which have greater conflict potential (such as revolutionary socialism).

The significance of pillarization is not placed within the proper context in the consociational literature. If they are plagued by "mutually reinforcing cleavages", it follows that the Netherlands are a deviant case *"prima facie* contrary to the crosscutting cleavage proposition". This is, however, qualified by reservations about "important exceptions". Important indeed; the socio-economic and religious lines "do not coincide" and are in fact "crosscutting cleavages". As a result, the confessionals and especially the important Catholic party tended to take a middle of the road position (Lijphart, 1968: 89,92,113-121). In addition the heterogeneous secular parties stressed their religious tolerance and as early as in 1901 the socialist leader Troelestra (1928:252) wrote that he "regretted that the French socialists had become influenced by anti-clericalism, ... it could never be an objective of social democracy ... to hamper the free development of religious groups". Hence, after 1917 organizational segmentation was primarily based upon solidarity criteria which had lost their conflictual elements, but which did crosscut the remaining conflict lines.

Lijphart does not apply the central concept of pillarization with analytical consistency. The premise of the crucial "self-denying" hypothesis is that the elites indeed perceived that pillarization unleashes dangerous centrifugal forces: it precedes consociationalism and constitutes the source of the problems. Lijphart (1976:82) also argues that *verzuiling* was created, fostered and strengthened as part and parcel of the efforts to create stability. Yet, the extent of *verzuiling* serves as an index to show how intensely cleavaged society was, especially on political values. But if pillarization was a stabilizing *instrument,* then its extent only measures how successful the elites were in carving up society, not the magnitude of the value cleavages themselves.

While we accept the proposition that a limited amount of *verzuiling* existed before 1917 and that thereafter it was greatly expanded, Lijphart cannot, without undermining his self-denying hypothesis. Why would "prudent" elites, concerned about *verzuiling's* "inherent" centrifugal forces, respond by creating more of it? Unless they had fostered it for ulterior ends, the rational response would have been to dismantle *verzuiling* while it was still possible.

A more plausible alternative analysis is to locate the start of pillarization when confessional trade unions were being formed, and regard it as primarily a reaction to the socialist union movement. As socialist appeals were plainly based on widely felt grievances, with confessionally-affiliated workers equally suffering, the movement could not merely be discredited. Primarily out of necessity, and partly pressured by some socially concerned individuals within their own ranks, the confessional elites were forced to take affirmative counter-measures. Already in 1886 we find in Catholic circles the theme which was to become so familiar in the decades thereafter — that liberalism had caused the workers' wretched economic circumstances, and so gave birth to its bastard child, socialism. Leo XIII instructed priests that it was their imperative duty to take the initiative to create Catholic workers' organizations "if socialism conquers or threatens an area" (Doutreloux, 1906: 108: 130). In the same year as *Rerum Novarum* (1891), Orthodox Calvinists held their first Christian Social Congress, and the *Proces-Verbaal* expressed very similar ideas about the causes and solutions of the social evils, also arguing for the establishment of confessional trade unions, and reminding employers that unless they cooperated, social unrest or worse might be the result. The important point is that the explicit purpose of these efforts was to stake out a sphere of influence among the workers rather than promote a distinctive philosophy on labour relations. But in practice it became necessary to develop such a philosophical apparatus to justify the organizations they had created (Messing, 1975:30). Confessional leaders foresaw the loss of support from their workers who could not appreciate a contradiction between socialism and religiosity; the structures were created to teach them otherwise.

The school issue had been one strong emotional mobilization instrument to bolster group cohesion, but by 1917 *collective* emancipatory goals were largely achieved. Futher emancipation, such as the raising of the general living standard, could only be achieved through fundamental changes of society and the economy, which was hardly in line with the elites' objectives. Now the only way to ensure cohesion was to complete encapsulation by expanding pillarization. The goal was not to engage in overt combat or to make converts, but rather to retain the loyalty of the present and future generations. It becomes very evident that the elites were more concerned about their own dominance in the subculture, rather than system performance, when we look at the Catholic Episcopate's infamous 1954 *Mandement*.[3] It was not that ideological conflicts had developed between confessional and socialist organizations. On the contrary, cooperation and mutual understanding between the unions was excellent; the intention was to abort such forms of rapprochement. Not surprisingly, this was applauded in Calvanist circles, and while some Catholics were privately dismayed, on the whole they remained silent. Separateness was not a design to avoid conflict, and elites did not hesitate to stir up conflict if improved relations threatened group cohesion.

Liberal-pluralist assumptions about the process are also questionable. Prominent in both Lijphart's analysis and our own is the role of the Dutch elites in the creation of these organizations. But, from a pluralist perspective events did not fit with theoretical preconceptions about the development of society and structures. Particularly vulnerable is the liberal premise that society is composed of free agents, endowed with certain value and interest orientations, on which bases organizations develop via informal coalition formation and institutionalization: values lead to structures, a process from the bottom upwards. Logically, if different structures are performing similar functional tasks, as in the case of *verzuiling*, then this must have been the result of incompatible values or ideologies.

However, the formation of organizations such as confessional unions was in fact contrary to pluralist thought, imposed from the top down and established not to pursue functional interests but to encapsulate and preserve the religious subgroup's loyalty. Given the important role of structures in the creation and maintenance of values at the mass level, it becomes clear that instead of considering them primarily as the organizational reflection of values, emphasis should be placed on the function of pillarization as a system of social control to enable certain elites to consolidate and protect their position through the manipulation of these values. Not surprisingly, pillar-structures occur especially in the domains of

> ... education, the press, radio, television, youth-affairs, welfare and politics. After all, precisely the activities of these organizations are concerned with the value contrasts, and is pre-eminently via these mechanisms that the desired values can be implemented and perpetuated (Van Kemenade, 1968:57; also Van Doorn, 1956).

The theoretical significance of our historical interpretation is that because the liberal premises about the development of organizations and empirical reality do not match, the *pluralist linkage between values and organizations is not applicable*. Consequently, it is incorrect to assume that these pillar-organizations are structurally separate because they have such different ideological perspectives on their functional tasks. Logically they could have convergent, or at least not incompatible, ideological positions and/or similar goal orientations. No one would argue that separated goat-breeders associations reflect ideological incompatibility about functional activities, and so when organizations such as trade unions are involved why should this be automatically and unhesitatingly assumed. Our line of argument explains why such organizations could interact in a large number of joint service, administrative and advisory agencies during the pre-war period, and indeed achieve significant functional integration thereafter. This involved no drastic turnarounds because their values were never fundamentally incongruent.

The above analysis was primarily at the subcultural and organizational level, but what about the mass level values and attitudes? Considering the extent social control and the threat of religious and secular sanctions, were the members "free agents"? It would be unwarranted to assume that segregated membership necessarily also reflected mass political value plurality. Support of these types of political parties, trade unions, etc., was to a high extent based on transferred, rather than direct and affective loyalty, a fact of special significance to understand the developments during the 1960s. The question arises whether the Dutch system was a polyarchy. It scored high on the participation dimension with voting being compulsory, while public participation was open. Yet can it still be characterized as liberal-democratic if, within the polity, society is deliberately structured so that a cumulative majority of the population "naturally" displays one-dimensional patterns of public behavior and associations, particularly if the state is a guarantor of the mechanisms to perpetuate such patterns?

To recapitulate, we argued that the literature on the relation between pillarized structures and values is based on invalid premises, which open up three theoretical probabilities that greatly reduce the significance of *verzuiling* as a centrifugal force. These are that pillarization does not have to crystallize around the areas of greatest political conflict; the pillars themselves need not have incompatible ideologies on "universalistic issues", nor do the individual organizations on their functional tasks; and lastly, they may be oriented to internal control rather than outward combat.

II. A RE-EXAMINATION OF THE
HISTORICAL AND EMPIRICAL EVIDENCE:
THE BACKGROUND TO THE GREAT
PACIFICATION OF 1917

In addition to these theoretical weaknesses, the historical and empirical evidence submitted provides only weak support that consociationalism did take place (regardless of whether there was a need for it). Lijphart sought to explain the paradox of democratic stability despite wide divergence of substantive values. To find the explanatory crux he investigates the "resolution of substantive conflicts", namely the 1917 Great Pacification and the subsequent establishment of consociational rules of the game. The essence of his argument is that the "secret of success" lies in accommodative politics which is the "...settlement of divisive issues and conflicts where only minimal consensus exists. Pragmatic solutions are forged for all problems, even those with clear religious-ideological overtones..."

We begin our analysis with the theory's crown jewel, the Great Pacification. According to Lijphart, the political situation around 1910 was serious, with sharply drawn conflict lines and a peak of tension: both the school and franchise issues remained unresolved while the rivals hardened in their intention not to yield. Theoretically he must opt for this perspective to support his claim that this was a crucial episode which induced the elites to apply a "self-denying hypothesis" and set the basic patterns of accommodative politics consisting of:

> (1) the pre-eminent role of the top leaders in recognizing the problems and realistically finding solutions ... (2) participation of the leaders of *all* blocs in the settlement; and (3) the importance of the principle of proportionality in the substance of the settlement-state subsidy for confessional education and representation in future parliaments...[4]

Some scholars were struck that despite the magnitude of the conflicts, such bitter antagonists nevertheless managed to accommodate; others, by the exchange of significant concessions, which linked very diverse issues and so resembled package deals in international integration studies. A crucial question is whether these issues were indeed highly contested, forcing each party to obtain a cherished principle by having to make a repugnant concession.

The right to establish confessional schools had long been recognized, while the liberals accepted in 1885 that subsidization did not violate the existing constitution of 1848. With support of 19 liberals, such a subsidy bill passed in 1889 under the first confessional cabinet of MacKay. Subsequent bills in 1903 and 1905 provided higher subsidies, state recognition of confessional university degrees, and admission of confessional teachers to the pension funds. In 1913, full equality with public education was prevented only because the term of office of the Heemskerck cabinet expired before the final stage of such legislation. The elections led to the new cabinet which brought about the 1917 constitutional changes, which thus formed only a last stage of a gradual development, and did not introduce the proportionality principle. Moreover, confessionals and seculars had not been unceasingly pitted against each other because Liberal MPs had supported subsidy bills, and the Socialist Easter Congress in 1902 passed the Groninger school motion also advocating full subsidy (Rogier, 1956: 367). Conversely the confessional Christian Historical Party had reservations about subsidizing confessional universities (Bruijn, 1971: 44).

Similarly, suffrage had been a process of gradual extension, whereby from 1870 to 1910 the percentage of enfranchised adult males rose from 11 percent to 63 percent (Daalder, 1966: 417). Cleavage lines were not drawn between confessionals and seculars, but instead between parties within each bloc and often within the parties themselves. The conflict was ignited in 1894 by a law proposal of the (left-liberal) minister Tak van Poortvliet which would enfranchise all adult males (except charity recipients). The Protestant Anti-Revolutionary Party was split right down the middle: ten members under the leadership of Abraham Kuyper supported an extension of suffrage laws, ten others led by De Savornin Lohman rejected it. The latter group formed in 1898 the Free ARP, which became after some fusions the aristocratically tinted Christian Historical Party in 1903 (Tijn, 1975: 598; ARP, 1975: 28, 29, 39). Within the Catholic parliamentary group strong tensions developed between the rejectionist ''Bahlmannians'' and Schaepman's followers (a party had not yet been formed). Also, the Liberal Party split (Oud, 1959:32), but consolidated again after the turn of the century, and for the elections of 1913 the three liberal parties issued a ''concentration manifesto'' endorsing universal suffrage, which socialists had always advocated. Although formally extra-parliamentary, the 1913-1918 Cort van der Linden cabinet largely adopted the manifesto, placing priority on the suffrage issue. Independently, Anti-Revolutionaries and Catholics formulated their position in 1907. Some Catholics favoured outright universal suffrage, but the majority of the confessionals supported so called "organic criteria", which was rather elusive, meaning nothing more than "heads of families". Moreover, franchise extension would be advantageous because of their socio-economic support base.

Confessionals were thus in an excellent bargaining position; able to concede on something not rating very high on their value hierarchy in order to gain on something which did. Constitutional changes requiring a two-third majority made their cooperation imperative, and they bargained toughly with seculars by indicating that they were only willing to cooperate on the suffrage issue if their demands on the school issue were met (Welderen, 1955: 150-153). At the opening of parliament in 1913, the new prime minister promised the formation of a subsidy study committee composed of two members of each political *party*, i.e. of three liberal, two Protestant, Catholic and socialist parties. In October 1915 the government introduced the constitutional proposals on suffrage, but from confessional side all sorts of objections were raised. Meanwhile in the education committee bargaining continued, until in March 1916 the final details were hammered out; now that further stalling was unnecessary, the confessionals dropped their objections to the suffrage laws.

According to Daalder (1966:207) the change from a majoritarian to a proportional system was a natural corollary to universal suffrage — a matter of abstract justice. Perhaps, but probably not unrelated was, as in Sweden, the fear of survival which was induced by the electoral decline of the Calvinists (from 25 to 11 seats) with the socialists as main victors. This also clarifies the insistence on the apparently unnecessary *constitutional* anchoring of subsidy. It could not be undone by a simple majority, and strengthened the apparatus for mobilization of supporters to resist further electoral setbacks. Notes made by the future prime minister Colijn show that confessional support for the very formation of the Cort van der Linden cabinet had been preceded by shrewd political calculating (Puchinger, 1969: 13-14).

As we saw, already *before* the formation of this cabinet, political groups had, in principle, decided on the issues. The rational and calculating politicking that accompanied final implementation can hardly be considered elite "accommodation", and the Great Pacification reinforced our observation that the success of negotiations is dependent upon at least a minimum prior congruence on basics. Technical committees can promote and stretch a bargaining momentum, but cannot bridge ideological incompatibilities, only at best massage them.

III. ECONOMIC AFFAIRS AND THE SOCIO-ECONOMIC COUNCIL

In *The Politics of Accommodation* (Lijphart 1976:81), we read that "the two basic cleavages which divide the Dutch population are class and religion". Moreover, consociationalism is defined as a political process characterized by the settlement of *major* issues between the leaders of *all* the various pillars, i.e. Catholics, Protestants, Socialists and Liberals. Therefore, if "the main politically significant issues after 1917 have been social and economic" (Lijphart, 1968: 16, 118) and if the spirit of elite accommodation was so pervasive, then it is *imperative* that above all the economically based pillars should have been actively involved in the policy-making process.

Consociational theory would have predicted that, as in Great Britain during the depression years, all-party cabinets would have been formed.[5] In reality, up to 1939, the second largest party, the Socialists, was excluded from government. Cohen (1974:265) concludes: "there is no evidence of (their) participation in the consociational politics during this period". The Catholic party leader, Nolens, stated in 1925 that "only in the case of grave necessity" would his party be willing to cooperate with the Socialists, a policy rudely reaffirmed in 1932 by his successor Aalberse. Given such attitudes, and also contrasting the theory's requirement of effectiveness with the overall governmental stagnation during the inter-war period, it would be difficult to attach a consociational label to this era — especially if we consider that many 'consociational' events actually concerned the above party politics monarchy, while the remainder often involved minor religious issues which had lost the volatility in 1917. The heterogeneous class composition of the confessionals and of the Social and Economic Council cannot be regarded as consociational explanations.

A good test of the linkage between consociational theory and class relations concerns Lijphart's treatment of the operation of the Social and Economic Council (SER). Theoretical and descriptive statements are so intertwined that it appears that the latter support the theory, but upon closer examination it becomes clear that this is not the case. The Council is referred to as the crown on the intricate system of permanently established confederal organizations and the pinnacle of the "institutionalization of the process of negotiation among the bloc leaders", represents an evolutionary stage in a consociational process initiated in 1917. We read: "From informal and *ad hoc* contacts, it has moved to formal and more or less permanent institutions, and finally to official organizations anchored in the country's legal-constitutional framework" (Lijphart, 1968: 112-114). Similarly in Lijphart's important theoretical article (1969a:76): "The typical consociational devices are advisory councils ... These councils and committees may be permanent organs such as the powerful Social and Economic Council ..." and later references to the significance of the SER read "These overarching organizations are extremely important because they purposefully counter the centrifugal tendencies of pillarization" (Lijphart, 1973a: 32).

It is incorrect to argue that these economic bodies were created to facilitate relations between the pillars. To do so represents a subtle shift in the type of analysis, one with considerable impact on the validity of the consociational theory. Rather, the SER with its tripartite composition of representatives of employers and employees organizations and government appointed experts reflects the adaptation of the pre-World War II corporatist philosophies to new forms of capitalism and societal expectations in the post-war period.

Although five years of foreign occupation had interrupted the normal political process, after the war, the same political alignments and political elites re-emerged. The institutions created to meet the demands of the post-war period were built upon the foundations laid before, and partly during the war. These were of three types — ideological, legal and structural, and these intertwined background conditions had a significant impact on the establishment and development of the role of the Social and Economic Council in the policy-making process.

During the inter-war period the orientations of the subcultures were especially guided by corporatist types of reforms. Confessional parties wanted to reform the economy and the state because the existing liberal structures caused class antagonisms and broke-up the "natural-fabric" of God's society. The state was allowed a complementary role in those areas of society or the economy where private initiative was unable to ensure conditions based on justice and human dignity. The economy was to be reorganized into self-regulating corporations with limited guidance from the state and an overall goal of fostering harmonious relationships between the social partners. Orthodox Protestants based such reforms on their philosophy of "sovereignty in own circle" which was broadly similar to the Catholic "subsidiarity principle".

The confessionals hoped that such structures would neutralize the main source of intra-pillar conflict and thus foster internal cohesion of their subcultures. Social Democrats advocated so-called "functional decentralization", also involving the creation of intermediary bodies to regulate the economy, and hoped to achieve their version of industrial democracy without the necessity of creating an unwieldy state bureaucracy. Liberal circles were more reserved and not until World War II does an appreciation develop of ideas akin to the British Conservatives' notion that "organic unity" of the social classes should be encouraged to create stable expectations and hence allow more accurate planning and therefore secure business profits.

The influence of corporatist ideologies was reflected in the 1938 Constitution, to which a fifth chapter was added to sanction the creation of public legal corporative bodies, endowed with authoritative powers. This formed in 1950 the legal basis of the SER. The practice of dealing constitutionally with such agencies had started in 1922 when, on initiative of the Socialist leader Troelstra, amendments were passed making it possible to create functionally organized public-legal bodies and regulating the status of Standing Committees of Advice. This reflected Social Democratic concern that the expansion of governmental capabilities might lead to institutional overload and the fear that the quality of democracy would deteriorate because parliamentarians would be forced to sanction a multitude of decisions on matters they knew little about.

An important instrument in the area of labour relations was created by the 1937 law on Binding Collective Bargaining Agreements which gave the minister the power to nullify such agreements or declare them applicable to all workers with the industry. The latter greatly increased the mandate of recognized producer organizations and their potential sanctioning power gave the government invisible influence over collective bargaining processes. Moreover, according to Windmuller (1970:98), this power to intervene constituted an important legal precedent which formed the basis for the rigid wage controls during the 15 to 20 years after the war, especially after the Extraordinary Decree on Labour Relations

(BBA) was added which required that each agreement had to be sanctioned by a board of government mediators. Structurally, it was especially significant that pillarization in itself, and competition between the pillars, had fostered intra-pillar hierarchical centralization of producers' organizations. This facilitated the operation of the established system by restricting the number of legitimate actors who could reach authoritative decisions because they were able to exercise control over their members.

Before and after World War II the various parties and affiliated interest organizations had produced numerous detailed recommendations for economic summit organizations to serve as an umbrella over a structure of vertical and horizontal, self-regulating agencies with statutory competences. Although in this respect the 1950 law was unsuccessful, the Social and Economic Council itself acquired a central position in the formulation of post-war social and economic policies.[6] Wartime experience and changes of the economy caused a transformation in the relationship between government and private enterprise which developed an appreciation of its mutual advantages. Attitudes about the desirability of full employment, stable prices, and social security had been shaped by the trauma of the Great Depression. In the task of reconstruction, Western European governments perceived that the most appropriate means to meet expectations and requirements were those of indicative planning, which required the reduction of the area of the unpredictable to a manageable series of clear alternatives. Among other objectives, this involved a coordination of economic activities so that gains in one area would not be negated by losses in others. In the Netherlands, advice on such coordination became one of the prime tasks of the SER. The government was legally required to consult the Council before taking any final action on all social and economic measures. Compared with the bodies it replaced, the Council provided comprehensive rather than compartmentalized analyses and formulations of economic and social policies. Its published inter-related objectives were the "Magical Pentangle" of economic growth with balanced investments, stable and full employment, fair distribution of income, stable prices and balance of payments.

An important consequence recognized by the Dutch government and labour leaders (Suurhoff, 1945), was stated succinctly by Panitch (1977:76):

> The consequence of full employment was that trade unions were in a much stronger position than before to raise money wages. If these increases were passed

on in price increases, however, this had the effect, given the growth rate of productivity, of affecting a country's foreign competitiveness. If the increases were not passed on in an inflationary spiral, on the other hand, the motor force of the capitalist economy — profits — tended to be squeezed. It was this problem that provided the spur to state economic planning in the post-war era directed both at raising productivity (and hence economic growth) and inducing trade unions to cooperate in an incomes policy which would restrain money wage demands.

The three background conditions led to a high degree of formal institutionalization. Especially up to the mid-sixties, the members of SER shared common perspectives on economic objectives. Consequently, government adoption of the policy advice resulting from these tripartite deliberations was probable, with speedy parliamentary enactment facilitated by functional cross-linkages. Participation in the Council reflected the legitimate mandate of each functional group, but imposed in exchange responsibility to ensure that their constituents would faithfully adhere to the agreements. The Dutch pillarized and centralized structures were perfectly equipped to this end and accounted for the policy's remarkable effectiveness.

The confusion between advice, enactment and enforcement functions created an important political role for such intermediary agencies but limited public accountability. A major problem was the fragile basis of shared, but time bound, goals like reconstruction. A voluntaristic corporatist system can only be sustained by a unifying myth, which until the mid-sixties was the so-called "harmony model". Eventually, it started to collapse at the bottom, while at the national level interactions continued in the SER and Foundation. Union members had become alienated, leading to uncontrollable wildcat strikes, and culminating in a wage explosion. Erosion of pillarization made it no longer effective as an instrument of social control. In an attempt to reestablish contact with the aspirations of their members an ideological reorientation of especially the Socialist Party and unions took place. This had considerable impact on the policy-making process and collective bargaining, making it less amenable to corporatist and technocratic problem solving. However, the smooth transition to a "bargaining relationship" was only possible because it could be "bought" by large wage rises and economic expansion. Despite many proposals and calls from both left and right to reintroduce mechanisms of the harmony model, it is unlikely that a revived system would be able to sustain itself.

CONCLUSION

Consociationalism cannot, despite its claims, account for socio-economic stability without straying beyond its own parameters, leaving few conflicts which the theory can distinctively explain. Before the war quite a degree of ideological, corporativistic, parallellism had developed, to the concern of confessionals whose objective had always been to avoid legitimizing the socialists with either formal association at the national level or interactions at the mass level, since both would threaten their grip on the followers. But they were prepared to condone affairs that took place out of the limelight, such as joint participation of their unions in functional ventures, which had become quite extensive already before World War II (De Jong, 1956:188). Through this process, Social Democrats obtained national legitimacy, with economic equilibrium theories providing the final link between the corporatist ideas while allowing simultaneous social separation. This allowed rigid social control to continue to be applied, which is why pillarization kept on expanding. As Bishops' letters pointed out, there was absolutely no excuse to belong to a socialist organization because for each one a Catholic counterpart existed. This explains why the evidence of consociationalism on ideological and political values is so scarce, but that of pillarization so extensive. The Netherlands do not represent an atypically fragmented political culture, and there is no paradox that needs to be explained.

NOTES

The writing of an earlier draft of this chapter (February 1977) was made possible by a research-fellowship of the Social Science Faculty of the Erasmus University in Rotterdam, and financial assistance of The Canada Council and Council on European Studies. I am especially grateful for the encouragement of Dr. M. van Schendelen and Dr. L. Panitch, and I would also like to thank for commentary on an earlier draft, Professors Barry, Daalder, De Vree, Eisenstadt, Lijphart and Rosenthal. Professor Richard Rose and Richard Parry provided helpful editorial suggestions.

1. This cross-over effect should of course not be exaggerated; quantitatively, in both the USA and the Netherlands, party colour does serve as the best predictor via "cue-taking" (van Schendelen, 1976: 244-247).
2. Lehmbruch (1974:94) and Stiefbold (1974:149) make the opposite observation

about France. Referring to Converse and Dupeux, they note that at the mass level there tended to be only limited perception of political conflict, while "polarization of public opinion seems, to a considerable degree, to be largely an elite-induced phenomenon".

3. See Kruijt (1974:135) "We maintain the rule that the Holy Sacraments must be refused — and, in case of death without conversion, the ecclesiastical funeral also — to any Catholic who is known to be a member of a Socialist association, or who, without being a member, still regularly attends Socialist meetings, or is a regular reader of Socialist periodicals or papers". The significance here is not its issue, one of a long list of such bans, but the sharpness of its language at a time when communal relations had been good. Similarly, such a ban was issued in 1946, during the post-war fraternization period.

4. In Austria, the Constitution of 1920 was written by an all-party coalition and among others provided for proportional representation. The writing reflected a process of compromise and adjustment between political camps which had started the discussions from totally divergent positions. Yet civil war erupted in 1934. This illustrates that neither all-party participation, nor proportional representation, nor the instilling of "elite political culture" values are necessarily sufficient to avoid conflict, especially if it is rooted in genuine divergent values (see Diamant, 1960: 80-87).

5. In Great Britain in 1931, a meeting between the king and the three party leaders on how to handle the fall of the MacDonald Labour Government in the face of the severe economic crisis did lead to a National Government, headed by MacDonald (1931-35) and subsequent National and Coalition Governments until 1945.

6. If it had been successful, the Netherlands would have provided both an historically and comparatively unique example of a non-authoritarian corporatist system. However, the 1950 law provided only a framework, and its implementation met a similar fate to the 1933 corporatist *Bedrijfsraden Wet Verschuur,* which also contained the (confessional) voluntarism principle. Delegation of legal authority to bodies composed of both employers and employees, able to make binding decisions, was neither particularly popular among employers, nor pushed by unions in periods of economic expansion. Yet such control was precisely the objective of socialists' support for "corporatism".

REFERENCES

ALMOND, G.A. (1956) "Comparative Political Systems", *Journal of Politics* 18: 391-409.

ARP (1975) *Een Kleine Eeuw Kleine Luijden.* 's-Gravenhage: Stichting Kader- en Vormingswerk ARP.

BANK, J. (1978) *Opkomst en Ondergang van de Nederlandse Volksbeweging.* Deventer: Kluwer.

BRUIJN, L. De (1971) "Confessionele Politieke Stromingen", pp. 38-57 in A. Hoogerwerf (ed.) *Verkenningen in de Politiek,* Vol. II. Alphen aan de Rijn: Samsom.

COHEN, H.F. (1974) *Om de Vernieuwing van het Socialisme.* Leiden: Universitaire Pers.

DAALDER, H. (1966) "The Netherlands: Opposition in a Segmented Society" pp. 188-236 in R. Dahl (ed.) *Political Oppositions in Western Democracies.* New Haven: Yale University Press.

—— (1971) "On Building Consociational Nations: the Cases of The Netherlands and Switzerland" pp.107-124 in K. McRae (ed.) (1974) *Consociational Democracy.*

—— (1974) "The Consociational Democracy Theme", *World Politics* 26 (July): 604-622.

DOORN, J.A.A. Van. (1956) "Verzuiling een Eigentijds Systeem van Sociale Controle", *Sociologische Gids* 3 (March-April).

DIAMANT, A. (1960) *Austrian Catholics and the First Republic: Democracy, Capitalism and the Social Order, 1918-1934.* Princeton: Princeton University Press.

DOUTRELOUX, Mgr. (1906) "Het Arbeiders Vraagstuk" in P.J.M. Aalberse (ed.) *Sociale Studiën* 1(1). Leiden.

DREES, W. (1976) *Drees 90.* Naarden: Strengholt.

DUIJNSTEE, F.J.F.M. (1966) *De Kabinets-formaties 1946-1965.* Deventer: Kluwer.

FENNEMA, M. (1976) "Professor Lijphart en de Nederlandse Politiek", *Acta Politica* 11 (1): 54-77.

JACKSON, R. and M. STEIN (eds.) (1971) *Issues in Comparative Politics,* New York and Toronto: St. Martin's Press and Macmillan.

JONG, F. De. (1956) *Om de Plaats van der Arbeid. Een Geschiedkundig Overzicht van het Ontstaan en Ontwikkeling van het N.V.V.* Amsterdam: Uitgave NVV.

KEMENADE, J. Van. (1968) *De Katholieken en hun Onderwijs.* Meppel: Boom.

KRUIJT, J.P. (1959) "The Netherlands: the Influence of Denominationalism on Social Life and Organizational Patterns" pp.128-136 in K. McRae (ed.) (1974) *Consociational Democracy.*

LEHMBRUCH, G. (1967) "A Non-Competitive Pattern of Conflict Management in Liberal Democracies: The Case of Switzerland, Austria and Lebanon", pp.90-97 in K. McRae (1974) *Consociational Democracy.*

LIJPHART, A. (1968) *The Politics of Accommodation.* Berkeley: University of California Press.

—— (1969a) "Consociational Democracy", *World Politics* 21(2) 207-225 also pp.70-89 in K. McRae (ed.) (1974) *Consociational Democracy.*

—— (1969b) "Typologies of Democratic Systems", pp.46-79 in A. Lijphart (ed.) (1969) *Politics in Europe,* Englewood Cliffs, NJ: Prentice-Hall.

—— (1973) "Verzuiling", pp.24-38 in A. Hoogerwerf (ed.) *Verkenningen in de Politiek* Vol.2 (2nd ed.) Alphen a/d Rijn: Samsom.

—— (1975) *The Politics of Accommodation,* Revised edition. Berkeley: University of California Press.

—— (1976) "Repliek aan M. Fennema", *Acta Politica* 11(1): 78-86.

—— (1977) *Democracy in Plural Societies.* New Haven and London: Yale University Press.

LIPSET, S.M. and S. ROKKAN (1967) *Party Systems and Voter Alignments: Cross National Perspectives.* New York: The Free Press.

LOWI, T.J. (1969) *The End of Liberalism: Ideology, Policy, and the Crisis of Public Authority,* New York: W.W. Norton & Company, Inc.

McRAE, K.D. (1974) (ed.) *Consociational Democracy,* Toronto: McClelland and Stewart Limited.

MESSING, F.A.M. (1975) *De Emancipatie van de Arbeidende Klasse in Nederland,* Kampen.

OUD, J.P. (1959) "Binnenlandse Politieke Ontwikkeling", pp.29-60 in M. Rooij (ed.), Verbond van Nederlandsche Werkgevers (sponsor), *Ondernemend Nederland van 1899 tot 1959*. Leiden: Senfert Kroese.

PANITCH, L.V. (1977) "The Development of Corporatism in Liberal Democracies", *Comparative Political Studies* 10, 1 (April): 61-90.

PRESTHUS, R. (1973) *Elite Accommodation in Canadian Politics*, Toronto: Macmillan Company.

PUCHINGER, G. (1969) *Colijn en het Einde van de Coalitie, Geschiedenis van de Kabinetsformaties*. Kampen: Kok Uitgeverij.

ROGIER, L.J. (1956) *Katholieke Herleving*. 's-Gravenhage: Pax.

ROMME, C.P.M. (1962) "Sociale Democratie", *Sociale Wetenschap*, 4.

RUSTOW, D.A. (1955) *The Politics of Compromise: A Study of Parties and Cabinet Government in Sweden*. Princeton: Princeton University Press.

SCHENDELEN, M.P.C.M. Van. (1976) "Information and Decision Making in the Dutch Parliament", *Legislative Studies Quarterly* 1 (2): 231-250.

SLOTEMAKER DE BRUINE, J.R. (1931) *Christelijk Sociale Studiën:- IV*. Zutphen: Ruys Uitg. Mij.

STIEFBOLD, R.P. (1974) "Segmented Pluralism and Consociational Democracy in Austria", pp.117-177 M. Heisler (ed.) *Politics in Europe*. New York: David McKay Company, Inc.

STERNQUIIST, N. (1966) "Sweden: Stability or Deadlock?" pp.116-147 in R. Dahl (ed.) *Political Oppositions in Western Democracies*, New Haven: Yale University Press.

SUURHOFF, J.G. (1945) *Staking Ja of Neen?*, Amsterdam.

TIJN, Th. Van. (1975) "De Wording der Politieke-Partijorganizaties in Nederland", pp.590-601 in G. Beekelaar (ed.) *Vaderland's Verleden in Veelvoud*. 's-Gravenhage: Nijhoff.

TELDERSSTICHTING (1958) *De P.B.O. in Nederland*. 's-Gravenhage.

TROELSTRA, P.J. (1928) *Gedenkschriften* – II. Amsterdam: Querido.

WELDEREN RENGERS, W.J. Van (1955) *Schets ener Parlementaire Geschiedenis van Nederland*. IV – 1914-1918. 's-Gravenhage: Nijhoff.

WINDMULLER, J. (1970) *Arbeidsverhoudingen in Nederland*, Utrecht: Spectrum Uitg.

Publications of the Committee on Political Sociology

1. "Approaches to the Study of Political Participation", a special issue of *Acta Sociologica* VI: 1-2 (1962).
2. *Cleavages, Ideologies and Party Systems,* E. Allardt and Y. Littunen, eds., Helsinki: Westermarck Society, 1964.
3. *Party Systems and Voter Alignments,* S.M. Lipset and Stein Rokkan, eds., New York: Free Press, 1967.
4. *Party Systems, Party Organizations and the Politics of New Masses,* Otto Stammer, ed., Berlin: Free University, 1968.
5. "Social Structure, Party Systems and Voting Behaviour", Richard Rose and Derek Urwin, eds., a special issue of *Comparative Political Studies* II: 1 (1969).
6. *Citizens, Elections, Parties,* Stein Rokkan et al., Oslo: Universitetsforlaget; New York: D. McKay, 1970.
7. *Mass Politics,* Erik Allardt and Stein Rokkan eds., New York: Free Press, 1970.
8. *Opinion-Making Elites in Yugoslavia,* Allan Barton, Bogdan Denitch and Charles Kadushin, eds., New York: Praeger, 1973.
9. *Electoral Behavior: a Comparative Handbook,* Richard Rose, ed., New York: Free Press, 1974.
10. *International Almanack of Electoral History,* Thomas T. Mackie and Richard Rose, New York: Free Press, 1974.
11. *The Management of Urban Change in Britain and Germany,* Richard Rose, ed., Beverly Hills & London: Sage Publications, 1974.
12. *Contemporary Political Sociology,* Sage Professional Papers Series 06-001-024, Beverly Hills & London Vol. I, 1974-77.
13. *The American Intellectual Elite,* Charles Kadushin, Boston: Little, Brown, 1974.
14. *The Dynamics of Public Policy,* Richard Rose, ed., Beverly Hills & London: Sage Publications, 1976.
15. *Comparing Public Policies,* Jerzy Wiatr and Richard Rose, eds., Warsaw: Polish Academy of Sciences and Ossolineum Press, 1977.
16. *Elections without Choice,* Guy Hermet, Richard Rose and Alain Rouquié, eds., London: Macmillan, 1978.
17. *Legitimation of Regimes,* Bogdan Denitch, ed., Beverly Hills & London, Sage Publications, 1979.
18. "The Policy Implications of Direct Elections", Richard Rose and Helen Wallace, eds., a special issue of the *Journal of Common Market Studies* XVII: 4 (1979).
19. *Trends toward Corporatist Intermediation,* Philippe C. Schmitter & Gerhard Lehmbruch, eds., Beverly Hills & London, Sage Publications, 1979.
20. *Electoral Participation,* Richard Rose, ed., Beverly Hills & London, Sage Publications, 1980.

Notes on Contributors

Ole Borre is Professor of Political Sociology at the Institute of Political Science, University of Aarhus, Denmark. He has authored and co-authored various books (in Danish) and articles for international journals on Danish voting behaviour.

Walter Dean Burnham is Professor of Political Science at the Massachusetts Institute of Technology. He is the author of *Critical Elections and The Mainsprings of American Politics,* 1970, and editor of *The American Party Systems,* 1975.

Arend Lijphart is Professor of Political Science at the University of California at San Diego. He is the author of *Democracy in Plural Societies,* 1977, and many other books and articles.

Juan J. Linz is Pelatiah Perit Professor of Political and Social Science at Yale University. He is the author of numerous articles on Spanish politics and social structure which have been published in collective volumes and is the author of *Crisis, Breakdown and Reequilibration,* an introductory volume to *The Breakdown of Democratic Regimes.*

G. Bingham Powell, Jr. is Professor of Political Science at the University of Rochester, New York. Currently he is writing a book on Contemporary Democratic Performance. He is best known as co-author of *Comparative Politics: A Developmental Approach,* 1966, and *Comparative Politics: System, Process and Policy,* 1978. He has also published a number of works on Austrian politics and comparative political processess.

Richard Rose is Director of the Centre for the Study of Public Policy at the University of Strathclyde, Glasgow. He has published extensively in comparative politics, political sociology, and policy analysis. Volumes he has authored or co-authored include *Can Government Go Bankrupt?, What is Governing? Politics and Purpose in Washington, Governing without Consensus, Politics in England, The Problem of Party Government, Challenges to Governance,* and *Do Parties Make a Difference?*

William Schneider has taught at Harvard University and is currently a Visiting Fellow at the Hoover Institution at Stanford in California. He has written articles on public opinion and voting behaviour and is co-authoring a forthcoming book on confidence in institutions.

Ilja Scholten is currently completing a PhD dissertation at Carleton University, Ottawa, on the development of corporatism in the Netherlands.

Ofira Seliktar is a lecturer in the Department of Political Science at the University of Haifa, Israel, and Visiting Assistant Professor in the Political Science Department at Texas A&M University. She has written articles on electoral behaviour and political socialization in Israel.